2ND EDITION

Variations

THE ULTIMATE GUIDE

MICHAEL ZARNOCK

©2004 Michael Zarnock

©2004 Krause Publications photography

Published by

An F+W Publications Company

700 East State Street • Iola, WI 54990-0001
715-445-2214 • 888-457-2873
www.krause.com

Our toll-free number to place an order or obtain
a free catalog is (800) 258-0929.

Library of Congress Catalog Number: 2004100950

ISBN: 0-87349-738-4

Edited by Tracy Schmidt

Designed by Jamie Griffin

Printed in the United States

Dedication

This book is dedicated to
all the other Hot Wheels™ collectors out there
that have spent their lunch money,
dug through the car for a handful of change,
or used their ATM or Credit Card to buy
that one Hot Wheels car they couldn't leave the store without.
To the collector who just happens to stop in the same store every day,
whether it's before or after work, or both,
who checks every car on every peg, every day.
To the collector who likes to take their family for weekend rides,
just so they can find new places to look for Hot Wheels cars.
To the collector who plans family vacations around Hot Wheels events
or spends that vacation hunting down Hot Wheels cars
while the rest of the family is at the beach or amusement park.
To the collector who tries to claim Hot Wheels hunting as a business expense
by claiming they bought them as gifts for a client's children.
And finally...
To all the spouses, girlfriends, and boyfriends
that have put up with all of our craziness over the years,
who have heard us say:
"I just have to stop in here for a minute,"
and then hearing one of the kids in the back seat saying,
"Gee Dad, don't you have enough Hot Wheels already?"

Table of Contents

Acknowledgments

To my loving wife Tina,
Who has so graciously put up with my obsession,
including the late nights I have kept her awake with my research and typing.

To my son Cody,
Who has had to spend more than just a couple of his Birthdays at a
Hot Wheels event somewhere in the country and not at home.

To my son Christopher,
Who is now grown and living many miles away from me,
I miss having you close by.

I love you all more than you will ever know
and I thank you for allowing me the time to do what I do.

To Frank Veres,
A big THANKS for all these great photos!

To the wonderful people at Krause Publications.

To Paul Kennedy, "Acquisitions Editor"
Whose continued faith in me and this project keep it alive.

To Tracy Schmidt, my "Editor"
Whose dedication and perseverance to this project, along with her endless efforts of
having to go through the thousands of pictures and listings, including the many emails,
files and all of the other countless goings on behind the scenes that are all a part of what
has to happen to make sure things come together as well as they do.

Without you, this would not be the adventure it continues to be!
We did it again!
And for that, I thank you both, with all my heart!

Michael

Introduction

Welcome to the 2nd Edition of *Hot Wheels Variations The Ultimate Guide*! My name is Michael Zarnock and I really have to say thanks to everybody that made the 1st edition of this guide such a huge success. Since this book's first release, a great number of collectors have been able to build larger and more complete collections. Most have even found variations they never knew they had in their box of extras. It's also brought forth collectors from all over the world who send me letters about a few variations I missed. I am grateful to have the opportunity to include them also. Hey, I can't have them all, you know. Some of these people have been so nice as to send me some of those new-found variations, and I have included their names at the end of the introduction.

I have always said that I can't do it alone. I wrote this guide as a collector for collectors, and it's the help I get from all of you that makes it what it is.

This book is all about collector numbers and their variations. For those of you that don't already know what I'm talking about, read on and pay attention. If you are going to read any part of this guide, this is the part that you will really want to read. Believe me, when you're done, it's something you will never regret doing. There is a lot of information here that has taken myself, and many others, years to acquire. I wish I had something like this to keep me from making some costly mistakes when I first started.

Let's take the terms "collector number" and "Blue Card." These words describe a type of package and have brought upon their own meaning. These are very important words, and as you read on you will see just how important they truly are.

There has been a lot of confusion as to what is actually a collector number package, so let's start by defining a collector number package. The collector numbers from 1 to 1121 were produced by Mattel from 1989 to 1999. Packages were readily available in any store that sold Hot Wheels cars. Limited edition

cars or cars from clubs with collector numbers on the package are not included in this book. Only cars that were released by Mattel for retail sale by mass merchandisers are inckuded.

Now, there were packages produced before 1989 with small black collector numbers in a circle. These packages are known as "Experimental Packs," and are not considered a part of the collector numbers we are talking about. One of these experimental pack cards is creamy white at the top and fades to blue at the bottom. The small black circle with the collector number inside is at the left side of the name of the car, and is in the middle of the card. There is a checklist of cars with their respective numbers on the backs of these packages. (See picture A)

There are also cards that have the name and circle with number in it at the bottom of the card and a checklist on the back. Additionally, there are black cards that fade to light blue at the bottom that have no number on the front and a checklist with numbers on the back. None of these cards are what we are calling collector numbers or "Blue Cards."

Some people include the experimental packs in the collector numbers category because the numbers for those cars are pretty much the same as the "Blue Card" collector numbers packages. To do this is a major, and costly, misconception. The prices for these cards are nowhere near the value of the "Blue Cards." Others also hear "Blue Card" and take it to mean any card that has blue on it—any shade of blue from any year. It's not! Each card has its own name and value. You can see that in the first few pages of this book. This is where you need to know the difference between the cards. Collector numbers with value are on "Blue Cards." Blue Cards are just that, all blue. The only other color on the card is the collector number and that is white. This white collector number is in the card's lower right-hand corner.

For example, the difference in card value can be explained as follows: Let's

take the number 30, '80s Corvette. This car is found on the experimental card with the number 30, and has a value of approximately $25. Now, this same car on the "Blue Card" number 30 is valued at about $631. See what I mean by paying attention? How would you feel if you paid $631 for the car on the experimental card? Kind of sick I'd bet, and believe me, it has happened. But hey, it's on a card with the number 30 on it right? Well, right number, wrong card. You're going to see in the following pages just how much a piece of cardboard can really be worth.

This whole collector numbers and Blue Card craze was started with the same card. In 1989, Mattel developed the "All Blue Card" with large white collector numbers in the lower right-hand corner. This is the card that they stayed with, and these cards were in use from 1989 to 1994. The numbers are basically 1 to 274. A couple of numbers in that stretch were released after 1994, but not many. If someone says they have "Blue Cards" to sell or trade, and know what they are talking about, they are talking about numbers ranging from 1 to 274. These are the most highly sought-after cards by collectors. (See picture B)

After five years of pretty much the same style card, Mattel decided to make a change. The "Blue & White" cards showed up in 1995. There were reissues of cars with collector numbers on these new "Blue & White" cards. Same car, same number, new packaging. The cards changed to blue on the top half and white on the lower half, with blue collector numbers in the lower right-hand corner. (See picture C) At first, the cars stayed the same, but after a while, things began to change: color, interior, or wheels, but luckily one thing did stay the same—the collector numbers. Of course, cars that are on all Blue Cards do go for a little more than the same car on a Blue and White card. The older the package, the more the value.

As I said earlier, the Blue & White cards carried on the collector numbers theme. Some people call these cards

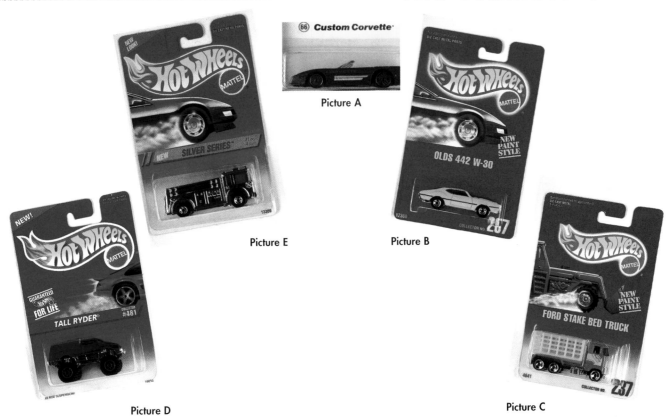

Picture A

Picture E

Picture B

Picture D

Picture C

"Blue Cards." They are not. These are "Blue & White cards." To repeat myself again, just because there is some blue on the card, doesn't mean it's a "Blue Card."

The year 1995 also brought about the "Series Cards." The series cards also have the collector numbers, but on the back of the card with the series name on the front. Only the cars that were not part of any series still had the collector numbers on the front of the card in the same place that the Blue Cards did. The series cards also increased the numbers past 274. The series cards started at number 275 with the "Race Team Series." In 1996, the card changed again with the collector numbers coming off the bottom of the card and added to the right side of the car name in a banner in the center of the card. (See picture D)

The year 1995 is also when many variations started showing up. In the first few series alone there were at least three variations of each car. That's when things got really crazy. There were all new cards, all new series cars along with collector number reissues with different wheels, colors, and windows. You name it, and it was happening. It was enough to make a person spend their lunch hour and their lunch money buying any available variation.

These collector numbers as we

know them went as far as 1121 and stopped in 1999. In the year 2000, Mattel started the collector numbers over at number 1 again, and has continued to do so in 2001 and 2002.

The prices in this book are for mint-packaged cars and are taken from actual sales. Whether it be from that auction site we all know about, at toy shows, or at some Hot Wheels Club meeting. Now remember, these prices are not written in stone. Cars have sold for less, but I have chosen to put down the highest steady price I have seen the car sell for. As time goes on, most prices go up.

I have been collecting, selling, trading, and watching this hobby for a long time. I have seen how most people who put prices on these cars take all the sales they know about and average them to make up the value of a car. To me that doesn't seem fair when we have an abundance of one car in one area of the country and only a handful in another. If there are a ton where YOU are, then you know not to pay a lot for it. But if you have never seen one, then you know it's rare. It's all in how bad you want it and what you're willing to pay for it. Saying this brings me to mention how these prices actually come about. Simply put, supply and demand. If the demand

is great and the supply is small, the price will be high. If the demand is small, no matter how small the supply, the price will be low. Someone has to want it to make it worth something.

What it all boils down to is this: Know what you're getting before you get it, ask questions, do your homework, read, read, and read some more until you know what you're doing, and most of all, use your head! That is what guides are for, to guide you in the right direction. As your host on this trip, I hope I've put things well enough into perspective that you are able to go forth and enjoy your journey. You may not always agree with the pricing, but you can't argue with a full-color picture and a detailed description.

All I can say from here is, best of luck and most of all…remember to have fun, it is a hobby!

Michael

Note: All of our internal page vehicle photos were taken by Frank Veres.

What Is A Variation?

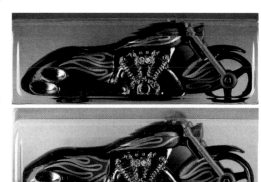

The #192 Corvette Stingray (left) has readily apparent color variations. Others, like the #519 Scorchin' Scooter (right) have more subtle variations in their tampos.

As with most of us, I have stopped and started my collecting many times as life permits. During my most recent collecting period, I have become obsessed with collector number packages. After a while and a lot of money, I ran out of numbered cards that were available to me. Either they were too expensive or just not available. So with that said and done, I kept searching for cars in the same places over and over hoping to find something new. In this diligent search of looking at the same cars over and over, I started noticing that some of the cars looked a little different. Some cars had different colors, or had different interiors, wheels, windows, or bases. There were variations of the cars that I already had. Cool, I said to myself. I can still feed my Hot Wheels habit. Habit? Well, it does get very addictive, doesn't it?

Variations. This word brings shakes and shivers to some people while others could care less. Well, this book is dedicated to those of us who do care about all those crazy variations. If you're as fanatical as I am, I would fathom a guess that you have searched the Internet and any publications for all information possible on variations—the new stuff that is being found, the older stuff that is and isn't around, and anything that anyone can tell you to watch out for.

This is where I come in. Many of you diehard collectors, and even some of you Newbies, might recognize my name from the Internet. Since the mid 1990s I have maintained quite a large Web site with my collection of variations listed by number and

added new information on variations when found. I also listed some good advice for the new collector (Newbie as they are called). Unfortunately, I no longer have any variations listed on the Internet because people decided to help themselves to the information and turn around and sell it as their own.

A lot of you have asked me to share my so-called expertise and views on the variation thing with you, since collecting variations has become a large part of the Hot Wheels collecting persona. In this book I have documented every variation I have been able to find. As we all know, variations are found all over the country, different things go to different places. The variation thing has only come about in the past couple years or so, and I'm sure you might find that there are some I have missed. As time goes on, there are more and more variations being found and I'm sure we will be seeing some very interesting things happening with these cars. Since the release of the first edition of this guide there have been a lot more collectors actively searching for new variations. More eyes find more things. So, if you have a couple or know of a few variations I may have missed, please let me know about them. You can e-mail me at CollectorNumbers@aol.com or write to me at PO Box 185, Marcy, NY 13403. Either way, I will check into it and get back to you. If you would like to stop by my Web site to see what I am up to, just type AOL Keyword "Zarnock" and it will take you to many links. The site has information as to where I will be, personal photos, and info including ordering information for my latest books.

As in the past, I will only document a car that I can actually say I have seen, not ones that are just rumors. I don't like chasing after something that isn't real, and I'm sure you don't either. The listings in this book were put together over the years with the exchange of information from collectors like yourself. Without the interaction of other collectors from all over the country, I would only know about the cars that were released in my area. Now what fun would that be? So, communication will keep this guide fresh from one edition to the next. If you find something out of the ordinary, let me know about it. I will look for it here. If I can't find one, I will have to have you send me a picture or even better, send me one (packaged of course), so I can prove that it does actually exist. If you send me one I will gladly pay for the car and the shipping.

Let's talk about variations. What is a variation?

A variation is something that has changed during the production of a car after it has been released.

There are wheel changes, name changes, interior changes, windows, tampos, even totally different car colors—these are all variations. These are cars that are made in short runs of who knows how many—but not too many.

To be a variation there has to be more than one of the car and it must be still in the package to be considered as a true collector number variation. There are several different kinds of variations. Transitional cars come when a car is changed from one style to the

A variation can be as simple as a set of different wheels, as on the #464 Blazer 4 X 4.

next. These are cars like the #816 Ferrari 308. When the car first came out it was bronze with a tan interior. It was later changed to a red body and they still had some tan interiors left. The tan interiors were put into the red cars until they were gone and then they used the new black interiors. The tan interior cars were very small numbers and are very rare.

There are cars that are made with a different color interior or wheel or shades of color paint during the normal production run because the parts or paint ran out before the rest of the cars were finished. Sometimes they run out of parts while running production and they have to get parts from another bin or other parts get mixed into the bin. You have to remember that these little cars are made in a factory where people get paid to make them. They don't care if they all look the same, they just need to get them out the door. Just like your boss at work tells you, "I don't care how you get it done, just get it done!"

Most of the time, variations are not planned, they just happen. Other times, variations are made purposely just to change things up a bit. Sometimes there are cars made with leftover parts from a previous style car. Cars like the GM Ultralite with "Police" tampo or the "Blood Red" Wildcat. These cars were

a leftover from the Demo Man series. They had painted bodies left over from other runs and put the new stuff on to release them as new collector numbers. All these things are variations, and now you can see why there are very few of them!!!

Putting a cash value on these cars has been very difficult because of their rarity. Demand determines the price. Some people pay a lot of money for variations and others could care less. I look at it this way, if you put a value of $25 on a Treasure Hunt car that has a 10,000-25,000 production run, then what kind of value can you put on something that has a run of 500 or maybe even less? This leads to the supply and demand rule. The fewer there are of something, and the more people that want it, makes it worth a higher amount.

Remember that a variation has to be the physical change of a car. If the car is in the wrong package or is upside down or backwards, it's not a variation. Those are just packaging errors. You might find a car that has a different front wheel than the back ones or one with a part missing, but unless you have a handful of them or know other people that have one or two, these are not variations, but one-of-a-kinds. Don't get me wrong, these are indeed something

neat to have in your collection, only because you are the only person that has one. Remember, there has to be more than one of the car, and it must still be in the package to be considered as a true collector number variation.

I hope you enjoy the list that I have painstakingly put together, and I hope it helps you to build a collection that you will be as proud of as I am of mine. I would like to take the time and space to mention some of the collectors that I have had the opportunity to talk with, meet, and whose collections I have seen with my own eyes. These people are just as nuts as I am about variations. Without the exchange of information from each other we would not be up on all the things to be looking for. Be a good collector and exchange information whenever you can.

Thanks Guys!!!!

Amy Boulan   Mark "Ace" Barber
Jim Garbaczewski   Greg Hall
Raymond Adler   Paul Hansen
Kevin Allen   Carl Pomponio
Jerry Amerson   Jim Speckeen

The # 415 Roll Patrol models shown above are a great example of an interior color.

It's Always Been Hot Wheels Cars For Me!

As a child I was fascinated with cars—any kind of cars. My dad was a body man and I would go with him sometimes to the shop. I saw a lot of cars and trucks when I was growing up. I was always trying to soup-up my Matchbox and slot cars to make them look as real as the cars on the street. I used to read *Hot Rod* magazine and would drool at all the California Custom cars.

It was the greatest time to be a 10-year-old boy in love with American Muscle cars. I can still remember hearing the deep rumbling sound and feeling the ground shake as a classic piece of horsepower cruised past me.

My obsession with Hot Wheels cars began one day back in 1968, as I was riding my Stingray bicycle with the tall sissy bar and Redline slick rear tire down to the local shopping center to look at the models. I walked into a local department store named "W.T. Grants" and saw a new display of die-cast cars. Well, when I saw "Hot Wheels with California Custom Styling," I went nuts! All these way cool cars with mag wheels and Redline tires already on them. Blowers popping out of the hood, side pipes or Zoomies, and trick paint—I was in Hod Rod heaven.

I didn't know which one of the eight cars I should get. I did know one thing though, I didn't have sixty-eight cents to buy one, so I had to race home and ask my mom. I raced into the house like I was getting chased by a rabid dog, screaming, "MOM, MOM!" I tried telling her about the cool cars I just saw at Grants and how I needed a dollar to get one, but the words got all messed up.

After I calmed down, she gave me the dollar. The first car I bought was the Silhouette. I loved custom stuff and that was the wildest thing there. I also remembered seeing the Silhouette on an episode of *Mission Impossible*. Needless to say, I fell in love with that car.

My mother still reminds me of the time that I bought everyone in the family Hot Wheels cars for Christmas gifts. I knew they wouldn't want them and would give them to me. Not a bad idea for a 10 year old. Too bad it didn't work. I couldn't part with them, so I had to buy everybody new gifts. Every birthday or holiday, everyone knew what to get me. My aunt was just recently cleaning out a drawer and found a list of cars I sent with her on a trip to California.

People have asked how I would compare Hot Wheels to other die-cast cars and I really can't give a straight answer. I guess it is all in what you like and what you are looking to get from it. Another question they ask is, "What are your favorite cars?" That's like asking which one of your kids do you like best? I like most of the "real" looking cars. I like a lot of the new cars Mattel is putting out. The '56 Ford Panel is way cool. The Mustang Mach I, '70 Road Runner, Tow Trucks and anything that can carry another vehicle (of course), Shelby Cobra, '57 T-Bird, Corvettes, '65 Mustang, and the list goes on.

I am also a package collector. I like the different styles of packages from the many eras of Hot Wheels cars. Like I said, it's all about the memories for me. Hot Wheels cars are something that can get me away from the stress of the adult world where everyone at work and home depends on you to be the pillar of strength. Hot Wheels cars relax me and bring me back to the easygoing childhood I once knew. Hot Wheels cars have always brought me pleasure, whether it's looking at the cars, playing with them when I was a child, or even today with my boys. For me, Hot Wheels cars have given me a consistency for the past 35-plus years. I would guess by now you can tell I keep everything in the original package. My saying is: "Preserve the toy, preserve the boy."

I've made many friends collecting these toy cars from 1968. I run across other enthusiasts every time I go to the store or at any Hot Wheels function I have the opportunity to attend across the country. There is a kind of camaraderie amongst us collectors. The diverse types of people that collect Hot Wheels cars ranges just like the variations I collect, they are all the same, yet different, each in their own way. It's a great time to be a kid, no matter how old you are!

#1 Old Number 5

#10 Baja Breaker

#29 Tail Gunner

15 Tank Truck

These are some of my prized possessions.

To Open Or Not To Open?

It's been a controversial topic for many of us, and I want to give my opinion on the subject for what it's worth.

I try to keep all my stuff still in the original packaging. That's what this book is all about, "collector numbers packages." I'm just one of those guys that likes to see things as they once came, unmolested. I have friends that like to take them out of the package because they like to play with them and display them that way. There are other people whose collection has been that way since the beginning, and they figure that's the way they should keep it. I've seen a guy take a MOC (mint on card) Redline Race Team Trailer that he just paid $140 for, rip it open, and put it on his shelf. It's all up to you what you want to do with your money and your collection. Which leads me to my next statement…the money thing!

Some people out there collect because they like it, some purchase for the sake of investment, and others land somewhere in between. Many people say the cars won't be worth much later on if they are loose. In my observation over the years, this has been true in many cases for many reasons.

I collect variations of the cars that are in the collector numbers packages. People ask, "Are you a cardboard collector or a car collector?" My response is they are both a very important part of the collection. These cars are in the United States released packages with collector numbers on them. This is where the packaging makes all the difference. The international packages do not have numbers on them and many times have different names for the cars than those in the U.S. packaging. Some internationally packaged cars also come in different colors and with different wheels. So finding an "International Only" released car in a U.S. package with the right name is quite a rarity.

I have a few in my collection that I don't think I would trade for a '95 Treasure Hunt car. One of these would be the #344, 1995 Model Series #8- Camaro convertible, red with black Malaysia base, black interior and clear window, with gold 7-spoke wheels. The gold 7-spoke wheels are what make it such a rarity. Only the internationally released Camaros had the gold 7-spoke wheels. Yes, there are a bunch out there, but not in the U.S. packaging. There is also the #342, 1995 Model Series #2 Mercedes SL, black & grey with red interior and gold 7-spoke wheels. This is where the packaging is very important.

Did I remember to say VERY?

Many cars are out there in abundance. For one reason or another, the same car has been released many times in the same color and wheels, but in a different play set, 5-pack, or other type of blister pack. If you're a loose collector, this means nothing to you except that you can get it just about anywhere for fifty cents.

Let's take the 1995 light-blue Race Team Series Funny Car with basic wheels. It's everywhere, right? It was released in the 2-pack from K-B Toys, in the Race Team 5 pack, or in the "Race Team Series," and is #278. They are everywhere in those packages, or in someone's collection loose, and in many sandboxes. But did you know that it's the very same car that's in the elusive #271 package that is valued at over $3,500? Same car out of the package, 50 cents, in the #271 package, $3,500. I have been told that there are only six of them known to exist. If someone buys one and is the opening-type collector, that will make the remaining five worth even more.

How about the Collector #51 package? It's the yellow '40s Woodie. This car can be found in many different packages from early releases for as little as $5, but on the all-blue card #51 package, it's between $1500 and $2400 if you can find one.

I believe that this is good enough reason for opting not to open the package. You also have to consider the variation thing. Many 5-pack cars are released that don't come in blister packs. If it's loose it has very little value, but packaged in the numbered blister, you have a well-sought-after piece.

This leads to the supply and demand rule. Cars are worth the most when there are fewer of them and more people want them. Also remember that card condition is a key factor. Buy what you like in the best condition you can afford but most of all, keep having fun!

Some Cars ARE Harder To Find

Some cars are always harder to find than others—not that they are made lesser numbers than others, but for other reasons. For example:

Construction vehicles are always in demand. That's why they are a little higher priced and quite hard to find at times. Some people who them for their train sets, grandma buys them for the kids to play with in the backyard, and there are some people that are just plain nuts about construction vehicles.

Police and Fire vehicles are also popular with train people, grammas for the grandkids, and don't forget, some people out just collect police stuff or just fire stuff or even both. This means that these too are hard to come by because they are bought up by the handful when found.

The '55 and '57 Chevys are other cars that are always in demand. Over the years there have been countless numbers of people that have owned a real one or their Uncle Bob's friend's nextdoor neighbor's brother had one. This is one of the many reasons these Chevys are hard to come by. People buy them to customize them to the way they looked when they had one, or want to make it look like the one they never had. Whatever the case may be, these cars are bought up in bunches whenever possible.

The '67 Camaros are always hard to find, especially when they look like a normal production car. The case with the Camaro is just like that of the '57 Chevy; somebody owned one at one time or has always wanted to have one. These cars you will usually find customized in a real street version. I believe that is the biggest reason the 1995 Treasure Hunt Camaro is

so hard to buy. It's not that they made any less than the other 1995 Treasure Hunt cars, but it came in a true street version. It was white with orange rally stripes, the correct colors I might add, and had big tires, just like the ones you see on the street. It is the ultimate custom car without having to take it out of the package and anything with it.

Anytime you have a Hot Wheels car with Real Riders tires (rubber tires) it is very much in demand. In 1995, Mattel reissued the Real Rider Series in their new four-car series sets. The run was shorter than realism-desiring collectors anticipated.

VW Bugs—do I have to say anything more? I think there are more people who collect VW Bugs than any other car. The Bug is just one of those cute little cars that everybody likes. These too are always in short supply, and if there is a variation, it is even harder to find.

Sometimes there are vehicles around and no one ever notices them. One example is the Peterbilt Dump Truck, (page 38) collector number 100. This dump truck came with white basic wheels. There is no chrome on the wheels and they are painted white. These are just like the wheels found on the #273 Super Cannon. This truck is very hard to find for a couple reasons. One reason is that you have to really look close to tell the difference between the white and the chrome wheels. You won't pick it out unless you are looking for it. Another reason is that there were not that many made. If you do come across one, you'll be very lucky.

There have been a few cars that have gotten through the inspectors for one reason or another that should not have been out there. By this, I mean cars that were only meant to be for international release, not U.S. release. In the 1995 season, there were cars for the international line that were the same as the U.S. releases, but had one minor difference. These cars had gold 7-spoke wheels. If you have any Canadian release Model Series cars from 1995, you will see cars like:

#1	Speed Blaster	green	chrome window	g7sp
#2	Mercedes SL	black & gray	red int	g7sp
#5	Power Pistons	burgundy	silver int	g7sp
#8	Camaro Conv.	green	gray int	g7sp
#8	Camaro Conv.	red	black int	g7sp
#9	Power Pipes	dark blue	pink int	g7sp
#10	Ferrari 355	yellow	black int	g7sp
#11	Power Rocket	purple	chrome int	g7sp

As I said earlier, these cars were all in the 1995 U. S. releases in the same colors and interiors but had different wheels. Somehow, some of these cars got put into U.S. released blister packs. The only two that I know of are the #8 red Camaro Convertible and the #2 black and gray Mercedes SL. The key here is to pay attention to the package. Sometimes international packaging is found here in the States so you

might get used to seeing those cars. If you pass it up as being an international package and don't notice it's a U.S. package, you miss out. I say it time and time again, it's all in paying attention. Anytime something like this happens, it makes for a very desirable piece for collectors who leave their cars in the packages.

Treasure Hunt Cars

There is always so much talk and debate about Treasure Hunt cars that I'm devoting a section to them alone.

1. What is a Treasure Hunt?

A Treasure Hunt car is a series car just like all the others. There are 12 cars per series year, one for each month of the year. Some of these Treasure Hunt cars have synthetic rubber tires and look much different than the other series cars, making them more appealing to collectors. These cars are on cards just like the other series cars and have series banners. The one thing that makes them really stand out is that they have either a dollar sign "$" on them or a picture of a treasure chest along with the series banner saying "Treasure Hunt." The banner has always been the color green, like money.

At first, these cars were very limited in production. The first year they were released was 1995. There was a production run of 10,000 for each car. This number was printed in the upper left-hand corner of the card's face. With production numbers being that low, they were indeed a treasure to find, and worth all the commotion they created.

In 1996, the production number was increased to 25,000 for each car, giving the collector a better chance of finding them. This number was also printed on the card's face. This was the last year any production numbers were printed on the cards. It seems as time went on, the production numbers have increased and are not released to the public anymore.

The Treasure Hunt Series cars are well worth the extra efforts of collectors.

2. How come I never find a Treasure Hunt car on the pegs?

Well, there are many different reasons you may never find a Treasure Hunt car on the pegs.

Most stores stock their shelves overnight or first thing in the morning. There are collectors and others standing at the door when the store opens to be the first one in the toy aisle. These people are there every day. They get to know the routine of the store and the stockers. They will always grab the Treasure Hunt cars first and leave for the next store. Unless you are one of those people, you are not going to get that Treasure Hunt. You also have to remember the odds of having a Treasure Hunt car being placed on the pegs that day. Read question #3 below.

3. Are there Treasure Hunt cars in every case?

I opened a case and there was not a Treasure Hunt car in there! There were 72 cars, but somebody must have taken out the Treasure Hunt car and replaced it with something else!

There are not Treasure Hunts in every case. More often than most, there are not. Treasure Hunt cars are only in selected cases. It used to be that the case codes on the side of the cases would denote if indeed there was a Treasure Hunt car or not in that case. That's why you hear so much about case codes, i.e. XXB or WWY. These letters are the last three letters in the lot numbers on the sides of the cases.

Mattel has gotten so much flack because of collectors and others bugging the store clerks for unopened cases that they changed their routine. Mattel still places Treasure Hunt cars in these predestined case codes, but randomly. This way, there is no real way to tell if there is, or is not, a Treasure Hunt in there.

There are Web sites out there that have the case codes and what people have found in them. So please don't think just because you have found an unopened case you are going to find a Treasure Hunt car. I have opened 50 or 60 cases in a year and only found three or four.

4. Is the stock person taking all the best cars from the back room?

Sometimes this is true, but in most stores it isn't. Many stores have policies on holding product for the employees, but that doesn't mean that they can't wait until a friend comes in and stock the shelves at that time.

A lot of collectors do make acquaintances with the clerks or department managers. Remember what your Mom said, "You catch more flies with honey than you do with vinegar!" Which means that if you are nice to people, you get a better reaction from them than you would if you get in their face and demand things. The clerks and managers don't like the flea market guys or the guys that start yelling about having no new cars on the shelves. So…get to know the people who work the floor. Talk to them, don't make a mess when you look through the cars. Pick up the mess that some other jerk left. If they ask if you are looking for anything special, don't say, "I'm looking for Treasure Hunts!" Just say, "I'm just looking for anything I don't have yet." All in all, don't be a jerk that they are not going to like. Believe me, after a while you will be amazed at what will happen.

5. How come all the good cars are gone when I get to the the store?

You have to look at it in a numbers way. There is usually one of a new car in each case when they first come out. So if it's new, everybody gets one when they need it, sometimes two. If you are not one of the collectors that go to every store, every day at 7 a.m. when they open, you are not going to get anything until all the other guys have their fill. Just like being the smallest kid at the table of seven older brothers and sisters. You get what's left. Now remember what I said. That is one car of each in each case. How many cases do you think the store puts out at a time? There are 72 cars in a case. The older cars come two to a case as time goes on. Do you think the store puts more than one or two cases out per day? The Wal-Mart by my house puts out maybe one case a day, and that is a lot compared to other stores.

Now, how many collectors are there where you live, and how many times do they go to the store?

That's why it's hard to find cars unless you aren't there every day. Don't think that you'll find new cars or Treasure Hunts just by stopping in at the local Wal-Mart every other week or so. If you have enough dedication and persistence, things eventually work out.

How To Use This Book

The camera icon shown at right indicates that there is a picture of a particular variation in this book.

The photos run in numerical order, with the exception of the Fossil Fuel Series, which was too far away from the listings. The listings run in release order.

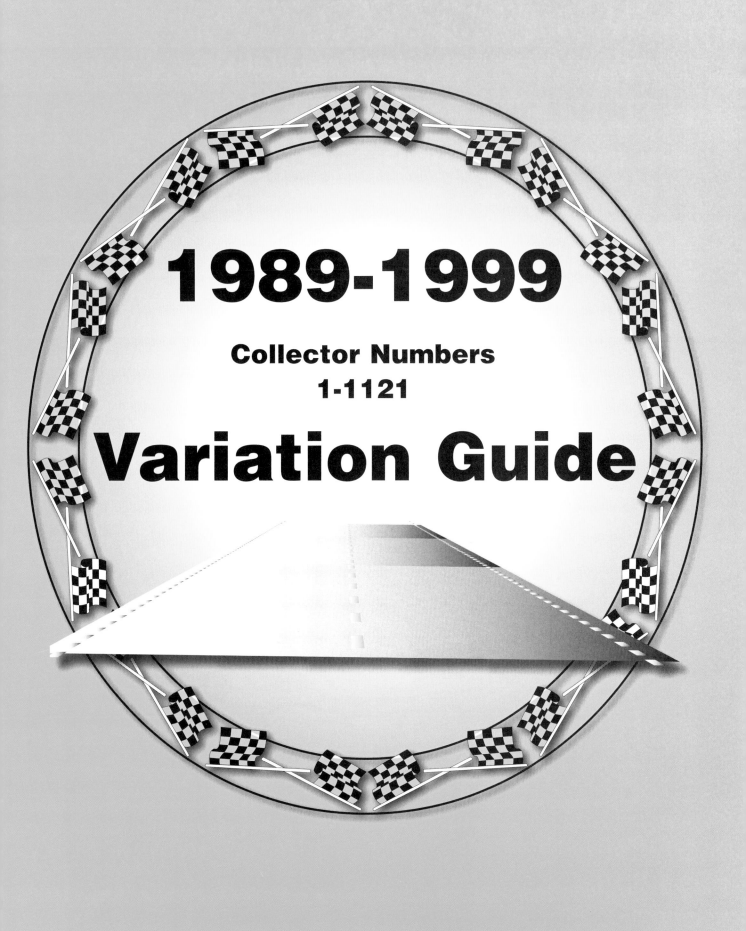

1989-1999

Collector Numbers
1-1121

Variation Guide

Non-Series Collector Number Packs

	Photo	No.	Name	Description	Price
☐	📷	1	Old Number 5	red enamel, matching red metal Malaysia base, louvers on hood, tan int., red, yellow & black tampo on hood w/"No. 5" & "Fire Dept." twice, black plastic ladder on each side, alw-bw	$180
☐	📷	2	Sol-Aire CX4	a. black with yellow, orange & blue stripe tampo, "33" on top & side, metal Malaysia base & int., yellow-tint window, uh	$32
☐	📷			b. same as (a) "33" on top only, no side tampo, metal Malaysia base & int., yellow-tint window, uh	$50
☐				c. same as (a), guh	$181
☐				d. same as (a), sho	$30
☐	📷	3	Wheel Loader	yellow enamel, yellow Malaysia base, black int., alw- yct	$10

Old Number 5

Sol-Aire CX4

Sol-Aire CX4

Wheel Loader

XT-3

Good Humor Truck

Blazer 4X4

Blazer 4X4

Troop Convoy

Vampyra

Vampyra

Baja Breaker

'31 Doozie

Roll Patrol

Peterbilt Tank Truck

Photo	No.	Name	Description	Price
❏ 📷	4	XT3	purple enamel, purple painted Malaysia base, white, yellow & red flame tampo, black canopy, bw	$12
❏	5	Good Humor Truck	a. white enamel, black plastic Malaysia base, with red & blue tampos, large rear window, blue int., clear window, asw-bw	$15
❏ 📷			b. same as (a), smaller rear window, asw-bw	$5
❏			c. same as (b), asw-t/b	$2
❏			d. same as (b), asw-5sp	$2
❏			e. same as (b), new larger tampos, asw-5sp	$2
❏			f. same as (b), asw-7sp	$2
❏	6	Blazer 4X4	a. black w/yellow, red & white tampo, metal Malaysia base, yellow int., yellow-tint window, alw-ct	$60
❏			b. same as (a), alw-cts	$70
❏ 📷			c. blue enamel, blue-tint metal Malaysia base, dark blue & light green side tampo w/red "Blazer" & three thin stripes, light green "4X4" on bottom of door, light green rectangle w/dark blue outline on hood w/three thick red stripes and light green "Blazer" twice, yellow-tint window, gray int., alw-ct	$25
❏ 📷			d. same as (b), alw-cts	$36
❏ 📷	7	Troop Convoy	olive w/matching olive painted Malaysia base, green, brown & tan camouflage on cover, alw-bbw	$300
❏ 📷	8	Vampyra	a. dark purple with white, orange & red wing tampo, metal Malaysia base, chrome engine, asw-bw	$25
❏ 📷			b. light purple with white, orange & red wing tampo, metal Malaysia base, chrome engine, asw-uh	$25
❏	9	unreleased		—

Photo		No.	Name	Description	Price
❏	📷	10	Baja Breaker	white enamel, metal Malaysia base, black, red & yellow tampo, metal base, red int., clear window, asw-ct	$250
❏	📷	11	'31 Doozie	maroon enamel, metal Malaysia base, tan top, maroon int., blue-tint window, asw-ww	$117
❏	📷	12	Roll Patrol	olive w/ matching olive metal Malaysia base, tan, green & brown camouflage on hood, black plastic roll bar, green plastic interior & spare tire, clear window, alw-bbw	$500
		13	unreleased		——
		14	unreleased		——
❏	📷	15	Peterbilt Tank Truck	yellow metal cab, metal Malaysia base, silver met. painted metal tank w/red "Shell" & yellow "Shell" logo outlined in red on side, alw-bw	$60
❏	📷	16	Earth Mover	yellow enamel, matching yellow painted metal Malaysia base, black seat, alw-yct	$104
❏	📷	17	Suzuki QuadRacer	yellow plastic, black-tinted metal base, blue seat, black handlebars, alw-yct	$56
❏	📷	18	Mercedes 540K	black enamel, metal Malaysia base, tan plastic top, tan int., clear window, asw-bw	$103
❏	📷	19	Shadow Jet	yellow enamel, metal Malaysia base, red "Intercooled" tampo on rear wing, blue "F-3" tampo on top, yellow int., smoked canopy, bw	$140
❏	📷	20	Rocketank	olive w/olive painted metal base	$25
❏	📷	21	Nissan Hardbody	a. white enamel, black Malaysia base, red & blue tampo, black int. clear window, alw-ct	$165
❏				b. same as (a), alw-cts	$190
❏	📷	22	Talbot Lago	white enamel w/metal Malaysia base, chrome int., smoked window, ww	$25
❏		23	'80s Firebird	a. black enamel, black plastic Malaysia base, yellow outline bird on hood, yellow "Formula" w/ yellow stripe on side, red int., clear window, asw-bw	$84

Earth Mover

Shadow Jet

Suzuki Quadacer

Rocketank

Mercedes 540K

Nissan Hardbody

Talbot Lago

'80s Firebird

Hiway Hauler

Hiway Hauler

'65 Mustang Convertible

Command Tank

'37 Bugatti

'37 Bugatti

Photo	No.	Name	Description	Price
☐	23	'80s Firebird	b. yellow enamel w/black taillights, green bird with red "30" on hood, red int., clear window, asw-bw	$30
☐ 📷			c. same as (b), asw-bw	$16
☐ 📷	24	Hiway Hauler	a. red enamel cab, metal Malaysia base, white container box with long Pepsi tampo, black int., red-tint window alw-bw	$30
☐			b. turquoise enamel cab, metal Malaysia base, white container box with Ocean Pacific tampo, tan int., blue-tint window, alw-bw	$12
	25	unreleased		—
☐	26	'65 Mustang Convertible	a. turquoise enamel, metal Malaysia base, black side tampo, tan int., clear window, asw-ww	$30
☐ 📷			b. metal flake blue, metal Malaysia base, white side tampo, tan int., clear window, asw-ww	$22
☐			c. white enamel, metal Malaysia base, red side tampo, tan int., clear window, asw-ww	$180
The '65 Mustang Convertible is the same as the "Parking Plate" cars and was carried at KB Toys.				
☐ 📷	27	Command Tank	olive w/light green, tan & brown camouflage on top & sides, tan star on side, olive base	$25
☐	28	'37 Bugatti	a. yellow enamel, yellow plastic fenders, metal Malaysia base, red cove, chrome int., blue-tint window, asw,-bw	$75

	Photo	No.	Name	Description	Price
❑	📷	28	'37 Bugatti	b. same as (a), asw-ww	$35
❑	📷			c. blue enamel, yellow plastic fenders, metal Malaysia base, gray cove, chrome int., blue-tint window, asw-ww	$20
❑				d. blue enamel, blue plastic fenders, metal Malaysia base, gray cove, chrome int., blue-tint window, asw-ww	$12
❑	📷			e. same as (d), chrome int., blue-tint window, asw-bw	$45
❑				f. same as (d), asw-7sp	$5
❑	📷	29	Tail Gunner	a. olive green, olive painted Malaysia base, light green, tan & brown camouflage, black window, alw-bct	$125
❑				b. same as (a), alw-bcts	$150
❑	📷	30	'80s Corvette	blue enamel, matching blue painted metal Malaysia base, red, white & yellow tampo w/88 & Corvette on sides, tan & red int. w/tan bag in back, clear window, alw-gho	$631
❑		31	Classic Cobra	a. red enamel, metal Malaysia base, two yellow & black stripes on hood, black int., clear window, alw-bw	$7
❑				b. same as (a), black painted metal Malaysia base, alw-3sp	$6
❑	📷			c. same as (a), metal Malaysia base, alw-7sp	$10
❑				d. same as (a), black plastic Malaysia base, alw-7sp	$5
❑				e. same as (a), black painted metal Malaysia base, alw-7sp	$5
❑	📷	32	Sharkruiser	a. gray with gray painted Malaysia base, chrome engine, sho	$15
❑				b. same as (a), uh	$7
❑	📷	33	Camaro Z28	a. purple enamel, black plastic Malaysia base, yellow, green & orange side tampo, black window, bw	$11
❑				b. same as (a), black plastic Malaysia base w/skids in front, bw	$15

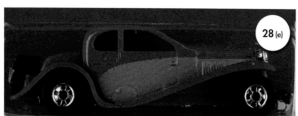

'37 Bugatti

Tail Gunner

'80s Corvette

Classic Cobra

Sharkruiser

Camaro Z28

Camaro Z28

Camaro Z28

Ferrari Testarossa

Bulldozer

Baja Bug

Ferrari Testarossa

Hot Bird

Photo	No.	Name	Description	Price
❏	33	Camaro Z28	c. orange enamel, black plastic Malaysia base, with yellow, blue & purple side tampo, black window, bw	$11
❏			d. same as (c), uh	$90
❏			e. red enamel, black plastic Malaysia base with skids, yellow, black & blue side tampo, black plastic black window, gho	$35
❏			f. same as (e), bw	$11
❏			g. red enamel black painted Malaysia base, yellow, black & blue side tampo, black window, uh	$8
❏			h. red enamel, unpainted metal Malaysia base, yellow, black & blue side tampo, black window, uh	$6
❏ 📷	34	Bulldozer	yellow metal body, yellow plastic Malaysia base, black rubber treads, black plastic rollers	$33
❏	35	Ferrari Testarossa	a. red enamel, matching red painted Malaysia base, black & red int., clear window, uh	$10
❏ 📷			b. same as (a), tan & red int., uh	$12
❏			c. black enamel, black met. painted Malaysia base, tan & black int., clear window, guh	$8
❏			d. same as (c), g3sp	$6
❏ 📷			e. same as (c), gbbs	$2
❏			f. same as (c), asw-gbbs	$25
❏			g. same as (c), black int. and rear taillights, gbbs	$70
❏ 📷	36	Baja Bug	white with red & orange flames, purple "Blazen Bug," metal Malaysia base, red int., bw	$125
❏ 📷	37	Hot Bird	a. black w/yellow bird tampo on hood, red & yellow stripe on roof & trunk, metal Malaysia base, red int., blue-tint window, gho	$22
❏			b. blue flake, blue-tint metal Malaysia base, yellow flames w/red outline on roof, hood, and side, white bird with yellow outline on hood, two white designs in front of flames on door, yellow "Firebird" on rocker panel behind front wheel, tan int., clear window, gho	$30
❏			c. same as (b), uh	$12

Photo	No.	Name	Description	Price
❑	37	Hot Bird	d. white enamel, blue-tint metal Malaysia base, red stripes w/blue rectangle & white stars tampo on hood, side has two blue stars on rear fender, blue "All American Firebird" on door w/three red ribbon stripes, red int. blue-tint window, gho	$25
❑			e. same as (d), red interior, uh	$16
❑			f. same as (d), tan interior, uh	$55
❑			g. same as (d), red interior, sho	$45
❑			h. same as (d), red interior, uh	$20
❑			i. same as (d), red interior, guh	$200
❑ 📷	38	Dump Truck	a. yellow enamel, metal Malaysia base, yellow metal dump box, alw-yct	$16
❑			b. same as (a), yellow plastic dump box, alw-yct	$7
❑	39	Monster Vette	a. yellow enamel, metal Malaysia base, red & purple flames on hood & side, black int., smoked window, alw-ct	$30
❑			b. same as (a), alw-cts	$100
❑ 📷			c. purple enamel, metal Malaysia base, red & blue flames & black int., smoked window, alw-ct	$60
❑			d. same as (c), alw-cts	$70
❑ 📷	40	Power Plower	black enamel, metal Malaysia base, orange, red & purple stripe, "Midnight Removal" on door, metal Malaysia base, red int., smoked window, asw-ct	$84
	41	unreleased		
❑	42	Oshkosh Snowplow	a. orange enamel painted metal cab, box & fenders, orange plastic plow blade, blue-tint metal Malaysia base, orange int., alw-oct	$35

Dump Truck

Monster Vette

Power Plower

Oshkosh Snowplow

Tall Ryder

Classic Caddy

Rescue Ranger

Rig Wrecker

Gulch Stepper

Gulch Stepper

Rolls Royce Phantom II

'40s Woodie

Delivery Truck

Zombot

Nissan 300 ZX

Nissan 300 ZX

Road Roller

Photo	No.	Name	Description	Price
❑	42	Oshkosh Snowplow	b. orange plastic cab & box, orange enamel painted metal fenders, orange plastic plow blade, blue-tint metal Malaysia base, orange enamel painted int., alw-ct	$30
❑			c. same as (b), alw-ct	$25
❑			d. light olive green enamel metal cab & box, light green enamel hood & fenders, green plastic plow blade, blue-tint metal Malaysia base, green enamel painted interior, alw-cts	$35
❑			e. green enamel metal cab & box, lighter green enamel hood & fenders, green plastic plow blade, blue-tint metal Malaysia base, green enamel painted interior, alw-ct	$25
❑			f. light olive green plastic cab & box, green painted metal fenders, green plastic plow blade, blue-tint metal Malaysia base, green enamel painted int., alw-cts	$30
❑ 📷			g. same as (f), alw-ct	$25
❑			h. light olive green plastic cab & box, matching enamel painted metal hood & fenders, green plastic plow blade, blue-tint metal Malaysia base, green interior, alw-ct	$25
❑ 📷	43	Tall Ryder	a. silver flake, black plastic between metal Malaysia base, red & yellow stripe, yellow & blue "Tall Rider" tampo on side, black window, alw-ct	$46
❑			b. same as (a), alw-cts	$65
❑ 📷	44	Classic Caddy	a. blue w/black plastic fenders, metal Malaysia base, tan int., asw-ww	$15
❑			b. same as (a), asw-5sp	$3
❑			c. same as (a), asw-t/b	$2
❑ 📷	45	Rescue Ranger	red enamel, chrome Malaysia base, white & black "Rescue Unit" w/red & yellow HW logo on door, yellow "Emergency" in black panel on rear w/white "Oxygen" & "First Aid+," yellow insert, black int., smoked window, alw-bw	$20
❑ 📷	46	Rig Wrecker	white enamel w/"Steves Towing" tampo, chrome Malaysia base, chrome int., clear window, asw-bw	$101
❑	47	'57 Chevy	a. turquoise, chrome Malaysia base, blue-tint int. & window, uh	$100
❑			b same as (a), gho	$350
	48	unreleased		—
❑ 📷	49	Gulch Stepper	a. red enamel with black plastic spacer & bumpers between a metal Malaysia base, yellow & white stripes with turquoise outlined side tampo, side has white oval with red "BELL," white square with red "15" outlined in turquoise, yellow oval with red "Pennzoil" on side and turquoise rectangle tampo, black window & tire on hood, alw-ct	$54
❑ 📷			b. same as (a), alw-cts	$75
❑			c. same as (a), no "Pennzoil" tampo, alw-ct	$20
❑ 📷	50	Rolls Royce Phantom II	met. blue, metal Malaysia base, black int., tan top, clear window, alw-ww	$405
❑ 📷	51	'40s Woodie	yellow enamel fenders & hood, light brown wood sides, chrome engine & grille, black painted roof, blue-tint window, black int., asw-bw	$2,400
❑ 📷	52	Delivery Truck	white enamel, "Larry's Mobile Tune-up," blue, red & yellow tampo, black plastic Malaysia base, red int., clear window, asw-bw	$32
❑ 📷	53	Zombot	a. gold chrome w/purple chrome gun, metal Malaysia base, sho	$15
❑			b. same as (a), uh	$15
❑ 📷	54	Nissan 300 ZX	a. met. red, metal Malaysia base, yellow 300 ZX tampo on hood, yellow stripe on roof, tan int., clear window, uh	$33
❑			b. white enamel, matching white painted metal Malaysia base, yellow, red and blue stripes on roof & hood, white & yellow "300" and red "ZX" outlined in blue on hood, large white and yellow "300" with red design outlined in blue on door, small red "Nissan" on fender behind front wheel, black interior & bumpers, clear window, asw-uh	$90
❑			c. same as (a), asw-gho	$130
❑ 📷	55	Road Roller	yellow enamel, black plastic Malaysia base, black inserts & rollers	$25
❑	56	Bronco 4-Wheeler	a. white enamel, metal Malaysia base, white plastic cap, red, yellow & blue stripe tampo, w/ "Built Ford Tough" on side, red & yellow flames on hood, red motorcycle on rear, red int., smoked window, asw-ct	$55

Bronco 4-Wheeler

Sheriff Patrol

3-Window '34

Sheriff Patrol

Blown Camaro Z28

Lamborghini Countach

Blown Camaro Z28

Alien

Alien

Photo	No.	Name	Description	Price
☐ 📷	56	Bronco 4-Wheeler	b. turquoise enamel, metal Malaysia base, white plastic cap, red & white stripe side tampo w/red "Bronco," red & white stripes w/"Ford" on hood, metal base, red motorcycle on rear, red int., blue-tint window, asw-ct	$25
☐ 📷	57	3-Window '34	purple w/purple fenders, black running boards, metal Malaysia base, light green, dark blue & red side tampo, chrome int., clear window, bw	$35
☐	58	Blown Camaro Z28	a. turquoise enamel, metal Malaysia base, dark blue & white tampo on hood with small yellow Z28 on nose, white & blue stripes with large white "Camaro" and yellow Z28 on side, chrome engine through hood, gray int., blue-tint window, gho	$65
☐ 📷			b. same as (a), uh	$60
☐			c. same as (a), bw	$80
☐ 📷	59	Sheriff Patrol	a. blue flake, metal Malaysia base, both doors white, black & yellow "Sheriff" on front door w/yellow & black star, "Sheriff 701" on roof, black int., blue-tint window, asw-bw	$15
☐ 📷			b. black enamel, metal Malaysia base, both doors white, blue & yellow "Police" on front doors & roof, blue & yellow star on front door & hood, small blue "Radar Equipped" on rear door, tan int., blue-tint window, asw-bw	$10
☐			c. same as (b), turquoise & yellow "Police" on front doors & roof, turquoise & yellow star on front door & hood, asw-bw	$15

Photo	No.	Name	Description	Price
☐	59	Sheriff Patrol	d. black enamel, metal Malaysia base, both doors white, blue & yellow "Police" on front doors & roof, blue & yellow star on front door & hood, larger blue "Radar Equipped" on rear door, tan int., blue-tint window, asw-7sp	$5
☐ 📷	60	Lamborghini Countach	white enamel, matching white painted Malaysia base, light blue & red stripes on side, red int., smoked window, uh	$13
	61	unreleased		—
☐ 📷	62	Alien	a. dark red plastic & silver flake, metal Malaysia base, metal int., smoked canopy, uh	$7
☐ 📷			b. red plastic & silver flake, metal Malaysia base, metal int., smoked canopy, uh	$5
☐			c. light red plastic & silver flake, metal Malaysia base, metal int., smoked canopy, 5sp	$4
☐			d. same as (c), 7sp	$4
☐ 📷	63	Radar Ranger	a. silver flake w/red, black & blue tampo, metal Malaysia base, chrome radar dish, black int., clear window, alw-cts	$40
☐			b. same as (a), alw-ct	$9
☐			c. same as (a), alw-bct	$40
☐			d. same as (a), alw-t/b	$3
☐			e. same as (a), unchromed gray radar dish, alw-t/b	$10
	64	unreleased		—
☐	65	VW Bug	a. turquoise enamel, metal Malaysia base, yellow, orange & magenta tampo on roof & side, tan int., clear window, bw	$41
☐ 📷			b. red enamel, metal Malaysia base, white & yellow flames with blue outline on front, top, and sides, white int., clear window, bw	$30
☐			c. same as (b), turquoise outlined flames, bw	$27
☐ 📷	66	Custom Corvette	dark red met., black plastic Malaysia base w/two slots from "Billionth Car" edition, yellow, white, and blue side stripe tampo, yellow & blue stripe on hood & trunk, blue "Corvette" on hood & sides, tan int., blue-tint window, uh	$45
☐			b. same as (a), black Malaysia base, w/o slots, uh	$50

Radar Ranger

'32 Ford Delivery

VW Bug

T-Bucket

Custom Corvette

Ferrari F40

Chevy Stocker

School Bus

Chevy Stocker

School Bus

Ambulance

Bus

	Photo	No.	Name	Description	Price
☐	📷	67	'32 Delivery	yellow enamel, yellow plastic fenders, metal Malaysia base, orange, red & blue stripe tampo on sides, "Delivery" tampo in blue, yellow int., clear window, bw	$35
☐		68	T-Bucket	a. yellow enamel, metal Malaysia base, red & blue flames, red int., clear window, bw	$10
☐	📷			b. same as (a), 5sp	$12
☐	📷	69	Ferrari F40	a. red enamel, metal Malaysia base, yellow "Ferrari F40" on hood, "F40" & stripe on sides, tan int., clear window, uh	$10
☐				b. same as (a), guh	$5
☐				c. same as (a), g3sp	$9
☐				d. same as (a), g5sp	$7
☐				e. same as (a), gbbs	$3

🏁 The 1995 Treasure Hunt #2 Gold Passion was found as an error on the "Gold Metal Speed, collector numbers 69, Ferrari F40 card." There are many of them out there. If you are lucky enough to find one for sale you should be able to pick it up for $100.

	Photo	No.	Name	Description	Price
☐	📷	70	Chevy Stocker	a. black enamel, metal Malaysia base, light red, yellow stripe on side, white & red "3" on door, side tampo includes red & blue "V" (Valvoline) in white circle & "Union," gray int., clear window, bw	$15
☐	📷			b. same as (a), dark red, yellow stripe on side, white & red "3" on door, " Union & Valvoline" decal missing from side, gray int., bw	$15
☐	📷	71	Ambulance	a. white enamel, black plastic Malaysia base, blue "American" & stars side tampo, red & blue stripe on sides, black "Oxygen Supplies" & "First Aid" side tampos, white int., blue-tint window, asw-bw	$5
☐				b. same as (a), asw-7sp	$3
☐				c. same as (a), asw-t/b	$3
☐				d. yellow enamel, black plastic Malaysia base, black "Ambulance" side tampo, red stripe w/white "Rescue," black "Radio Dispatch" on door, black "Unit 5," & "City of Hot Wheels" logo box's side, yellow int., dark smoke window, asw-5sp	$2

Street Roader

Pontiac Banshee

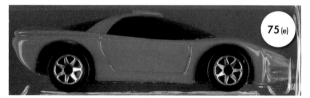

Pontiac Banshee

GT Racer

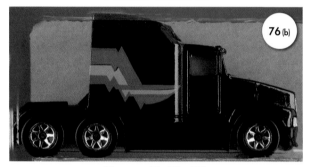

Kenworth Big Rig

GT Racer

Pontiac Banshee

Bywayman

Photo	No.	Name	Description	Price
☐	71	Ambulance	e. same as (d), asw-5dot	$2
☐			f. same as (d), asw-7sp	$4
☐ 📷	72	School Bus	a. yellow enamel w/thick black stripe on side, black Malaysia base, black int., clear window, asw-bw	$9
☐ 📷			b. School Bus name on card with black Prison Transport bus in package. Black w/white & gold stripe w/black "Police" in stripe, "Prisoner Transport" in white on side, gray plastic Malaysia base, blue int., clear window w/barred windows, asw-5dot	$20
☐		Bus (name change on card)	c. same as (b), asw-5dot	$2
☐ 📷			d. same as (c), clear window w/ no bars, asw-5dot	$31
☐ 📷	73	Street Roader	a. white enamel, black center insert, metal Malaysia base, red, blue & black tampo on hood & sides, black int., clear window, alw-ct	$15
☐			b. same as (a), alw-cts	$25
☐ 📷	74	GT Racer	a. purple enamel, metal Malaysia base, orange, dark blue & white stripe tampo, w/dark blue "5" on hood & sides, "Bell" & "V" tampo on sides, chrome pipes & rear wing, metal int., dark smoked window, uh	$20
☐			b. same as (a), missing "V" tampo on sides, uh	$15
☐ 📷			c. same as (b), bw	$15
☐ 📷	75	Pontiac Banshee	a. red enamel, dark red roof bar, dark smoked window, metal Malaysia base, asw-uh	$10

Photo	No.	Name	Description	Price
☐ 📷	55	Pontiac Banshee	b. red enamel, red roof bar, dark smoked window, metal Malaysia base, asw-uh	$4
☐			c. same as (b), Malaysia base, asw-guh	$200
☐			d. same as (b), asw-5sp	$4
☐ 📷			e. same as (b), asw-7sp	$10
☐	76	Kenworth Big Rig	a. black enamel, black plastic Malaysia base, red, orange & blue side tampo, gray window, alw-bw	$8
☐ 📷			b. same as (a), with dark red inside tampo, alw-7sp	$6
☐			c. same as (a), alw-7sp	$3
☐			d. same as (a), alw-t/b	$3
☐	77	Bywayman	a. maroon, metal Malaysia base, yellow & black eagle tampo on side, black "Eagle" & stars tampo in white ribbon on lower sides, red int., dark smoked window, asw-ct	$20
☐			b. same as (a), asw-wct	$150
☐ 📷			c. black enamel, metal Malaysia base, eagle with white head, yellow wings & blue outline on side, red int., roll bar & bed, dark smoked window, asw-ct	$12
☐			d. same as (c), turquoise outline on eagle tampo, asw-ct	$15
☐			e. blue flake, metal Malaysia base, yellow & black eagle tampo, black "eagle" & stars tampo in white ribbon on lower sides, red int., dark smoked window, asw-ct	$90
☐ 📷	78	Peterbilt Cement Truck	red enamel, metal Malaysia base, white plastic barrel, alw-bw	$100
☐ 📷	79	Big Bertha	olive w/green, tan & brown camouflage on top	$11
☐ 📷	80	Porsche 959	a. met. red, metal Malaysia base, orange & yellow tampos, tan int., clear window, asw-uh	$15
☐ 📷			b. red enamel, metal Malaysia base, white tampos & black "7," gray int., clear window, asw-uh	$14
☐ 📷			c. red enamel, metal Malaysia base, yellow & blue "59" tampo, gray int., clear window, asw-uh	$13

Peterbilt Cement Truck

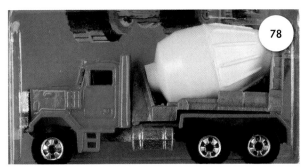

Big Bertha

Porsche 959

Porsche 959

Porsche 959

Porsche 959

Photo	No.	Name	Description	Price
☐ 📷	80	Porsche 959	d. same as (c), asw-sho	$20
☐	81	Ratmobile	a. white plastic body, metal Malaysia base, chrome engine, asw-uh	$5
☐ 📷			b. same as (a), asw-sho	$15
☐	82	Fire Eater	a. red enamel, chrome Malaysia base, black & yellow tampos, blue plastic insert, no logo, blue-tint int. & window, alw-bw	$8
☐			b. same as (a), yellow HW logo in front of rear wheel, alw-5sp	$3
☐ 📷			c. same as (a), alw-7sp	$4
☐			d. day-glo yellow enamel, chrome Malaysia base, red & black tampos, red HW logo in red outlined square, w/two red & black circles on side behind front wheel, red plastic insert, black interior, smoked window, alw-5sp	$3
☐ 📷			e. same as (d), alw-t/b	$2
☐	83	Tank Gunner	olive w/matching metal Malaysia base, light green, dark maroon & tan camouflage on sides, hood is same w/tan star, alw-bbw	$103
☐ 📷	84	Probe Funny Car	red enamel, metal Malaysia base, white "Motorcraft" tampos, smoked window, bw	$30
	85	unreleased		—
☐	86	Propper Chopper	a. white enamel, blue plastic Malaysia base & interior, red, blue & yellow tampo, yellow triangle at left of side tampo, blue-tint window	$65
☐ 📷			b. same as (a), red triangle at left side of tampo	$10
☐ 📷	87	Purple Passion	a. purple met., chrome Malaysia base, w/green & dark blue scallop tampo on hood & sides, red int., clear window, ww	$14
☐ 📷			b. purple met., chrome Malaysia base, w/light yellow & turquoise flames on hood & sides, tan int., clear window, ww	$9
☐			c same as (b), bright yellow & turquoise flames on hood & sides, ww	$9
☐ 📷	88	Thunderbird Stocker	a. red enamel, black plastic base, white "Motorcraft" tampos on hood & sides, black int. clear window, bw	$25
☐			b. same as (a), asw-bw	$30

Ratmobile

Probe Funny Car

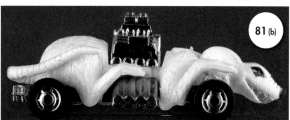

Fire-Eater

Propper Chopper

Fire-Eater

Purple Passion

Purple Passion 87 (b)

Purple Passion 87 (c)

T-Bird Stocker 88 (a)

T-Bird Stocker 88 (c)

Mini Truck 89 (b)

Mercedes 380 SEL 92 (a)

Mercedes 380 SEL 92 (b)

Mercedes 380 SEL 92 (c)

	Photo	No.	Name	Description	Price
☐	📷	88	Thunderbird Stocker	c. white & black enamel, black plastic Malaysia base, red stripe on side, yellow "Havoline 28" tampo on sides, black "28" on roof, black int., clear window, uh	$15
☐				d. same as (c), bw	$200
☐		89	Mini Truck	a. turquoise enamel, turquoise plastic Malaysia base, thin magenta, blue & yellow stripes, blue int., clear window, sho	$200
☐	📷			b. same as (a), uh	$10
☐				c. same as (b), thick dark purple, blue & yellow stripes	$10
		90	unreleased		—
		91	unreleased		
☐	📷	92	Mercedes 380 SEL	a. black enamel, black plastic Malaysia base, chrome front grille & headlights, tan int., clear window, asw-gho	$40
☐	📷			b. same as (a), uh	$12
☐	📷			c. same as (a), asw-sho	$15
		93	unreleased		—
☐	📷	94	Auburn 852	a. red w/red fenders, red int., clear window, metal Malaysia base, asw-ww	$20
☐				b. same as (a), asw-bw	$200
☐	📷	95	'55 Chevy	a. white enamel, gray pearl plastic Malaysia base, orange, yellow & magenta side tampo, dark magenta window, bw	$16
☐	📷			b. same as (a), skids on front of base	$20
☐				c. yellow enamel, gray pearl plastic Malaysia base, magenta, orange & blue side tampo, dark magenta window, bw	$17

Auburn 852

Nissan Custom "Z"

'55 Chevy

Nissan Custom "Z"

'55 Chevy

Ford Stake Bed Truck

	Photo	No.	Name	Description	Price
❏		95	'55 Chevy	d. same as (c), skids on front of base	$22
		96	unreleased		—
		97	unreleased		—
❏	📷	98	Nissan Custom "Z"	a. met. red, metal Malaysia base, yellow "300ZX" twice on hood, two yellow pinstripes on roof, tan int., clear window, uh	$12
❏	📷			b. same as (a), sho	$20
❏				c. same as (a), guh	$200
❏	📷	99	Ford Stake Bed Truck	met. blue, chrome Malaysia base, yellow stake rack, yellow, red & white door tampo, chrome int., clear window, asw-bw	$9
❏	📷	100	Peterbilt Dump Truck	a. red w/red plastic dump box, metal Malaysia base, clear window & int., asw-bw	$5
❏	📷			b. same as (a), asw-wbw	$75
❏				c. same as (a), asw-3sp	$5
❏				d. same as (a), asw-7sp	$3
		101	unreleased		—
❏	📷	102	Surf Patrol	a. yellow enamel, metal Malaysia base, red tampos, thick white "Rescue" tampo, light red int., clear window, asw-ct	$3
❏				b. yellow enamel, metal Malaysia base, red tampos, thin white "Rescue" tampo & "City of Hot Wheels" logo, dark red int., smoked window, asw-ct/b	$2
❏	📷	103	Range Rover	white enamel, black Malaysia base, blue & red side stripe, tan int., clear window, asw-ct	$8
❏		104	Turbo Streak	a. day-glo red w/matching painted rear wing & front spoiler, unpainted metal Malaysia base, blue & pink "Tune-up Masters" tampo, bw	$75
❏	📷			b. same as (a), unpainted wing & front spoiler	$15
❏				c. same as (b), blue & white "Tune-up Masters" tampo	$10
❏	📷	105	Peugeot 205 Rallye	white enamel, metal Malaysia base, red, yellow, blue, & black tampos, w/"2" tampo on hood & sides, gray int., clear window, alw-bw	$91

Photo	No.	Name	Description	Price
☐ 📷	106	VW Golf	a. white w/pink, green & blue tampos, pink Malaysia base & int., clear window, asw-bw	$50
☐			b. red w/white & black side stripes, yellow "GTI", black Malaysia base, tan int., clear window, asw-bw	$10
	107	unreleased		—
☐ 📷	108	Ramp Truck	a. white enamel, metal Malaysia base, white plastic ramp w/dark blue, yellow & red tampos, clear window, asw-bw	$41
☐			b. same as (a), white plastic ramp with turquoise, yellow & red tampos, asw-bw	$12
	109	unreleased		—
☐	110	Trailbuster	a. turquoise w/pink, yellow & black tampo, metal Malaysia base, pink int., clear window, asw-ct	$25

100 (a)

Peterbilt Dump Truck

105 (a)

Peugot 205 Rallye

100 (b)

Peterbilt Dump Truck

106 (a)

VW Golf

102 (a)

Surf Patrol

108 (a)

Ramp Truck

103

Range Rover

110 (b)

Trailbuster

104 (b)

Turbo Streak

111

Street Beast

Limozeen

Pontiac Fiero 2M4

Speed Shark

Roll Patrol

Pontiac Fiero 2M4

Mazda MX-5 Miata

Pontiac Fiero 2M4

Ferrari 250

Photo		No.	Name	Description	Price
☐	📷	110	Trailbuster	b. same as (a), blue replaces black in side tampo, asw-ct	$15
☐	📷	111	Street Beast	turquoise & white, metal Malaysia base, blue & pink tampos, turquoise int., clear window, asw-ww	$5
☐	📷	112	Limozeen	white enamel chrome Malaysia base, pink, orange & blue side tampos, white int., smoked window, asw-ww	$15
☐		113	Speed Shark	a. maroon w/white, pink & yellow tampos, chrome window, chrome Malaysia base, pink int., bw	$45
☐	📷			b. purple w/white, pink & yellow tampos, chrome window, chrome Malaysia base, pink int., bw	$7
☐				c. black w/red, orange & yellow tampos, orange-tint window, red int., chrome Malaysia base, bw	$5
☐				d. black w/red, orange & yellow tampos, orange-tint window, red int., chrome Malaysia base, 5sp	$3
☐	📷	114	Pontiac Fiero 2M4	a. red enamel, very blue-tint metal Malaysia base, red, white & blue flag tampo on hood & sides, white pinstripe w/white "Fiero" below black painted rear side window, black int., clear window, asw-uh	$8
☐				b. same as (a), red enamel, metal base, asw-bw	$85
☐				c. black enamel, metal Malaysia base, red, yellow & blue confetti side tampo, white, red & blue "Fiero" on hood, red int., clear window, asw-sho	$25
☐				d. same as (c), black enamel, metal base, asw-uh	$15
☐				e. same as (c), black enamel, metal base, asw-uh	$30
☐	📷			f. same as (c), black enamel, black painted metal Malaysia base, asw-bw	$20

Photo	No.	Name	Description	Price
☐ 📷	115	Roll Patrol	olive, matching olive painted metal Malaysia base, green, tan & brown camouflage on hood, black int., clear window, asw-bct	$27
☐ 📷	116	Mazda MX-5 Miata	a. red enamel, matching red painted metal Malaysia base, yellow, pink & green "Miata" tampo on hood, tan int., clear window, asw-bw	$10
☐			b. same as (a), no hood tampo, asw-bw	$13
☐ 📷	117	Ferrari 250	a. yellow enamel, chrome Malaysia base and pipes, black "7" in dark yellow circle on door, magenta "Ferrari" tampos on hood and sides black int., clear window, bw	$17
☐			b. same as (a), red "Ferrari" tampos on hood & sides, bw	$15
☐			c. yellow enamel, yellow plastic Malaysia base, black "7" in yellow circle, red "Ferrari" tampos on hood & sides, chrome pipes, black int., clear window, bw	$12
☐			d. same as (c), black pipes, bw	$9
☐			e. same as (d), 7sp	$5
☐	118	Ferrari 348	a. yellow enamel, black plastic Malaysia base, red, turquoise & white hood tampo, black & yellow int., clear window, uh	$6
☐ 📷			b. same as (a), sho	$15
	119	unreleased		——
	120	unreleased		——

Ferrari 348

Toyota MR2 Rally

Lamborghini Diablo

Zender Fact 4

Zender Fact 4

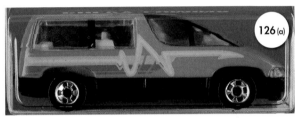

Chevy Lumina

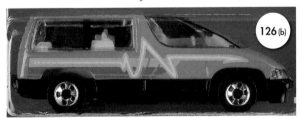

Chevy Lumina

Power Plower

Power Plower

128

Baja Breaker

129 (a)

Suzuki QuadRacer

131 (a)

Nissan Hardbody

131 (d)

Nissan Hardbody

133 (b)

Shadow Jet

134

Mercedes 540K

135 (b)

'32 Ford Delivery

136 (a)

'56 Flashsider

136 (c)

'56 Flashsider

136 (e)

'56 Flashsider

137

Blimp

Photo	No.	Name	Description	Price
	121	unreleased		—
☐ 📷	122	Toyota MR2 Rallye	a. white enamel, black plastic Malaysia base, red, orange & yellow tampos, chrome front lights, red int., clear window, asw-sho	$22
☐			b. same as (a), asw-uh	$8
☐			c. same as (b), black front lights, uh	$20
☐ 📷	123	Lamborghini Diablo	red enamel, matching red painted Malaysia base, yellow "Diablo" tampo, tan int., smoked window, uh	$6
	124	unreleased		—
☐ 📷	125	Zender Fact 4	a. silver flake, black plastic Malaysia base, yellow "Fact 4" above right headlight, white "Zender" on nose, yellow "Fact 4" in front of rear wheel above rocker panel, black int., clear window, uh	$15
☐			b. same as (a), no tampo on side, uh	$7
☐ 📷			c. same as (b), sho	$15
☐			d. same as (b), guh	$150
☐ 📷	126	Lumina Minivan	a. red enamel, black plastic Malaysia base, pink, yellow & blue stripes on side, tan int. with narrow rear seat, clear window, black painted top, black pillar on side of windshield, asw-bw	$8
☐			b. same as (a), wider rear seat, no black pillar on side of windshield, asw-bw	$20
☐			c. same as (a), wide rear seat, alw-bw	$25
☐ 📷	127	Power Plower	a. purple flake, metal Malaysia base, dark blue, yellow & orange tampos on hood & sides, yellow int., clear window, asw-ct	$20
☐ 📷			b. lt. purple enamel, metal Malaysia base, lt. blue, yellow & orange tampos on hood & sides, yellow int., clear window, asw-ct	$12
☐			c. dark purple enamel, metal Malaysia base, light blue, yellow & orange tampos on hood & sides, yellow int., clear window, asw-ct	$18
☐ 📷	128	Baja Breaker	met. purple, blue-tint China base, yellow tampo on sides, red int., clear window, alw-bw	$3
☐ 📷	129	Suzuki QuadRacer	a. white w/blue seat, black handlebars, black-tint metal Malaysia base, alw-yct	$12
☐			b. same as (a), alw-ct	$29
	130	unreleased		—
☐ 📷	131	Nissan Hardbody	a. white enamel, black plastic Malaysia base, red & blue tampos on hood & sides, blue-tint window, pink int., front end & roll bar, ct	$48
☐ 📷			b. black enamel, black plastic Malaysia base, light green, blue & pink tampos on hood, roof & sides, "10" in green on hood, "10" in pink on door, blue-tint window, pink int., front end, roll bar, alw-ct	$12
☐			c. same as (a), alw-cts	$25
☐			d. black enamel, black metal Malaysia base, light green, blue & pink tampos on hood, roof & sides, green & yellow "10" hood, pink & blue "10" on door, blue-tint window, pink int., front end & roll bar, alw-ct	$17
☐			e. black enamel, black plastic Malaysia base, green, blue & yellow tampos on roof, hood & sides, yellow & blue "10" on door, green & blue "10" on hood, blue-tint window, yellow int., front end & roll bar, alw-ct	$6
☐			f. same as (e), alw-bct	$15
☐			g. same as (e), alw-ct/b	$4
☐			h. red enamel, black plastic Malaysia base, black & white checkered flag tampos on hood & sides, yellow & black "1" on hood & sides black int., smoked window, alw-ct/b	$3
	132	unreleased		—
☐	133	Shadow Jet	a. purple met., metal Malaysia base, green "Inter Cooled" tampo on rear wing, "F-3" in yellow, purple int., yellow-tint canopy, bw	$14
☐ 📷			b. same as (a), small front bw	$20
☐			c. same as (a), yellow "Inter Cooled" tampo on rear wing, "F-3" in green, bw	$20
☐ 📷	134	Mercedes 540K	white enamel, metal Malaysia base, tan top, red int., clear window, asw-bw	$12

Flashfire

Hiway Hauler

Flashfire

Hiway Hauler

Shock Factor

Recycling Truck

Shock Factor

	Photo	No.	Name	Description	Price
☐		135	'32 Ford Delivery	a. white enamel, turquoise plastic fenders, metal Malaysia base, turquoise, pink & blue side tampo, turquoise int., clear window, bw	$7
☐	📷			b. same as (a), 7sp	$6
☐	📷	136	'56 Flashsider	a. turquoise enamel, chrome Malaysia base, pink, yellow & blue side tampo, black window, sho	$35
☐				b. same as (a), uh	$7
☐	📷			c. same as (a), 5sp	$5
☐				d. same as (a), 5dot	$3
☐	📷			e. same as (d), chrome window, 5dot	$37
☐				f. same as (a), asw-5dot	$15
☐	📷	137	Blimp	gray plastic body w/black "Goodyear" on side, white gondola w/black window tampo	$9
		138	unreleased		—
		139	unreleased		—
☐	📷	140	Flashfire	a. black enamel, black plastic Malaysia base, green, yellow & pink side tampo, red int. & side insert, yellow-tint canopy, sho	$15
☐				b. same as (a), uh	$6
☐				c. same as (a), t/b	$3
☐	📷			d. same as (a), 5sp	$12

Photo	No.	Name	Description	Price
❑	140	Flashfire	e. same as (a), 5dot	$4
❑			f. same as (a), w5dot	$8
❑ 📷	141	Shock Factor	a. black enamel, metal Malaysia base, metal body w/red plastic engine, driver & side pods, red, blue & yellow tampos on sides & wing, ct	$45
❑			b. same as (a), dull pink plastic engine, driver & side pods, ct	$10
❑ 📷			c. same as (a), bright pink plastic engine, driver & side pods, ct	$10
❑ 📷	142	Hiway Hauler	a. red enamel cab, chrome Malaysia base, white box w/blue Kool-Aid tampo, thin red ribbon, yellow "Wacky Warehouse," black window, alw-bw	$15
❑ 📷			b. same as (a), thick red ribbon, alw-bw	$15
❑	143	Recycling Truck	a. orange metal cab, black plastic Malaysia base, orange plastic box w/yellow & blue "Recycler" tampo on side, box closed at top, black window, alw-bw	$10
❑			b. same as (a), box open at top	$5
❑ 📷			c. same as (a), asw-7sp	$5
❑			d. day-glo green metal cab, white plastic Malaysia base, light green plastic box w/white stripe & red "Recycling," "Dept. of Sanitation," "45" & "City of Hot Wheels" logo on side, black window, alw-t/b	$4
❑ 📷			e. same as (d), asw-5sp	$10
❑			f. same as (d), asw-7sp	$4
❑ 📷	144	Oshkosh Cement Mixer	white plastic body, red barrel, blue painted fenders & blue plastic Malaysia base, blue painted seat, asw-bw	$6
❑	145	Tractor	a. yellow metal body & bucket, yellow plastic Malaysia base, cab & hydraulics, ytt	$10
❑ 📷			b. same as (a), alw-ytt	$20
❑			c. red metal body & bucket, red plastic Malaysia base, cab & hydraulics, ct front wheel & tt rear	$6
❑			d. red metal body & bucket, dark red plastic Malaysia base, red cab & hydraulics, ct front wheel & tt rear	$6
❑			e. same as (c), t/b front wheel & tt rear	$4
❑ 📷			f. red metal body & bucket, dark red plastic Malaysia base, black cab & hydraulics, t/b front wheel & tt rear.	$25

The Tractor 145 (f) variation was a Canadian release in a U.S. package, found only at KB-Toys.

Recycling Truck

Tractor

Oshkosh Cement Mixer

Tractor

Photo	No.	Name	Description	Price
❏	145	Tractor	g. green metal body & bucket, light green plastic Malaysia base, yellow cab & hydraulics, yt/b front wheel & ytt rear	$4
❏			h. same as (g), exhaust stack shortened for safety	$3
❏	146	Bulldozer	yellow metal body, yellow plastic base & blade, one-piece black treads & rollers, black seat & grille	$8
❏	147	Tank Truck	a. red enamel, matching red plastic Malaysia base, chrome window & tank w/blue "Unical 76" the "76" is in an orange circle, asw-bw	$6
❏			b. same as (a), dark red plastic Malaysia base asw-bw	$6
❏			c. same as (a), asw-7sp	$5
❏			d. orange enamel, matching orange plastic Malaysia base, chrome window & tank w/blue "Unical 76," the "76" is in an orange circle, asw-7sp	$7
❏			e. same as (d), asw-t/b	$4
❏			f. white enamel, orange plastic Malaysia base, black tank w/white "Water Dust Control" & yellow stripes on side, black "Road Dept." on door w/"City of Hot Wheels" logo, asw-3sp	$2
❏			g. same as (f), asw-5sp	$4
❏	148	Porsche 930	a. green flake, metal Malaysia base, pink, yellow & blue tampos, rose-tint int. & window, asw-bw	$50
❏			b. purple enamel, metal Malaysia base, yellow & black side tampo, in yellow, black int., dark smoked window, asw-bw	$45
❏			c. red w/yellow & black side tampo, "Porsche 930" in white, metal Malaysia base, black int., dark smoked window, asw-bw	$5
❏			d. same as (c), asw-5sp	$3
❏	149	BMW 850i	a. blue enamel, blue plastic Malaysia base, white, pink & yellow tampos on hood & sides, tan int., clear window, asw-uh	$5
❏			b. same as (a), asw-sho	$15
❏			c. same as (a), asw-gr	$6
❏	150	BMW 323	a. black enamel, black plastic Malaysia base, white "M3" & red & blue slash tampo on side, "BMW" embossed on rear plate, tan int., clear window, alw-bw	$8

Tractor

Bulldozer

Tank Truck

Tank Truck

Porsche 930

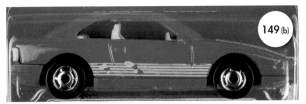

BMW 850i

BMW 850i

BMW 323

Ford Aerostar

Thunderstreak

Thunderstreak

'59 Cadillac

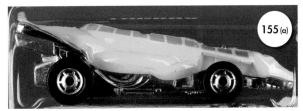

Turboa

Rodzilla

Photo	No.	Name	Description	Price
❏	150	BMW 323	b. same as (a), alw-uh	$8
❏			c. same as (b), no BMW on rear plate, alw-uh	$9
❏ 📷			d. same as (c), alw-sho	$15
❏ 📷	151	Ford Aerostar	met. purple w/yellow tampo on side, metal Malaysia base, chrome window, bw	$6
	152	unreleased		—
❏	153	Thunderstreak	a. dark blue & dark green, metal Malaysia base, HW logo on side pod, red stripe w/white "1" on front, bw	$7
The green #153 cars are supposedly leftovers from the "Zip-Lock" promotion with a repaint.				
❏ 📷			b. same as (a), white "1" missing on nose	$12
❏ 📷			c. yellow metal body w/yellow plastic side pods, metal Malaysia base, red & black tampos, black "Pennzoil" on side, bw	$11
❏ 📷	154	'59 Cadillac	a. white pearl, chrome Malaysia base, red int./clear window, ww/bw	$7
❏			b. cream pearl, chrome Malaysia base, red int., clear window, ww/bw	$35
❏ 📷	155	Turboa	a. yellow w/green tampo, blue-tint metal Malaysia base, uh	$5
❏			b. same as (a), sho	$15
❏ 📷	156	Rodzilla	a. purple plastic body w/light purple plastic Malaysia base, yellow eyes, white teeth, sho	$15

Photo	No.	Name	Description	Price
❏ 📷	156	Rodzilla	b. reddish-purple plastic body and head, light purple plastic Malaysia base, yellow eyes, white teeth, uh	$5
❏ 📷			c. reddish-purple plastic body, purple plastic head, dark purple painted metal Malaysia base, yellow eyes, white teeth, uh	$15
❏ 📷	157	'57 Chevy	a. yellow w/red flames over white w/blue stripe on sides, blue-tint int. & window, uh	$26
❏			b. same as (a), sho	$35
❏ 📷	158	Mercedes-Benz Unimog	white enamel metal cab & box, metal Malaysia base, white plastic rear box cover w/red, green & black tampo, red plastic fenders & int., clear window, alw-ct	$10
❏ 📷	159	Big Bertha	light gray painted metal body & treads, brown & black camouflage, white star on rear gray plastic turret & Malaysia base	$12
❏ 📷	160	Command Tank	white painted body, dark gray, light gray & black camouflage, white plastic treads, base & turret	$7
❏	161	Roll Patrol	a. light gray enamel w/matching Malaysia base, white, black & light brown camouflage tampo on hood only, black int. & spare tire, clear window, alw-bbw	$12
❏			b. same as (a), asw-ct	$15
❏ 📷			c. same as (a), asw-bct	$12
❏			d. light gray enamel w/matching Malaysia base, white, black & light brown camouflage w/white star on hood, white, black & light brown camouflage on side, black int., clear window, asw-bct	$20
❏ 📷	162	'65 Mustang Conv.	a. red w/yellow side tampo, metal Malaysia base, cream int., clear window, asw-ww	$15
❏			b. orange-ish red, yellow side tampo, metal Malaysia base, cream int., clear window, asw-ww	$8
❏ 📷			c. blood red, yellow side tampo, metal Malaysia base, tan int., clear window, asw-ww	$25
❏			d. same as (b), asw-5sp	$5
❏ 📷			e. same as (b), asw-7sp	$8
❏ 📷	163	Talbot Lago	red flake, metal Malaysia base, orange-tint window & int., ww	$15
❏ 📷	164	Mercedes 540K	a. blue flake, metal Malaysia base, light blue top, red int., clear window, asw-bw	$6
❏			b. same as (a), asw-3sp	$4

156 (b)

Rodzilla

156 (c)

Rodzilla

157 (a)

'57 Chevy

158

Mercedes-Benz Unimog

Big Bertha

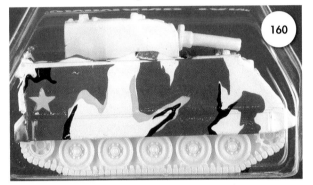

Command Tank

Roll Patrol

'65 Mustang Convertible

'65 Mustang Convertible

'65 Mustang Convertible

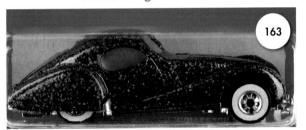

Talbot Lago

Photo	No.	Name	Description	Price
❏	164	Mercedes 540K	c. same as (a), asw-5sp	$4
❏			d. same as (a), asw-t/b	$4
❏			e. same as (a), asw-5dot	$4
❏ 📷	165	Suzuki QuadRacer	a. bright pink body, blue seat, black handlebars, black-tinted metal Malaysia base, alw-ct	$9
❏ 📷			b. dull pink body, blue seat, black handlebars, black-tinted metal Malaysia base, alw-ct	$8
❏ 📷	166	Vampyra	a. black plastic body, blue-tint metal Malaysia base, yellow, green & purple wing tampo, green & yellow eyes, sho	$40
❏ 📷			b. black plastic body, metal Malaysia base, yellow, green & purple wing tampo, green & yellow eyes, bw	$8
❏			c. same as (b), uh	$12
❏			d. black plastic body, metal Malaysia base, no wing tampo, green & yellow eyes, uh	$8
❏ 📷	167	'80s Firebird	a. orange enamel, black plastic Malaysia base, purple & pink lightning bolt tampos on side & hood, purple int., clear window, asw-bw	$6
❏			b. same as (a), extra lightning bolt on rear fender	$15
❏ 📷	168	GT Racer	black enamel, metal Malaysia base, yellow, pink, purple & red stripes on sides, roof & hood, "5" on sides & hood, silver window, bw	$8
❏ 📷	169	Sol-Aire CX4	a. candy blue, black plastic Malaysia base, pink, purple & orange tampos, "2" on front & sides, black int., clear window, sho	$15
❏			b. same as (a), uh	$12

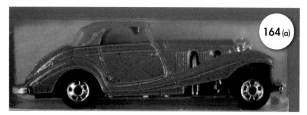

Mercedes 540K

Vampyra

Suzuki QuadRacer

Vampyra

'80's Firebird

Suzuki QuadRacer

GT Racer

Photo	No.	Name	Description	Price
❑	169	Sol-Aire CX4	c. candy blue, metal Malaysia base, pink, purple & orange tampos, "2" on front & sides, metal int., clear window, uh	$6
❑ 📷	170	Chevy Stocker	pink flake, metal Malaysia base, yellow int., yellow-tint window, bw	$7
❑ 📷	171	VW Bug	a. met. purple, metal Malaysia base, orange, green & yellow tampos on roof, hood & sides, red int., clear window, bw	$9
❑			b. same as (a), 3sp	$4
❑ 📷	172	Mazda MX-5 Miata	a. yellow enamel w/matching yellow painted Malaysia base, w/pink, blue & black side tampos, pink int., clear window, asw-bw	$5
❑			b. same as (a), asw-lime green star wheel	$7
❑			c. same as (a), asw-5sp	$125
❑			d. same as (a), asw-7sp	$50
❑			e. met. burgundy w/matching metal Malaysia base, red HW logo, tan int., clear window, asw-7sp	$8
❑			f. met. burgundy w/matching metal Malaysia base, yellow & orange side pinstripe, yellow HW logo on front fender high behind wheel, tan int., smoked window, asw-3sp	$4
❑			g. same as (f), asw-5sp	$4
❑			h. same as (f), asw-screacher wheels	$200
	173	unreleased		
❑ 📷	174	Limozeen	light blue flake, chrome Malaysia base, light yellow int., clear window, ww	$7
❑ 📷	175	Ferrari 348	a. white pearl, black plastic Malaysia base, pink, red & purple tampo on hood & roof, red & white int., clear window, sho	$15

Photo	No.	Name	Description	Price
☐	175	Ferrari 348	b. same as (a), uh	$10
☐ 📷	176	Lamborghini Diablo	a. blue flake, metal Malaysia base, light blue rear wing & bumper, red int., red-tint window, uh	$10
☐			b. same as (a), dark blue rear wing & bumper, uh	$8
☐ 📷	177	Zender Fact 4	a. purple flake, orange plastic Malaysia base, orange int., clear window, sho	$15
☐			b. same as (a), uh	$8
☐	178	Hot Bird	black flake, metal Malaysia base, pink int., rose-tint window, uh	$10
☐ 📷	179	Porsche 959	a. met. purple, metal Malaysia base, yellow, pink & gray tampos, gray #5 on sides, chrome window, asw-sho	$15
☐			b. same as (a), asw-uh	$9
	180	unreleased		—
☐ 📷	181	Pontiac Fiero 2M4	a. light green mf., metal Malaysia base, light yellow int., clear window, asw-sho	$15
☐			b. same as (a), asw-uh	$7
☐ 📷	182	Shadow Jet	a. green enamel, metal Malaysia base, green "Inter Cooled" on rear wing, blue "F-3" smoked canopy, green int., bw	$8
☐			b. same as (a), yellow "Inter Cooled" on rear wing, bw	$6
☐			c. same as (b), 5sp	$4
☐ 📷	183	VW Golf	a. dark green flake, chrome Malaysia base, yellow int., yellow-tint window, asw-bw	$30
☐ 📷			b. pink flake, chrome Malaysia base, yellow int., yellow-tint window, asw-bw	$14
☐			c. same as (b), black Malaysia base, asw-bw	$8
☐ 📷	184	Mercedes 380 SEL	a. blue flake, metal Malaysia base, yellow int., yellow-tint window, asw-sho	$15
☐			b. same as (a), asw-uh	$10
☐ 📷	185	Propper Chopper	a. white enamel, black plastic Malaysia base, hook, tail & int., black stripes w/thin yellow "Police" & yellow star over dark red circle side tampo outlined in black, small, gray rotors, blue-tint window	$7
☐			b. same as (a), black stripes w/thick yellow "Police"	$7
☐ 📷			c. yellow enamel, black Malaysia base, black "Unit 4 Search + Rescue" tampo, dark red stripe w/white "Rescue" & "City of Hot Wheels" logo red HW logo at rear above black plastic hook, rotors, tail & window	$5

169 (a)

Sol-Aire CX4

172 (a)

Mazda MX-5 Miata

170

Chevy Stocker

174

Limozeen

171 (a)

VW Bug

175 (a)

Ferrari 348

Lamborghini Diablo

Shadow Jet

Zender Fact 4

VW Golf

Hot Bird

VW Golf

Porsche 959

Mercedes 380 SEL

Pontiac Fiero 2M4

Propper Chopper

Photo		No.	Name	Description	Price
☐		185	Propper Chopper	d. same as (c), lighter red side stripe	$3
☐	📷			e. same as (c), orange plastic Malaysia base & tail, black rotors & window	$4
☐	📷	186	Ford Aerostar	a. white enamel, red, yellow & blue "Speedie Pizza" tampo w/phone #, chrome window, bw	$12
☐				b. same as (a), no phone #	$12
☐	📷	187	Ramp Truck	a. yellow enamel metal cab, metal Malaysia base, white plastic ramp w/blue, red & yellow tampo, black window, asw-bw	$5
☐				b. same as (a), asw-t/b	$7
☐				c. same as (a), asw-7sp	$3
☐		188	Hummer	a. light brown metal body w/matching gun on roof, black plastic Malaysia base, brown, orange & black camouflage everywhere, black star on hood, black window, asw-ct	$9
☐	📷			b. tan metal body w/matching gun on roof, black plastic Malaysia base, light brown, white & black camouflage everywhere, black star on hood, black window, asw-ct	$12

Photo	No.	Name	Description	Price
❑ 📷	188	Hummer	c. light brown plastic body w/matching gun on roof, black painted metal Malaysia base, brown, orange & black camouflage on roof, trunk & sides only, asw-ct	$6
❑			d. light brown plastic body, no gun on roof, black painted Malaysia base, brown, orange & black camouflage on roof, trunk & sides only, asw-t/b	$4
❑			e. white w/black "Anti-Drug Unit" tampo on side, "City of Hot Wheels" logo, metal Malaysia base, thin antenna, black window, asw-t/b	$3
❑			f. same as (e), silver painted Malaysia base, thin antenna, asw-t/b	$3
❑			g. same as (f), silver painted Malaysia base, fat antenna, asw-t/b	$4
❑ 📷	189	Gleamer Patrol	a. dark chrome texture, metal Malaysia base, tan int., smoked window, asw-bw	$8
❑			b. chrome texture, metal Malaysia base, tan int., smoked window, asw-bw	$12
❑			c. same as (b), black int., smoked window, asw-bw	$8
❑ 📷	190	'57 T-Bird	a. light gold chrome texture, metal Malaysia base, black int., smoked window, bw	$8
❑ 📷			b. dark gold chrome texture, metal Malaysia base, black int., smoked window, bw	$8
❑	191	Aeroflash	a. dark pink chrome texture, metal Malaysia base, black window, uh	$8
❑			b. light pink chrome texture, metal Malaysia base, black window, guh	$10
❑			c. dark pink chrome texture, metal Malaysia base, black window, guh	$10
❑			d. dark pink chrome texture w/silver painted Malaysia base, black window, guh	$20
❑ 📷	192	Corvette Stingray	a. green chrome texture, metal Malaysia base, black int., smoked window, bw	$25
❑ 📷			b. silver chrome texture, metal Malaysia base, black int., smoked window, bw	$10
❑			c. same as (b), uh	$10
❑ 📷	193	Porsche 959	a. pink chrome texture, metal Malaysia base, dark smoked window, asw-uh	$8
❑ 📷			b. silver chrome texture, metal Malaysia base, dark smoked window, asw-uh	$12
❑ 📷	194	Blimp	a. gray plastic body, red & light yellow "Hot Wheels" tampo, white gondola w/black tampo windows	$5
❑			b. same as (a), bright red & yellow "Hot Wheels" tampo	$5
❑			c. same as (a), silver gondola w/black tampo windows	$2
❑ 📷	195	Troop Convoy	light gray w/brown, white & black camouflage on top of canopy, white star & "US ARMY" on hood, alw-bbw	$8
❑ 📷	196	3-Window '34	a. white enamel, pink plastic fenders, black running boards & int., metal Malaysia base, pink, orange & black lines & star side tampo, asw-bw	$40
❑			b. white enamel, purple plastic fenders, black running boards & int., metal Malaysia base, purple, orange & black lines & star side tampo, asw-bw	$10

Propper Chopper

Ford Aerostar

Ramp Truck

Propper Chopper

Photo	No.	Name	Description	Price
❏	196	3-Window '34	c. lime yellow enamel, purple plastic fenders, black running boards & int., metal Malaysia base, orange, magenta, & light green side tampo, clear window, asw-bw	$175

The 3-Window '34 (c) variation car was also released in a 5 pack and only brings $10 or so loose.

Photo	No.	Name	Description	Price
❏	197	Corvette Split Window	a. light blue w/red, magenta & yellow tampo on hood, roof & trunk, (1 rivet) chrome Malaysia base, red int., clear window, asw-ww	$5
❏ 📷			b. same as (a), (2 rivet) chrome Malaysia base, asw-ww	$10
❏			c. same as (a), (2 rivet) chrome Malaysia base, asw-ww	$15
❏			d. same as (a), (1 rivet) gray Malaysia base, asw-bw	$25
❏			e. same as (a), (2 rivet) chrome Malaysia base, asw-5sp	$11
❏			f. same as (a), (2 rivet) gray plastic Malaysia base, asw-5sp	$5
❏ 📷	198	Path Beater	a. day-glo yellow w/orange, blue & white side tampo, blue-tint metal Malaysia base, w/ smaller front bumper gray int., roll bar & bed, blue-tint window, asw-ct	$15
❏ 📷			b. day-glo yellow w/orange, blue & white side tampo, metal Malaysia base, gray int., roll bar & bed, blue-tint window, asw-ct	$5
❏ 📷			c. same as (b), asw-bct	$20
❏			d. same as (b), asw-t/b	$2
❏			e. day-glo yellow w/orange, blue & white side tampo, blue-tint metal Malaysia base, gray int., roll bar & bed, blue-tint window, asw-ct	$2
❏ 📷	199	Double Demon	a. bright yellow plastic body, green tampo, chrome insert, metal Malaysia base, alw-uh	$6
❏			b. light yellow plastic body, black tampo, black insert w/yellow HW logo, metal Malaysia base, alw-uh	$15

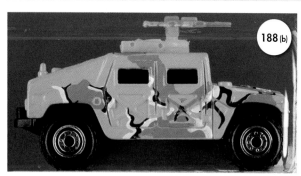

188 (b)

Hummer

188 (c)

Hummer

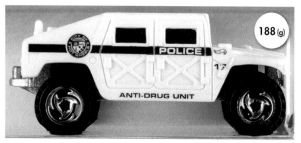

188 (g)

Hummer

189 (a)

Gleamer Patrol

190 (a)

'57 T-Bird

190 (b)

'57 T-Bird

192 (a)

Corvette Stingray

Corvette Stingray

Troop Convoy

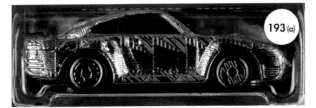

Porsche 959

3-Window '34

Porsche 959

Corvette Split Window

Blimp

Path Beater

	Photo	No.	Name	Description	Price
☐	📷	199	Double Demon	c. dark yellow plastic body, black tampo, black insert w/yellow HW logo, metal Malaysia base, alw-uh	$6
☐		200	Custom Corvette	a. white pearl, black Malaysia base, red side tampo, yellow, red & black tampo on hood, red int., clear window, uh	$5
☐				b. dark met. purple, black Malaysia base, light gray int., clear window w/red HW logo, uh	$5
☐				c. same as (b), 5sp	$5
☐	📷			d. same as (b), 7sp	$7
☐				e. same as (b), bbs	$3
☐	📷	201	Oshkosh Snowplow	a. orange plastic cab & box, orange metal fenders, int., & hood, metal Malaysia base, oct	$5
☐	📷			b. same as (a), bct	$12
☐				c. same as (a), ot/b	$3
☐				d. gray plastic cab & box w/white & black "Fresno Feed Co." metal burgundy fenders, int. & hood, t/b	$5
The #201 Oshkosh Snowplow (d) variation dried up real quick; maybe someone from Fresno bought them all.					
☐	📷	202	'93 Camaro	a. purple enamel, black plastic Malaysia base, yellow & orange "Camaro" tampo on side, clear window, white int., alw-uh	$10
☐				b. same as (a), gray int., uh	$6
☐				c. same as (b), long exhaust pipe, smoked window, gray int., uh	$5

198 (b)

Path Beater

198 (c)

Path Beater

199 (a)

Double Demon

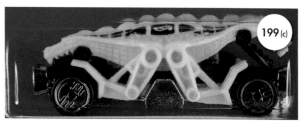

199 (c)

Double Demon

200 (d)

Custom Corvette

201 (a)

Oshkosh Snowplow

Photo	No.	Name	Description	Price
❑	203	Jaguar XJ220	a. met. silver, black plastic Malaysia base, black int., clear window, uh	$5
❑ 📷			b. same as (a), guh	$10
❑			c. dark met. blue, black plastic Malaysia base, black int., clear window, uh	$5
❑			d. same as (c), guh	$6
❑ 📷			e. lighter dark met. blue, black plastic Malaysia base, gray int., clear window, asw-gbbs	$20
❑			f. lighter dark met. blue, black plastic Malaysia base, gray int., clear window, gbbs	$3
❑			g. dark met. blue, black plastic Malaysia base, gray int., clear window, gbbs	$3
❑			h. lighter dark blue met, black plastic Malaysia base, black int., clear window, gbbs	$3
❑	204	Oscar Mayer Wienermobile	a. dark red plastic hot dog, two-piece matching tan Malaysia base, dark smoked window, bbw	$5
❑ 📷			b. dark red plastic hot dog, two-tone tan Malaysia base (dark bottom), dark smoked window, bbw	$5
❑			c. red plastic hot dog, tan matching Malaysia base, smoked window, bbw	$5
❑ 📷			d. red plastic hot dog, tan matching Malaysia base, smoked window, bw	$12
The Oscar Mayer Wienermobile with the chrome basic wheel is rare; these cars were the same as the promo.				
❑			e. red plastic hot dog, two-tone tan Malaysia base (dark top), smoked window, 7sp	$3
❑			f. red plastic hot dog, matching tan Malaysia base, smoked window, 7sp	$3
❑			g. red plastic hot dog, matching tan Malaysia base, smoked window, 5dot	$3
❑			h. red plastic hot dog, matching tan Thailand base, smoked window, 5sp	$5
❑	205	Treadator	a. red enamel metal body w/orange plastic scoops, chrome fenders, engine & canopy, black treads & Malaysia base	$5
❑			b. day-glo green metal body w/dark purple plastic scoops, purple fenders, engine & canopy black treads & Malaysia base	$8
❑			c. same as (b), HW logo on front wing	$4

	Photo	No.	Name	Description	Price
❑	📷	205	Treadator	d. dull green enamel metal body w/dark purple plastic scoops, purple fenders, engine & canopy, purple HW logo on front left wing	$4
❑	📷	206	Pipe Jammer	a. yellow enamel, black painted metal Malaysia base, chrome int., uh	$6
❑				b. yellow enamel, black painted Malaysia base, undipped dull chrome int., uh	$8
❑	📷	207	Vector "Avtech" WX-3	a. dark lavender pearl w/matching top, black plastic Malaysia base, tan int., smoked window, uh	$8
❑	📷			b. dark pearl lavender w/light lavender pearl top, black plastic Malaysia base, tan int., smoked window, uh	$8
❑				c. lavender pearl w/matching top, black plastic Malaysia base, tan int., smoked window, uh	$5
❑				d. lavender pearl w/matching top, black plastic Malaysia base, tan int., smoked window, 5sp	$6
❑		208	Avus Quattro	a. met. silver w/black plastic Malaysia base, red int., clear window, uh	$3
❑	📷			b. same as (a), 5sp	$5
❑	📷	209	Lexus SC400	met. black, black plastic Malaysia base, white int., clear window, uh	$5
❑		210	Dodge Viper RT/10	a. red enamel, black plastic Malaysia base, black int., clear windshield, uh	$5
❑				b. same as (a), guh	$7
❑	📷			c. same as (a), 5sp	$100
❑				d. red enamel, black plastic China base, black int., gold logo on clear windshield, bbs	$15

The red Viper with chrome bbs wheels is the same car that was re-released as the 1996 Treasure Hunt car. It is harder to find in the 210 package than it is to find in the Treasure Hunt package.

❑				e. yellow enamel, black plastic Malaysia base, black int., clear windshield, guh	$10
❑				f. same as (e), clear windshield w/red HW logo, guh	$12
❑				g. met. green, black plastic Malaysia base, black int., clear windshield w/red HW logo, guh	$6
❑				h. same as (g), g3sp	$5

Oshkosh Snowplow

'93 Camaro

Jaguar XJ220

Jaguar XJ220

Oscar Mayer Wienermobile

Oscar Mayer Wienermobile

Treadator

Avus Quattro

Pipe Jammer

Lexus SC400

Vector "Avtech" WX-3

Viper RT/10

Vector "Avtech" WX-3

Twin Mill II

Photo	No.	Name	Description	Price
❏	210	Dodge Viper RT/10	i. same as (g), 5sp	$175
❏			j. same as (g), g5sp	$8
❏			k. same as (g), gbbs	$5
❏	211	Twin Mill II	a. day-glo yellow, black plastic Malaysia base, black window, uh	$40
❏ 📷			b. same as (a), chrome Malaysia base, uh	$17
❏			c. same as (a), gray plastic Malaysia base, uh	$8
❏ 📷	212	Silhouette II	a. met. purple w/chrome Malaysia base, white int., clear window, uh	$7
❏			b. same as (a), gray plastic Malaysia base, uh	$5
❏			c. same as (b), 5dot	$3
❏ 📷	213	'57 Chevy	a. aqua enamel, chrome Malaysia base, orange, yellow & magenta stripe tampo on side, "Chevy emblem" on door, blue-tint window & int., uh	$12
❏			b. same as (a), emblem not on door, uh	$6
❏			c. same as (b), guh	$35
❏			d. aqua enamel, chrome Malaysia base w/large '57, orange, yellow & magenta stripe tampo on side, blue-tint window & int., 5sp	$5
❏			e. same as (d), small '57 on base, 5sp	$5
❏			f. same as (d), no '57 on base, 5sp	$5
❏ 📷			g. same as (f), smoked window & black int.	$125
❏ 📷	214	Swingfire	a. dark met. blue & white, metal Malaysia base, white & yellow tampo on hood & top of fenders, white int., clear window, ww	$6

Photo	No.	Name	Description	Price
❑	214	Swingfire	b. same as (a), 5sp	$15
❑			c. same as (a), 7sp	$5
❑	214	Street Beast (name change on card)	d. dark met. blue & white, white & yellow tampo on hood & top of fenders, metal Malaysia base, white int., clear window, t/b	$4
❑	215	Auburn 852	a. light red enamel, black plastic fenders, metal Malaysia base, black int., clear windshield, ww	$10
❑ 📷			b. red enamel, black plastic fenders, metal Malaysia base, black int./clear windshield, ww	$10
❑			c. same as (a), 5sp	$5
❑			d. red enamel, dark brown fenders & 30th Anniversary logo on front fender behind wheel, metal Malaysia base, black int., clear window, asw-5sp	$65
❑ 📷	216	Fat Fendered '40	purple enamel, metal Malaysia base, yellow tampo on side outlined in red, black int., clear window, bw	$20
❑ 📷	217	'40s Woodie	a. turquoise & black w/magenta & yellow stripes on hood & rear fender, metal Malaysia base, yellow int., clear window, bw	$6
❑			b. same as (a), 5sp	$4
❑			c. same as (a), 5dot	$2
❑			d. same as (a), 7sp	$2
❑ 📷	218	Street Roader	met. light green, metal Malaysia base, blue, magenta & orange tampo on hood & sides, gray int., smoked window, alw-ct	$70
❑ 📷	219	Gulch Stepper	day-glo yellow, metal Malaysia base, orange, red & black side tampo, black window, alw-ct	$6
❑ 📷	220	Bywayman	a. white pearl, metal Malaysia base, pink & orange tampo w/gray stripe on hood & sides, black int., clear window, ct	$12
❑			b. same as (a), blue int., ct	$5
❑			c. same as (b), blue-tint metal Malaysia base, blue int., ct	$5
❑			d. same as (b), t/b	$3
❑ 📷	221	Range Rover	a. met. black, gray plastic Malaysia base, orange stripe & white "Range Rover" on sides, tan int., clear window, ct	$5
❑			b. same as (a), t/b	$3

Silhouette II

Swingfire

'57 Chevy

Auburn 852

'57 Chevy

Fat Fendered '40

'40's Woodie

Gulch Stepper

Street Roader

Bywayman

Photo	No.	Name	Description	Price
❑ 📷	222	Blazer 4X4	a. light blue flake, metal Malaysia base, yellow int./blue-tint window, alw-ct	$11
❑			b. same as (a), alw-bct	$15
❑ 📷			c. same as (a), dark blue flake, alw-ct	$15
❑ 📷	223	Baja Bug	red flake, metal Malaysia base, black int., bw	$31
❑	224	Zombot	a. light blue chrome body, metal Malaysia base, purple chrome gun, uh	$9
❑ 📷			b. blue chrome body, metal Malaysia base, pink chrome gun, uh	$9
❑ 📷			c. dark chrome body, metal Malaysia base, pink chrome gun, uh	$7
❑			d. dark chrome body, metal Malaysia base, purple chrome gun, uh	$7
❑			e. dark chrome body, metal Malaysia base, orange gun, uh	$5
❑ 📷			f. chrome body, metal Malaysia base, orange gun, 7sp	$5
❑			g. undipped dull chrome body, metal Malaysia base, 7sp	$6
❑ 📷	225	Limozeen	a. black flake, chrome Malaysia base, bright red int., clear window, ww	$12
❑			b. same as (a), dull dark red int., ww	$12
❑	226	Ferrari 348	a. day-glo pink, black plastic Malaysia base, yellow, white & black tampo on hood, white & black stripe on roof, black & red int., clear window, uh	$6
❑			b. same as (a), smoked window, uh	$9
❑			c. same as (b), all red int., smoked window, uh	$200
❑ 📷			d. same as (a), clear window, 5sp	$5
❑			e. black enamel, black Malaysia base, yellow, white & magenta tampo on hood, white & magenta stripes on roof, black & red int., clear window, 5sp	$5
❑ 📷			f. same as (e), 7sp	$10
❑	227	Lamborghini Diablo	a. yellow enamel, metal Malaysia base, black "Diablo" on side, gray int., red-tint window, uh	$5
❑ 📷			b. same as (a), 5sp	$7
❑			c. purple pearl, black painted metal Malaysia base, purple int., clear window w/gold logo, t/b	$3
❑			d. light purple pearl, black painted Malaysia base, purple int., clear window w/gold logo, 5sp	$5

Photo	No.	Name	Description	Price
❏	227	Lamborghini Diablo	e. dark purple pearl, black painted metal Malaysia base, purple int., clear window w/gold logo, 5dot	$5
❏	228	Zender Fact 4	a. met. blue, black Malaysia base, white "Zender" on front, yellow "Fact 4" on top of fender, gray int., smoked window, uh	$6
❏			b. same as (a), clear window, uh	$25
❏			c. same as (a), black int., dark smoked window, uh	$10
❏ 📷			d. day-glo green, black Malaysia base, yellow, magenta & white tampo on hood & roof, black int., clear window, uh	$6
❏			e. day-glo green, black Malaysia base, orange, black & white tampo on hood & roof, black int., dark smoked window, uh	$10
❏			f. day-glo green w/orange, black & white tampo on hood & roof, black Malaysia base, black int., clear window, uh	$25

Range Rover

Blazer 4X4

Blazer 4X4

Baja Bug

Zombot

Zombot

Zombot

Limozeen

Ferrari 348

Ferrari 348

Mercedes 380 SEL

Lamborghini Diablo

XT-3

Zender Fact 4

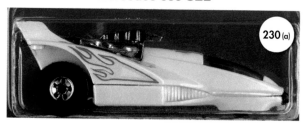

XT-3

Photo	No.	Name	Description	Price
❏	228	Zender Fact 4	g. maroon, black China base, black & gold tampo on hood & side, tan int./clear window, 5sp	$2
❏ 📷	229	Mercedes 380 SEL	pink flake, metal Malaysia base, black int., smoked window, uh	$11
❏ 📷	230	XT-3	a. white pearl w/matching painted Malaysia base, black nose & int., yellow, white & red flames, red-tint canopy, bw	$6
❏			b. same as (a), blue-tint canopy, bw	$50
❏ 📷			c. dark blue flake, white Malaysia painted base, black nose & int., white logo on rear wing, blue-tint canopy, bw	$5
❏			d. same as (c), white logo reversed on rear wing, blue-tint canopy, bw	$7
❏			e. light blue flake w/white Malaysia painted base, black nose & int., white logo on rear wing, blue-tint canopy, bw	$5
❏			f. dark blue flake w/white Malaysia painted base, black nose & int., white logo on rear wing, blue-tint canopy, 5sp	$5
❏			g. light blue flake w/white Malaysia painted base, black nose & int., white logo on rear wing, blue-tint canopy, 5sp	$5
❏	231	Mini Truck	a. day-glo orange, orange plastic Malaysia base, blue, white & black tampos, blue int., clear window, uh	$5
❏			b. same as (a), asw-uh	$40
❏			c. same as (a), alw-uh	$25
❏ 📷			d. same as (a), 5sp	$3
❏			e. same as (a), t/b	$3
❏			f. same as (a), 5dot	$3
❏			g. same as (a), w5dot	$8
❏ 📷	232	Lamborghini Countach	a. red enamel, red painted Malaysia base, rear wing is a separate wing casting white & black stripe side tampos, black int., dark smoked window, uh	$8
❏			b. red enamel, red painted Malaysia base, rear wing is molded as part of the body, support for wing is not flush to the body and is inset white & black stripe side tampos, tan int./ smoked window, uh	$8

Photo	No.	Name	Description	Price
❏	232	Lamborghini Countach	c. red enamel, red painted Malaysia base, rear wing & body molded as one, support flush with rear, white & black stripe side tampos, black int., dark smoked window, guh	$10
❏ 📷			d. white enamel, white Malaysia base, rear wing support is set in and not flush with the rear of car, red int./clear window, 5dot	$15
❏			e. same as (d), rear wind support is flush with rear of car, clear window, 5dot	$20
❏			f. same as (d), inset wing support, smoked window, 5dot	$2
❏			g. same as (e), flush wing support, smoked window, 5dot	$5
❏	233	Toyota MR2 Rally	a. black enamel, black Malaysia base, orange, purple & lavender stripes on hood & sides, red int., clear window, uh	$100
❏ 📷			b. same as (a), 3sp	$35
❏ 📷			c. same as (a), 5sp	$50
			**The black MR2 cars were only found at Kmart stores.**	
❏ 📷			d. white enamel, black Malaysia base, orange, purple & lavender stripes on hood & sides, red int., clear window, asw-uh	$8
❏			e. same as (d), orange, purple & pink stripes on hood & sides, uh	$5
❏			f. same as (e), 3sp	$2
❏			g. same as (e), t/b	$2
❏			h. same as (e), 5dot	$2
❏			i. white enamel, black plastic Malaysia base, purple, light green & blue enamel tampos on sides & hood, purple int., blue-tint window, bbs	$4
❏			j. same as (i), blue pearl replaces enamel blue in tampo on side & hood	$4
❏	234	Nissan Custom "Z"	a. met. purple, metal Malaysia base, yellow stripes on roof & hood, "300 ZX" on hood twice, black int., clear window, uh	$6
❏			b. same as (a), guh	$6
❏			c. same as (a), g3sp	$4
❏ 📷			d. same as (a), g5sp	$4
❏			e. same as (a), gbbs	$4
❏ 📷	235	Turbo Streak	a. day-glo yellow, metal Malaysia base, red HW logo on side, chrome engine, bw	$10

Mini Truck

Toyota MR2 Rally

Lamborghini Countach

Toyota MR2 Rally

Lamborghini Countach

Toyota MR2 Rally

Toyota MR2 Rally

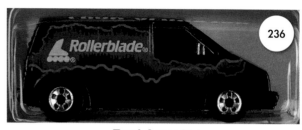

Ford Aerostar

Nissan Custom "Z"

Ford Stake Bed Truck

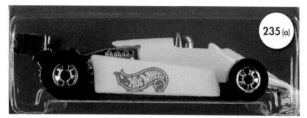

Turbo Streak

Hiway Hauler

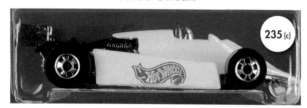

Turbo Streak

Photo	No.	Name	Description	Price
☐	235	Turbo Streak	b. same as (a), dark-tinted chrome engine, bw	$12
☐ 📷			c. same as (a), black chrome engine, bw	$12
☐ 📷	236	Ford Aerostar	black enamel, metal Malaysia base, aqua, yellow, purple & red tampo on side, chrome window, bw	$8
☐	237	Ford Stake Bed Truck	a. red cab w/bright yellow & white tampo, yellow plastic stake rack, chrome Malaysia base, chrome int., clear window, bw	$8
☐			b. red cab w/yellow & white tampo, yellow plastic stake rack, chrome Malaysia base, chrome int., clear window, bw	$6
☐			c. same as (b), smoked window, 3sp	$3
☐			d. same as (b), smoked window, 5sp	$5
☐			e. same as (b), clear window, 7sp	$4
☐			f. same as (b), smoked window, 7sp	$4
☐ 📷			g. same as (b), gray plastic Malaysia base, smoked window, 7sp	$5
☐ 📷	238	Hiway Hauler	a. purple enamel cab, white box w/dark green, dark blue & dark purple tampo, HW logo on front bumper, chrome Malaysia base, black window, alw-bw	$30
☐			b. same as (a), no HW logo on front bumper, bw	$10
☐			c. same as (b), light green, light blue & light purple tampo on box, bw	$10
☐	239	Mercedes-Benz Unimog	a. light brown metal cab & box w/brown, orange & black camouflage, green rear box cover, tan plastic fenders & int., clear window, alw-ct	$14
☐			b. same as (a), green changed to olive on rear box cover, wct	$5
☐ 📷			c. same as (b), bct	$12

Photo	No.	Name	Description	Price
❑	239	Mercedes-Benz Unimog	d. same as (b), wt/b	$4
	240	unreleased		—
	241	unreleased		—
❑	242	'93 Camaro	a. blue enamel, gray Malaysia base, white panel on sides with large red & yellow HW logo, black "1" & "25th Anniversary" logo on side, red stripe on bottom, "Jack Baldwin" twice in white on roof w/red Chevy bow tie, HW logo in yellow w/2 logos on rear spoiler, "Camaro" in white on clear windshield, white int., uh	$150
❑ 📷			b. same as (a), bw	$40
❑			c. met. blue instead of blue enamel, uh	$200
❑			d. light blue met., gray plastic Malaysia base, white on sides, red & yellow HW logo, black # 1 & "25th Anniversary" logo on side, red stripe on bottom, "Jack Baldwin" twice in white on roof w/red Chevy bow tie, HW in yellow w/2 logos on rear spoiler, "Camaro" in white on clear windshield, white int., bw	$8
❑			e. same as (d), darker met. blue	$6
❑ 📷		Camaro Race Car (name change)	f. dark met. blue, gray plastic Malaysia base, white on sides, red & yellow HW logo, red "1" on side & red stripe on bottom, red Chevy bow tie, no "Jack Baldwin" on roof, HW in yellow w/2 logos on rear spoiler, "Camaro" in white on clear windshield, white int., t/b	$3
❑			g. same as (f), 5sp	$3
	243	unreleased		—
❑	244	No Fear Race Car	a. black enamel, black painted Malaysia base, red "No Fear" on nose, rear wing, side body & pod, "Racer" & "1" on side body, "1" & HW logo on nose, "Goodyear" in white on front wing, black plastic driver, bw	$5
❑			b. same as (a), 7sp	$4
❑ 📷			c. same as (a), 5dot	$3
❑ 📷			d. same as (c), "No Fear" missing from tampos, 5dot	$5
❑ 📷			e. same as (c), "No Fear & "Racer" missing from tampos, 5dot	$7
❑ 📷			f. same as (c), no side tampo at all, red "1" & HW logo on nose only, "Goodyear" in white on front wing, 5dot	$9
❑ 📷	245	Driven To The Max	a. day-glo orange, metal Malaysia base, blue & red "Driven To The Max" on sides, red HW logo on side by driver, gray plastic wing & driver, large rear bw	$5

Mercedes-Benz Unimog

1993 Camaro

1993 Camaro

No Fear Race Car

No Fear Race Car

Hot Wheels Variations

	Photo	No.	Name	Description	Price
❏		245	Driven To The Max	b. day-glo yellow w/purple & dark blue tampo on top & sides, day-glo plastic wing & driver, large rear 5sp	$3
❏	📷	246	Shadow Jet II	a. black-tint chrome body, black flake painted Malaysia base, white HW logo on rear, chrome driver, clear canopy, uh	$4
❏				b. chrome body, black flake painted Malaysia base, white HW logo on rear, chrome driver, clear canopy, uh	$4
❏				c. same as (b), 3sp	$4
❏				d. same as (b), 5sp	$4
❏				e. same as (b), 5dot	$3
❏	📷	247	Rigor Motor	dark red met., metal Malaysia base, white skulls & radiator, chrome int., clear canopy, bw	$3
❏		248	Splittin' Image II	a. dark met. blue, blue plastic Malaysia base, white HW logo on front fender top, chrome canopy, engine & headlights, uh	$12
❏				b. same as (a), puh	$6
❏				c. same as (a), pink & white HW logo on front fender top, puh	$5
❏				d. dark met. blue, blue plastic Malaysia base, white HW logo on front fender top, pink canopy, engine & headlights, puh	$7
❏	📷			e. dark met. blue, blue plastic Malaysia base, orange HW logo on front fender top, pink canopy, engine & headlights, o7sp	$11
❏	📷			f. dark met. blue, blue plastic Malaysia base, orange HW logo on front fender top, pink canopy, 7sp	$18
❏	📷			g. dark met. blue, blue plastic Malaysia base, orange HW logo on front fender top, chrome canopy, 7sp	$4
❏	📷	249	Fuji Blimp	white plastic w/dark green stripe, white gondola w/green & red "Fuji Film" tampo	$4
❏		250	Talbot Lago	a. black flake, metal Malaysia base, chrome int., clear window, ww	$5
❏	📷			b. same as (a), 7sp	$3
❏	📷	251	Gulch Stepper	a. red w/black & yellow tampo on roof & sides, metal Malaysia base, black window, tire on hood & spacer between body & base, ct	$10
❏				b. black w/yellow & red tampo on roof & sides, black window, tire on hood & spacer between body & base, metal Malaysia base, ct	$9
❏				c. same as (b), roof tampo reversed, ct	$50
❏				d. same as (b), ct/b	$5
❏	📷	252	Street Roader	a. white enamel, metal Malaysia base, pink tampo with dark blue outline on sides & hood, "Suzuki" in grille, blue int. & spacer between body & base, blue-tint window, ct	$10
❏	📷			b. same as (a), purple tampo with dark blue outline on sides & hood, ct	$25
❏	📷			c. white enamel, metal Malaysia base, dark pink tampo with dark blue outline on sides & hood, no "Suzuki" in grille, blue int. & spacer between body & base, blue-tint window, ct	$15
❏				d. same as (c), pink tampo with dark blue outline on sides & hood, ct/b	$7
❏		253	Mercedes 380SEL	a. met. maroon, metal Malaysia base, tan int., red HW logo in rear clear window, uh	$5
❏				b. same as (a), dark met. maroon, uh	$4
❏	📷			c. same as (b), dark met. maroon, 5sp	$7
❏				d. same as (a), 5sp	$5
❏				e. same as (a), t/b	$4
❏				f. same as (a), 7sp	$4
❏		254	Sol-Aire CX-4	a. met. blue, white plastic Malaysia base, white sides w/red & yellow HW logo & red "1," white int., clear window, guh	$7
❏				b. same as (a), gbbs	$6
❏	📷			c. same as (a), 7sp	$5
❏	📷	255	BMW 850i	a. dark met. blue, black plastic Malaysia base, red int., red HW logo in rear smoked window, uh	$4
❏				b. same as (a), guh	$20

No Fear Race Car

No Fear Race Car

Driven To The Max

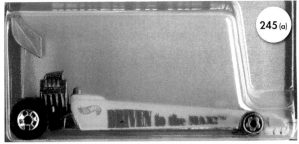

Shadow Jet II

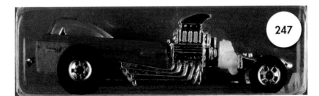

Rigor Motor

Splittin' Image II

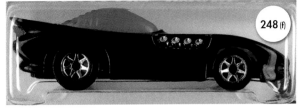

Splittin' Image II

Splittin' Image II

Fuji Blimp

Talbot Lago

Gulch Stepper

Photo	No.	Name	Description	Price
❑	255	BMW 850i	c. same as (a), clear window, guh	$10
❑			d. same as (c), black HW logo in rear clear window, guh	$5
❑			e. same as (d), black HW logo in rear clear window, g3sp	$5
❑			f. same as (d), black HW logo in rear clear window, gbbs	$3
❑ 📷	256	'80s Firebird	fluorescent red, black plastic Malaysia base, green, blue & yellow ribbons on sides, green bird on hood, light yellow int., black window, bw	$11
❑	257	3-Window '34	a. met. silver, metal Malaysia base, gray fenders, running boards & int., yellow, orange & red flames, tinted window, asw-bw	$15
❑			b. same as (a), large rear bw	$15

Photo	No.	Name	Description	Price
☐	257	3-Window '34	c. same as (a), 3sp	$3
☐ 📷			d. same as (a), 7sp	$15
☐	258	Blazer 4x4	a. silver-blue pearl, metal Malaysia base, blue pearl, magenta & black tampos on hood & sides, gray int., blue-tint window, red HW logo on side window, alw-ct	$10
☐			b. same as (a), dark blue replaces pearl blue in tampo, alw-ct	$8
☐ 📷			c. same as (b), purple HW logo on front fender & red HW logo on side window, alw-ct	$10
☐ 📷			d. same as (b), magenta HW logo on front fender, alw-ct	$10
☐			e. same as (b), red HW logo on side window, alw-bct	$20
☐	259	Lumina Minivan Taxi	a. yellow enamel, yellow plastic Malaysia base, black squares & "taxi" tampo on hood & sides, black int., clear window, bw	$5
☐ 📷			b. same as (a), 5sp	$7
☐	260	Twin Mill II	a. dark blue, gray plastic Malaysia base, two red & white stripes on roof & hood, white HW logo on rear window, red window, chrome engines, alw-uh	$20
☐			b. same as (a), orange window, alw-uh	$5
☐ 📷			c. same as (b), alw-5sp	$20
☐			d. same as (b), alw-5dot	$4
☐			e. same as (b), alw-w5dot	$8
☐			f. same as (d), chrome Malaysia base, alw-5dot	$20
☐	261	Cybercruiser	a. purple flake, metal Malaysia base, purple chrome driver & engine, uh	$5

252 (a)

Street Roader

252 (b)

Street Roader

253 (c)

Mercedes 380SEL

254 (c)

Sol-Aire CX4

255 (a)

BMW 850i

256

80's Firebird

257 (d)

3-Window '34

Blazer 4X4

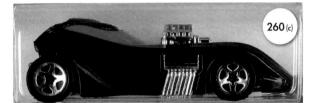

Lumina Minivan

Blazer 4X4

Twin Mill II

Cybercruiser

Photo		No.	Name	Description	Price
❏	📷	261	Cybercruiser	b. same as (a), black painted metal Malaysia base, uh	$30
❏		262	1993 Camaro	a. met. blue, gray plastic Malaysia base, white on sides, red & yellow HW logo, black "1" & "25th Anniversary" logo on side, red stripe on bottom, "Jack Baldwin" twice in white on roof w/red Chevy bow tie, HW in yellow w/2 logos on rear spoiler, "Camaro" in white on clear windshield, white int., guh	$8
❏	📷			b. same as (a), darker met. blue, guh	$7
❏				c. light shade of red enamel, black Malaysia base, white HW logo on rear, white int., clear window, uh	$5
❏				d. red enamel, black Malaysia base, white HW logo on rear white int., clear window, uh	$5
❏				e. same as (d), tan int., uh	$5
❏				f. red enamel, gray plastic Malaysia base, gold HW logo on rear, tan int., clear window, uh	$7
❏				g. same as (f), white HW logo on rear, Tan int. clear window, 5sp	$4
❏	📷			h. same as (f), gold HW logo on rear, tan int. clear window, 5sp	$7
❏	📷	263	Mean Green Passion	green, chrome Malaysia base, olive & blue flames on hood & sides, tan int., clear window, ww	$15
❏		264	Lexus SC400	a. dark met. red, black plastic Malaysia base, white-ish int., clear window, uh	$10
❏				b. same as (a), tan int., clear window, uh	$7
❏				c. met. maroon, black plastic Malaysia base, tan int., clear window, uh	$5
❏				d. same as (c), 3sp	$4
❏				e. same as (c), t/b	$3
❏	📷			f. same as (c), 5sp	$4
❏				g. same as (c), 5dot	$3
❏				h. same as (c), w5dot	$8
❏				i. same as (c), 7sp	$5
❏	📷	265	Oldsmobile Aurora	a. turquoise pearl, gray plastic Malaysia base, gray int., clear window, bw	$15
❏				b. same as (a), smoked window, bw	$9
❏				c. same as (a), black plastic window, bw	$10

Photo	No.	Name	Description	Price
❑	265	Oldsmobile Aurora	d. black enamel, black plastic Malaysia base, white & gold side stripe w/"Police" & "City of Hot Wheels" logo on sides, white roof w/#54 in black, white interior, blue-tint window, b7sp	$5
❑	266	'59 Cadillac	a. lavender pearl, chrome Malaysia base, white int., ww	$10
❑			b. light lavender pearl, chrome Malaysia base, white int., 7sp	$6
❑			c. light purple pearl, chrome Malaysia base, white int., 7sp	$6
❑ 📷			d. blue pearl, chrome Malaysia base, gold, black & rose tampos on sides, gold, black & rose tampos on sides, black int., smoked window, gbbs	$4
❑	267	Olds 442 W-30	a. yellow enamel, chrome Malaysia base, black stripes on hood scoops, black int., red HW logo in rear clear window, bw	$5
❑			b. same as (a), 7sp	$8

This car and all Olds 442 bodies hereafter are a new casting that started with the Blue & White card. You can tell by the wheel well openings, they are bigger and not round as the early casting. The two inside lines of the hood scoops come out farther than the outside lines.

Photo	No.	Name	Description	Price
❑			c. yellow enamel, chrome Malaysia base, black stripes on bigger hood scoops, black int., red HW logo in rear clear window, 7sp	$3
❑ 📷			d. same as (c), gray plastic Malaysia base, 7sp	$15
❑			e. same as (c), chrome Malaysia base, 5sp	$15
❑			f. same as (c), gray plastic Malaysia base, 5sp	$5
❑			g. same as (c), 5dot	$3
❑	268	GM Lean Machine	a. neon yellow plastic body, black painted Malaysia base, black canopy, uh	$8
❑ 📷			b. same as (a), smoked canopy, uh	$7
❑			c. same as (b), 3sp	$4

1993 Camaro

1993 Camaro

Mean Green Passion

Lexus SC400

Oldsmobile Aurora

'59 Cadillac

'59 Cadillac

'59 Cadillac

Olds 442 W-30

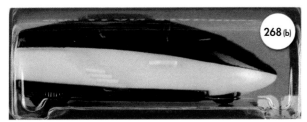

GM Lean Machine

Oshkosh Cement Mixer

Chevy Stocker

Chevy Stocker

	Photo	No.	Name	Description	Price
❑		268	GM Lean Machine	d. same as (b), t/b	$4
❑				e. same as (b), 5dot	$4
❑				f. same as (b), 5sp	$4
❑				g. same as (b), 7sp	$7
❑		269	Oshkosh Cement Mixer	a. yellow plastic body & Malaysia base, yellow painted fenders, black barrel, bw	$4
❑	📷			b. same as (a), 5sp	$3
❑				c. same as (a), 7sp	$4
❑				d. same as (a), t/b	$3
❑	📷	270	Chevy Stocker	a. pink flake, metal Malaysia base, yellow int., yellow-tint window, guh	$5
❑	📷			b. pink flake, metal Malaysia base, red int., smoked window, guh	$80
❑	📷			c. met. gold, metal Malaysia base, red int., smoked window, guh	$35
❑	📷	271	Funny Car	light met. blue, metal Malaysia base, red & yellow over white HW logo on hood & sides, white "F/C 1" & "Goodyear" tampo on sides w/racing decals, bw-Yes that's right!	$3,500
❑		272		unreleased	—
❑	📷	273	Tail Gunner	white enamel, metal Malaysia base, gray, blue & black camouflage on roof, hood & sides, gray int., front end & guns on rear bed, dark smoked window, wct	$8
❑		274	Super Cannon	a. olive w/matching olive metal Malaysia base, green, light green, tan & yellow camouflage, black plastic guns & front window, wbw	$4
❑	📷			b. same as (a), w5sp	$10

Chevy Stocker

Funny Car

Tail Gunner

Super Cannon

Race Team Series

Photo	No.	Name	Description	Price
❑ 📷	275	Lumina Stocker	a. light blue met. w/red & yellow HW logo over white on hood, white "1" on hood, roof & doors, red bow tie on hood & trunk, racing decals & yellow HW on sides, white int., clear window, uh	$5
❑			b. same as (a), Pontiac front end with two-sided grille in bumper	$135
❑			c. dark blue met. w/red & yellow HW logo over white on hood, white "1" on hood, roof & doors, red bow tie on hood & trunk, racing decals & yellow "Hot Wheels" on sides, white int., clear window, uh	$5
❑			d. same as (c), 7sp	$5
❑ 📷	276	Hot Wheels 500	a. light blue met., metal Malaysia base, white w/red stripe & HW logo on nose, "Goodyear" twice on front spoiler, HW in yellow on side pod, large HW logo on sides & rear white painted wing, gray plastic driver, bw	$5
❑ 📷			b. same as (a), dark met. blue, bw	$7
❑ 📷			c. same as (b), uh	$20
❑			d. same as (b), 7sp	$7
❑ 📷	277	Side Splitter	a. light met. blue, metal Malaysia base, red & yellow over white HW logo on hood & sides, white F/C 1 & "Goodyear" tampo on sides w/racing decals, bw	$8
The Side Splitter 277 (a) variation is the same car that is in the "271" package for $3500. See what packaging does for prices!				
❑ 📷			b. same as (a), dark met. blue, bw	$7
❑			c. same as (b), dark met. blue, 5sp	$5
❑ 📷	278	Dragster	a. light met. blue w/white on top & small red stripes, white "1," "T/F" & large red & yellow HW logo on sides, metal Malaysia base & engine, white plastic rear wing & driver, bw	$5
❑			b. same as (a), dark met. blue, bw	$8
❑			c. same as (b), 5sp	$4

Race Team Series, Lumina Stocker

Race Team Series, Side Splitter

Race Team Series, Hot Wheels 500

Race Team Series, Side Splitter

Race Team Series, Hot Wheels 500

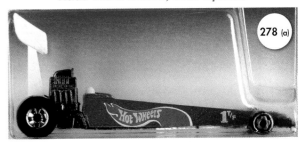

Race Team Series, Dragster

Race Team Series, Hot Wheels 500

Krackle Car Series

Photo	No.	Name	Description	Price
❑ 📷	280	Sharkruiser	a. blue & yellow met. cracked paint, metal Malaysia base, lime plastic teeth, engine & int., red HW logo between exhaust, uh	$5
❑			b. same as (a), silver painted Malaysia base, uh	$8
❑			c. same as (a), 7sp	$5
❑			d. same as (a), silver painted Malaysia base, 7sp	$8
❑ 📷	281	Turboa	a. purple & red met. cracked paint, metal Malaysia base, red plastic int., uh	$5
❑			b. same as (a), silver painted Malaysia base, red HW logo on rear wing, uh	$8
❑			c. purple & red met. cracked paint, metal Malaysia base, red plastic int., gray HW logo right side of cockpit, 7sp	$5
❑			d. same as (c), silver painted Malaysia base, 7sp	$8
❑	282	'63 Split-Window	a. aqua & orange met. cracked paint, chrome Malaysia 1 rivet base, white int., black HW logo on front orange-tint window, asw-bw	$7
❑			b. same as (a), chrome Malaysia 2 rivet base, asw-bw	$6
❑ 📷			c. same as (a), gray Malaysia 2 rivet base, asw-bw	$10
❑			d. same as (a), chrome Malaysia 2 rivet base, asw-5sp	$7
❑			e. same as (a), gray Malaysia 2 rivet base, asw-5sp	$9
❑	284	Flashfire	a. purple & yellow met. cracked paint, black plastic Malaysia base, purple chrome engine, yellow int. & side insert, yellow-tint canopy w/red HW logo, uh	$5
❑			b. same as (a), 5sp	$5
❑ 📷			c. same as (a), 7sp	$10
❑ 📷			d. purple & orange met. cracked paint, black plastic Malaysia base, blue chrome engine, orange int. & side insert, orange canopy w/green HW logo, 5sp	$20

Krackle Car Series, Sharkruiser

Krackle Car Series, Flashfire

Krackle Car Series, Turboa

Krackle Car Series, Flashfire

Krackle Car Series, '63 Split-Window

Steel Stamp Series

Photo	No.	Name	Description	Price
❑	285	Steel Passion	a. met. black, chrome Malaysia base, rose & silver cove tampo, gold side stripe, rose, gold & silver tampo on hood, red int., tinted window, gold logo on side, asw-ww	$8
❑			b. same as (a), clear window, ww	$15
❑ 📷			c. same as (a), tinted window, 7sp	$7
❑	287	Zender Fact 4	a. met. dark burgundy (almost black) w/rose & blue specs, black plastic Malaysia base, gold side stripe, white int., smoked window, gold HW logo on top of rear spoiler, uh	$5
❑			b. same as (a), gold HW logo on side, 3sp	$3
❑			c. same as (a), gold HW logo on top of rear spoiler, 5sp	$4
❑ 📷			d. same as (a), clear window, gold HW logo on side, 5sp	$20
❑	289	'56 Flashsider	a. met. burgundy chrome Malaysia base, gold, rose & light blue side tampo, chrome window, gold logo on rear fender, uh	$6
❑			b. same as (a), 5sp	$7
❑ 📷			c. same as (a), 7sp	$20
❑	290	#4-'57 Chevy	a. dark met. blue, chrome Malaysia base, rose, silver & light blue side tampo, rose HW logo in rear window, blue-tint window & int., uh	$6
❑			b. same as (a), smoked window & interior, 5sp	$50
❑			c. same as (a), 5sp	$7
❑ 📷			d. same as (a), 7sp	$20

Steel Stamp Series, Steel Passion

Steel Stamp Series, '56 Flashsider

Steel Stamp Series, Zender Fact 4

Steel Stamp Series, '57 Chevy

Pearl Driver Series

Photo	No.	Name	Description	Price
☐	292	Pearl Passion	a. lavender pearl, chrome Malaysia base, green HW logo on side above rear wheel, light yellow int., tinted window, asw-ww	$8
☐ 📷			b. same as (a), 7sp	$7
☐	293	VW Bug	a. pink pearl, metal Malaysia base, gray int., clear window, red logo in white circle on rear, bw	$7
☐ 📷			b. same as (a), 5sp	$15
☐			c. same as (a), 7sp	$12
☐ 📷	295	Talbot Lago	a. blue pearl, metal Malaysia base, red HW logo in white circle on rear, chrome int., blue-tint window, ww	$8
☐			b. same as (a), 7sp	$5
☐	296	Jaguar XJ220	a. white pearl, black plastic Malaysia base, white int., white HW logo on rear smoked window, uh	$5
☐ 📷			b. same as (a), 3sp	$4
☐			c. same as (a), 5sp	$4
☐			d. same as (a), 7sp	$10

Pearl Driver Series, Pearl Passion

Pearl Driver Series, Talbot Lago

Pearl Driver Series, VW Bug

Pearl Driver Series, Jaguar XJ220

Dark Rider Series

	Photo	No.	Name	Description	Price
❑	📷	297	Splittin' Image	a. black met., black plastic Malaysia base, red HW logo on top front fender, black-tint chrome engine & canopy, black-tint 6sp	$10
❑				b. same as (a), black-tint 7sp	$4
❑		298	Twin Mill II	a. black met., black plastic Malaysia base, black-tint chrome engines, black window, red HW logo on rear, black-tint 6sp	$10
❑	📷			b. same as (a), alw-black-tint 6sp	$15
❑				c. same as (a), black-tint 7sp	$4
❑	📷	299	Silhouette II	a. black met., black-tint chrome Malaysia base, black int., clear window, red HW logo on rear, black-tint chrome engine, black-tint chrome 6sp	$10
❑				b. same as (a), black plastic Malaysia base, black-tint chrome 6sp	$8
❑				c. same as (b), black-tint chrome 7sp	$4
❑	📷	300	Rigor Motor	a. met. black, met. black painted Malaysia base, black-tint chrome engine & int., clear canopy, white skulls & radiator, red HW logo on rear, black-tint 6sp	$10
❑				b. same as (a), black-tint 5sp	$4
❑				c. same as (a), black-tint 7sp	$6
❑				d. met. black, metal China base, red chrome engine & int., red-tint window, white skulls & radiator, dull red HW logo on rear, bbs	$3

The number 300 Rigor Motor is one of a few cars that were re-released in 1997 as a collector number and is not really part of the series.

Dark Rider Series, Splittin' Image

Dark Rider Series, Silhouette II

Dark Rider Series, Twin Mill II

Dark Rider Series, Rigor Motor

Roarin' Rods Series

	Photo	No.	Name	Description	Price
❑	📷	303	Street Roader	a. orange w/black tampos on hood & sides, black int., dark smoked window, metal Malaysia base, black HW logo on side, alw-oct	$3
❑				b. same as (a), alw-ct	$25
❑	📷	304	Roll Patrol	a. white w/black tampos on hood & sides, black-tint metal Malaysia base, black int., dark smoked window, black HW logo on side, asw-yct	$20
❑	📷			b. same as (a), asw-yct	$4
❑	📷			c. same as (b), black painted Malaysia base, asw-yct	$15
❑		305	Classic Cobra	a. neon yellow, metal Malaysia base, silver tampos, olive int., silver HW logo on side, smoked window, alw-7sp	$10
❑				b. same as (a), black-tint metal Malaysia base, alw-7sp	$15
❑				c. same as (a), black-tint metal Malaysia base, alw-5sp	$50

☐	📷	305	Classic Cobra	d. same as (a), black plastic Malaysia base, alw-7sp	$5
☐		302	#4-Mini Truck	a. tan, tan plastic Malaysia base, black tampos, tan int. & bed, chrome speakers in bed, chrome engine, black logo on side, smoked window, uh	$5
☐	📷			b. same as (a), orange plastic Malaysia base, 5sp	$55
☐				c. same as (a), 5sp	$4
☐				d. same as (a), 7sp	$8

Roarin' Rods Series, Mini Truck

Roarin' Rods Series, Roll Patrol

Roarin' Rods Series, Street Roader

Roarin' Rods Series, Roll Patrol

Roarin' Rods Series, Roll Patrol

Roarin' Rods Series, Classic Cobra

Hot Hubs Series

Photo	No.	Name	Description	Price
☐ 📷	307	Cybercruiser	burgundy flake, metal Malaysia base, purple chrome driver & engine, black logo in white box on rear, blue swirl wheel w/orange tire	$7
☐ 📷	308	Vampyra	a. purple w/yellow & red eyes, black-tint metal Malaysia base, gold-tint chrome engine, gold logo on side of wing, green 6sp wheel w/black tire	$9
☐			b. purple w/yellow & red eyes, black painted metal Malaysia base, gold-tint chrome engine, gold logo on side of wing, green swirl wheel w/black tire	$4
☐			c. purple w/yellow & red eyes, black painted metal China base, gold-tint chrome engine, gold logo on side of wing, bbs	$3
The Vampyra 308 (c) variation car is one of a few that were re-released in 1997.				
☐ 📷	310	Shadow Jet	day-glo green flake w/purple "Inter Cooled" tampo on rear wing, red "F-3" tampo on top, red logo on top, yellow nose, metal Malaysia base, green int., yellow-tint canopy, yellow swirl wheel w/purple tire	$9
☐ 📷	311	Suzuki QuadRacer	a. yellow body w/purple seat, black handlebars, black-tint Malaysia base, red logo on rear fender, yellow swirl wheel w/black tire	$10

❑	📷	311	Suzuki QuadRacer	b. greenish yellow w/purple seat, black handlebars, black-tint Malaysia base, red logo on rear fender, yellow swirl wheel w/black tire	$20
❑				c. greenish yellow w/purple seat, black handlebars, black-tint Malaysia base, red logo on rear fender, greenish yellow Tiger Paw wheel	$40
❑				d. light yellow w/purple seat, black handlebars, black-tint China base, red logo on rear fender, cts	$3

The Suzuki QuadRacer 311 (d) variation is one of a few that were re-released in 1997.

307

Hot Hubs Series, Cybercruiser

308 (a)

Hot Hubs Series, Vampyra

310

Hot Hubs Series, Shadow Jet

311 (a)

Hot Hubs Series, Suzuki QuadRacer

311 (b)

Hot Hubs Series, Suzuki QuadRacer

Speed Gleamer Series

	Photo	No.	Name	Description	Price
❑	📷	312	3-Window '34	aqua chrome w/aqua running boards, int. & fenders, metal Malaysia base, gold logo in rear blue-tinted window, 7sp	$4
❑		313	T-Bucket	a. purple pearl, black-tint metal Malaysia base, red logo in white box on rear, blue-tint chrome engine, white int., clear window, 5sp	$35
❑	📷			b. purple pearl, met. black painted metal Malaysia base, red logo in white box on rear, blue chrome engine, white int., purple-tint window, 5sp	$5
❑				c. purple pearl, black painted metal Malaysia base, red logo in white box on rear, purple chrome engine, white int., purple-tint window, 5sp	$5
❑	📷			d. purple pearl w/black painted metal Malaysia base, red logo in white box on rear, purple-tint chrome engine, white int., purple-tint window, 7sp	$20
❑	📷	315	Ratmobile	a. black plastic rat body w/gray painted Malaysia base, red logo on chrome engine, uh	$3
❑				b. same as (a), 7sp	$4
❑		316	Limozeen	a. gold flake, gold chrome Malaysia base, white int., smoked window, red logo on rear, asw-ww	$15
❑	📷			b. same as (a), asw-7sp	$15

Anytime you have a Hot Wheels car with Real Riders tires it is very much in demand because of its realism. In 1995, Mattel reissued the Real Rider Series in their new four car series sets. Everyone became excited because the cars were cool, and customizers were going to have a supply of Real Riders tires for their new projects. As it would happen, the Real Rider Series of 1995 was a very short run.

Speed Gleamer Series, 3-Window '34

Speed Gleamer Series, Ratmobile

Speed Gleamer Series, T-Bucket

Speed Gleamer Series, Limozeen

Speed Gleamer Series, T-Bucket

Real Rider Series

Photo	No.	Name	Description	Price
📷	317	Dump Truck	day-glo yellow w/yellow dump box, black int. & window, metal Malaysia base, red logo in white box on rear, day-glo yellow wheel w/"Real Rider" rubber tire	$30
📷	318	Mercedes Unimog	met. silver metal cab & box, day-glo orange plastic fenders, int. & rear box cover, metal Malaysia base, red logo in white box on rear, orange wheels w/knobby Real Rider rubber tires	$25
	319	unreleased		——
📷	320	'59 Cadillac	rose pearl, chrome Malaysia base, white int., red logo on clear windshield, chrome wheels w/whitewall Real Rider tires	$45
📷	321	Corvette Stingray	met. green, metal Malaysia base, gold HW logo on rear fender behind wheel, clear window & int., gray wheels w/Goodyear Real Rider tires	$75

Real Rider Series, Dump Truck

Real Rider Series, Mercedes Unimog

Real Rider Series, '59 Cadillac

Real Rider Series, Corvette Stingray

Silver Series

Photo		No.	Name	Description	Price
❏	📷	322	Fire Eater	a. chrome body, chrome Malaysia base, blue insert, blue-tint window & interior, asw-bw	$15
❏				b. chrome body, chrome Malaysia base, yellow & black tampos, red insert, blue-tint window & int., asw-bw	$8
❏				c. same as (a), asw-7sp	$5
❏	📷	323	Rodzilla	a. chrome body w/white eyes & teeth, gold chrome engine, metal Malaysia base, red logo on top rear arm, uh	$4
❏				b. chrome body w/white eyes & teeth, gold chrome engine, silver painted metal Malaysia base, red logo on top rear arm, uh	$10
❏				c. chrome body w/white eyes & teeth, gold chrome engine, metal Malaysia base, red logo on top rear arm, 7sp	$4
❏				d. collector number card (no series) chrome body w/white eyes & teeth, gold chrome engine, metal China base, red logo on top rear arm, 5sp	$3

The Rodzilla 323 (d) variation is one of a few that were re-released in 1997.

Photo		No.	Name	Description	Price
❏	📷	325	Propper Chopper	chrome body, yellow & black "Police" side tampo, black Malaysia base, int. & tail, blue-tint window, gray rotors, red logo on side	$3
❏		328	School Bus	a. chrome body, black plastic Malaysia base, thick black stripe & "School Bus" on side, "Emergency Exit" on rear door, black logo on rear, white int., clear window, asw-bw	$10
❏				b. same as (a), tinted window, asw-bw	$20
❏				c. same as (a), asw-3sp	$15
❏				d. same as (a), asw-5sp	$4
❏	📷			e. same as (a), asw-7sp	$4

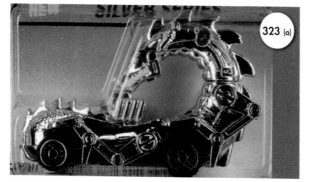

Silver Series, Fire Eater

Silver Series, Rodzilla

Silver Series, Propper Chopper

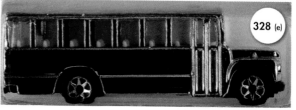

Silver Series, School Bus

Photo Finish Series

For some reason the Photo Finish Series has become really hard to find. They were not very appealing, so my guess is that collectors did not grab extras.

Photo	No.	Name	Description	Price
☐ 📷	331	Aerostar	white enamel, metal Malaysia base, orange photo on side, silver window, no logo, 7sp	$10
☐ 📷	332	Blimp	white body, "Hot Wheels" city photo on side, black gondola, no logo	$10
☐ 📷	333	Tank Truck	candy blue, chrome Malaysia base, white tank w/orange & dark blue photo on side, chrome window, no logo, 7sp	$10
☐ 📷	335	Hiway Hauler	green pearl, chrome Malaysia base, white box w/NYC photo on side, black window, asw-7sp	$20

The 335 Hiway Hauler has become very rare since September 11, 2002.

Photo Finish Series, Aerostar

Photo Finish Series, Tank Truck

Photo Finish Series, Blimp

Photo Finish Series, Hiway Hauler

Racing Metals Series

When the Racing Metals Series came out, there were all kinds of different shades in the chrome. The shades that really made a difference in the variations were the ones for the Ramp Truck. For some reason there was color added to the mix. The best way to distinguish these is through a side-by-side comparison.

Photo	No.	Name	Description	Price
☐ 📷	336	Race Truck	dark-tint chrome, black painted metal Malaysia base, red & white tampos on side & hood, yellow "Hot Wheels" on smoked windshield, red int., bed & roll bar, ct	$5
☐	337	Ramp Truck	a. chrome cab, metal Malaysia base, purple plastic ramp w/large red & yellow HW logo & blue lettering on side, black window w/yellow HW logo across windshield, 7sp	$5
☐ 📷			b. blue-tint chrome cab, metal Malaysia base, purple plastic ramp w/large red & yellow HW logo & blue lettering on side, large yellow & red over white HW logo on roof, black window w/yellow HW across windshield, 7sp	$8
☐			c. pink-tint chrome cab, metal Malaysia base, purple plastic ramp w/large red & yellow HW logo & blue lettering on side, black window w/yellow HW across windshield, 7sp	$35
☐ 📷			d. same as (c), pink chrome cab, 7sp	$50
☐ 📷	338	Camaro Racer	a. light blue-tint chrome, gray Malaysia base, large HW logo on sides & hood, "Jack Baldwin" in white on roof, red bow tie on roof & hood, two HW logos on rear spoiler w/yellow HWs, white int., clear window, 5sp	$8
☐			b. same as (a), no "Jack Baldwin" on hood	$5
☐ 📷	340	Dragster	light blue-tint chrome w/large red & yellow HW logo on sides, white on top of nose w/red stripe, white int. & rear wing, metal engine & Malaysia base, 5sp	$5

There were cars reissued after 1997 with the same number as they had in their respective series. They are easy to identify because they don't have the series information on the cards anymore, just the collector number. I am including them where they fall, but will mention that they were a later release and not part of the original series.

Racing Metals Series, Race Truck

Racing Metals Series, Ramp Truck

Racing Metals Series, Ramp Truck

Racing Metals Series, Camaro Racer

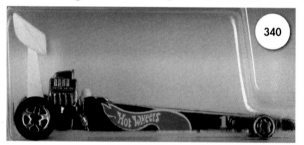

Racing Metals Series, Dragster

1995 Model Series

Mattel did not put the collector numbers in order for the 1995 Model series cars. Therefore, they are listed below in the series' release order.

Photo	No.	Name	Description	Price
☐ 📷	343	#1-Speed Blaster	a. met. blue, black plastic Malaysia base, chrome engine & window, red logo in white box on rear, uh	$51
☐			b. met. blue, chrome Malaysia base, engine & window, red logo in white box on rear, uh	$10
☐ 📷			c. met. blue, pink chrome Malaysia base, engine & window, longer pipes at rear, uh	$45
☐ 📷			d. met. blue, pink chrome Malaysia base, engine & window, red logo in white box on rear, uh	$5
☐			e. same as (d), 5sp	$5
☐			f. met. green, chrome Malaysia base, engine & window, red logo in white box on rear, 3sp	$3
☐			g. same as (f), t/b	$3
☐			h. same as (f), 5sp	$3
☐			i. same as (f), 5dot	$3
☐ 📷			j. same as (f), 7sp	$35

Photo	No.	Name	Description	Price
❑	343	#1-Speed Blaster	k. met. green, gray plastic Malaysia base, engine & window, red logo in white box on rear, 5dot	$10
❑			l. collector numbers card (no series) met. green, chrome Malaysia base, engine & window, red logo in white box on rear, 5dot	$3
❑ 📷	342	#2-Mercedes SL	a. red enamel, matching red plastic Malaysia base, tan int., clear window, red logo in white box on rear, alw-uh	$5
❑ 📷			b. same as (a), dark red plastic Malaysia base, alw-uh	$7
❑			c. same as (a), alw-5sp	$5
❑			d. same as (b), dark red plastic Malaysia base, alw-5sp	$5
❑ 📷			e. black met., gray Malaysia plastic base, tan int. clear window, red logo in white box on rear, alw-5sp	$35
❑			f. same as (e), red int., clear window, alw-5sp	$3
❑			g. same as (f), alw-7sp	$3
❑			h. black met, gray Malaysia plastic base, red int., clear window, red logo in white box on rear, alw-g7sp	$40

The Mercedes SL 342 (h) variation is one of those cars that were for other than U.S. release, & are rare when found in a U.S. collector number package.

Photo	No.	Name	Description	Price
❑			i. same as (f), alw-bbs	$7
❑			j. same as (i), collector numbers card (No Series), alw-bbs	$3
❑	341	#3-'58 Corvette	a. day-glo pink, pink plastic Malaysia base, chrome int. & engine, red logo in white box on trunk, bw	$5
❑ 📷			b. same as (a), 7sp	$7
❑			c. light purple pearl met., purple plastic Malaysia base, chrome int. & engine, white logo on trunk, clear window, 7sp	$7
❑			d. candy purple met., purple plastic Malaysia base, chrome int. & engine, white logo on trunk, clear window, 5sp	$12
❑			e. same as (d), 7sp	$4
❑ 📷			f. same as (a), gray int. & engine, no chrome, no origin base, 7sp	$10
❑			g. collector numbers card (no series) purple pearl, purple plastic Malaysia base, chrome int. & engine, white logo on trunk, clear window, 5dot	$3
❑			h. same as (g), collector numbers card (no series), 5sp	$8
❑			i. collector numbers card (no series) purple pearl, purple plastic Malaysia base, chrome int. & engine, white logo on trunk, clear window, 7sp	$3

341 (f)

1995 Model Series, '58 Corvette

342 (b)

1995 Model Series, #2-Mercedes SL

342 (a)

1995 Model Series, Mercedes SL

342 (e)

1995 Model Series, #2-Mercedes SL

Photo	No.	Name	Description	Price
☐ 📷	345	#4-Speed-A-Saurus	a. green plastic, metal Malaysia base, chrome engine, bw	$3
☐			b. green plastic, metal Malaysia base, chrome engine, 5sp	$3
☐			c. collector numbers card (no series) purple plastic, metal Malaysia base, chrome engine, 5sp	$2
☐	347	#5-Power Rocket	a. bronze plastic body, metal Malaysia base, gray int., blue-tint canopy, HW logo on side, uh	$30
☐ 📷			b. same as (a), 5sp	$10
☐			c. same as (a), 7sp/rear-5sp/fr	$15

I saw this car listed in another book as being just the 5sp version, but there it was 7sp on the rear and 5sp on the front! I have this car personally.

Photo	No.	Name	Description	Price
☐		Power Pistons (name change)	d. burgundy plastic body, metal Malaysia base, gray int., blue-tint window, HW logo on side, 3sp	$4
☐ 📷			e. same as (d), 5sp	$5
☐			f. same as (d), 7sp	$25
☐			g. collector numbers card (no series) burgundy plastic body, silver painted metal Malaysia base, gray int., blue-tint window, gray logo on side, t/b	$2
☐			h. same as (g), 3sp	$2
☐	346	#6-Hydroplane	met. blue, white plastic Malaysia base, chrome int., clear canopy, large HW logo on top of rear wing & each side, red "1" over white on rear wing side	$3
☐	348	#7-Dodge Ram	a. dark met. green, gray plastic Malaysia base, green cap, chrome int., smoked window, red logo in white box on rear, alw-5sp	$4
☐			b. same as (a), dark gray plastic Malaysia base from the 1996 Ram Treasure Hunt, alw-5sp	$10
☐			c. same as (a), alw-5dot	$3
☐ 📷			d. same as (a), alw-w5dot	$8

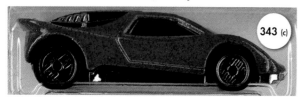

1995 Model Series, #1-Speed Blaster (343 a)

1995 Model Series, #1-Speed Blaster (343 c)

1995 Model Series, #1-Speed Blaster (343 d)

1995 Model Series, #1-Speed Blaster (343 j)

1995 Model Series, #8-Camaro Convertible (344 c)

1995 Model Series, #4-Speed-A-Saurus (345 a)

1995 Model Series, #5-Power Rocket (347 b)

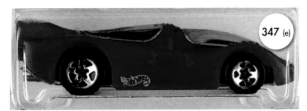

1995 Model Series, #5-Power Pistons

1995 Model Series, #9-Power Pipes

1995 Model Series, #7-Dodge Ram

1995 Model Series, #10-Ferrari 355

Photo	No.	Name	Description	Price
❑	348	#7-Dodge Ram	e. same as (c), collector number card (no series), alw-5dot	$3
❑	344	#8-Camaro Convertible.	a. met. teal, black plastic Malaysia base, gray int., red HW logo on clear windshield, alw-uh	$7
❑			b. same as (a), alw-3sp	$4
❑			c. same as (a), alw-5sp	$4
❑			d. red enamel, black plastic Malaysia base, black int., clear window, yellow HW logo on rear fender, alw-3sp	$3
❑			e. same as (d), alw-t/b	$3
❑			f. red enamel, black plastic Malaysia base, black int., clear window, yellow HW logo on rear fender, alw-g7sp	$40

The Camaro Convertible 344 (f) variation is one of those cars for other than U.S. release & is rare when found in a U.S. collector number package.

Photo	No.	Name	Description	Price
❑			g. same as (d), alw-5sp	$5
❑			h. same as (g), no series on card, just collector number, alw-5sp	$3
❑			i. same as (g), plastic India base, alw-5sp	$3
❑			j. same as (h), black plastic Malaysia base, alw-5sp	$3
❑	349	#9-Power Pipes	a. dark blue plastic body, silver painted metal Malaysia base, red logo in white box on rear, chrome int., purple canopy, 3sp	$3
❑			b. same as (a), 5sp	$3
❑ 📷			c. same as (a), 7sp	$5
❑			d. same as (b), collector numbers card (no series) dark blue plastic body, silver painted metal Malaysia base, red logo in white box on rear, chrome int., purple canopy, 5sp	$2
❑			e. collector numbers card (no series) dark blue plastic body, silver painted metal Malaysia base, red logo in white box on rear, chrome int., purple canopy, 5dot	$2
❑	350	#10-Ferrari 355	a. yellow enamel, metal Malaysia base, black int., clear window, red logo on rear plate, asw-3sp	$4
❑			b. same as (a), asw-t/b	$3
❑			c. same as (a), asw-5sp	$5
❑			d. same as (a), silver painted Malaysia base, asw-5sp	$7
❑			e. same as (a), asw-7sp	$4
❑			f. same as (a), silver painted Malaysia base, asw-7sp	$7
❑ 📷			g. same as (a), asw-5dot	$4
❑			h. same as (a), asw-w5dot	$8
❑			g. yellow enamel, metal Malaysia base, black side stripe w/"Ferrari," black window, red logo on rear, 5sp	$8

Photo	No.	Name	Description	Price
❏ 📷	351	#11-Power Rocket	a. purple plastic body with light silver flakes, metal Malaysia base, orange stripe tampo & gray lettering, chrome driver & engine, orange HW logo behind rear wheel, extended tip on engine front, 5sp	$7
❏			b. purple plastic w/light silver flakes, silver painted Malaysia base, orange stripe side tampo w/"EXP 3510" & gray lettering, chrome driver & engine, orange HW logo behind rear wheel, tip cut short on front of engine, 3sp	$4
❏			c. same as (b), t/b	$3
❏			d. same as (b), 5sp	$5
❏			e. same as (b), 5dot	$4
❏			f. same as (b), w5dot	$8
❏			g. same as (b), collector number card (no series), 5dot	$2
❏ 📷	352	#12-Big Chill	a. white enamel, black plastic Malaysia base, chrome canopy, black treads, metal rollers, pink ski	$12
❏			b. same as (a), orange ski	$8
❏ 📷			c. white enamel, black plastic Malaysia base, day-glo orange "Shredder" tampo, blue tampo on front & sides, chrome canopy, black treads, metal rollers, orange ski	$5
❏			d. white enamel, black plastic Malaysia base, black tampo, chrome canopy, black treads, metal rollers, orange ski	$5
❏			e. same as (d), collector number card (no series)	$4

1995 Model Series, #11-Power Rocket

1995 Model Series, #12-Big Chill

1995 Model Series, #12-Big Chill

1995 Treasure Hunt Series

Photo	No.	Name	Description	Price
❏ 📷	353	#1-Olds 442	met. blue w/white scoops, chrome Malaysia base, white int., clear window, red HW logo in rear window, chrome wheel redline "Real Rider" tires	$70
❏ 📷	354	#2-Gold Passion	a. gold flake, gold chrome Malaysia base, black cove w/gold pinstripe, lavender tampo on door to rear fender, black, gold & lavender tampo on hood, black HW logo on rear fender skirt, white int., clear window, gold wheel Real Rider tires	$75
❏ 📷		(Ferrari F40 on card) #69	b. same as (a), on Ferrari card	$100
❏	355	#3-'67 Camaro	a. white enamel, orange "SS" stripes on hood & trunk, metal Malaysia base, orange int., clear window, chrome wheel Real Rider tires	$400

Photo		No.	Name	Description	Price
❏	📷	355	#3-'67 Camaro	b. same as (a), gray wheel Real Rider tires	$350
❏	📷	356	#4-'57 T-Bird	dark met. purple, chrome Malaysia base, clear window & int., white HW logo in rear window, white line Real Rider tires	$65
❏	📷	357	#5-VW Bug	day-glo green, metal Malaysia base, purple int., clear window, red HW logo in white box on rear, purple swirl wheel w/chrome rim	$125
❏	📷	358	#6-'63 Split-Window	met. blue, chrome Malaysia base, white int., red HW logo on front clear window, chrome wheel white line Real Rider tires	$75
❏	📷	359	#7-Stutz Blackhawk	met. black, metal Malaysia base, red int., gold HW logo in front clear window, chrome wheel redline Real Rider tires	$50
❏	📷	360	#8-Rolls-Royce	dark met. red, metal Malaysia base, tan plastic top, dark red HW logo in white oval on rear, red int., clear window, red 6sp wheel w/chrome rim	$50
❏	📷	361	#9-Classic Caddy	light met. green body, olive plastic fenders, metal Malaysia base, tan int., clear window, red HW logo on front fender, gold 6sp	$50
❏	📷	362	#10-Classic Nomad	met. teal, metal Malaysia base, white int., red HW logo in front clear window, chrome swirl wheel	$60
❏	📷	363	#11-Classic Cobra	dark met. green, metal Malaysia base, two wide gold stripes on hood & trunk, tan int., clear window, gold chrome 6sp	$70
❏	📷	364	#12-'31 Doozie	yellow enamel, black plastic fenders, top & int., metal Malaysia base, red HW logo on side, clear window, yellow 6sp	$50

1995 Treasure Hunt Series, #1-Olds 442

1995 Treasure Hunt Series, #4-'57 T-Bird

1995 Treasure Hunt Series, #2-Gold Passion

1995 Treasure Hunt Series, #5-VW Bug

1995 Treasure Hunt Series, #2-Gold Passion
(Ferrari F40 on card)

1995 Treasure Hunt Series, #6-'63 Split-Window

1995 Treasure Hunt Series, #3-'67 Camaro

1995 Treasure Hunt Series, #7-Stutz Blackhawk

1995 Treasure Hunt Series, #8-Rolls Royce

1995 Treasure Hunt Series, #9-Classic Caddy

1995 Treasure Hunt Series, #10-Classic Nomad

1995 Treasure Hunt Series, #11-Classic Cobra

1995 Treasure Hunt Series, #12-'31 Doozie

1996 First Editions

Photo	No.	Name	Description	Price
❏	378	#1-'96 Mustang	a. met. red, metal Malaysia base, red HW logo on rear spoiler, silver headlights, tan int., clear window, asw-3sp	$7
❏			b. same as (a), asw-t/b	$7
❏			c. same as (a), asw-5sp	$9
❏			d. same as (a), asw-5dot	$7
❏ 📷			e. same as (a), asw-7sp	$25
❏ 📷	367	#2-Chevy 1500 Pickup	a. met. silver, metal Malaysia base, silver int., smoked window, large HW logos on hood & bed, orange, blue & black side tampos, orange number on roof & door, yellow letter alw-b7sp	$12
❏			b. same as (a), asw-b7sp	$3
❏			c. same as (b), silver painted metal Malaysia base, asw-b7sp	$12
❏			d. silver w/metal China base, silver int., clear window, large HW logos on hood only, orange, blue & black side tampos, orange number on roof & door, 5sp	$3
❏ 📷	382	#3-'70 Dodge Daytona	a. red enamel, chrome Malaysia base, tan int., gold logo in front of rear wheel, clear window, asw-gbbs	$3
❏			b. same as (a), black interior, asw-gbbs	$175
The '70 Dodge Daytona 382 (b) card has the "New" in the upper left-hand corner.				
❏			c. same as (a), asw-g7sp	$3
❏			d. same as (a), asw-7sp	$50
❏			e. same as (a), asw-t/b	$3
❏	373	#4-Street Cleaver	a. yellow plastic body, yellow painted Malaysia base, chrome engine, 5sp	$4
❏			b. same as (a), 5sp	$10
❏			c. same as (a), alw-5sp	$12
❏			d. same as (b), flame tampo, 3sp	$10
❏			e. same as (a), t/b	$4
❏			f. same as (a), 5dot	$4
❏			g. same as (a), alw-5dot	$4
❏			h. same as (a), w5dot	$8

Photo	No.	Name	Description	Price
☐ 📷	373	#4-Street Cleaver	i. yellow plastic body, yellow painted Malaysia base, gray engine, alw-5dot	$10
☐	370	#5-Rail Rodder	a. black plastic body, metal Malaysia base, chrome engines & drivers (wheels), HW logo on orange & dark red side stripe, greenish yellow "Railrodder" tampo, small rear b5sp	$8
☐			b. same as (a), large rear 5sp	$5
☐ 📷			c. black plastic body, metal Malaysia base, gray engines & drivers, HW logo on orange & dark red side stripe, light green "Railrodder" tampo, large rear 5sp	$10
☐			d. black plastic body, metal China base, chrome engines & drivers, HW logo on orange & red side stripe, yellow "Railrodder" tampo, large rear 5sp	$4
☐ 📷	372	#6-Customized VW Drag Bus	met. blue, metal China base, large HW logo on side w/yellow "Fahrvergnugen," orange int., clear window, 5sp/front	$65
You might notice here that there are two cars with the same "collector number." I have no idea why it happened.				
☐	369	#7-Road Rocket	a. light green plastic body w/transparent blue plastic top, metal Malaysia base, blue HW logo on side, gbbs	$2
☐			b. same as (a), g7sp	$20

🏁 🏁 The 369 card had "New" at the top. The back had cars #4, 5, & 6 listed. Notice the name of
🏁 🏁 #6—it says "Rocket Shot." We all know that the #6 FE was the Drag Bus (#372). I have no
idea why the number was changed, except that the #369 was issued to the "Sizzlers" that was
also later changed to the "Turbo Flame."

Photo	No.	Name	Description	Price
☐ 📷	371	#7-Road Rocket	a. light green plastic body w/transparent blue plastic top, metal Malaysia base, blue HW logo on side, red HW logo on top of rear wing, gbbs	$10
☐			b. same as (a), blue HW logo on side only, gbbs	$3

🏁 The Road Rocket 371 (b) variation has the card with 371 "Coolest To Collect" in the upper 🏁
corner and the FEs listed on the back as #7, 8 & 9.

1996 First Editions, #2-Chevy 1500 Pickup

1996 First Editions, #7-Road Rocket

1996 First Editions, #8-Sizzlers

1996 First Editions, #6-Customized VW Drag Bus

1996 First Editions, #5-Rail Rodder

1996 First Editions, #4-Street Cleaver

Photo	No.	Name	Description	Price
☐ 📷	369	#8-Turbo Flame	a. white pearl plastic body, metal Malaysia base, large HW logo on sides, orange-tint window, chrome engine, 5sp	$6
☐	369	#8-Sizzlers (name change)	b. white pearl plastic body, metal Malaysia base, large HW logo on sides, orange-tint window, chrome engine, 5sp	$3
	**This Sizzlers is the same as the "Turbo Flame." Rumor has it that Mattel had to use the "Sizzlers" name or lose it.**
☐			c. white pearl plastic body, metal Malaysia base, large HW logo on sides, orange-tint window, chrome engine, 5dot	$15
☐			d. white pearl plastic body, silver painted metal Malaysia base, large HW logo on sides, orange-tint window, chrome engine, 5sp	$8
☐			e. white pearl plastic body, metal Malaysia base, large HW logo on sides, orange-tint window, gray engine, 5sp	$10
☐	374	#9-Radio Flyer Wagon	a. red enamel, metal Malaysia base, white "Radio Flyer" tampo on sides, black seat, white logo on rear, chrome engine, 5sp	$4
☐			b. same as (a), gray engine, 5sp	$15
☐			c. same as (a), silver painted metal Malaysia base, 5sp	$8
☐ 📷			d. same as (a), metal China base, bw	$5
☐			e. same as (a), metal China base, bw rear/5sp front	$8
☐	375	#10-Dogfighter	a. met. red, black plastic Malaysia base, yellow, red & white side tampo, tan propeller chrome engine, seat & suspension, red logo on tail, 5sp	$3
☐ 📷			b. same as (a), gray engine, 5sp	$10
☐			c. same as (a), t/b	$2
☐			d. same as (a), 5dot	$2
☐ 📷	376	#11-Twang-Thang	silver flake, pearl plastic Malaysia base, red transparent guitars w/chrome strings on side, chrome int., clear window, blue logo on rear, 5sp	$2
☐	377	#12-Ferrari F50	a. red enamel, gray plastic Malaysia base, yellow Ferrari on rear spoiler (snuck out in a US package), asw-7sp	$30
☐ 📷			b. red enamel, gray plastic Malaysia base, black int., yellow HW logo on rear spoiler, clear window, asw-bbs	$3
☐ 📷			c. (new casting) dark red w/gray plastic China base, black int., yellow HW logo on rear spoiler, clear window, asw-bbs	$2
☐			d. Collector number card (no series) dark red enamel, gray plastic India base, black int., yellow logo on rear spoiler, clear window, asw-bbs	$2

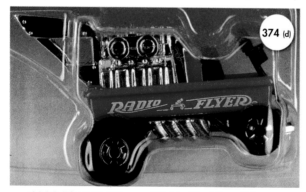

1996 First Editions, #9-Radio Flyer Wagon

1996 First Editions, #10-Dogfighter

1996 First Editions, #11-Twang Thang

1996 First Editions, #12-Ferrari F50

1996 First Editions, #1-'96 Mustang

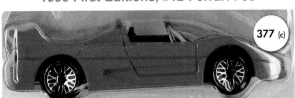

1996 First Editions, #12-Ferrari F50

Race Truck Series

Photo	No.	Name	Description	Price
☐	380	Dodge Ram 1500	a. red, red plastic Malaysia base, yellow & black #4 on roof & door, yellow & black Ram tampo on hood, silver "DODGE" tampo on rear fender, yellow & silver HW logo in front of rear wheel, red int., alw-yellow letter b7sp	$3
☐			b. same as (a), no hood or roof tampo, alw-yellow letter b7sp	$15
☐ 📷			c. same as (a), no letters on tires, alw-b7sp	$10
☐ 📷			d. met. gray, red & black #4 on door, white "DODGE" tampo on rear fender, red & yellow over white HW logo in front of rear wheel, red & black "Ram" tampo on hood, gray plastic China base, red front & rear bumpers, int. & bed, smoked window, alw-5sp	$3
☐	381	Ford LTL (Kenworth T600)	a. met. silver, red plastic Malaysia base, white, red & blue tampos on sleeper sides, blue window, yellow letter large b7sp	$10

The #381 was supposed to be the Ford LTL, but for some reason it did not make it into production and they used the Kenworth T600 instead.

Photo	No.	Name	Description	Price
☐ 📷		Kenworth T600	b. same as (a), name was changed on package	$5
☐ 📷	382	'56 Flashsider	a. met. black, chrome Malaysia base, gray & red #1 & stripe on sides w/racing decals, gray & red #1 on roof, white Chevrolet on hood w/large red bow tie, white Chevrolet twice & small red bowtie on bed cover, red logo on rear, chrome window, yellow letter b7sp	$9
☐			b. same as (a), red HW logo on door, yellow letter b7sp	$7
☐			c. same as (b), no letters on b7sp	$15
☐	383	Nissan Truck	a. met. dark blue, chrome Malaysia base, red & white tampos, HW logo on door, yellow front end, int. & roll bar, clear window, alw-ct	$125
☐			b. same as (a), gray front end, int. & roll bar, chrome engine, HW logo on door, alw-ct	$3
☐ 📷			c. same as (b), alw-bct	$20

Race Truck Series, Dodge Ram 1500

Race Truck Series, Kenworth T600

Race Truck Series, Dodge Ram 1500

1996 First Editions, #3-'70 Dodge Daytona

Race Truck Series, '56 Flashsider

Race Truck Series, Nissan Truck

Flamethrower Series

	Photo	No.	Name	Description	Price
❏	📷	384	'57 T-Bird	a. white pearl, chrome Malaysia base, copper & green flames, 2 flames on rear fender, 5 flames on trunk, gold HW logo in rear window, clear window & int., 7sp	$8
❏				b. white pearl, chrome Malaysia base, fading pink & green flames, day-glo pink HW logo on rear fender, 4 flames on trunk, clear window & int., 7sp	$10
❏				c. white pearl, chrome Malaysia base, fading pink & green flames, gold HW logo in rear window, 5 flames on trunk, 2 flames on rear fender, clear window & int., 7sp	$7
❏	📷			d. white pearl, chrome Malaysia base, full bright pink & green flames, day-glo pink HW logo on rear fender, 5 flames on trunk, clear window & int., 7sp	$7
❏				e. white pearl, chrome Malaysia base, light pink & green flames, 2 flames on rear fender, 4 flames on trunk, gold HW logo in rear window, clear window & int., 7sp	$9
❏				f. white pearl, chrome Malaysia base, light pink & green flames, day-glo pink HW logo on rear fender & gold HW logo in rear window, clear window & int., 4 flames on trunk, 7sp	$45
❏	📷	385	Hydroplane	a. yellow w/yellow, red & blue flames on sides & rear wing, chrome engine & int., black plastic Malaysia base, smoked canopy	$3
❏				b. same as (a), flames on wing backwards, chrome engine & int	$30
❏				c. same as (a), no flames on top of rear wing	$15
❏	📷	386	Range Rover	a. red enamel, chrome Malaysia base, gold & magenta flames on hood, roof & side, red logo in rear window, tan int., clear window, asw-ct	$5
❏				b. same as (a), flames missing from rear fender, magenta logo on rear fender, ct	$3
❏		387	Oshkosh Snowplow	a. black plastic cab & box, metal Malaysia base, yellow & blue flames on door, top of box, hood & top of rear fenders, black enamel metal nose, fenders & int., black-tint chrome, alw-ct	$4
❏	📷			b. same as (a), alw-bct	$10

Flamethrower Series, '57 T-Bird

Flamethrower Series, '57 T-Bird

385 (a)

Flamethrower Series, Hydroplane

387 (b)

Flamethrower Series, Oshkosh Snowplow

386 (a)

Flamethrower Series, Range Rover

Space Series

	Photo	No.	Name	Description	Price
☐	📷	388	Radar Ranger	white pearl, black painted Malaysia base, orange, blue & red tampos, red HW logo on nose, chrome dish, orange int. & insert clear canopy, alw-ct	$3
☐				b. same as (a), red HW logo on side	$5
☐	📷	389	GM Lean Machine	a. white pearl top, blue plastic lower body, metal Malaysia base, orange "HWSA," blue "Hot Wheels Space Administration," red "V" on nose, rear deck behind canopy has three red stripes & two rectangles w/red "No Step" & two other tampos. Red HW is on rear, two red stripes and three white dots on rear fender, thin orange strip with white "SEARCH" on side & two red stripes in front by nose, orange painted taillights, black canopy, 5sp	$3
☐				b. same as (a), unpainted taillights, 5sp	$15
☐				c. same as (a), red "HWSA" on nose & red HW logo on up on rear deck by the stripes	$15
	📷	390	Alien	a. blue plastic forward part of body, white pearl lower & rear, metal Malaysia base, orange "HWSA" with white "Hot Wheels Space Administration" & two red stripes on front, white "Rescue," & orange stripe on side, two red slashed tampos on body over rear wheels, red HW logo by rear tire, black canopy, 5sp	$3
☐				b. same as (a), red HW logo at center of rear deck on top	$5
☐		391	Treadator	a. silver-blue pearl, black plastic Malaysia base, orange scoops & nose, red "HWSA" on both front wings red HW logo on right front wing, blue chrome engine & canopy	$4
☐	📷			b. same as (a), red HW logo on left front wing	$5
☐				c. same as (a), red HW logo facing front on top of rear wing	$7
☐				d. white pearl, black plastic Malaysia base, orange scoops & nose, red "HWSA" & logo on left front wing, blue chrome engine & canopy	$15

388

Space Series, Radar Ranger

389 (a)

Space Series, GM Lean Machine

Space Series, Alien

Space Series, Treadator

Race Team Series II

	Photo	No.	Name	Description	Price
☐		392	#1-Ramp Truck	a. met. blue, metal Malaysia base, white ramp w/large HW logo & blue lettering on side, clear window, asw-5sp	$3
☐	📷			b. same as (a), asw-7sp	$8
☐				c. met. blue, metal China base, white ramp w/large HW logo & blue lettering on side, smoked front window w/HW logo, asw-5sp	$3
☐	📷	393	Baja Bug	met. blue, metal Malaysia base, large HW logo on hood & side, yellow "Hot Wheels" on roof, white int., 5sp	$5
☐	📷	394	'57 Chevy	met. blue, chrome Malaysia base, metal engine sticking out of hood, white sides & large HW logo & red #1, white bow tie & HW logo on trunk, blue-tint window & int., 5sp	$4
☐	📷	395	Bywayman	a. met. blue, metal Malaysia base, large HW logos on hood & sides, white bow tie on hood, white int. & roll bar, clear window, asw-ct	$4
☐				b. same as (a), asw-t/b	$15

Race Team Series II, Ramp Truck

Race Team Series II, '57 Chevy

Race Team Series II, Baja Bug

Race Team Series II, Bywayman

Mod Bod Series

	Photo	No.	Name	Description	Price
☐		396	Hummer	a. pink plastic body, w/green, purple met. painted Malaysia base, green, magenta & yellow tampos, logo above rear wheel, green-tint window, asw-ct	$4
☐	📷			b. same as (a), asw-ct/b	$40

Photo	No.	Name	Description	Price
☐ 📷	397	School Bus	met. purple, yellow plastic Malaysia base, orange, green & yellow tampos on roof & sides, orange int., clear window, asw-7sp	$4
☐ 📷	398	VW Bug	light blue, metal Malaysia base, magenta, green & yellow tampos on sides, roof & hood, green int., clear window, 7sp	$5
☐	399	'67 Camaro	a. bright green enamel, red stripes, metal Malaysia base, large logos on sides & roof, red int. w/open steering wheel, clear window, 5sp	$7
☐			b. same as (a), closed steering wheel, 5sp	$5
☐			c. same as (b), asw-5sp	$25
☐			d. same as (b), yellow HW logo in rear tinted window, 5sp	$31
☐ 📷			e. same as (b), 7sp	$60

Mod Bod Series, Hummer

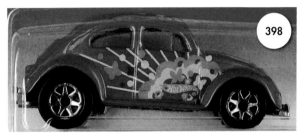

Mod Bod Series, VW Bug

Mod Bod Series, School Bus

Mod Bod Series, '67 Camaro

Dark Rider Series II

Photo	No.	Name	Description	Price
☐ 📷	400	Big Chill	a. met. black, black plastic Malaysia base, black-tint chrome engine & canopy, black treads, metal rollers, gray HW logo on side, black ski	$3
☐ 📷			b. silver flake, black plastic China base, chrome engine & canopy, black treads, metal rollers, black HW logo on side, orange ski	$3
☐ 📷	401	Street Beast	met. black, black painted Malaysia base, black int., clear window, gray HW logo on trunk, black-tint 7sp	$3
☐ 📷	402	Thunderstreak	met. black & black-tint side pods, black painted Malaysia base, black plastic driver, gray HW logo on nose, black-tint 7sp	$3
☐ 📷	403	Power Pistons	black-tint chrome, black painted Malaysia base, black int., clear canopy, gray logo in front of rear wheel, black-tint 7sp	$3

Dark Rider Series II, Big Chill

Dark Rider Series II, Big Chill

Dark Rider Series II, Street Beast

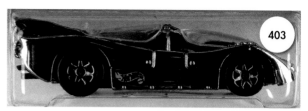

Dark Rider Series II, Power Pistons

Dark Rider Series II, Thunderstreak

Sports Car Series

	Photo	No.	Name	Description	Price
❑	📷	404	Porsche 930	met. silver, metal Malaysia base, red, white & black tampos, black int., smoked window, 7sp	$3
❑	📷	405	Custom Corvette	a. purple pearl, black Malaysia base, green & yellow tampos on hood, sides & trunk, football on hood, yellow helmet on sides, red logo on smoked windshield, gray int., 5sp	$45
❑				b. same as (a), 7sp	$4
❑	📷			c. same as (b), red HW logo on smoked windshield & yellow HW logo on front fender, 7sp	$30
❑				d. same as (b), yellow logo on front fender, asw-7sp	$3
❑	📷			e. same as (b), red logo on windshield, red int., 7sp	$50
❑	📷	406	Shelby Cobra 427 S/C	a. white pearl w/black, red & blue tampos, metal Malaysia base, black int., clear window, blue logo behind driver, alw-5sp	$55
❑				b. same as (a), alw-7sp	$3
❑	📷	407	'59 Caddy	a. met. black, chrome Malaysia base, yellow & orange flames on sides, "Slam Dunk" tampo on hood w/ball & net, white int., red logo on clear windshield, 7sp	$3
❑				b. same as (a), ww7sp	$150

Sports Car Series, Porsche 930

Sports Car Series, Custom Corvette

Sports Car Series, Custom Corvette

Sports Car Series, Shelby Cobra 427 S/C

Sports Car Series, Custom Corvette

Sports Car Series, '59 Caddy

Splatter Paint Series

	Photo	No.	Name	Description	Price
❑	📷	408	Rescue Ranger	a. day-glo orange w/blue splatters, orange plastic Malaysia base, blue insert & lights on roof, blue int., red logo on blue-tint windshield, t/b	$7
❑				b. same as (a), 5sp	$3
❑				c. same as (b), black int., red logo on smoked windshield, 5sp	$5

The Rescue Ranger is a popular car because it is really heavy and is used for racing.

	Photo	No.	Name	Description	Price
❑	📷	409	Funny Car	white w/red & yellow splatters, metal Malaysia base, clear window, 5sp	$5
❑	📷	410	'55 Chevy	a. yellow w/red splatters, red plastic Malaysia base, red logo on magenta-tint windshield, t/b	$7
❑				b. same as (a), 5sp	$3
❑	📷	411	'80s Camaro	white w/blue & black splatters, metal Malaysia base, white int., red logo on clear windshield, 5sp	$2

Splatter Paint Series, '55 Chevy

Splatter Paint Series, Rescue Ranger

Splatter Paint Series, '80s Camaro

Splatter Paint Series, Funny Car

Street Eaters Series

	Photo	No.	Name	Description	Price
❑	📷	412	Speed Machine	a. light green pearl, metal Malaysia base, red yellow & black tampos, red int., red-tint canopy, yellow logo on rear, 7sp	$10
❑				b. same as (a), 5sp	$3
❑	📷	413	Silhouette II	a. purple pearl, red plastic Malaysia base, red, green & white tampos, red int., orange-tint canopy, red logo on rear, chrome engine, 5sp	$4
❑				b. same as (a), red logo on front fender, 5sp	$3
❑	📷	414	Propper Chopper	a. blue enamel w/red, orange & white tampos, orange Malaysia base, blue rotors & tail, orange int., clear window, white logo on side	$15
❑				b. same as (a), blue-tint window	$3
❑				c. same as (a), orange China base, clear window	$2
❑	📷	415	Roll Patrol	a. light brown w/red, white & black tampos, orange painted Malaysia base, light orange int., black logo on side, black roll bar, clear window, yct	$10
❑	📷			b. same as (a), dark orange int., ytc	$10
❑				c. same as (a), light orange interior, yt/b	$4
❑				d. same as (b), dark orange interior, yt/b	$4
❑				e. same as (d), very dark orange int., yt/b	$8

Street Eaters Series, Speed Machine

Street Eaters Series, Silhouette II

Street Eaters Series, Propper Chopper

Street Eaters Series, Roll Patrol

Street Eaters Series, Roll Patrol

Fast Food Series

Photo	No.	Name	Description	Price
☐	416	Pizza Vette	a. white plastic body w/pepperoni tampos, black painted metal Malaysia base, black window, HW logo behind front wheel, 3sp	$3
☐ 📷			b. same as (a), 5sp	$10
☐ 📷	417	Pasta Pipes	white plastic body, black painted metal Malaysia base, orange & yellow tampos, chrome int., blue-tint canopy, HW logo on rear, 3sp	$3
☐ 📷	418	Sweet Stocker	white, black painted Malaysia base, red, orange, green & purple candy tampos, yellow int., yellow-tint window, red HW logo on trunk, 3sp	$20
☐	419	Crunch Chief	a. white, black painted Malaysia base, red, orange, green & purple tampos, HW logo behind front wheel, no int., yellow-tint window, 3sp	$4
☐ 📷			b. same as (a), 7sp	$10

Fast Food Series, Pizza Vette

Fast Food Series, Pasta Pipes

Fast Food Series, Sweet Stocker

Fast Food Series, Crunch Chief

Silver Series II

	Photo	No.	Name	Description	Price
❑	📷	420	Dump Truck	a. chrome cab, metal Malaysia base, chrome dump box, red logo on top of box, black grille, ct/b	$20
❑				b. same as (a), black dump box, no HW logo, ct/b	$5
❑		421	'40s Woodie	chrome body, metal Malaysia base, black int., gold HW logo in side clear window, 5sp	$3
❑				b. same as (a), gold HW logo in rear clear window, 5sp	$5
❑	📷			c. same as (a), gold HW logo in side clear window, 7sp	$6
❑	📷	422	'57 Chevy	chrome, metal Malaysia base, no int., black logo in rear orange-tint window, 5sp	$5
❑	📷	423	Oscar Mayer Wienermobile	chrome hot dog, chrome Malaysia base, yellow band, red & white "Oscar Mayer" tampo, dark smoked window, b5sp	$5

Silver Series II, Dump Truck

Silver Series II, '57 Chevy

Silver Series II, '40s Woodie

Silver Series II, Oscar Mayer Weinermobile

Fire Squad Series

	Photo	No.	Name	Description	Price
❑		424	Ambulance	a. day-glo green, chrome Malaysia base, yellow & black "Fire Dept." &"City of Hot Wheels" logo w/white background in center, black HW logo behind rear wheel, white int. & rear doors, smooth rear step, blue-tint window, asw-5sp	$8
❑				b. same as (a), 7sp	$8
❑	📷			c. same as (b), ribbed rear step, 7sp	$5
❑	📷			d. red enamel, chrome Malaysia base, yellow & black "Fire Dept." & "City of Hot Wheels" logo w/red background in center, black HW logo behind rear wheel, ribbed rear step, white int. & rear doors, blue-tint windows5sp	$10
❑				e same as (d), 3sp	$25
❑				f. same as (d), 7sp	$4
❑				g. same as (f), "City of Hot Wheels" logo w/yellow background in center, 7sp	$10
❑	📷	425	Rescue Ranger	yellow enamel, chrome Malaysia base, red & black tampo on door, black outline "Fire Dept" on hood, red rear insert & lights on roof, black int., black logo on side behind door, smoked window, 5sp	$3
❑		426	Flame Stopper	a. yellow enamel, black plastic Malaysia base, red & black side tampos, black logo on rear door, black window, black boom, alw-yct	$50
❑	📷			b. same as (a), alw-yt/b	$3

Photo	No.	Name	Description	Price
❑	426	Flame Stopper	c. same as (a), black plastic China base, alw-cts	$2
❑	427	Fire Eater	a. red enamel, chrome Malaysia base, yellow & black tampos, black logo on front door, blue insert, blue-tint window & int., 5sp	$4
❑ 📷			b. same as (a), gray pearl plastic Malaysia base, 5sp	$100
❑			c. same as (a), 7sp	$20
❑			d. same as (c), gray pearl plastic Malaysia base	$80

Fire Squad Series, Ambulance

Fire Squad Series, Flame Stopper

Fire Squad Series, Ambulance

Fire Squad Series, Fire Eater

Fire Squad Series, Rescue Ranger

1996 Treasure Hunt Series

Photo	No.	Name	Description	Price
❑ 📷	428	#1-'40s Woodie	a. day-glo yellow hood & fenders, tan wood grain plastic body, metal Malaysia base, black int., gold logo in side rear smoked window, yellow wheel w/yellow rim, yellowwall Real Rider tires	$40
❑			b. same as (a), yellow wheel w/silver rim, yellowwall Real Rider tires	$75
❑			c. same as (a), yellow wheel w/gold rim, yellowwall Real Rider tires	$150
❑ 📷	437	#2-Auburn 852	gold w/black flakes, metal Malaysia base, gold fenders & int., clear window, gold logo in white box on trunk, gold chrome wheel whitewall Real Rider tires	$35
❑ 📷	430	#3-Ferrari 250	met. gray, gray plastic Malaysia base, red stripe on hood & trunk, gold logo in white box on rear plate, red int., clear window, chrome wheel Real Rider tires	$35
❑ 📷	431	#4-Jaguar XJ220	met. green, black plastic Malaysia base, gold logo on rear smoked window, g6sp	$30
❑ 📷	432	#5-'59 Caddy	red enamel, chrome Malaysia base, tan int., silver side stripe & "Eldorado" tampo gold logo on clear windshield, chrome wheel whitewall Real Rider tires	$50
❑ 📷	433	#6-Dodge Viper RT/10	a. white enamel, black plastic Malaysia base, 2 blue stripes on hood & trunk, black int., gold logo on clear windshield, w6sp	$60

Photo	No.	Name	Description	Price
☐ 📷	433	#6-Dodge Viper RT/10	b. red enamel, black plastic China base & int., gold logo on clear windshield, alw-bbs	$10

Some people say the Dodge Viper RT/10 (b) variation is not a Treasure Hunt. I say, "If it looks like a duck, walks like a duck & sounds like a duck, it's a duck!" This car is packaged in the Treasure Hunt package, it's a Viper and has the same windshield and logo and collector number. It's no different than any other variation. It's a Treasure Hunt.

Photo	No.	Name	Description	Price
☐ 📷	434	#7-'57 Chevy	met. purple, chrome Malaysia base, purple-tint window & int., gold logo in rear window, chrome wheel "Goodyear" "Real Rider" tires	$60
☐ 📷	435	#8-Ferrari 355	white pearl, metal Malaysia base, tan int., clear window, gold logo on rear plate, gold star wheel	$30
☐ 📷	436	#9-'58 Corvette	met. silver, gray plastic Malaysia base, red cove, chrome bumpers, red int., clear windshield, gold logo in white box on trunk, chrome wheel whitewall Real Rider tires	$60
☐ 📷	429	#10-Lamborghini Countach	a. day-glo orange w/matching painted Malaysia base, tan int., clear window, c6sp	$30
☐			b. same as (a), chrome star wheel	$150
☐ 📷	438	#11-Dodge Ram 1500	met. maroon w/maroon cap, dark gray plastic Malaysia base, gray int., clear window, gold logo in white box on rear, chrome wheel Real Rider tires	$35
☐ 📷	439	#12-'37 Bugatti	met. blue, metal Malaysia base, red int., clear window, gold logo in white oval on trunk, c6sp	$25

1996 Treasure Hunt Series, #1-'40s Woodie

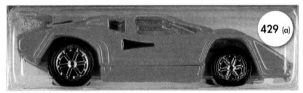

1996 Treasure Hunt Series, #10-Lamborghini Countach

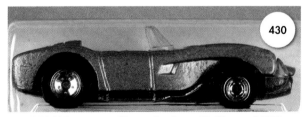

1996 Treasure Hunt Series, #3-Ferrari 250

1996 Treasure Hunt Series, #4-Jaguar XJ220

1996 Treasure Hunt Series, #5-'59 Caddy

1996 Treasure Hunt Series, #6-Dodge Viper RT/10

1996 Treasure Hunt Series, #6-Dodge Viper RT/10

1996 Treasure Hunt Series, #7-'57 Chevy

1996 Treasure Hunt Series, #8-Ferrari #355

1996 Treasure Hunt Series, #9-'58 Corvette

1996 Treasure Hunt Series, #2-Auburn 852

1996 Treasure Hunt Series, #11-Dodge Ram 1500

1996 Treasure Hunt Series, #12-'37 Bugatti

Non-Series Collector Number Packs

Photo	No.	Name	Description	Price
❏	440	Monte Carlo Stocker	a. dark blue met, gray plastic Malaysia base, race team tampos, white #1 on roof & door, gray & red stripe on bottom side, white int., clear window, alw-yellow letter b7sp	$3
❏ 📷			b. same as (a), no letter/alw-b7sp	$10
❏ 📷	441	Chevy Stocker	black enamel, metal Malaysia base, red & white #1 on roof & door, white "Chevrolet" on rear fender & hood, racing decals & HW logo on side, red int., clear window, 7sp	$5
❏	442	Ferrari F40	a. white pearl, metal Malaysia base, large yellow & black Ferrari shield logo on hood, tan int., smoked window, red logo on rear plate, 5sp	$3
❏ 📷			b. same as (a), small yellow & black Ferrari hood emblem, 7sp	$2
❏			c. same as (b), w5dot	$8
❏	443	Ferrari 348	a. met. black, yellow & black Ferrari logo on hood, red int., yellow HW logo on rear clear window, black plastic Malaysia base, 5sp	$8
❏ 📷			b. same as (a), 7sp	$4
❏			c. same as (a), 5dot	$5
❏ 📷	444	Aeroflash	white w/yellow, green & blue tampo, day-glo orange painted Malaysia base & int., orange-tint window, red HW logo behind rear wheel, g7sp	$2
❏	445	Jaguar XJ220	a. met. green, gray plastic Malaysia base, gray int., red HW logo on rear clear window, 5sp	$3
❏ 📷			b. same as (a), 7sp	$22
❏ 📷	446	'32 Ford Delivery	a. very dark blue (almost black), metal Malaysia base, white"Ford" on side, black int., clear window, white HW logo on rear, 3sp	$20
❏			b. same as (a), 7sp	$2
❏	447	'63 Split-Window	a. met. green, chrome Malaysia base, tan int., red HW logo on clear windshield, asw-3sp	$4
❏			b. same as (a), asw-5sp	$4
❏ 📷			c. same as (a), asw-7sp	$4
❏			d. same as (a), asw-t/b	$50
❏ 📷			e. same as (a), gray plastic Malaysia base, asw-3sp	$8
❏ 📷			f. same as (a), gray Malaysia base, asw-7sp	$8
❏ 📷	448	'67 Camaro	a. yellow enamel, metal no origin base, black stripes on hood & trunk, black int., yellow HW logo on rear smoked window, 5sp	$7

440 (b)

Monte Carlo Stocker

446 (a)

'32 Ford Delivery

441

Chevy Stocker

447 (c)

'63 Split-Window

442 (b)

Ferrari F40

447 (e)

'63 Split-Window

443 (b)

Ferrari 348

447 (f)

'63 Split-Window

444

Aeroflash

448 (a)

'67 Camaro

445 (b)

Jaguar XJ220

449 (b)

Camaro Z-28

Photo	No.	Name	Description	Price
❑	448	'67 Camaro	b. same as (a), metal Malaysia base, 5sp	$10
❑			c. same as (b), silver met. painted engine compartment, 5sp	$5
❑			d. same as (c), 5dot	$8
❑	449	Camaro Z-28	a. day-glo orange, black painted Malaysia base, black int., smoked window, orange "Camaro" on windshield, orange HW logo on rear window, 3sp	$5
❑ 📷			b. same as (a), 5sp	$3
❑	450	Corvette Stingray	a. white pearl, metal Malaysia base, blue-tint window & int., blue logo on rear fender, 3sp	$3
❑			b. same as (a), asw-3sp	$20

Photo	No.	Name	Description	Price
❏	450	Corvette Stingray	c. same as (a), 5sp	$3
❏ 📷			d. same as (a), 7sp	$10
❏ 📷	451	3-Window '34	a. day-glo pink, metal Malaysia base, pink plastic fenders & runningboards, pink int., black logo on rear, rose-tint window, 3sp	$15
❏			b. same as (a), 7sp	$4
❏ 📷	452	Ferrari 250	a. met. green, green plastic base, yellow & black Ferrari logo on nose, red HW logo in white box on rear, dark tan int., chrome pipes, clear window, 5sp	$15
❏			b. same as (a), 5dot	$3
❏			c. same as (a), 7sp	$3
❏	453	Audi Avus	a. red enamel, black plastic Malaysia base, white int., smoked canopy w/red & black painted tampo, white HW logo on rear, alw-5sp	$10
❏			b. same as (a), alw-7sp	$10

The only difference in pricing with the #453 Audi Avus (a) and (b) variations is that the package says "Audi Avus." These were short lived until they were renamed "Avus Quattro."

Photo	No.	Name	Description	Price
❏		Avus Quattro (name change)	c. same as (a), w/name change on card alw-5sp	$3
❏ 📷			d. same as (b), just name change on card, alw-7sp	$3
❏			e. same as (c), t/b	$3
❏	454	Zender Fact 4	a. white pearl, gray plastic Malaysia base, blue "Zender" on nose, gold "Fact 4" on top of fender, gray int., blue-tint window, blue logo on rear spoiler, 5sp	$3
❏ 📷			b. same as (a), 7sp	$3
❏	455	'65 Mustang Convertible	a. gold flake, metal Malaysia base, white side stripe, no HW logo, white int., smoked window, asw-3sp	$4
❏			b. same as (a), asw-5sp	$5
❏ 📷			c. same as (a), asw-7sp	$7
❏ 📷			d. dark met. blue, metal China base, white side stripe, white int., clear window, white HW logo behind rear wheel, asw-5sp	$3
❏	457	Pontiac Banshee	a. met. black, metal China base, neon-yellow int., clear canopy w/black band, red HW logo windshield, asw-5sp	$3

Corvette Stingray

450 (d)

Avus Quattro

453 (d)

3-Window '34

451 (a)

Zender Fact 4

454 (b)

Ferrari 250

452 (a)

'65 Mustang Convertible

455 (c)

'65 Mustang Convertible

Enforcer

Pontiac Banshee

'80s Firebird

Speed Shark

Pontiac Fiero 2M4

Zombot

Blazer 4X4

Photo	No.	Name	Description	Price
☐ 📷	457	Pontiac Banshee	b. same as (a), asw-bbs	$6
☐			c. purple pearl, metal China base, black int. clear canopy w/black band, white logo on rear window, asw-5sp	$3
☐ 📷	458	Speed Shark	met. lavender, chrome China base, purple int., purple-tint window, white log on rear spoiler, 5sp	$3
☐ 📷	460	Zombot	black over silver, day-glo orange China base, orange plastic gun, 2 red HW logos on bottom of feet, 5sp	$3
☐ 📷	461	Enforcer	candy met. purple, metal China base, silver painted windows, gray plastic guns & rockets, silver HW logo on nose, alw-5sp	$3
☐	462	'80s Firebird	a. met. blue, blue plastic China base, white int., red HW logo on clear windshield, asw-5sp	$3
☐ 📷			b. same as (a), asw-bbs	$3
☐	463	Fiero 2M4	a. day-glo yellow, metal China base, black Fiero logo on hood, black stripe on side, black int., clear window, red logo in front of rear wheel, asw-5sp	$3
☐ 📷			b. same as (a), asw-bbs	$5
☐ 📷	464	Blazer 4X4	a. met. dark blue, blue-tint metal China base, yellow int., blue-tint window, no logo, alw-ct	$3
☐ 📷			b. same as (a), alw-cts	$6
☐ 📷	467	Peugeot 405	a. met. dark green, green plastic China base, white plastic spacer between body & base, white int., red HW logo in rear clear window, asw-5sp	$4

Photo	No.	Name	Description	Price
❑	467	Peugeot 405	b. met. silver, black plastic China base, purple & orange side tampo, black plastic spacer between body & base, black int. & purple logo on side in orange stripe, clear window, black int. asw-5sp	$3
❑ 			c. same as (b), asw-bbs	$3
❑ 	468	GT Racer	a. day-glo orange, metal China base, black window, large HW logo on black rear wing, 5sp	$5
❑			b. day-glo orange, metal China base, black window, blue stripe & black lettering on sides, black logo behind rear tire, black rear wing & engine, 5sp	$5
❑			c. same as (b), bbs	$5
❑			d. light olive pearl, metal China base & int., thin red side stripe & black lettering, black logo behind rear wheel, dark smoked window, black rear wing & engine, 5sp	$5

The GT Racer is really heavy and used for racing.

Photo	No.	Name	Description	Price
❑ 	469	Hot Bird	a. met. gold, metal China base, white int., tinted window, red HW logo on rear plate, 5sp	$5
❑			b. met. gold, metal China base, black hood bird, clear window, black int., purple HW logo on rear plate, 5sp	$3
❑ 			c. same as (b), bbs	$3
❑ 	470	Turbo Streak	a. white body, white painted China base, met. dark blue side pods, white plastic driver, large HW logo on white rear wing, 5sp	$4
❑			b. same as (a), purple tampo added to side pod & HW logo, 5sp	$3
❑ 	471	Velocitor	a. dark met. blue, white painted China base, large HW logo on hood, red int. & spacer between body & base, clear window, 5sp	$4

Blazer 4X4

464 (b)

Turbo Streak

470 (a)

Peugeot 405

467 (a)

Velocitor

471 (a)

GT Racer

468 (a)

Velocitor

471 (b)

Hot Bird

469 (a)

Buick Stocker

472 (a)

Street Beast

BMW M1

VW Golf

VW Golf

Forklift

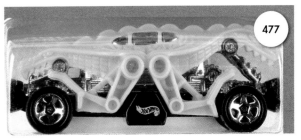

Double Demon

Dragon Wagon

Photo	No.	Name	Description	Price
☐ 📷	471	Velocitor	b. black enamel, black painted China base, large HW logo on rood & hood, red "Mattel" & racing decals on sides, red int. & spacer between body & base, red logo behind rear wheel, 5sp	$3
☐			c. same as (b), bbs	$7
☐ 📷	472	Buick Stocker	a. day-glo yellow, black painted China base, black int., red HW logo on clear windshield, 5sp	$3
☐			b. day-glo yellow, black painted metal China base, red tampos on sides, light blue tampos on hood, black int., clear window, red HW logo on side, 5sp	$3
☐			c. same as (b), bbs	$4
☐ 📷	473	Street Beast	a. teal pearl w/matching painted China base, gray int. & rear louvers, red logo on tinted windshield, 5sp	$3
☐			b. silver & gray two tone, gray painted China base, black int. & rear louvers, red logo on clear windshield, 5sp	$3
☐ 📷	473	BMW M1 (name change)	c. same as (b), name change on card, 5sp	$3
☐ 📷	474	VW Golf	a. met. black, black plastic China base, red int., yellow HW logo in clear back window, asw-5sp	$5
☐ 📷			b. black enamel, black plastic China base, yellow "Fahrvergnugen" & red driver guy on sides, red int., clear window, red HW logo on front fender in front of wheel, asw-5sp	$3
☐			c. same as (b), asw-bbs	$3
☐ 📷	475	Forklift	yellow enamel, metal China base, black cage & seat, yellow forks, red HW logo on side, large bw front/medium 5sp rear	$5

Photo		No.	Name	Description	Price
❑	📷	477	Double Demon	day-glo green plastic body, magenta chrome insert, black painted China base w/green logo on side, alw-5sp	$3
❑	📷	478	Dragon Wagon	day-glo yellow w/orange eyes, teal pearl painted China base, red HW logo on rear, alw-5sp	$3
❑	📷	479	Computer Warrior	black over blue, day-glo orange painted China base, chrome engine 2 red logos on bottom of feet, 5sp	$3
❑	📷	481	Tall Ryder	a. candy met. green, metal China base, chrome spacer between body & base, chrome window, white logo on rear, alw-cts	$4
❑	📷			b. yellow pearl met., silver painted metal China base, purple & green side tampos, black spacer between body & base, black window, red logo on door, alw-cts	$4
❑				c. same as (b), pearl met. gold, alw-cts	$3
❑	📷	482	Earth Mover	yellow plastic cab, yellow painted China frame, black seat & exhaust, red HW logo on side, alw-cts	$5
❑	📷	483	Thunder Roller	met dark red, chrome China base, red HW logo on front bumper, tan int., clear window, large bw rear, large 5sp front	$5
❑	📷	484	Grizzlor	a. white plastic body, orange plastic engine, metal China base, red HW logo on rear, 5sp	$3
❑	📷			b. white plastic body w/painted black spots & red collar, red painted China base, chrome engine, red HW logo on rear, 5sp	$5

479

Computer Warrior

482

Earth Mover

481 (a)

Tall Ryder

483

Thunder Roller

481 (b)

Tall Ryder

484 (a)

Grizzlor

484 (b)

Grizzlor

Evil Weevil

Sting Rod

Command Tank

Big Bertha

Troop Convoy

Rocket Shot

Photo	No.	Name	Description	Price
📷	485	Evil Weevil	light orange plastic body w/light green eyes, unpainted metal exhaust, day-glo orange painted China base, no logo, alw-5sp	$3
📷	486	Command Tank	purple pearl w/flat black camouflage & "Nite Force" tampo on side, black plastic turret, rear door & China base, silver HW logo on side rear	$5
📷	487	Troop Convoy	a. met. gray metal cab, day-glo orange plastic roof & rear bed, black canopy, black painted China base, gold HW logo on hood, alw-5sp	$15
			b. met. dark green metal cab w/matching painted metal China base, green plastic bed, tan roof & canopy, light blue & tan tampo on hood & door, light blue HW logo on door, alw-5sp	$5
📷	488	Sting Rod	dark met. gray, day-glo orange painted China base, orange plastic guns & rockets, red logo on nose, alw-cts	$3
📷	489	Big Bertha	a. dark met. gray, day-glo orange plastic turret, gray plastic China base, gold HW logo on front	$12
			b. dark purple pearl w/flat black camouflage, silver "Nite Force" tampo & HW logo on rear, black plastic turret & China base	$5
		Tough Customer (name change)	c. light purple pearl w/flat black camouflage, silver "Nite Force" tampo & HW logo on rear, black plastic turret & China base	$4
📷	491	Rocket Shot	a. met. gray body & tracks, day-glo orange plastic top w/gray rocket, gray plastic China base, silver HW logo on front	$10
			b. purple pearl w/flat black camouflage & silver "Nite Force" tampo, silver logo on front, black top w/purple rocket, black plastic China base	$5
📷	492	Swingfire	a. day-glo orange metal body, gray plastic int. & China base, silver logo on front, 5sp	$10

Swingfire

Ferrari Testarossa

Porsche 911 Targa

BMW 850i

Mercedes 500SL

Corvette Coupe

Ferrari 308GT

Chevy Nomad

Photo	No.	Name	Description	Price
❏	492	Swingfire	b. white enamel, gray plastic China base, w/blue "Snow Patrol" tampo on side & hood, light blue logo on door, light blue int., 5sp	$5
❏ 📷	493	Porsche 911 Targa	a. day-glo yellow, black plastic China base & int., yellow in rear clear window, alw-5sp	$8
❏			b. same as (a), asw-5sp	$3
❏ 📷	494	Mercedes 500SL	dark met. gray, black painted China base, red int., yellow HW logo on clear windshield, asw-5sp	$2
❏	496	Ferrari 308GT	a. red enamel, black plastic China base, black int., yellow HW logo on tinted windshield, asw-5sp	$3
❏ 📷			b. same as (a), asw-bbs	$57
❏	497	Ferrari Testarossa	a. white pearl, black plastic China base & int., red HW logo on clear windshield, asw-5sp	$3
❏ 📷			b. same as (a), asw-bbs	$5
❏	498	BMW 850i	a. met. silver, red int., black plastic China base, yellow logo on rear clear window, asw-5sp	$3
❏ 📷			b. same as (a), asw-bbs	$3
❏ 📷	499	Corvette Coupe	a. met. dark green, black plastic China base, red int., red HW logo on rear clear window w/painted black top, asw-5sp	$6
❏			b. same as (a), asw-bbs	$4
❏ 📷	502	Chevy Nomad	a. met. red, metal Malaysia base, tan int. w/open steering wheel, clear window, gold HW logo on rear, g7sp	$7
❏			b. same as (a), closed steering wheel, g7sp	$4
❏	503	'80s Corvette	a. dark candy met. red, metal Malaysia base, gray int., clear window w/black painted top, black HW logo on rear, asw-3sp	$3

Photo	No.	Name	Description	Price
❏	503	'80s Corvette	b. same as (a), asw-t/b	$3
❏ 📷			c. same as (a), asw-5sp	$75
❏			d. same as (a), asw-bbs	$3
❏	504	Camaro Z-28	a. white pearl, black painted Malaysia base, blue-tint window, no int., gold HW logo behind rear wheel, 3sp	$3
❏ 📷			b. same as (a), 5sp	$3
❏	505	1993 Camaro	a. met. black, black plastic Malaysia base, clear window, yellow HW logo on rear, tan int., alw-5sp	$3
❏			b. same as (a), alw-t/b	$3
❏			c. same as (a), alw-bbs	$4
❏ 📷			d. same as (a), alw-yellow letter/b7sp	$25
❏ 📷	506	Nissan 300ZX	met. purple w/matching painted metal China base, gold tampos on side & hood, purple int., clear window, gold HW logo on front right of hood, asw-5sp	$3
❏ 📷	507	Peugeot 205 Rallye	black, blue & purple body with silver "205" tampo on door, orange painted metal China base, silver HW logo in front of rear wheel, alw-5sp	$30
❏			b. same as (a), bare metal China base, alw-5sp	$51

'80s Corvette

Nissan 300ZX

Camaro Z-28

Peugeot 205 Rallye

1993 Camaro

1997 First Editions

Photo	No.	Name	Description	Price
❏ 📷	509	#1-Firebird Funny Car	dark met. blue, metal Malaysia base, large HW logo on hood & sides, white 1 f/c tampo on side w/racing decals, metal int., clear window, 5sp	$5
❏ 📷	513	#2-Ford F-150	red enamel, gray plastic Malaysia base, chrome int., bed & bumpers, smoked window, red HW logo in white box on rear plate, alw-5sp	$3
❏ 📷	512	#3-Excavator	white enamel, black plastic Malaysia base & tracks, dark blue side tampo, gray plastic boom & bucket	$25
❏ 📷	520	#4-Saltflat Racer	a. light red plastic body, chrome engine & int., clear window, silver painted Malaysia base w/racing decals on front fender, 5sp	$4
❏ 📷			b. dark red plastic body, chrome engine & int., clear window, silver painted Thailand base w/racing decals on front fender, 5sp	$3
❏ 📷	517	#5-'59 Chevy Impala	a. light purple pearl, chrome Malaysia base, gray & black stripe & orange tampo on side, white int., clear window, gray logo on fender skirt, asw-g7sp	$35

1997 First Editions, #1-Firebird Funny Car

1997 First Editions, #7-Way 2 Fast

1997 First Editions, #12-25th Countach

1997 First Editions, #11-'97 Corvette

1997 First Editions, #3-Excavator

1997 First Editions, #11-'97 Corvette

1997 First Editions, #2-F-150

1997 First Editions, #10-Mercedes C-Class

Photo	No.	Name	Description	Price
☐	517	#5-'59 Chevy Impala	b. same as (a), asw-gbbs	$4
☐	518	#6-BMW Z3 Roadster	a. met. silver, metal Malaysia base, w/dark blue, light blue & red stripe on door, red HW logo on door, red int., clear window, asw-5sp	$6
☐ 📷		#6-BMW M Roadster (name change)	b. same as (a), name change, asw-5sp	$3
☐			c. same as (a), black painted Malaysia base, asw-5sp	$10
☐			d. same as (a), asw-5dot	$25
☐			e. same as (a), asw-3sp	$3
☐	514	#7-Way 2 Fast	a. orange enamel, metal Malaysia base "no tm,", black & white squares & red HW logo on roof, chrome int., 5sp	$5
☐			b. same as (a), w/"tm" on base, 5sp	$3
☐ 📷			c. same as (a), silver painted metal Thailand base, 5sp	$4
☐			d. same as (a), asw-5dot	$25
☐			e. same as (a), asw-3sp	$3

  #8 in the 1997 First Edition Series was never produced. I know it was pictured on the 1997 poster. The 1970 Barracuda #523 was meant to be the #8 car, but it was never packaged as such. Instead, it was released as a regular collector numbers vehicle.

Photo		No.	Name	Description	Price
☐	📷	519	#9-Scorchin' Scooter	a. met. purple, metal engine & pipes, orange, blue & silver flames, black painted seat, gray forks & handlebars, chrome wheel w/black spokes	$5
☐				b. same as (a), "A" under rear fender	$7
☐	📷			c. same as (b), blue-tint metal engine & pipes	$10
☐	📷	516	#10-Mercedes C-Class	black enamel, gray plastic Malaysia base & int., silver #3 on roof & rear door, silver "Mercedes Benz" on rear fender, silver HW logo on front lower door, gray interior, clear window, asw-gbbs	$3
☐	📷	515	#11-'97 Corvette	a. met. green, black plastic Malaysia base, tan int., HW logo stamped in rear smoked window, alw-bbs	$3
☐	📷			b. same as (a), dark met. green, alw-bbs	$3
☐	📷	510	#12-25th Countach	yellow pearl, black plastic Malaysia base, black int., gold HW logo on clear windshield, asw-5dot	$3

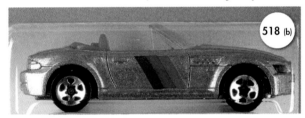

1997 First Editions, #5-'59 Chevy Impala

1997 First Editions, #9-Scorchin' Scooter

1997 First Editions, #6-BMW M Roadster

1997 First Editions, #4-Saltflat Racer

1997 First Editions, #9-Scorchin' Scooter

1997 First Editions, #4-Saltflat Racer

Non-Series Collector Number Packs

Photo		No.	Name	Description	Price
☐	📷	523	1970 Plymouth Barracuda	sublime enamel, chrome China base, black side stripe, black hood scoop, black int., tinted window, black HW logo behind front wheel, asw-5sp	$7
☐				b. same as (a), white floorboards, asw-5sp	$10
☐	📷	524	GMC Motor Home	race team met. blue w/large logo on side, gray plastic India base, white int., clear window, bw	$25
☐	📷	525	Trail Buster	black enamel, metal India base, red side stripes, red-over-white logo on side rear, black int., clear window, alw-bw	$4
☐	📷	526	Neet Streeter	yellow enamel, metal India base, magenta & black side tampo, black hood scoop, black int., red HW logo on side, bw	$5
☐	📷	527	Second Wind	white enamel, blue plastic India base & int., blue "6" in red circle & red HW logo on side blue-tint window, bw	$3
☐	📷	528	Beach Blaster	a. white enamel, gray plastic India base, purple & red side tampo, red int., clear window, red HW logo behind rear wheel, bw	$2
☐				b. same as (a), "Indja" on base instead of "India"	$5

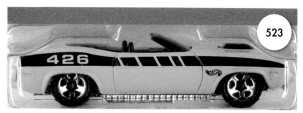

523

1970 Plymouth Barracuda

524

GMC Motor Home

525

Trail Buster

526

Neet Streeter

527

Second Wind

528 (a)

Beach Blaster

Phantom Racers Series

Photo	No.	Name	Description	Price
❑	529	Power Rocket	a. transparent green body, metal Malaysia base, white HW logo on side, pink transparent canopy, chrome int., chrome engine, 3sp	$10
❑ 📷			b. same as (a), orange transparent canopy, 3sp	$3
❑	530	Power Pistons	a. transparent red body, metal Malaysia base, white HW logo in front of rear wheel, gray int., clear canopy, 3sp	$3
❑ 📷			b. same as (a), 5sp	$4
❑ 📷	531	Power Pipes	transparent blue body, metal Malaysia base, purple-tint canopy, chrome int., red HW logo in white box on rear, 3sp	$3
❑	532	Road Rocket	a. transparent orange body, metal Malaysia base, lime transparent top, chrome engine, white HW logo behind front wheel, 3sp	$4
❑ 📷			b. same as (a), t/b	$3

529 (b)

Phantom Racers Series, Power Rocket

530 (b)

Phantom Racers Series, Power Pistons

531

Phantom Racers Series, Power Pipes

532 (b)

Phantom Racers Series, Road Rocket

Race Team Series III

	Photo	No.	Name	Description	Price
❏	📷	533	Hummer	a. dark blue pearl plastic body w/small antenna, metal Malaysia base, 2 large HW logos on roof, red "1" & racing decals on sides, gray windows, asw-ct/b	$3
❏				b. same as (a), large antenna, asw-ct/b	$4
❏				c. same as (b), silver painted Malaysia base, asw-ct/b	$6
❏		534	Chevy 1500 Pickup	a. met. blue, metal Malaysia base, large HW logo on hood & sides, white on sides w/red lettering & racing decals, white int., smoked window, asw-3sp	$9
❏				b. same as (a), asw-5sp	$4
❏				c. same as (a), silver painted Malaysia base, asw-5sp	$7
❏				d. same as (a), asw-5dot	$5
❏	📷			e. same as (a), asw-7sp	$35
❏	📷	535	#3-3-Window '34	a. met. blue, metal Malaysia base, white on side & large HW logo, white & orange flames on hood, blue int. & running boards, smoked window, 5sp	$4
❏	📷	536	#4-'80s Corvette	met. blue w/large logo on hood & sides, white on sides w/red "1" & racing decals, clear window w/transparent blue painted roof, white int., metal Malaysia base, asw-5sp	$3
❏				b. same as (a), clear window w/dark blue painted roof, asw-5sp	$5
❏				c. same as (a), asw-5dot	$3

Race Team Series II, Hummer

Race Team Series II, 3-Window '34

Race Team Series II, Chevy 1500 Pickup

Race Team Series II, '80s Corvette

Heat Fleet Series

	Photo	No.	Name	Description	Price
❏		537	Police Cruiser	a. light green enamel, dark purple plastic Malaysia base, orange & purple flames on hood & sides, light purple int., clear window, purple HW logo behind rear wheel, asw-3sp	$10
❏				b. same as (a), asw-5sp	$3
❏				c. same as (a), asw-5dot	$3
❏	📷			d. same as (a), asw-7sp	$10
❏		538	School Bus	a. dark green enamel, black plastic Malaysia base, orange & purple flames on roof & sides, red HW logo on rear of roof, clear window, white int., asw-3sp	$5
❏				b. same as (a), asw-5sp	$3
❏				c. same as (b), clear window w/bars from the Police Bus, asw-5sp	$75
❏	📷			d. same as (a), asw-7sp	$3
❏				e. dark green enamel, black plastic China base, orange & purple flames on roof & sides, red HW logo on rear of roof, clear window, white int., asw-5sp	$3
❏		539	Peterbilt Tank Truck	a. maroon met. metal cab w/flames on hood, black plastic tank w/flames & red HW logo on side, chrome Malaysia base & window, asw-5sp	$5

	Photo	No.	Name	Description	Price
❏		539	Peterbilt Tank Truck	b. same as (a), asw-7sp	$3
❏	📷			c. same as (b), no HW logo on side, asw-7sp	$15
❏			Peterbilt Fuel Tanker (name change)	d. same as (a), asw-t/b	$3
❏	📷	540	Ramblin' Wrecker	a. black enamel, chrome Malaysia base, flames on sides, red plastic boom, smoked window, yellow HW logo on side rear, chrome interior, asw-7sp	$5
❏				b. same as (a), asw-t/b	$5

Heat Fleet Series, Police Cruiser

Heat Fleet Series, Peterbilt Fuel Tanker

Heat Fleet Series, School Bus

Heat Fleet Series, Ramblin' Wrecker

Biff! Bam! Boom! Series

	Photo	No.	Name	Description	Price
❏		541	Mini Truck	a. red enamel, black plastic Malaysia base, white, yellow & black tampos, black logo on side rear, & int., smoked window, 3sp	$3
❏	📷			b. same as (a), t/b	$9
❏				c. same as (a), 5sp	$7
❏		542	Limozeen	a. pearl blue, chrome Malaysia base, silver & magenta tampos, white int., magenta HW logo on front fender, smoked window, asw-5dot	$30
❏	📷			b. same as (a), asw-5sp	$4
❏				c. same as (b), no bullet holes on front fender, asw-5sp	$8
❏				d. same as (c), undipped chrome Malaysia base, asw-5sp	$7
❏		543	VW Bug	a. met. green, metal Malaysia base, yellow, white, red & black tampos, black HW logo in front of rear wheel, black int., clear window, 5sp	$5
❏				b. same as (a), no HW logo, 5sp	$5
❏				c. same as (a), black HW logo in front of rear wheel, 7sp	$50
❏	📷			d. same as (c), no HW logo, 7sp	$65
❏	📷	544	Range Rover	purple pearl w/orange, black, light blue & white tampos, chrome Malaysia base, black HW logo behind rear wheel, gray int., clear window, asw-ct/b	$3

Biff! Bam! Boom! Series, Mini Truck

Biff! Bam! Boom! Series, VW Bug

Biff! Bam! Boom! Series, Limozeen

Biff! Bam! Boom! Series, Range Rover

Quicksilver Series

	Photo	No.	Name	Description	Price
☐	📷	545	Chevy Stocker	a. red plastic body, metal Malaysia base, yellow, white & black tampo on hood & sides, black window, white HW logo behind rear wheel, asw-3sp	$2
☐				b. same as (a), silver painted Malaysia base, asw-3sp	$4
☐	📷	546	Aeroflash	a. purple plastic body, white painted Malaysia base, white, red & black tampos on hood & roof, white window, white HW logo on rear, 3sp	$2
☐	📷			b. same as (a), asw-3sp	$8
☐	📷	547	Ferrari 308	white pearl plastic body w/blue, lavender & black tampos, black painted metal Malaysia base, black window, light blue HW logo on nose, 5dot	$2
☐	📷	548	T-Bird Stock Car	a. blue plastic body, metal Malaysia base, orange, yellow & black tampos, black window, white HW logo behind rear wheel, 5sp	$2
☐				b. same as (a), silver painted Malaysia base, 5sp	$4

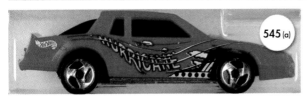

Quicksilver Series, Chevy Stocker

Quicksilver Series, Ferrari 308

Quicksilver Series, Aeroflash

Quicksilver Series, T-Bird Stock Car

Quicksilver Series, Aeroflash

Speed Spray Series

	Photo	No.	Name	Description	Price
❑	📷	549	Hydroplane	white w/aqua, yellow & black tampo on sides & top, blue plastic Malaysia base, chrome int., clear canopy, black HW logo on top of scoop	$3
❑	📷	550	Street Roader	a. white enamel, metal Malaysia base, brown mud tampo & red "Dirty Dog" on door & hood, red int. & spacer between body & clear window, red HW logo on side rear, alw-ct/b	$3
❑				b. same as (a), silver painted metal Malaysia base	$10
❑	📷	551	XT-3	blue enamel, white painted Malaysia base, white tampo on sides, orange-tint canopy, orange nose tip, metal engine, white logo on side, 5sp	$3
❑	📷	552	Funny Car	pearl magenta, metal Malaysia base, white, yellow & black tampos on side, clear window, black HW logo behind rear wheel, 5sp	$4

Speed Spray Series, Hydroplane

Speed Spray Series, XT-3

Speed Spray Series, Funny Car

Speed Spray Series, Street Roader

Spy Print Series

	Photo	No.	Name	Description	Price
❑	📷	553	Stealth	a. purple plastic body, metal Malaysia base, white on side w/red & black tampos, purple-tint window, chrome int., black HW logo over front wheel, 3sp	$3
❑				b. same as (a), silver painted Malaysia base, 3sp	$4
❑				c. same as (a), t/b	$3
❑				d. same as (b), silver painted Malaysia base, t/b	$4
❑		554	Alien	a. blue enamel, metal Malaysia base, white plastic top, black, blue & red tampos, white & blue int., smoked canopy, red HW logo on front left, 3sp	$3
❑	📷			b. same as (a), t/b	$4
❑		555	Sol-Aire CX4	a. dark met. maroon, black plastic Malaysia base, white sides w/black & green tampos, black window, black logo behind rear wheel, 3sp	$3
❑	📷			b. same as (a), t/b	$4
❑	📷	556	#4-Custom Corvette	black enamel, black plastic Malaysia base, yellow, red & white tampos, gray int., smoked window, red & white HW logo on nose, 3sp	$2

Spy Print Series, Stealth

Spy Print Series, Alien

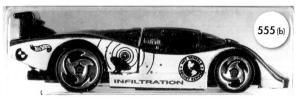

Spy Print Series, Sol-Aire CX4

555 (b)

Spy Print Series, Custom Corvette

556

Street Beast Series

	Photo	No.	Name	Description	Price
☐	📷	557	Mercedes-Benz Unimog	black enamel cab & box, red plastic fenders & int., metal Malaysia base, tan rear box cover w/black HW logo & black & red tampo, clear window, alw-ct/b	$2
☐	📷	558	Jaguar XJ220	a. orange enamel, black plastic Malaysia base, black & gold tampos on side & hood, black int., clear window, black logo behind rear wheel, yt/b	$2
☐				b. same as (a), no side tampo, yt/b	$8
☐	📷	559	Blown Camaro	a. day-glo yellow pearl, metal Malaysia base, black & green pearl tampos on hood & sides, black int., clear window, HW logo on hood, ot/b	$3
				b. same as (a), no origin base, ot/b	$5
☐	📷	560	Corvette Stingray	white enamel, metal Malaysia base, yellow, red & black tampos on hood & roof, blue-tint window & int., black HW logo on roof, yt/b	$3

557

Street Beast Series, Mercedes-Benz Unimog

559 (a)

Street Beast Series, Blown Camaro

560

Street Beast Series, Corvette Stingray

558 (a)

Street Beast Series, Jaguar XJ220

White Ice Series

	Photo	No.	Name	Description	Price
☐	📷	561	Speed Machine	white pearl, metal Malaysia base, white int., red-tint window, black HW logo on rear, 3sp	$2
☐	📷	562	Shadow Jet	a. white pearl, metal Malaysia base, white int., yellow-tint canopy, yellow plastic nose, light gold-tint chrome engines& fuel tanks, black HW logo on top behind canopy, 5sp	$2
☐				b. same as (a), chrome engines & fuel tanks, 5sp	$5
☐	📷	563	Splittn' Image II	white pearl, white plastic Malaysia base, blue-tint chrome canopy, engine & headlights, gray plastic side pipes, black HW logo behind left headlight, 3sp	$2
☐	📷	564	Twin Mill II	white pearl, white plastic Malaysia base, red-tint window, white int., pink chrome engines, black HW logo on rear, alw-5sp	$2

White Ice Series, Speed Machine

White Ice Series, Splittin' Image II

White Ice Series, Shadow Jet

White Ice Series, Twin Mill II

Dealer's Choice Series

Photo		No.	Name	Description	Price
☐	📷	565	Silhouette II	a. pearl blue, black plastic Malaysia base, white & red tampos on side, white tampos on hood, gold int. & engine, clear canopy, gold HW logo behind front wheel, 5dot	$2
☐				b. same as (a), 5sp	$4
☐		566	Street Beast	a. white & gold, metal Malaysia base, black, gold & red tampos on hood & sides, gold int., clear window, red HW logo behind seats, 5dot	$2
☐	📷			b. same as (a), 7sp	$9
☐		567	Baja Bug	a. met. red, metal Malaysia base, white, black & red tampo on side, white & black tampo on hood, white int., white HW logo on door above spade, 5sp	$5
☐				b. same as (a), silver painted Malaysia base, 5sp	$8
☐	📷			c. same as (a), asw-5sp	$7
☐	📷	568	'63 Corvette	a. black enamel, red plastic Malaysia base w/"63 Corvette," red, white & gold tampo on hood, red & white tampo on side, red "Q" & heart on roof, red HW logo on right side hood, red int., clear window, asw-5dot	$3
☐				b. same as (a), dark red int., asw-5dot	$4
☐				c. same as (a), red plastic Malaysia base, without "63 Corvette," asw-5dot	$4
☐				d. same as (a), asw-5sp	$15

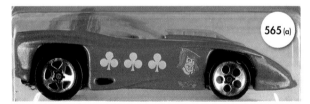

Dealer's Choice Series, Silhouette II

Dealer's Choice Series, Street Beast

Dealer's Choice Series, Baja Bug

Dealer's Choice Series, '63 Corvette

Rockin' Rods Series

Photo		No.	Name	Description	Price
☐	📷	569	Twang Thang	dark met. red, black plastic Malaysia base, black & white tampo on nose, magenta tampo behind chrome seats, chrome engine, black guitars on side w/chrome strings, white HW logo behind front wheel, clear window, 5sp	$2
☐	📷	570	Ferrari 355	a. black enamel, metal Malaysia base, green pearl, purple, white & orange tampos, purple int., clear window, red & white HW logo in front of rear wheel, asw-3sp	$3
☐				b. same as (a), asw-5sp	$3
☐	📷	571	Turbo Flame	a. purple plastic body, black painted Malaysia base, red, yellow, black & white tampo on side, yellow-tint window, yellow HW logo on side up by chrome engine, 5sp	$5
☐	📷		(new card)	b. purple plastic body, black painted Malaysia base, red, yellow, black & white tampo on side, more red & less lightning, yellow-tint window, yellow HW logo on side up by chrome engine, 5sp	$2
☐		572	Porsche 930	a. pearl dark green, metal Malaysia base, brown, yellow & white tampos, black int., smoked window, brown & white HW logo behind rear wheel, asw-3sp	$50
☐	📷			b. same as (a), asw-5sp	$3
☐				c. same as (a), asw-5dot	$2

Rockin' Rods Series, Twang Thang

Rockin' Rods Series, Ferrari 355

Rockin' Rods Series, Turbo Flame

Rockin' Rods Series, Turbo Flame Porsche 930

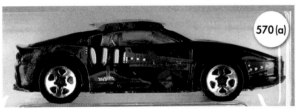

Rockin' Rods Series, Turbo Flame

Blue Streak Series

Photo		No.	Name	Description	Price
☐	📷	573	Olds 442	dark candy blue, large silver logo on trunk, chrome Malaysia base, black int., blue-tint window, asw-3sp	$5
☐	📷	574	Nissan Truck	candy blue, black plastic Malaysia base, black int. & roll bar, blue-tint window, chrome engine, large silver HW logo on hood, alw-ct/b	$20
☐	📷	575	'55 Chevy	a. candy blue, chrome Malaysia base, black window, large silver HW logo on trunk, 3sp	$5
☐				b. candy blue, black plastic Malaysia base, black window, large silver HW logo on trunk, 3sp	$20
☐	📷	576	Speed Blaster	a. candy blue, chrome Malaysia base, chrome window & engine, large HW logo on hood, 3sp	$20
☐				b. same as (a), black plastic Malaysia base,3sp	$4

Blue Streak Series, Olds 442

Blue Streak Series, '55 Chevy

Blue Streak Series, Nissan Truck

Blue Streak Series, Speed Blaster

Non-Series Collector Number Packs

Photo	No.	Name	Description	Price
☐ 📷	577	Police Cruiser	a. black enamel, black plastic Malaysia base, white doors w/gold & red "Auto City Police" tampo, gold "Emergency" on rear fender, red logo on rear door, white & gold "96" & blue lights on roof, gold & white logo & gold "Police" on trunk, tan int., smoked window, asw-b7sp	$4
☐ 📷			b. white enamel, white plastic Malaysia base, black int., blue-tint window & blue lights on roof, red & gold side stripe w/"Fire Dept. Chief" & "01" in gold & black, "City of Hot Wheels" logo on front door, white logo on rear fender, black "01" on roof, gold & black "Fire Dept" on trunk, asw-5sp	$6
☐			c. same as (b), asw-3sp	$8

Police Cruiser

Police Cruiser

1997 Treasure Hunt Series

Photo	No.	Name	Description	Price
☐ 📷	578	#1-'56 Flashsider	met. green, chrome Malaysia base, orange & lavender tampo on hood, chrome window, black bed cover, orange logo on rear, 5sp	$25
☐ 📷	579	#2-Silhouette II	white enamel, white plastic Malaysia base & int., blue-tint canopy, blue-tint chrome engine, red logo on rear, w3sp	$15
☐ 📷	580	#3-Mercedes 500SL	black enamel, black plastic Malaysia base, silver luggage rack tampo on trunk, silver "SL500" tampo on side, silver logo on rear, clear window, white int., alw-5sp	$15
☐ 📷	581	#4-Street Cleaver	black plastic, gold painted Malaysia base, red & gold tampo w/gold HW logo, gold-tint chrome engine, alw-5sp	$20
☐ 📷	582	#5-GM Lean Machine	met. burgundy & chrome, black painted Malaysia base, black tampos, chrome canopy, black HW logo on side, 5sp	$12
☐ 📷	583	#6-Hot Rod Wagon	yellow enamel, metal Malaysia base, gold-tint chrome engine & rear wing, black seat & handle, red HW logo on rear, y5sp	$35
☐ 📷	584	#7-Olds Aurora	purple pearl w/silver stripe & "Aurora" on side, chrome Malaysia base, small silver tampo on hood, gray int., clear window, silver HW logo behind rear wheel, asw-5sp	$11

Photo	No.	Name	Description	Price
❑ 📷	585	#8-Dogfighter	met. green, yellow plastic Malaysia base, gold & black tampos on sides, orange prop, gold-tint chrome engine & suspension, black HW logo on tail, 5sp	$20
❑ 📷	586	#9-Buick Wildcat	silver flake, gray plastic Malaysia base, red stripes, met. black window, chrome engine, red & white logo on rear, alw-3sp	$15
❑ 📷	587	#10-Blimp	blue plastic w/large HW logo on side, white gondola w/black window & "T.H. 97" tampo	$12
❑ 📷	588	#11-Avus Quattro	met. gold, black plastic Malaysia base, black "Avus" on side, black "Audi" logo on hood, red HW logo in front of rear wheel, white int., smoked canopy w/gold & black, alw-t/b	$12
❑ 📷	589	#12-Rail Rodder	white pearl plastic body, metal Malaysia base, pink-tint chrome engines & smoke stack, chrome drivers (wheels), red flame outline w/one orange flame at the end, red HW logo at end of flame tampo on side, b5sp	$25

1997 Treasure Hunt Series, #1-'56 Flashsider

1997 Treasure Hunt Series, #2-Silhouette II

1997 Treasure Hunt Series, #3-Mercedes 500SL

1997 Treasure Hunt Series, #4-Street Cleaver

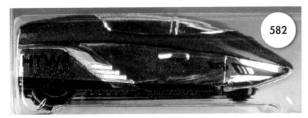

1997 Treasure Hunt Series, #5-GM Lean Machine

1997 Treasure Hunt Series, #6-Hot Rod Wagon

1997 Treasure Hunt Series, #7-Olds Aurora

1997 Treasure Hunt Series, #8-Dogfighter

1997 Treasure Hunt Series, #9-Buick Wildcat

1997 Treasure Hunt Series, #10-Blimp

1997 Treasure Hunt Series, #12-Rail Rodder

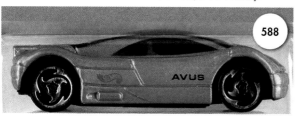

1997 Treasure Hunt Series, #11-Avus Quattro

Non-Series Collector Number Packs

Photo	No.	Name	Description	Price
❑	590	Porsche 911	a. red enamel, metal Malaysia base, black int., smoked window, black HW logo on nose, asw-t/b	$15
❑			b. same as (a), large rear t/b	$3
❑ 📷			c. same as (a), asw-5sp	$15
❑			d. same as (a), large rear 5sp	$9
❑			e. same as (a), large rear 5dot	$4
❑	591	Porsche 959	a. silver-blue pearl, metal Malaysia base, black int., smoked window, blue HW logo on rear spoiler, asw-t/b	$3
❑ 📷			b. same as (a), asw-5sp	$3
❑			c. same as (b), metal China base, asw-5sp	$3
❑	592	Porsche 930	a. pearl blue, metal Malaysia base, black int., smoked window, white logo on nose, asw-t/b	$3
❑ 📷			b. same as (a), asw-5sp	$3
❑ 📷	593	Skullrider	a. dark pink chrome body, metal Malaysia base, black int. & engine, black HW logo behind passenger's head, 5sp	$4
❑ 📷			b. same as (a), very light pink chrome body, almost no color	$3
❑ 📷	594	GM Ultralite	a. white & black enamel w/gray "SAPD" & police logo on sides, black, gray & white tampo on hood, no HW logo, black painted windows. This is the same as the "Demo Man" series car except for the wheels. Notice the "Warner" name on the black plastic Malaysia base, 7sp	$10

It seems likely some painted bodies still around from the Demo Man series that ended up as the #594 GM Ultralite.

Photo	No.	Name	Description	Price
❑			b. same as (a), 5dot	$15
❑			c. white & black enamel w/no tampos or HW logo, black plastic Malaysia base, black painted windows, 3sp	$3
❑ 📷			d. same as (c), 7sp	$3
❑ 📷		Police Car (name change)	e. same as (c), just name change on card	$3
❑ 📷	595	Corvette Sting Ray III	a. dark met. purple, purple plastic Malaysia base, gray int., clear window, no logo, 5sp	$5
❑			b. same as (a), 7sp	$3
❑			c. same as (a), 3sp	$25
❑ 📷			d. met. dark blue, black plastic Malaysia base, white int., smoked window, silver HW logo on nose, 3sp	$3

Porsche 911

GM Ultralite

Porsche 959

GM Ultralite

Porsche 930

GM Ultralite

Skullrider

Corvette Sting Ray III

Skullrider

Corvette Sting Ray III

Photo	No.	Name	Description	Price
❑	595	Corvette Sting Ray III	e. same as (a), 5dot	$25
❑ 📷	596	Pontiac Salsa	a. orange enamel, chrome Malaysia base, silver flake window, light gray int., no HW logo, alw-3sp	$25
❑			b. same as (a), black plastic Malaysia base, alw-3sp	$2
❑ 📷			c. same as (b), alw-t/b	$20
❑			d. same as (b), alw-7sp	$3
❑ 📷	597	Buick Wildcat	a. candy red or blood red, black plastic Malaysia base, black engine, black window, no HW logo, alw-7 sp	$20

I think the #597 Buick Wildcat car was another leftover from the Demo Man series.

❑ 📷			b. same as (a), red enamel, alw-7sp	$3
❑			c. same as (b), asw-3sp	$5
❑			d. met. green, gray plastic Malaysia base, gray engine, black window, no HW logo, alw-3sp	$7
❑			e. same as (d), dark met. green, asw-3sp	$7

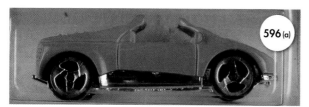

Pontiac Salsa

Camaro Wind

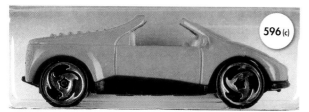

Pontiac Salsa

Nissan Custom "Z"

Buick Wildcat

Nissan Custom "Z"

Buick Wildcat

Commando

Turboa

Photo		No.	Name	Description	Price
❑		597	Buick Wildcat	f. same as (e), chrome engine, 3sp	$5
❑	📷	598	Turboa	butterscotch pearl, metal China base, red, silver & black tampo, gold chrome seat, engine & pipes, red HW logo on back of head, 5sp	$2
❑	📷	599	Camaro Wind	white enamel, metal China base, yellow, orange & red flames on nose & sides, pink chrome window, engine & side pipes, red HW logo behind side window, bbs	$4
❑	📷	600	Nissan Custom "Z"	a. light blue enamel, metal China base, magenta, silver & black tampo on side, magenta HW logo behind front wheel, black int., clear window, bbs	$4
❑				b. same as (a), 5sp	$44
❑				c. same as (a), dark met. blue, bbs	$6
❑	📷			d. same as (c), 5sp	$10
❑	📷	601	Commando	candy brown pearl, metal China base, black & gold side tampo, gold HW logo on door, black int. & engine, clear window, alw-cts	$6
❑	📷	602	Sharkruiser	black enamel, gray painted China base, red chrome engine, seat & teeth, silver HW logo above front wheel, bbs	$3
❑	📷	603	BMW 325i	yellow enamel w/red & black tampos on hood & sides, gray painted metal China base, black HW logo behind front wheel, black int., clear window, asw-bbs	$2

Photo	No.	Name	Description	Price
❏	604	Ferrari 308 GTS	a. yellow & black enamel, black plastic China base, black & yellow Ferrari logo on hood, black int., clear windshield w/yellow logo, asw-5sp	$6
❏			b. same as (a), asw-bbs	$27
❏	605	Mercedes 2.6	met. gold, black plastic China base, red painted taillights, silver painted grille, black int., clear window, gold HW logo in rear window, asw-bbs	$2
❏	606	Mercedes 300TD	dark met. green, gray plastic China base, red painted taillights, silver painted grille, gray int., red HW logo in rear clear window, asw-5sp	$3
❏	607	Fat Fendered '40	aqua enamel, metal China base, yellow, orange & purple side tampo, black int., white logo in clear side window, asw-5sp.	$12

The #607 along with the #216 Fat Fendered '40 are very heavy and were bought up for racing. I expect these to become very hard to find still in the package.

Photo	No.	Name	Description	Price
❏	608	Porsche 911 Targa	met. silver, black plastic China base, black painted door handle, black int., red logo in rear clear window, alw-5sp	$2
❏	609	Jaguar XJ40	dark blue, black plastic China base, red painted taillights, silver painted rear plate & front grille, white int., white HW logo in rear blue-tint window, asw-bbs	$3
❏	610	Land Rover MkII	orange enamel, black plastic China base, blue & white side tampos, black int., clear window, no HW logo, alw-5sp	$10
❏	611	Fire-Eater II	red enamel, gray plastic China base, silver tampos on side, gray plastic ladder, dark blue-tint window, silver HW logo on side, asw-5sp	$2
❏	612	'57 T-Bird	aqua enamel, metal China base, chrome bumpers, white int., red HW logo in clear windshield, asw-bw	$10

Sharkruiser (602)

Mercedes 300TD (606)

BMW 325i (603)

Fat Fendered '40 (607)

Ferrari 308 GTS (604 b)

Mercedes 2.6 (605)

Porsche 911 Targa (608)

Jaguar XJ40 (609)

Land Rover MkII

Fire-Eater II

'57 T-Bird

London Bus

Ford XR4Ti

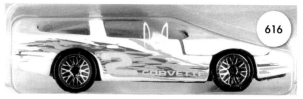

'80s Corvette

Flame Stopper II

Chevy Stocker

London Taxi

Photo	No.	Name	Description	Price
❏ 📷	613	London Bus	red enamel, black plastic China base, white side strip w/red & black tampos, black window, gold HW logo on rear, asw-5sp	$9
❏ 📷	615	Ford XR4Ti	met. silver, black plastic China base, butterscotch & purple side tampos, purple "4" & blue "Ford" oval on hood, purple HW logo behind front wheel, red int. & taillights, clear window & headlights, asw-5sp	$2
❏ 📷	616	'80s Corvette	white enamel, black plastic China base, yellow & blue side tampo w/gray #2 & Corvette, blue int./black dashboard, black painted top, gold HW logo in rear clear window, asw-bbs	$4
❏ 📷	617	Flame Stopper II	red enamel, gray plastic China base & boom w/bucket, red & white side tampos, dark smoked window, black logo on door, asw-5sp	$2
❏ 📷	618	Chevy Stocker	white enamel, metal China base, silver & blue side stripe w/red & blue tampos, silver & blue tampo on hood w/red & blue "Huffman Racing," purple int., clear window, red logo behind rear wheel, asw-5sp	$20

The #618 Chevy Stocker is another car bought up by racing fans, most of these have been taken out of the package and are going to be hard to find.

Photo	No.	Name	Description	Price
☐ 📷	619	London Taxi	yellow enamel, metal China base, black & white squared side stripe, black "London Cab Co." on rear fender, red "See City of Hot Wheels" on side, black HW logo behind front wheel, black int., clear window, asw-5sp	$7
☐ 📷	620	Ford Transit Wrecker	light blue enamel, white plastic China base, white & red tampos, white plastic boom, black hook & window, red HW logo behind rear wheel, asw-5sp	$5
☐ 📷	622	City Police	black enamel, black China base, white & yellow side stripe w/black tampos & "City of Hot Wheels" logo, black tampo on white roof w/blue light, gold "Police" on trunk, dark gray int. & bumpers, red logo above rear wheel, alw-b5sp	$3
☐ 📷	623	Mustang Cobra	a. dark pink pearl, black plastic China base, black stripe on hood, black "Mustang 5.0" on door, thin gold stripe on side, gold logo above 5.0 behind front wheel, black int., clear window, asw-bbs	$2
☐ 📷			b. same as (a), asw-5sp	$15
☐ 📷	624	Assault Crawler	olive plastic body, olive plastic China base, brown, green & tan camouflage	$5
☐ 📷	625	Classic Packard	black enamel, metal China base, black plastic fenders, black int., silver HW logo in rear clear window, asw-5sp	$5
☐ 📷	641	Wheel Loader	a. orange & black, metal China base, white HW logo on cab door, gray seat, engine & scoop, alw-cts	$5
☐			b. same as (a), gold HW logo on cab door, alw-cts	$4
☐ 📷	642	Forklift	a. white enamel, blue plastic cage, black plastic forks, small blue HW logo between wheels on side, metal China base, rear 5sp-front bw	$5
☐ 📷			b. same as (a), larger blue HW logo between wheels on side, rear 5sp-front bw	$5
☐ 📷			c. same as (b), dark blue plastic cage, rear 5sp-front bw	$5
☐ 📷	643	Digger	a. yellow enamel w/black "E 32" & City of HWs logo on side, black logo on side, gray plastic boom & scoop, yellow painted China base, (no HW flame on base above Digger), alw-5sp	$5
☐			b. same as (a), yellow painted China base, HW flame on base above Digger, alw-5sp	$4

Ford Transit Wrecker

City Police

Mustang Cobra

Mustang Cobra

Assault Crawler

Classic Packard

1998 First Editions

	Photo	No.	Name	Description	Price
☐	📷	637	#1-Escort Rally	a. white pearl w/pearl blue, red & black side tampos, gray plastic Malaysia, base w/"Ford Rally," pearl blue nose w/black & white headlights, white & yellow lettering, red int., smoked window, bbs	$10
☐				b. same as (a), gray plastic Malaysia base w/"Escort Rally," bbs	$2
☐	📷	640	#2-Slideout	purple pearl, gray plastic Malaysia base, black & white tampo on rear roll bar, orange & white "6" & racing decals in sides, white & black "6" & racing decals on side of top wing, orange wings, engine & rear push bar, orange HW logo on side below racing decals, 5sp	$5
☐	📷	634	#3-Dodge Sidewinder	a. day-glo orange, gray plastic Malaysia base, purple int. & bed cover, smoked window, white HW logo behind rear wheel, 5sp	$3
☐				b. same as (a), black HW logo behind rear wheel, 5sp	$15
☐	📷	633	#4-Dodge Caravan	a. dark met. burgundy, gray plastic Malaysia base, yellow, black & white side tampo, white int., smoked window, white HW logo on rear fender, alw-t/b	$5
☐	📷			b. same as (a), lighter met. burgundy, alw-t/b	$3
☐				c. same as (b), alw-5sp	$3
☐	📷	639	#5-Jaguar XK8	a. (48 on card) green pearl, gray plastic Malaysia base, black & white side tampo, white int., clear window, white HW logo behind rear wheel, bbs	$100
☐				b. same as (a), black int., bbs	$5
☐		638	#6-Jaguar D-Type	a. dark candy blue w/matching painted metal Malaysia base, white circle w/black "4" on front & rear, two white stripes on nose, white HW logo on rear, gray int., clear window, alw-5sp	$2

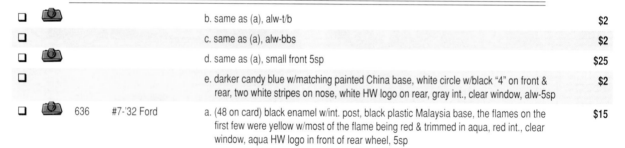

In 1998, there were three different headings on the cards issued for the 1998 First Editions. The first stating there were "48" cars in the series, the second stating "45" cars in the series, and the third stating 40 cars in the series. If you have cards with 48 on them add $5, cards with 45 on them add $3. The series ended up having 40 cars.

	Photo	No.	Name	Description	Price
☐	📷			b. same as (a), alw-t/b	$2
☐				c. same as (a), alw-bbs	$2
☐	📷			d. same as (a), small front 5sp	$25
☐				e. darker candy blue w/matching painted China base, white circle w/black "4" on front & rear, two white stripes on nose, white HW logo on rear, gray int., clear window, alw-5sp	$2
☐	📷	636	#7-'32 Ford	a. (48 on card) black enamel w/int. post, black plastic Malaysia base, the flames on the first few were yellow w/most of the flame being red & trimmed in aqua, red int., clear window, aqua HW logo in front of rear wheel, 5sp	$15

1998 First Editions, #4-Dodge Caravan

1998 First Editions, #3-Dodge Sidewinder

1998 First Editions, #4-Dodge Caravan

1998 First Editions, #8-'65 Impala

1998 First Editions, #7-'32 Ford

1998 First Editions, #7-'32 Ford

1998 First Editions, #1-Escort Rally

1998 First Editions, #6-Jaguar D-Type

1998 First Editions, #6-Jaguar D-Type

1998 First Editions, #5-Jaguar XK8

Photo		No.	Name	Description	Price

The very first releases of the # 7-'32 Ford were reported to have a driver by some collectors. What they saw was the casting post still inside. The post is where they break the body from the mold. This car is on the older Card with the rear of the Porsche and the card reads, "#7 of 48 Cars" and has the blister from the Slideout. Shortly after, the post was cleaned out and it got its own blister.

Photo		No.	Name	Description	Price
❑	📷	636	#7-'32 Ford	b. (48 on card) black enamel w/int. post, black plastic Malaysia base, mostly yellow flame w/red, trimmed in aqua, red int., clear window, aqua HW logo in front of rear wheel, 5sp	$11
❑				c. (48 on card) black enamel, black plastic Malaysia base, yellow flame w/red, trimmed in aqua, red int., clear window, aqua HW logo in front of rear wheel, 5sp	$10
❑				d. (40 on card) black enamel, black plastic Malaysia base, yellow flame w/red, trimmed in aqua, red int., clear window, aqua HW logo in front of rear wheel, 5sp	$6
❑				e. (40 on card) black enamel, black plastic Malaysia base, yellow flame w/red, trimmed in aqua, red int., clear window, aqua HW logo in front of rear wheel, t/b	$3
❑				f. (40 on card) black enamel, black plastic Thailand base, yellow flame w/red, trimmed in aqua, red int., clear window aqua HW logo in front of rear wheel, t/b	$3
❑	📷	635	#8-'65 Impala	candy purple, chrome Malaysia base, yellow & orange tampos on hood & sides, tan int., clear window, orange HW logo in front of rear wheel, asw-gbbs	$4
❑	📷	644	#9-'63 T-Bird	a. met. teal w/silver side trim, metal Malaysia base, white int., clear window, silver HW logo on rear fender, asw-5dot	$3
❑				b. same as (a), asw-t/b	$100
❑		645	#10-Dairy Delivery	a. white pearl, gray plastic Malaysia base, dark pink & teal side tampos, teal HW logo in front of rear wheel, aqua int., clear window, 5sp	$4
❑	📷			b. same as (a), bright pink & teal side tampos, 5sp	$4

Photo		No.	Name	Description	Price
❑	📷	645	#10-Dairy Delivery	c. same as (b), top pink stripe bends down to touch second pink stripe, 5sp	$4
❑				d. same as (c), gray plastic China base, 5sp	$4
❑		646	#11-Mercedes SLK	a. yellow enamel, metal Malaysia base, white side trim paint, black painted door handle, black HW logo on rear fender, black int., smoked window and headlights, asw-5dot	$12
❑	📷			b. yellow pearl, metal Malaysia base, silver side trim paint, black painted door handle, black HW logo on rear fender, black int., smoked window and headlights, asw-5dot	$20
❑	📷			c. same as (b), tan int., asw-5dot	$4
❑				d. same as (c), asw-5sp	$4
❑	📷	647	#12-Lakester	red enamel w/matching painted Malaysia base, yellow & orange "61" on top w/white lettering, black, yellow & white racing decals on sides, chrome engines, exhaust & int., clear canopy, alw-5sp	$3
❑	📷	648	#13-Hot Seat	a. white plastic, blue-tint metal Malaysia engine & base, black plastic seat & plunger, black HW logo on rear (no pun intended), 5sp	$3
❑				b. same as (a), metal Malaysia base, 5sp	$3
❑	📷	668	#14-Ford GT-90	white enamel, metal Malaysia base, small black Ford oval & GT90 tampos on side, black HW logo in front of rear wheel, blue int., smoked window, asw-3sp	$2

640

1998 First Editions, #2-Slideout

641 (a)

Wheel Loader

642 (a)

Forklift

642 (b)

Forklift

642 (c)

Forklift

643 (a)

Digger

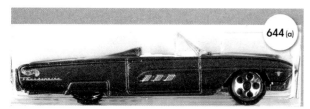

1998 First Editions, #9-'63 T-Bird

1998 First Editions, #11-Mercedes SLK

1998 First Editions, #10-Dairy Delivery

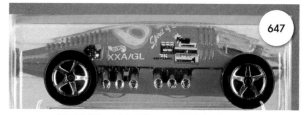

1998 First Editions, #12-Lakester

1998 First Editions, #10-Dairy Delivery

1998 First Editions, #13-Hot Seat

1998 First Editions, #11-Mercedes SLK

1999 First Editions, #1-1936 Cord

Photo	No.	Name	Description	Price
☐ 📷	652	#15-Pikes Peak Celica	a. yellow enamel, black plastic Malaysia base, black, red & white tampos on hood & roof, purple & red side tampo w/black & white "Pennzoil," black "No Fear" & purple "Toyota Express Lube," red int., dark smoked window, white HW logo on hood by windshield, asw-gbbs	$7
☐			b. same as (a), lavender & red side tampo w/black & white "Pennzoil," black "No Fear" & lavender "Toyota Express Lube," asw-gbbs	$5
☐ 📷			c. same as (b), black "No Fear" & lavender "Toyota Express," "Lube" is now in black, asw-gbbs	$3
☐ 📷	653	#16-Firebird	a. met. gold, gray plastic China base, black & white tampos, light tan int., tinted window, no HW logo, yellow letter b5sp	$2
☐			b. same as (a), darker met. gold, alw-yellow letter b5sp	$2
☐	661	#17-'70 Roadrunner	a. light Hemi Orange, chrome Malaysia base, short black stripe on trunk w/silver logo, the stripe on the trunk ran short of the rear window, black stripe on hood didn't come to the windshield either. Hood has black stripe w/silver "426 HEMI" & hood pins, black int., clear window, 5sp	$5
☐			b. Hemi Orange, chrome Malaysia base, black stripe, silver logo on trunk reaches rear window, black stripe w/silver "426 HEMI" & hood pins on hood reaches windshield, black int., clear window, 5sp	$3
☐ 📷			c. same as (b), 5dot	$20

Photo		No.	Name	Description	Price
☐	📷	665	#18-Mustang Cobra	a. black enamel, gray plastic Malaysia base, side tampos include: green wedge on side w/thin yellow stripe & orange "Mustang" & "OSO," misc. racing decals, yellow & green over white "11," "Cosen" tampo missing from rear fender, hood tampos include: green wedge w/thin yellow stripe, orange "Mustang," white "Team OSO," yellow & green over white "11," white Ford oval, "Team OSO" & HW logo on trunk, gray int., clear window, asw-gbbs	$10
☐				b. same as (a), w/"Cosen" added to rear fender, asw-gbbs	$3
☐	📷			c. same as (b), w/olive "11" on side, asw-gbbs	$5
☐				d. same as (b), w/trunk tampo reversed, asw-gbbs	$15

1999 First Editions, #1-1936 Cord

1998 First Editions, #23-Solar Eagle III

1998 First Editions, #21-Go Kart

1998 First Editions, #15-Pikes Peak Celica

1998 First Editions, #15-Pikes Peak Celica

1998 First Editions, #16-Firebird

1998 First Editions, #20-'40 Ford Pickup

1998 First Editions, #20-'40 Ford Pickup

1998 First Editions, #22-Super Comp Dragster

1999 First Editions, #3-'38 Phantom Corsair

1999 First Editions, #3-'38 Phantom Corsair

1998 First Editions, #19-Panoz GTR-1

1998 First Editions, #19-Panoz GTR-1

1998 First Editions, #19-Panoz GTR-1

1998 First Editions, #25-Tow Jam

1998 First Editions, #24-Tail Dragger

1998 First Editions, #17-'70 Roadrunner

1998 First Editions, #33-Bad Mudder

Photo	No.	Name	Description	Price
☐ 📷	665	#18-Mustang Cobra	e. same as (b), gray plastic Thailand base w/dark green wedge on side & hood, bright yellow (no green) "11" on side & hood, asw-gbbs	$8
☐			f. same as (e), dark olive wedge on side & hood, asw-bbs	$8
☐ 📷	657	#19-Panoz GTR-1	a. white enamel, black plastic China base, dark red & silver stripes on top of hood & rear fenders, dark red "66" & Panoz logo on hood, light blue panel w/red "66" on door, larger red HW logo behind rear wheel, misc. racing decals behind front wheel, blue int., clear window, bbs	$5
☐ 📷			b. white enamel, black plastic China base, bright red & silver stripes on top of hood & rear fenders, bright red "66" & Panoz logo on hood, light blue w/red "66" on door, small red HW logo behind rear wheel, misc. racing decals behind front wheel, blue int., clear window, bbs	$2
☐ 📷			c. same colors as (b), black plastic Malaysia base, smaller tampo on door that only covers door, bbs	$3
☐ 📷	654	#20-'40 Ford Pickup	a. light pearl blue, chrome Malaysia base, yellow, red tampo w/purple outline on door & rear fender, red & white HW logo on door, gray int., roll bar, tubs & wing, blue-tint window, 5sp	$20
☐			b. candy blue, chrome Malaysia base, yellow, red tampo w/purple outline on door & rear fender, red & white HW logo on door, gray int., roll bar, tubs & wing, blue-tint window, 5sp	$3
☐			c. same as (a), yellow & red door & rear fender tampo (purple outline is missing), 5sp	$8
☐ 📷			d. candy blue, chrome Thailand base, yellow & orange tampo w/purple outline on door & rear fender, red & white HW logo on door, gray int., roll bar, tubs & wing, blue-tint window, 5sp	$4
☐			e. dark candy blue, chrome China base, yellow tampo w/purple outline (orange 8 is missing from tampo), on door & rear fender, red & white HW logo on door, gray int., roll bar, tubs & wing, blue-tint window, 5sp	$8
☐			f. dark candy blue, chrome China base, yellow & orange tampo w/purple outline on door & rear fender, red & white HW logo on door, gray int., roll bar, tubs & wing, blue-tint window, 5sp	$4
☐ 📷	651	#21-Go Kart	day glo green w/black & orange tampo, white HW logo on side pod, metal chassis, day-glo painted metal Malaysia base, black seat, 5sp	$5

1998 First Editions, #33-Bad Mudder

1998 First Editions, #26-Customized C3500

1998 First Editions, #26-Customized C3500

1998 First Editions, #27-Super Modified

1998 First Editions, #18-Mustang Cobra

1998 First Editions, #18-Mustang Cobra

1998 First Editions, #18-Mustang Cobra

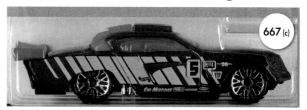

1998 First Editions, #34-At-A-Tude

Photo	No.	Name	Description	Price
☐ 📷	655	#22-Super Comp Dragster	a. black enamel, 3 decals on side including HW logo, black plastic fenders w/Malaysia, "1" or "2" under running board, gray roll cage, int. & wheelie bar, chrome exhaust & base, 5sp	$8
☐			b. same as (a), 5 decals on side including HW logo, 5sp	$4
☐ 📷	650	#23-Solar Eagle III	yellow plastic body, black mf. Malaysia base, blue solar cells on top, black & red tampos on side & nose, black canopy, no HW logo, black window	$2
☐ 📷	659	#24-Tail Dragger	a. met. purple, metal Malaysia base, pearl pink & blue pinstripe tampos on hood & sides, pearl blue HW logo in front of rear wheel, white int., clear window, bbs	$4
☐			b. same as (a), pearl pink & blue pinstripe tampos on hood only, no side tampo or HW logo, bbs	$15
☐			c. same as (a), no tampos or logo, bbs	$15
☐	658	#25-Tow Jam	a. red enamel, chrome Malaysia base, large HW logo on roof, logo covers almost all of the roof, metal boom, black sling, black window, 3sp	$50
☐ 📷			b. same as (a), small HW logo on roof, 3sp	$5
☐			c. same as (b), chrome Thailand base, 3sp	$5
☐ 📷	663	#26-Customized C3500	a. met. teal, gray plastic Malaysia base, long thin blue, magenta & white stripe down sides, magenta HW logo on side behind cab, thin black stripes above rocker panel, gray int., smoked window, 5dot	$15
☐ 📷			b. met. teal, gray plastic Malaysia base, short wide dark blue, purple & white stripe down sides, thick dark blue stripes on & above rocker panel, white HW logo on rear of bed cover, gray int., smoked window, 5dot	$4

Photo	No.	Name	Description	Price
☐ 📷	664	#27-Super Modified	a. black enamel body & Malaysia base, magenta, orange, yellow & white tampo on front w/white, black & red lettering, white logo on nose, metal engine chrome rear wing & roll cage, pink seat, front wing & rear push bar, bbs/2	$3
☐			b. bbs/2 rear & bbs front	$7

Bbs/2 is the second-generation wire wheel, it has a thicker tire and a smaller wheel. If you look at it quick, it looks a little like a rubber tire.

☐ 📷	669	#28-Chaparral 2	a. white enamel, black painted metal Malaysia base, black "66" in black circle on nose, gray plastic injection & exhaust, red logo on side in front of rear wheel, black int., clear window, bbs/2	$3
☐ 📷			b. same as (a), bbs/2 rear & bbs/front	$8
☐			c. same as (a), bbs	$8
☐ 📷			d. same as (a), bbs rear & bbs/2 front	$8
☐ 📷	670	#29-Mustang Mach I	a. day-glo orange, black plastic Malaysia base, black stripe on hood, black int. & rear louvers, blue-tint window, black HW logo on rear fender, 5sp	$40
☐			b. same as (a), asw-5sp	$60
☐ 📷			c. mustard yellow, black plastic Malaysia base, black stripe on hood, black int. & rear louvers, blue-tint window, black logo on rear fender, 5sp	$4

1998 First Editions, #34-At-A-Tude

1998 First Editions, #14-Ford GT-90

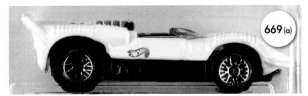

1998 First Editions, #28-Chaparral 2

1998 First Editions, #28-Chaparral 2

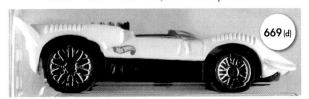

1998 First Editions, #28-Chaparral 2

1998 First Editions, #29-Mustang Mach I

1998 First Editions, #29-Mustang Mach I

1998 First Editions, #29-Mustang Mach I

1998 First Editions, #32-Chrysler Thunderbolt

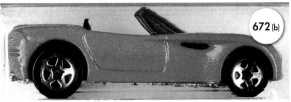

1998 First Editions, #35-Dodge Concept Car

1998 First Editions, #36-Whatta Drag

1998 First Editions, #31-Callaway C-7

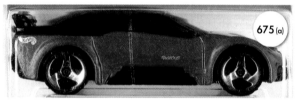

1998 First Editions, #30-Sweet 16 II

1998 First Editions, #37-Express Lane

1999 First Editions, #7-Pontiac Rageous

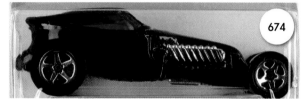

1999 First Editions, #25-Porsche 911 GT1-98

1999 First Editions, #25-Porsche 911 GT1-98

1998 First Editions, #37-Express Lane

Photo	No.	Name	Description	Price
☐ 📷	670	#29-Mustang Mach I	d. same as (c), asw-5sp	$20
☐			e. same as (c), 5dot	$25
☐ 📷	674	#30-Sweet 16 II	dark met. purple w/matching painted metal Malaysia base, purple-tint window, chrome engine, int. & front wheel drive unit, silver HW logo on rear, 5sp	$3
☐ 📷	677	#31-Callaway C-7	a. met. silver, black plastic Malaysia base, black & red lettering on hood, black lettering on sides & rear, orange dot above front wheel, black painted headlights, black plastic rear wing, front cowl, black int., black HW logo behind rear wheel, clear window, 5sp	$4
☐			b. same as (a), HW logo is black over red behind rear wheel, 5sp	$25
☐			c. same as (a), black plastic headlights, 5sp	$3
☐ 📷	671	#32-Chrysler Thunderbolt	a. silver pearl, black plastic Malaysia base, white int., purple-tint window, purple HW logo on trunk, 5dot	$2
☐			b. same as (a), 5sp	$30
☐ 📷	662	#33-Bad Mudder	a. white enamel, black plastic Malaysia base, "No Roof Tampo," dark blue wedge w/white oval & red outlined "8" on side, light blue pearl stripes, light red stripes & red, blue & black racing decals on sides, no logo, two decals side by side above "Chi Motors," light blue pearl "Goodyear" on front fender, large "Ford" oval on door, black int., asw-ct/b	$80

Photo	No.	Name	Description	Price
❏	662	#33-Bad Mudder	b. white enamel, black plastic Malaysia base, "No Roof Tampo," black wedge w/white & red "8" on side, dark blue enamel stripes, red stripes & red, blue & black racing decals in new places on sides, larger "Cosen" tampo only above larger "Chi Motors," dark blue enamel "Goodyear" on front fender, dark blue logo on rear fender, large "Ford" oval on door, black int., asw-ct/b	$50
❏ 📷			c. white enamel, black plastic Malaysia base, black & red rectangle w/white & red "8" & blue "Bousquette" & "Handy Cams" roof tampo, black wedge w/white & red "8" on side, dark blue enamel stripes, red stripes & red, blue & black racing decals in new places on sides, "Cosen" tampo only above "Chi Motors," dark blue enamel "Goodyear" on front fender, dark blue logo on rear fender, large "Ford" oval on door, black int., asw-ct/b	$5
❏			d. same as (c), all reds in tampo are much darker, asw-ct/b	$5
❏	667	#34-At-A-Tude	a. met. blue, black plastic Malaysia base, yellow stripes & black, red & white racing decals on sides, black HW logo in front of rear wheel on door, chrome int., orange-tint window, large rear bbs/small front bbs	$4
❏			b. same as (a), dark met. blue, large rear bbs/small front bbs	$4
❏ 📷			c. same as (a), alw-bbs	$20
❏ 📷			d. same as (a), asw-bbs	$15
❏	672	#35-Dodge Concept Car	a. pearl orange, metal Malaysia base, silver HW logo on trunk, silver painted headlights, smoked window, purple int., 5sp	$300
❏ 📷			b. same as (a), black int., 5sp	$3
❏			c. same as (b), metal China base, 5sp	$3
❏ 📷	673	#36-Whatta Drag	met. red, metal Malaysia base, yellow & green roof tampo, red & white HW logo on roof, chrome engine, rear wing & suspension, gray scoop, chrome int., orange-tint window, 3sp	$3
❏ 📷	678	#37-Express Lane	a. red plastic body, metal Malaysia base, white side tampo w/red "Express Lane," black seat & steering wheel, smaller white HW logo on rear plate, metal engine, 5sp	$3

1999 First Editions, #24-Baby Boomer

1998 First Editions, #38-Cat-A-Pult

1998 First Editions, #39-Fathom This

1999 First Editions, #9-Tee'd Off

1999 First Editions, #9-Tee'd Off

	Photo	No.	Name	Description	Price
❑	📷	678	#37-Express Lane	b. dark red plastic body, metal China base, white side tampo w/red "Express Lane," black seat & steering wheel, small white HW logo on rear plate	$3
❑		681	#38-Cat-A-Pult	a. red enamel, metal Malaysia base, faint white stripe down hood, white oval w/black "64" on nose, red HW logo above oval on hood, black int., orange-tint window, asw-5sp	$25
❑				b. same as (a), black HW logo above oval on hood, asw-5sp	$10
❑	📷			c. same as (b), bright white stripe down hood, black HW logo, asw-5sp	$3
❑				d. same as (c), asw-3sp	$3
❑	📷	682	#39-Fathom This	a. white enamel, black & white props, red "Experimental" tampo & HW logo on top of white plastic pontoons, orange windows	$4
❑				b. same as (a), HW logo on side of white plastic pontoons	$3
❑		684	#40-Double Vision	a. met. red, gray plastic Malaysia base, white & black tampos, white HW logo on rear fender behind wheel, gray engines w/chrome Super Chargers, gray seat, clear canopy, gbbs	$2
❑	📷			b. same as (a), gray engines w/chrome Super Chargers in backwards, gbbs	$8

683 (c)

1999 First Editions, #9-Tee'd Off

684 (b)

1998 First Editions, #40-Double Vision

Tattoo Machines

	Photo	No.	Name	Description	Price
❑	📷	685	'57 T-Bird	light pearl blue, chrome Malaysia base, white & black tampo on hood & sides, black HW logo on rear fender by taillight, blue-tint window & int., 3sp	$2
❑		686	'93 Camaro	a. day-glo green, black plastic Malaysia base, black & white side tampo, black & white HW logo on side in front of rear wheel, white int., smoked window, alw-3sp	$2
❑	📷			b. same as (a), alw-t/b	$2

The Tattoo Machines '93 Camaro with the tri-blade wheel was really rare when it first came out, and was trading for cars in the $40 range. They were in the first few cases delivered, and only a few were found. All the others were with the 3-spoke wheel. To have one of the tri-blade cars was to have a have a very good piece in your collection. Then, a few months after it was in production, Mattel put out the tri-blade variation as a normal release. As a result, the values fell.

	Photo	No.	Name	Description	Price
❑	📷	687	Stutz Blackhawk	a. met. red, metal Malaysia base, white & black side tampos, red & white HW logo behind rear wheel, white int., tinted window, asw-3s	$2
❑				b. same as (a), dark met. red, asw-3sp	$2
❑	📷			c. same as (a), dark met. burgundy, asw-3sp	$2
❑		688	Corvette Stingray	a. orange enamel, yellow sides w/black & orange tampos, metal Malaysia base, black int., smoked window, black HW logo behind front tire, 3sp	$2
❑	📷			b. same as (a), t/b	$8

Tattoo Machines Series, '57 T-Bird

Tattoo Machines Series, Stutz Blackhawk

Tattoo Machines Series, '93 Camaro

Tattoo Machines Series, Corvette Stingray

Tattoo Machines Series, Stutz Blackhawk

Techno Bits Series

	Photo	No.	Name	Description	Price
☐	📷	689	Shadow Jet II	a. black plastic body, metal Malaysia base, orange side tampo w/thin yellow outline, white & light green tampos on side over the orange, chrome int., white, orange, light green, & yellow tampos on front, orange & white HW logo on side toward rear, green-tint window, b5sp	$3
☐				b. same as (a), white & dark green tampos on side over the orange, white, orange, dark green, yellow & brown tampos on front, b5sp	$4
☐	📷			c. black plastic, metal Malaysia base, brown side tampo w/thin yellow outline, white, light green & orange tampos on side over the brown, white, orange, light green, & yellow tampos on front, orange & white HW logo on side toward rear, chrome int., green-tint window, b5sp	$15
☐				d. black plastic, metal Malaysia base, brown side tampo w/thin yellow outline, white, light green orange tampos on side over the brown, & white, brown, light green & yellow tampos on front, orange & white HW logo on side toward rear, chrome int., green-tint window, b5sp	$10
☐		690	Power Pistons	a. purple plastic, metal Malaysia base, yellow, black & gray side tampos, gold int., yellow-tint window, 3sp	$2
☐				b. same as (a), bbs	$2
☐	📷			c. same as (a), t/b	$2
☐	📷			d. dark purple plastic body, metal Malaysia base, yellow, black & gray side tampos, gold int., yellow-tint window, t/b	$4
☐		691	Shadow Jet	a. met. blue, metal Malaysia base, gold & silver tampo on top, silver, black & gold tampo on side pod, red & silver HW logo on top of rear wing, gold chrome engine & exhaust, black int., black plastic nose, smoked canopy, 5sp	$6
☐	📷			b. same as (a), purple met., 5sp	$2
☐	📷			c. same as (a), very dark purple met. (looks black), 5sp	$25
☐	📷	692	Radar Ranger	day-glo green, black painted Malaysia base, black, purple & white tampos, black plastic radar dish, purple plastic insert, purple & yellow HW logo behind canopy on side, red-tint canopy, ct/b	$2

Techno Bits Series, Shadow Jet II

689(a)

Techno Bits Series, Shadow Jet II

689(c)

Techno Bits Series, Power Pistons

690(c)

Techno Bits Series, Power Pistons

690(d)

Techno Bits Series, Shadow Jet

691(b)

Techno Bits Series, Shadow Jet

691(c)

Techno Bits Series, Radar Ranger

692

Tropicool Series

	Photo	No.	Name	Description	Price
❑	📷	693	Ice Cream Truck	a. white enamel, black plastic Malaysia base, yellow, red, green & black stripes, "Rasta Fruits & Veggies" & Rasta Dude w/green & yellow hat on side, white HW logo in red stripe behind rear wheel, green int., clear window, asw-5sp	$10
❑				b. same as (a), black HW logo in white stripe behind rear wheel, asw-5sp	$4
❑	📷			c. same as (b), yellow, red, green & black stripes, "Rasta" only, asw-5sp	$8
❑		694	Baja Bug	a. white enamel, metal Malaysia base, dark red, black, yellow & green stripes w/Rasta Dude on door, yellow & red tampo w/Rasta Dude on hood, "Bug'n Taxi" in white in side & hood, red int., black & white HW logo on side behind door, large rear 5sp	$7
❑				b. same as (a), bright red in tampos, large rear 5sp	$5
❑				c. same as (a), metal India base, large rear 5sp	$5
❑	📷			d. same as (a), metal Malaysia base, asw-5sp	$8
❑		695	'35 Cadillac	a. red enamel, metal Malaysia base, yellow, white, red & green side tampo, black plastic fenders, light gray int., smoked window, white tampo w/large logo behind side window, asw-bbs	$3
❑				b. same as (a), asw-3sp	$4
❑	📷			c. same as (a), asw-5sp	$10
❑	📷	696	Corvette Convertible	a. day-glo green w/blue, white & black side tampo, black plastic Malaysia base w/o "Custom Corvette," blue int., smoked window, blue logo on rear fender, 3sp	$6
❑				b. same as (a), black plastic Malaysia base w/"Custom Corvette," 3sp	$4
❑				c. same as (b), bbs	$2

Tropicool Series, Ice Cream Truck

Tropicool Series, Ice Cream Truck

Tropicool Series, Baja Bug

Tropicool Series, Classic Cadillac

Tropicool Series, Corvette Convertible

Low 'N Cool Series

Photo	No.	Name	Description	Price
☐ 📷	697	Mini Truck	day-glo yellow, black plastic Malaysia base, light green & yellow tampos outlined in orange & dark blue on hood & sides, black int. & rear bed, smoked window, chrome engine, shifter & rear speakers, dark blue HW logo on rear fender behind wheel, g3sp	$2
☐ 📷	698	'59 Impala	a. green pearl, chrome Malaysia base, dark purple & black side tampo, white HW logo on rear fender, white int., smoked window, asw-gbbs	$4
☐			b. same as (a), light purple pearl & black side tampo, gbbs	$3
☐ 📷	699	'59 Cadillac	a. rose pearl, chrome Thailand base, yellow & blue tampos on sides & hood, white int., smoked window, yellow HW logo on front fender by headlight, asw-gbbs	$5
☐ 📷			b. same as (a), pink pearl, chrome Thailand base, gbbs	$5

You really have to put the (a) and (b) variations of the #699, '59 Cadillac cars side-by-side to see the difference.

☐ 📷	716	Limozeen	black flake w/pearl tampo & gold stripe on side, gold-tint chrome Malaysia base, white int., smoked window, gold HW logo on rear fender, asw-gbbs	$4

Low 'N Cool Series, Mini Truck

Low 'N Cool Series, '59 Impala

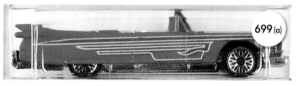

Low 'N Cool Series, '59 Cadillac

Low 'N Cool Series, '59 Cadillac

Non-Series Collector Number Packs

	Photo	No.	Name	Description	Price
☐	📷	700	Shock Factor	yellow enamel & blue plastic, metal China base, black, red & white tampos on side & rear wing, black HW logo on side by scoop, blue plastic driver, alw-bw	$3
☐	📷	702	Lumina Van	a. dark green met., black plastic China base, three thin silver stripes w/"Lumina" on sides, tan int., smoked window, silver HW logo on rear fender, bbs	$4
☐				b. same as (a), 5sp	$4
☐	📷	712	Tipper	a. blue enamel, black plastic China base, white tip box w/yellow & black w/small "BD" tampo in blue, black & white HW logo on box side, black int., smoked window, asw-5sp	$2
☐	📷			b. dark blue enamel, black plastic China base, white tip box w/yellow & black w/large "BD" tampo in blue, black & white logo on box side, black int., smoked window, asw-5sp	$3
☐		714	Talbot Lago	blue enamel w/black fenders, black painted metal base, bbs	$274
☐	📷	715	1996 Mustang GT	white enamel, metal China base, thin black stripe w/yellow & orange tampos trimmed in black on sides, yellow logo in tampo behind front wheel, silver painted headlights, red int., clear window, asw-5sp	$30

Shock Factor

Tipper

Lumina Van

1996 Mustang GT

Tipper

Low 'N Cool Series, Limozeen

Biohazard Series

	Photo	No.	Name	Description	Price
☐	📷	717	Hydroplane	a. (red car on card) dark day-glo green, yellow "Biohazard Removal" tampo on pontoons, yellow w/black over brown Biohazard Removal logo on pontoons, black over brown (mostly black) designs on pontoons, black behind canopy w/yellow "unit 4" & red HW logo, black plastic Thailand base, chrome int., clear canopy	$25
☐				b. same as (a), yellow w/black over red "Biohazard Removal" logo on pontoons, black plastic Thailand base, black int., clear canopy	$15
☐	📷			c. day-glo green, yellow "Biohazard Removal" tampo on pontoons, yellow w/black over brown Biohazard Removal logo on pontoons, black over brown (mostly black) designson pontoons, black behind canopy w/yellow "unit 4" & red HW logo, black plastic Thailand base, black int., smoked canopy	$4

Photo	No.	Name	Description	Price
☐	717	Hydroplane	d. same as (c), yellow w/black over dark brown Biohazard Removal logo on pontoons	$4
☐			e. bright day-glo green, yellow "Biohazard Removal" tampo on pontoons, yellow w/brown over black Biohazard Removal logo on pontoons, black behind canopy w/yellow "unit 4" & red HW logo, black plastic Malaysia base, black int. smoked canopy	$5
☐ 📷	718	Flame Stopper	a. day-glo pink, black plastic Thailand base w/long headlights, yellow w/ black over brown biohazard removal, yellow "Caution High Pressure Foam Flow" over black rectangle behind rear wheel, black window, black plastic boom w/rivets, alw-yct/b	$3
☐			b. same as (a), black plastic Malaysia base w/small headlights, boom has larger rivets & part number, smaller logo behind rear side window	$3
☐ 📷			c. same as (a), black plastic China base, smaller HW logo behind rear side window, black & yellow biohazard logo on body between wheels	$3
☐ 📷	719	Recycling Truck	a. day-glo yellow metal cab, black window, day-glo yellow plastic waste container with black & red over yellow side tampo, thin white lettering outlined in black, red over black HW logo on side, this tampo is very hard to read, black plastic Malaysia base, asw-t/b	$5
☐ 📷			b. same as (a), with much better tampo, yellow & red over black side tampo, larger white over black lettering, red over black HW logo on side, asw-t/b	$3
☐ 📷	720	Rescue Ranger	a. black enamel, chrome Malaysia base, dark red, yellow & white side tampos, red HW logo on side in left yellow rectangle, day-glo yellow plastic insert, yellow-tint window & interior, alw-5sp	$4
☐			b. same as (a), alw-5dot	$3

Biohazard Series, Hydroplane

Biohazard Series, Hydroplane

Biohazard Series, Flame Stopper

Biohazard Series, Flame Stopper

Biohazard Series, Recycling Truck

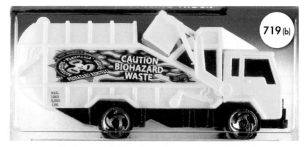

Biohazard Series, Recycling Truck

Biohazard Series, Rescue Ranger

Dash 4 Cash Series

Photo	No.	Name	Description	Price
❏	721	Jaguar XJ220	a. silver w/black on sides, black plastic Malaysia base, black stripes on hood & roof, magenta outlined tampo on hood, silver "Fast Cash" & magenta outlined tampo on sides, silver & black HW logo on rear fender behind rear wheel, light purple int., clear window, bbs	$5
❏			b. same as (a), dark purple int., bbs	$5
❏			c. same as (a), light purple int., 3sp	$3
❏			d. same as (c), dark purple int., 3sp	$3
❏			e. same as (c), no roof, hood stripes, or tampo, light purple int., 3sp	$10
❏			f. same as (a), light purple int., asw-3sp	$15
❏ 📷			g. same as (a), light purple int., t/b	$40
❏	722	Ferrari F40	a. light yellow gold, metal Malaysia base, black & white tampos on hood & sides, white logo on front fender, tan int., tinted window, gbbs	$4
❏ 📷			b. This is a transition piece. Light yellow gold body w/dark gold rear engine cover, black & white with tampos on hood & sides, white HW logo on front fender, metal Malaysia base, tan int., tinted window, gbbs	$10
❏			c. dark gold, metal Malaysia base, black & white with tampos on hood & sides, white HW logo on front fender, tan int., tinted window, gbbs	$3
❏ 📷	723	Audi Avus	black enamel, black plastic Thailand base, white, dark red & yellow side tampos, gold & black tampos on smoked canopy, dark red HW logo in front of rear wheel, white int., alw-gbbs	$3
❏	724	Dodge Viper RT/10	a. white pearl, black plastic Thailand base, pearl blue side tampo, red & black tampo & red & white logo on hood, red int., smoked window, alw-t/b	$3
❏ 📷			b. same as (a), small front-t/b	$15
❏			c. same as (a), black plastic China base, alw-t/b	$3

Dash 4 Cash Series, Jaguar XJ220

Dash 4 Cash Series, Audi Avus

Dash 4 Cash Series, Ferrari F40

Dash 4 Cash Series, Dodge Viper RT/10

Race Team Series IV

Photo	No.	Name	Description	Price
❏ 📷	725	'67 Camaro	a. met. blue w/white sides & large HW logo, metal no origin base, red #1 on rear fender, white "1" & yellow "Hot Wheels" on roof, dark red stripe below white on rear fender, white bowtie in front of rear wheel, white int., tinted window, 5sp	$5
❏			b. same as (a), metal Malaysia base, 5sp	$4
❏			c. same as (a), metal no origin base, asw-5sp	$20
❏ 📷	726	Mercedes C-Class	met. blue w/white sides & large HW logo, black plastic Thailand base, large HW logo on hood w/white "1," red "1" on rear fender, dark red stripe below white on rear fender, white "Bridgestone" on rear pcst above rear tire, white int., smoked window, asw-5sp	$3
❏ 📷	727	Shelby Cobra 427 S/C	met. blue w/white sides & large HW logo, metal Malaysia base, red "1" on rear fender, dark red stripe below white on rear fender, white "Ford" above logo on door, yellow "Hot Wheels" above trunk, large HW logo on hood, white "1" on nose, white int., smoked window, alw-5sp	$3

Photo	No.	Name	Description	Price
☐ 📷	728	'63 Corvette	met. blue w/white sides & large HW logo, chrome 2-rivet Malaysia base, red "1" on rear fender, dark red stripe below white on rear fender, white "Goodyear" above logo on door, yellow "Hot Wheels" & large white "1" on roof, large logo & small "1" on hood, white int., tinted window, asw-5sp	$8

Race Team Series IV, '67 Camaro

Race Team Series IV, Shelby Cobra 427 S/C

Race Team Series IV, Mercedes C-Class

Race Team Series IV, '63 Corvette

Artistic License Series

When they named this series "Artistic License Series," they really meant it. They used artistic license on most of these cars.

Photo	No.	Name	Description	Price
☐ 📷	729	Alien	a. white enamel & white plastic, metal Thailand base, black, yellow & red tampos on side & front, thin yellow "Alien" in black box on side, thin white "Alien" in red box on front, black HW logo in front of rear wheel, white int., tinted canopy, 3sp	$8
☐			b. white pearl & white plastic, metal Thailand base, black, yellow & red tampos on side & front, thick yellow "Alien" in black box on side, thin white "Alien" in red box on front, black HW logo in front of rear wheel, white int., tinted canopy, 3sp	$3
☐ 📷	730	'57 Chevy	a. gray plastic body w/chrome engine through hood, metal Malaysia base, orange, black, red & white girl tampo on sides, white dotted stripe on roof & trunk, black & white HW logo on rear fender, dark smoked window, t/b	$3
☐			b. same as (a), t/b wheels put on backwards, large in front, small in rear (It's more of an error, but there are enough of these out there to mention.)	$10
☐			c. same as (a), asw-t/b	$20
☐	731	VW Bug	a. white pearl, metal Malaysia base, red, dark blue, light green & black tampos on roof & sides, red & white HW logo on rear of roof, black int., blue-tint window, 5dot	$4
☐ 📷			b. same as (a), asw-5dot	$15
☐			c. same as (a), tampos on roof only, 5dot	$10
☐	732	1970 Barracuda	a. black enamel, chrome Maylasia base, white tampos on hood & sides, orange & blue over white twist on trunk, orange & blue twist w/orange HW logo on door, day-glo dark orange int. & hood scoop, smoked window, asw-3sp	$3
☐			b. same as (a), tampo colors reversed on door, blue & orange twist w/blue HW logo on door, asw-3sp	$3
☐ 📷			c. black enamel, chrome China base, white tampos on hood & sides, orange & blue over white twist on trunk, orange & blue twist w/orange HW logo on door, day-glo light orange int. & hood scoop, smoked window, asw-5sp	$3
☐ 📷			d. same as (c), tampo colors reversed on door, asw-5sp	$3

Artistic License Series, Alien

Artistic License Series, '57 Chevy

Artistic License Series, VW Bug

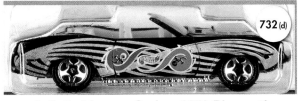

Artistic License Series, 1970 Plymouth Barracuda

Artistic License Series, 1970 Plymouth Barracuda

Mixed Signals Series

Photo	No.	Name	Description	Price
☐ 📷	733	Street Roader	white pearl w/yellow, red & black street sign tampos on sides, yellow int. & spacer between body & metal Malaysia base, black logo above rear wheel, smoked window, alw-ct/b	$2
☐ 📷	734	'80s Corvette	met. green, metal Malaysia base, black, white & yellow road sign tampos on sides, black int., smoked window w/black top, black HW logo above rear wheel, asw-bbs	$2
☐ 📷	735	Nissan Truck	pearl orange met., black plastic Malaysia base, yellow, red, black & white road sign tampos on sides, black int. & roll bar, clear window, chrome engine, white HW logo above rear wheel, alw-ct/b	$2
☐ 📷	736	School Bus	a. yellow enamel, black plastic Malaysia base, black, red, white & green road sign tampos on sides, black int., clear window, black HW logo on rear door, asw-5dot	$3
☐			b. same as (a), black HW logo on side behind rear wheel, asw-5dot	$3
☐			c. same as (a), black logo on side behind rear wheel, rear door outline missing, asw-5dot	$3
☐			d. yellow enamel, black plastic Thailand base, black, red, white & green road sign tampos on sides, black int., clear window, larger black HW logo on rear door, asw-5dot	$3
☐			e. same as (d), black HW logo on rear door, asw-5dot	$3

Mixed Signals Series, Street Roader

Mixed Signals Series, Nissan Truck

Mixed Signals Series, '80s Corvette

Mixed Signals Series, School Bus

Flyin' Aces Series

	Photo	No.	Name	Description	Price
❑	📷	737	1970 Dodge Daytona Charger	a. met. green, tan Malaysia base, w/white stripes on hood, red stripe on nose & top of rear wing, white, gold, black & red tampos on sides, red & black over white HW logo on rear fender, black int., clear window, asw-5dot	$3
❑				b. same as (a), asw-5sp	$4
❑	📷	738	Dogfighter	a. black enamel w/white, gold, red & yellow tampos on tail, yellow plastic Malaysia base & prop, chrome seat, engine & suspension, dark red HW logo on tail, 5dot	$3
❑				b. same as (a), 5sp	$4
❑				c. same as (a), 3sp	$3
❑		739	Sol-Aire CX4	a. yellow enamel, black plastic Malaysia base, black, red & white tampos on nose & rear wing, black & gray stripes w/red & white HW logo on side, red, white, gold & black tampos on side, black int., clear window, 5sp	$3
❑	📷			b. same as (a), black & white stripes w/red & white HW logo on side, 3sp	$4
❑	📷			c. same as (a), black & gray stripes, 3sp	$3
❑	📷			d. yellow enamel, black plastic Malaysia base, black, red & white tampos on nose & rear wing, black & white stripes w/red & white logo on side, red, white, gold & black tampos on side, black int., clear window, 5dot	$30
❑	📷	740	XT-3	met. gray w/red, black, green & white tampos, orange painted metal Malaysia base, black canopy & nose, blue-tint metal engine, red & white logo in front of engine on top of side pod, 5sp	$2

Flyin' Aces Series, 1970 Dodge Charger Daytona

Flyin' Aces Series, Sol-Aire CX4

Flyin' Aces Series, Dogfighter

Flyin' Aces Series, Sol-Aire CX4

Flyin' Aces Series, Sol-Aire CX4

Flyin' Aces Series, XT-3

Sugar Rush Series

	Photo	No.	Name	Description	Price
❑	📷	741	Mazda MX-5 Miata	a. orange enamel w/matching orange painted Thailand base, yellow & black "Reese's" tampo on hood, trunk & sides, yellow & black HW logo on rear fender, bright yellow headlights & gas cap, black int., smoked window, asw-5sp	$5
❑				b. same as (a), mustard yellow headlights & gas cap, 5sp	$3
❑	📷	742	Funny Car	white enamel w/brown sides & gray "Hershey's" tampo, metal Malaysia base, small white "Milk Chocolate" & gray HW logo behind rear wheel, brown stripe w/brown "Milk Chocolate" twice on hood, black window, 5sp	$5

Photo	No.	Name	Description	Price
☐ 📷	743	'95 Camaro	dark met. blue, black plastic Malaysia base, white stripe on side & hood w/red "Crunch," white "Nestles" on hood, trunk & side, white "Milk Chocolate with Crisped Rice" on door & rear spoiler, red & white logo on front fender behind wheel, black int., clear window, alw-5sp	$4
☐ 📷	744	'96 Mustang Convertible	yellow enamel, metal China base, dark blue stripe on hood & rear spoiler, dark blue, yellow & white "Butterfinger" tampo on sides, dark blue logo behind rear wheel, black int., clear window, asw-5sp	$5

Sugar Rush Series, Mazda MX-5 Miata

Sugar Rush Series, '95 Camaro

Sugar Rush Series, Funny Car

Sugar Rush Series, '96 Mustang Convertible

Tech Tones Series

Photo	No.	Name	Description	Price
☐ 📷	745	Buick Wildcat	a. black enamel w/green met. inlay, light green plastic Malaysia base, with "93 Warner" silver painted window, chrome engine, white HW logo on rear, alw-3sp	$5
☐			b. same as (a), no "93 Warner" on base	$3
☐ 📷	746	Silhouette II	a. black enamel, purple plastic Malaysia base, magenta met. inlay, white int., clear canopy, pink chrome engine, white HW logo on rear canopy, 5dot	$5
☐			b. same as (a), black logo on rear canopy, 5dot	$3
☐ 📷	747	Speed Machine	black enamel w/met. gold inlay, metal Malaysia base, gold int., clear canopy, white HW logo on rear, t/b	$3
☐ 📷	748	Avus Quattro	black enamel w/dark red met. inlay, dark red plastic Malaysia base, white int., clear canopy w/red & black tampos, red HW logo on rear of canopy, alw-gbbs	$3

Tech Tones Series, Buick Wildcat

Tech Tones Series, Speed Machine

Tech Tones Series, Silhouette II

Tech Tones Series, Avus Quattro

1998 Treasure Hunt Series

Photo	No.	Name	Description	Price
☐ 📷	749	#1-Twang Thang	black enamel w/blue chrome guitars, black plastic Malaysia base, chrome engine, exhaust & int., clear window, pearl blue "Treasure Hunt '98" & HW logo on nose, 5sp	$15
☐ 📷	750	#2-Scorchin' Scooter	met. red, metal Malaysia engine, yellow & black tampo on sides, yellow & black HW logo on front fender by axle, black forks, chrome rim w/black spokes	$40
☐	751	#3-Kenworth T600A	a. dark candy purple, chrome Malaysia base, silver, orange & purple tampo w/silver HW logo on side of sleeper, black window, alw-3sp	$25
☐ 📷			b. same as (a), undipped chrome Malaysia base, alw-3sp	$35
☐ 📷	752	#4-3-Window '34	orange enamel, metal Malaysia base, yellow orange & red tampo on sides, orange plastic fenders, black running boards & int., yellow & orange HW logo in front of rear window, clear window, chrome engine & grille, 5dot	$35
☐ 📷	753	#5-Turbo Flame	chrome body, black painted Malaysia base, green, yellow & black side tampo, yellow & black HW logo behind front wheel, black engine, green-tint canopy & rear, chrome int., 5sp	$15
☐ 📷	754	#6-Saltflat Racer	black plastic body, gold painted Thailand base, gold chrome engine, front drive, int. & roll bar, red & black tampo on front fender, red-tint window, red & white HW logo on front fender, 5sp	$15
☐ 📷	755	#7-Street Beast	red enamel & white plastic, metal Malaysia base, black & gold tampos, white int, red-tint window, black HW logo on rear fender, asw-gbbs	$15
☐ 📷	756	#8-Road Rocket	chrome body w/clear top, metal Malaysia base, black "TH-" & red "98" on side, black & red HW logo on clear rear wing, black roll bar & engine, 3sp	$15
☐ 📷	757	#9-Sol-Aire CX4	white pearl w/flag tampo on sides, blue w/white stars on nose, flag tampo on top of rear engine cover, blue plastic Malaysia base & int., clear canopy, blue HW logo behind rear wheel, wbbs	$15

1998 Treasure Hunt Series, #1-Twang Thang

1998 Treasure Hunt Series, #2-Scorchin' Scooter

1998 Treasure Hunt Series, #3- Kenworth T600A

1998 Treasure Hunt Series, #4-3-Window '34

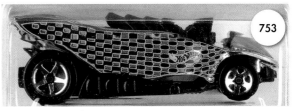
1998 Treasure Hunt Series, #5-Turbo Flame

1998 Treasure Hunt Series, #6-Saltflat Racer

1998 Treasure Hunt Series, #7-Street Beast

	Photo	No.	Name	Description	Price
❑	📷	758	#10-'57 Chevy	met. green metal body & metal engine through hood, gold-tint chrome Thailand base, gold, black & silver tampo on sides, white & silver logo in front of rear wheel, yellow-tint window & int., 3sp	$35
❑	📷	759	#11-Stingray III	silver pearl, black plastic Malaysia base, w/black stripes & Corvette logo on hood, black & white tampo on sides, black & white HW logo on door, red int., smoked window, 3sp	$25
❑	📷	760	#12-Way 2 Fast	olive flake, metal Thailand base, orange stripes & white circle w/gold & orange "1" on roof, orange stripe & white circle w/gold & orange "1" on side, gold "Treasure Hunt 98" on roof twice & once on side, white "Treasure Hunt Special" behind rear wheel, orange HW logo in front of rear wheel, chrome int. & engine, gold plastic radiator shell, 5sp	$20

1998 Treasure Hunt Series, #8-Road Rocket

1998 Treasure Hunt Series, #11-Stingray III

1998 Treasure Hunt Series, #9-Sol-Aire CX4

1998 Treasure Hunt Series, #12-Way 2 Fast

1998 Treasure Hunt Series, #10-'57 Chevy

Non-Series Collector Number Packs

	Photo	No.	Name	Description	Price
❑	📷	761	Flame Stopper	red enamel, black plastic Malaysia base, white stripe below doors w/gold & black "Fire Dept" & "City of Hot Wheel's" logo, gold & black "31" behind black rear window, white HW logo behind rear wheel, gray plastic boom w/part number on side, alw-ct/b	$2
❑	📷	765	Oshkosh P-Series	a. light met. blue metal nose & fenders, blue-tint metal Malaysia base, white plastic cab & box, gray plastic plow blade, met. blue seats, white HW logo on hood, alw-ct/b	$4
❑				b. same as (a), dark met. blue, alw-ct/b	$4
❑	📷	767	Mercedes 380 SEL	white pearl w/met. gold painted metal Malaysia base, tan int., red HW logo in rear clear window, gold chrome grille & headlights, asw-t/b	$2
❑	📷	768	Lamborghini Countach	black enamel, black plastic Malaysia base, red int., clear window, gold HW logo in front window, asw-5dot	$2
		769	unreleased		——
❑	📷	770	Lexus SC400	a. met. blue, black plastic Malaysia base, white int., smoked window, white HW logo on rear plate, asw-bbs	$5
❑				b. met. purple, black plastic Malaysia base, white int., smoked window, white HW logo on rear plate, asw-bbs	$3
❑	📷			c. same as (b), clear window, asw-bbs	$15
❑	📷			d. same as (b), dark met. purple, asw-bbs	$3
❑		771	'56 Flashsider	a. yellow pearl, chrome Malaysia base, pink & blue side tampo, black window, pink HW logo on rear fender, 5dot	$3

761

Flame Stopper

765 (a)

Oshkosh P-Series

767

Mercedes 380 SEL

768

Lamborghini Countach

770 (a)

Lexus SC400

	Photo	No.	Name	Description	Price
❏	📷	771	'56 Flashsider	b. same as (a), asw-5dot	$15
❏	📷	773	Hot Wheels 500	day-glo yellow, blue-tint metal Malaysia base, black, white & orange tampos on side pod, side of front wing, nose & rear deck, black plastic driver, yellow letter b/7sp	$3
❏	📷	774	Ramp Truck	dark met. green w/large HW logo on roof, metal China base, met. gray plastic ramp w/yellow, blue & red tampo on side, smoked window, asw-5sp	$3
❏	📷	778	Speed Blaster	a. met. blue, black plastic Malaysia base, red & white side tampo, white HW logo & "C778" in front of rear wheel, chrome window & engine, 3sp	$4
❏	📷			b. same as (a), met. purple, 3sp	$7
❏	📷			c. same as (a), dark burgundy, 3sp	$3
❏		779	Big Chill	a. blue enamel w/white flames on sides, HW logo on front between chrome driver & white skis, white plastic Thailand base w/black front wheel	$8
❏	📷			b. same as (a), white plastic China base w/white front wheel	$3
❏		780	'58 Corvette	a. aqua enamel w/chrome engine through hood, aqua plastic Malaysia base, silver painted headlights, smoked window, chrome int., exhaust, bumpers & grille, white box w/red & white HW logo on trunk, 5dot	$6
❏	📷			b. same as (a), asw-5dot	$15
❏	📷			c. same as (a), flat hood & met. silver painted engine, 5dot	$5
❏				d. aqua enamel w/hood, aqua plastic Malaysia base, silver painted headlights, silver met. painted engine, smoked window, chrome int., exhaust, bumpers & grille, rear bumper has much smaller license plate, white box w/red & white logo on trunk, 5dot	$8
❏	📷	781	Lamborghini Diablo	a. met. red, black painted Malaysia base, tan int., tinted window, red met. plastic rear wing & bumper, gold HW logo on windshield, asw-5sp	$3
❏				b. same as (a), 5dot	$3
❏	📷	782	Radar Ranger	met. gold w/black & white tampos, blue-tint metal Malaysia base, chrome radar dish, black logo on front right, black insert & seat, clear canopy, alw-ct/b	$3
❏	📷	783	Twin Mill II	silver pearl w/magenta & black side tampo, black plastic Malaysia base, chrome engines, black window, magenta HW logo in front of rear wheel, alw-bbs	$3
❏		784	Ferrari Testarossa	(red car on card) a. met. silver w/yellow & black Ferrari logo on hood, black painted Malaysia base, black int., clear window, black logo on rear plate, 5dot	$5

770 (c)

Lexus SC400

770 (d)

Lexus SC400

771 (b)

'56 Flashsider

773

Hot Wheels 500

774

Ramp Truck

778 (a)

Speed Blaster

778 (b)

Speed Blaster

778 (c)

Speed Blaster

779 (b)

Big Chill

780 (b)

'58 Corvette

780 (c)

'58 Corvette

781 (a)

Lamborghini Diablo

782

Radar Ranger

783

Twin Mill II

Photo		No.	Name	Description	Price
❑	📷	784	Ferrari Testarossa	b. same as (a), 5sp	$5
❑	📷		Ferrari F512M (name change/blue car on card)	c. same as (a), 5dot	$3
❑				d. same as (c), 5sp	$3
❑	📷	787	'57 Chevy	met. purple metal body w/blue-tint metal engine through hood, chrome Thailand base, black & red side tampo w/red "'57" & white "Chevy," black int., smoked window, white HW logo on rear fender, t/b	$4
❑	📷	788	Mercedes 540K	a. met. purple, metal Malaysia base, light blue stripe on side, light blue HW logo on door, light blue plastic top, black int., clear window, asw-bbs	$4
❑	📷			b. same as (a), alw-bbs	$7
❑				c. same as (a), 3sp	$3
❑	📷	791	Treadator	a. met. blue w/white scoops & nose, black plastic Thailand base & treads, chrome canopy, engine & fenders, white HW logo on front left wing	$3
❑				b. same as (a), undipped chrome canopy, engine & fenders	$5

Ferrari Testarossa

Ferrari Testarossa

'57 Chevy

Mercedes 540K

Mercedes 540K

Treadator

Camaro Race Car

Auburn 852

Tractor

'96 Camaro Convertible

Dodge Ram 1500

Propper Chopper

Flashfire

'40s Woodie

Driven to the Max

Photo	No.	Name	Description	Price
☐ 📷	792	Camaro Race Car	white pearl w/orange squares on sides and black plastic Malaysia base, black outlined "4" & "Bousquette Racing," black square w/orange outlined "4" on roof, black w/white "Bousquette Racing" twice on hood, white & orange HW logo on rear fender, black int., clear window, alw-5sp	$3
☐ 📷	793	Auburn 852	black enamel w/met. gold plastic fenders & int., metal Malaysia base, gold tampo on hood & behind seat, gold HW logo on rear deck, gold chrome headlights, grille & windshield frame w/tinted window, asw-gbbs	$6
☐ 📷	795	Tractor	candy silver, black plastic Malaysia base, black plastic cab & hydraulics, black HW logo on nose, c/tt rear-ct/b frt	$3
☐ 📷	796	'96 Camaro Convertible	white enamel, gray plastic India base, orange stripes on sides, hood & trunk, orange int., smoked window, white & orange HW logo on rear fender above rear tire, alw-w5sp	$3
☐	797	Dodge Ram 1500	a. red enamel w/red plastic rear cap, white plastic Maylaysia base, white tampos on front & rear fenders w/"Dodge Ram X-Tra" between, light yellow plastic bumpers, int. & spacer between body and smoked window, alw-5dot	$4
☐ 📷			b. red enamel w/red plastic rear cap, white plastic China base, white tampos on front & rear fenders w/"Dodge Ram X-Tra" between, yellow plastic bumpers, int. & spacer between body and tinted window, alw-5sp	$3
☐ 📷	798	Propper Chopper	blue enamel w/gold, black, blue & white POLICE tampos, black plastic tail, rotors, hook, int. & China base, blue-tint window gold & white HW logo on side rear by tail	$3
☐	802	Flashfire	a. met. gold, light gold Thailand base, pink, green & yellow side tampos, gold chrome engine, black rear spoiler, side panel, exhaust & int., smoked canopy, no HW logo, 5dot	$5
☐			b. same as (a), green HW logo on rear deck, 5dot	$3
☐ 📷			c. same as (b), alw-5dot	$10
☐ 📷	803	'40s Woodie	white pearl hood & fenders, black & gold pinstripes on side of hood, metal Malaysia base, chrome engine through hood, tan wood grain plastic body, white enamel roof w/orange, black & gold pinstripes, orange & white logo on front of roof, smoked window, black int., 5sp	$8
☐ 📷	808	Driven to the Max	white pearl w/magenta & dark blue tampos, blue-tint metal engine & Thailand base, magenta & dark blue HW logo on side, white "Hot Set-up" on side, hot pink plastic driver & spoiler, 5sp	$3

Photo		No.	Name	Description	Price
❑	📷	812	GM Lean Machine	met. green & met. gold plastic body, metal Malaysia base, gold seat, smoked canopy w/white logo, t/b	$3
❑	📷	813	Ferrari 355	a. black enamel, metal Malaysia base, yellow & black Ferrari logo on hood & door, yellow int., yellow-tint window, white HW logo on rear fender, asw-3sp	$90
❑				b. same as (a), asw-5sp	$4
❑		814	Speed-A-Saurus	a. glossy teal plastic dinosaur, orange painted Malaysia base, gold-tint chrome engine & exhaust, magenta HW logo on left rear tail, large rear 5sp	$3
❑	📷			b. same as (a), dull teal plastic dinosaur, large rear 5sp	$4
❑	📷			c. same as (a), med. rear 5sp	$7
❑	📷	815	Mercedes 500 SL	met. green, black plastic Thailand base, red, gold & black stripes on hood & sides, tan int., smoked window, gold chrome headlights & grille, gold HW logo on front fender behind wheel, alw-3sp	$3
❑	📷	816	Ferrari 308	a. met. bronze w/yellow & black Ferrari logo on hood, black painted metal Malaysia base, yellow HW logo on rear plate, tan int., smoked window, 5dot	$3
❑				b. same as (a), met. brown, 5dot	$4

GM Lean Machine

Mercedes 500 SL

Ferrari 355

Ferrari 308

Speed-A-Saurus

Ferrari 308

Ferrari 308

Speed-A-Saurus

Porsche 928

Photo	No.	Name	Description	Price
☐	816	Ferrari 308	c. same as (a), met. bronze, 5sp	$3
☐ 📷			d. same as (b), met. brown, 5sp	$5
☐			e. same as (d), met. brown, black int., 5sp	$20
☐ 📷			f. red enamel w/yellow & black Ferrari logo on hood, red painted metal Malaysia base, yellow HW logo on rear plate, black int., smoked window, 5sp	$3
☐			g. same as (f), tan int., 5sp	$25
☐ 📷	817	Porsche 928	white pearl, metal Malaysia base, red HW logo on nose, black window, bbs	$3
☐ 📷	818	Porsche Carrera	a. met. red, metal Malaysia base, tan int., smoked window, yellow logo on rear fender, g5sp	$3
☐			b. met. red w/flames, metal Malaysia base, tan int., smoked window, yellow logo on rear fender, g5sp (This is a Candian release car that got out in a US package.)	$20
☐ 📷	820	Zender Fact 4	green flake w/gold & black tampos on hood & sides, black plastic China base, gold HW logo on clear windshield, black int., bbs	$3
☐ 📷	821	'96 Mustang Convertible	white enamel, metal China base (same as #715), thin black stripe w/yellow & orange tampos trimmed in black on sides, yellow logo in tampo behind front wheel, silver painted headlights, red int., clear window, asw-5sp	$4
☐ 📷	822	Camaro Z28	met. teal, metal no origin base, gray int., clear window, yellow HW logo behind rear wheel, 3sp	$5
☐ 📷	823	Sol-Aire CX4	met. blue, white plastic Malaysia base, white sides w/large HW logo & red "1," large HW logo & red bow tie on nose, white "1" on top of right front fender, yellow "Hot Wheels" on rear wing, yellow "Goodyear" behind rear wheel, white int., clear window, gbbs	$4
☐ 📷	827	Radio Flyer Wagon	a. red enamel, metal Malaysia base, white "Radio Flyer" side tampo, white HW logo on rear, chrome motor, black seat & handle, 5sp	$5
☐			b. red enamel, metal China base, white "Radio Flyer" side tampo, smaller white HW logo on rear, chrome motor, black seat & handle, 5sp	$4
☐			c. same as (b), metal Thailand base, 5sp	$6

818 (a)

Porsche Carrera

820

Zender Fact 4

821

'96 Mustang Convertible

822

Camaro Z28

823

Sol-Aire CX4

827 (a)

Radio Flyer Wagon

Porsche Carrera

Baja Bug

Ferrari Testarossa

Baja Bug

Radio Flyer Wagon

Baja Bug

Rail Rodder

Photo	No.	Name	Description	Price
❏ 📷	829	Porsche Carrera	met. silver, metal Malaysia base, red HW logo behind front wheel, red int., clear window, t/b	$3
❏ 📷	834	Ferrari Testarossa	a. black enamel, gloss black painted India base, yellow "Ferrari" w/yellow & black Ferrari logo on hood, tan & black int., clear window, yellow HW logo on rear deck, bw	$3
❏			b. same as (a), semi-gloss black painted India base, bw	$5
❏ 📷	835	Baja Bug	a. dark met. blue, metal India base, large HW logo on sides & white "Nithia" on door, white int., all medium bw	$5
❏ 📷			b. same as (a), met. blue, all medium bw	$5
❏ 📷			c. red enamel, metal India base, black & mustard tampos on side w/"Dakar RALLY 1," tan int., large rear bw	$12
❏			d. same as (c), all medium bw	$15
❏ 📷	837	Radio Flyer Wagon	met. blue w/white "Radio Flyer" side tampo, metal China base, smaller white HW logo on rear, chrome motor, white seat & handle, 5sp	$4

Photo	No.	Name	Description	Price
☐ 📷	850	Rail Rodder	a. gray plastic body, metal Malaysia base, gold-tint chrome engines & drivers, yellow & black side tampos w/green fade "Rail Rodder," black HW logo & "Engine 5" on cab side, b5sp	$3
☐			b. same as (a), metal China base	
☐ 📷	851	Treadator	a. light blue pearl w/white plastic scoops & nose, light day-glo green plastic Thailand base & treads, silver & black tampo on tail, silver HW logo on side by scoop, chrome canopy, engine, exhaust & fenders	$5
☐ 📷			b. same as (a), light purple pearl	$3
☐			c. same as (b), light purple pearl, undipped chrome canopy, engine, exhaust & fenders	$7
☐ 📷			d. same as (a), purple pearl tampo	$6
☐ 📷	852	Rigor Motor	a. candy purple met., metal Malaysia base, gold "Rigor Motors Racing" on side, gold-tint engine, fuel tank & seat, yellow-tint canopy, white plastic skulls & radiator, all medium g5sp	$7
☐ 📷			b. same as (a), large rear g5sp	$3
☐			c. same as (a), large rear g3sp	$34
☐			d. same as (a), metal China base, large rear g5sp	$4
☐			e. same as (a), metal Thailand base, large rear g5sp	$5
☐	853	Camaro Z28	a. day-glo yellow plastic body, metal Malaysia base, blue, red, white & black side tampo, large black & white "4" on side w/red & white HW logo behind front wheel, black window, 5dot	$5
☐			b. same as (a), black painted metal Malaysia base, 5dot	$3
☐ 📷			c. same as (b), 5sp	$10

Treadator

Rigor Motor

Treadator

Rigor Motor

Camaro Z28

Treadator

Porsche 959

Porsche 959

Ferrari F50

Porsche 930

T-Bird Stocker

Hummer

Hummer

Bronco

	Photo	No.	Name	Description	Price
❑	📷	854	Porsche 959	a. white enamel, metal Malaysia base, pink & black tampo on door & front fender w/large black "2," black "High Bank Racing" & red HW logo on rear fender, black int., smoked window, asw-t/b	$5
❑	📷			b. same as (a), orange & black tampo on door & front fender, asw-t/b	$3
❑				c. same as (b), asw-3sp	$7
❑				d. white enamel, metal China base, pink & black tampo on door & front fender w/large black "2," black "High Bank Racing" & red HW logo on rear fender, black int., smoked window, asw-bbs	$3
❑	📷	855	Ferrari F50	purple pearl w/silver, red & black side tampo, black plastic Malaysia base, silver HW logo on rear fender by spoiler, smoked window, black int., asw-t/b	$3
❑	📷	856	Porsche 930	a. met. red, metal Thailand base, orange, white & black tampo on side, white HW logo behind rear wheel, black int., smoked window, asw-3sp	$4
❑				b. same as (a), metal Malaysia base, asw-3sp	$3
❑	📷	857	T-Bird Stocker	orange plastic body w/magenta, silver, black & white side tampo, black HW logo behind front wheel, black painted Thailand metal base, black window, 5dot	$3
❑	📷	858	Hummer	a. white plastic body, black painted Malaysia base, black zebra stripes & orange "Hummer Racer," yellow "Jungle" w/orange outline, red-tinted window, black HW logo on rear, asw-ct/b	$6
❑	📷			b. same as (a), yellow "Jungle" w/red outline & red "Hummer Racer"	$3
❑	📷	859	Bronco	red enamel w/white plastic bed cap, blue-tint metal Thailand base, black plastic motorcycle on rear, black & white side tampo, white HW logo above tampo on door, black int., smoked window, asw-ct/b	$5
❑	📷	860	Road Rocket	white plastic w/dark blue top, metal Thailand base, light green & silver tampo on side w/silver logo, 3sp	$3
❑	📷	861	Twin Mill II	met. gold, black plastic Malaysia base, magenta & black side tampo, chrome engines, black window, magenta HW logo in front of rear wheel, large bbs rear, small bbs front	$3

	Photo	No.	Name	Description	Price
❑	📷	862	Pontiac Salsa	met. red, chrome Malaysia base, yellow & blue side tampo, dark blue HW logo on side above tampo, black int., black window, alw-5dot	$3
❑	📷	863	Oshkosh Cement Mixer	day-glo yellow plastic body, black plastic Malaysia base, silver painted metal fenders, black plastic barrel w/yellow, green & black tampos, asw-3sp	$4
❑	📷	864	Tank Truck	a. very dark met. burgundy (looks black), black plastic Malaysia base, white, orange & blue tampo on cab side, chrome tank w/red & blue stripes & chrome lettering, chrome outline logo in red stripe by exhaust stack, chrome window, headlights & grille, asw-5dot	$5
❑	📷			b. same as (a), met. burgundy, asw-5dot	$3
❑	📷	865	Ford F-150	white enamel, black plastic Malaysia base, orange side tampo w/large orange "M," small black "M" & logo on rear fender, small black "M" in orange dot behind front wheel, chrome bumpers, bed & int., smoked window, alw-3sp	$3
❑	📷	866	Ferrari 250	a. met. gold, black plastic Thailand base, black circle w/white "16" on door & black "Classic Racer," yellow & black Ferrari logo on nose, black HW logo in middle of rear fender behind wheel, chrome grille & side pipes, black int., smoked window, bbs	$4
❑				b. same as (a), black plastic Malaysia base, bbs	$3
❑		867	'97 Corvette	a. met. blue w/red, white, silver & black side tampos, red HW logo middle of door above tampo, red tampo, white bowtie & silver lettering on hood, silver & white box w/black "1" on door & hood, white int., tinted window, red plastic Thailand base, alw-5sp	$4
❑	📷			b. same as (a), met. dark blue, alw-5sp	$3
❑		868	Range Rover	a. met. green, chrome Thailand base, red w/white outline & blue tampos, misc. decals on side w/white HW logo on door, gold Land Rover logo on door & hood, tan int., smoked window, asw-ct/b	$4

Road Rocket — 860

Tank Truck — 864 (a)

Twin Mill II — 861

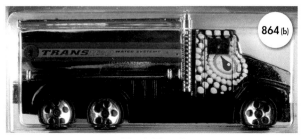

Tank Truck — 864 (b)

Pontiac Salsa — 862

Ford F-150 — 865

Oshkosh Cement Mixer — 863

Ferrari 250 — 866 (a)

'97 Corvette

Olds 442

Range Rover

Rig Wrecker

Power Pipes

Hydroplane

Chevy Stocker

Pit Crew Truck

Photo	No.	Name	Description	Price
❑ 📷	868	Range Rover	b. same as (a), met. dark green, asw-ct/b	$3
❑ 📷	869	Power Pipes	black plastic body, orange painted Thailand base, brown & yellow side tampo, white HW logo behind front wheel, gold-tint chrome scoops & int., orange-tint canopy, ot/b	$3
❑ 📷	870	Chevy Stocker	purple plastic body, black painted Malaysia metal base, orange, gray & white side tampo, two skulls on front fender, one skull on rear fender, gray logo on right upper side of door, black window, gt/b	$3
❑ 📷	871	Olds 442	met. blue, chrome Thailand base, white sides & large HW logo & misc. racing decals, white "1" on rear fender above wheel, white "Richard" on door above logo, white int., smoked window, asw-5sp	$4
❑	872	Rig Wrecker	a. white enamel, black plastic Thailand base, black diamond tampo on side, red & blue tampo on door, red "1" w/black outline on side w/black "Pit Crew" and black "Tow Rig" w/red outline, red & yellow HW logo on side by fuel tank, red plastic boom, chrome int., grille & exhaust stacks, smoked window, asw-5dot	$5
❑ 📷			b. same as (a), asw-t/b	$6
❑ 📷	873	Hydroplane	white enamel, black plastic Malaysia base, red & black "Harbor Patrol" on pontoons, red tampo w/"City of Hot Wheels" logo on pontoons, white numbers on left pontoon only, large dark blue HW logo on top of rear wing, chrome engine, black int., smoked canopy	$3
❑	874	Pit Crew Truck	a. candy gray, red plastic Thailand base & int., red, blue & white side tampos, gold HW logo behind rear wheel above blue stripe, blue-tint window, asw-5dot	$3
❑ 📷			b. same as (a), asw-t/b	$7

Police Car

'95 Camaro

Bywayman

Gulch Stepper

Chevy 1500

Mercedes 380 SEL

	Photo	No.	Name	Description	Price
❑	📷	875	Police Car	black enamel, black plastic Thailand base, white roof w/black "01" & red lights, white "State Police" & stripe on side w/"City of Hot Wheels" logo on door, red & white HW logo behind front fender, gray int., tinted window, asw-5sp	$5
❑	📷	876	Bywayman	a. red enamel, metal Thailand base, silver, black & gold side tampos, silver HW logo behind rear wheel, white int., roll bar & bed, tinted window, asw-ct/b	$3
❑				b. same as (a), blue-tint metal Thailand base, asw-ct/b	$4
❑	📷	877	Chevy 1500	gray plastic body, black painted metal India base, red, yellow, black & white side tampos, white "Powercharger," black "Racing" on rear fender, white HW logo behind rear wheel, black int. & bed cover, clear window, asw-t/b	$3
❑		881	'95 Camaro	a. black enamel w/red, yellow & white side tampo, white "Buckle Up & Hold On" tampo on rear fender, red HW logo behind rear wheel, red int., smoked window, black plastic India base, alw-3sp	$3
❑	📷			b. same as (a), alw-5sp	$15
❑	📷	884	Gulch Stepper	yellow pearl, blue-tint metal Thailand base, magenta side tampo w/black & white "Gulch Stepper" & cactus, black window & spacer between body & base, white HW logo on rear fender, alw-ct/b	$3
❑	📷	889	Mercedes 380 SEL	black enamel, met. gold painted metal Malaysia base, gold chrome grille & headlights, thin gold stripe on side w/"Custom 380 SL" on rear fender, gold HW logo behind rear wheel on fender, tan int., tinted window, asw-gbbs	$3
❑	📷	890	BMW M Roadster	a. white enamel, metal Malaysia base, two wide black stripes on hood & trunk, black on side w/white outline "Roadster" & red "Nicholas Leasing," black HW logo behind rear wheel, red int. smoked window, asw-3sp	$3
❑				b. same as (a), metal Thailand base	$4
❑	📷	894	Toyota MR2	white enamel, black plastic Thailand base, red & gray on side w/large black "TOYOTA" & misc. racing decals, red tampo on roof w/black "TOYOTA" twice and "Saferoil" over red "36," red & gray tampo on hood w/black "TOYOTA," "Chosen Performance" & "4t" tampo, black logo behind rear wheel, light gray int., smoked window, asw-bbs	$3

Photo		No.	Name	Description	Price
☐	📷	899	'56 Flashsider	a. silver pearl, chrome Thailand base, large dark red HW logo on side, small dark blue flames on both fenders, dark blue"Adrian" & red "My other Hot Wheels is a car" on door, red & blue stripe on bottom of cab, red & blue # 42 on lower left corner of door, red "Hot Wheels" & dark blue "Fan" fender, black window, 5sp on rear	$7
☐	📷			b. same as (a), light red in color	$4
☐		908	Ford F Series CNG Pickup	a. met. purple, black plastic Malaysia base, light green, orange & yellow tampos on hood, roof & side, white HW logo high on rear fender by taillight, chrome int., bumpers & bed, smoked window, alw-3sp	$15
☐	📷			b. same as (a), alw-5sp	$3

BMW M Roadster

Toyota MR2

'56 Flashsider

'56 Flashsider

Ford F-Series, CNG Pickup

1999 Treasure Hunt Series

Photo		No.	Name	Description	Price
☐	📷	929	#1-Mercedes 540K	red enamel, metal Malaysia base, gold over black stripe on top of door, black panels w/gold pinstriping on hood & trunk, gold "TR" on trunk, chrome grille & headlights, black plastic top, clear window, asw-5sp	$25
☐	📷	930	#2-T-Bird Stocker	blue enamel, gray plastic Malaysia base, black & yellow side tampo w/white & red "12," white "T. HUNTER" on rear fender w/misc. racing decals on side, large white & red "12" on roof, black hood w/white "T. HUNTER" & misc. racing decals, yellow logo on rear fender, yellow int., clear window, asw-5sp	$10
☐	📷	931	#3-'97 Corvette	pearl lavender, black plastic Thailand base, red & white stripe over gold on hood & side, "Nineteen 98" in black on rocker panel, yellow int., smoked window, alw-5dot	$25
☐	📷	932	#4-Rigor Motor	day-glo yellow, black painted metal Malaysia base & exhaust, black, orange & silver flames on top behind chrome engine, white skulls, chrome fuel tank & int., yellow-tint canopy, black HW logo on rear, g5sp	$15
☐	📷	933	#5-Ferrari F512M	a. yellow enamel, metal Malaysia base, silver "Ferrari" on rear of engine cover, yellow & black rectangle "Ferrari" emblem on front, white & red "TH" emblem on rear plate, red & silver painted taillights, silver & black painted lights in front bumper, black int., clear window, chrome star wheel	$20
☐				b. same as (a), black painted metal Malaysia base, chrome star wheel	$85

	Photo	No.	Name	Description	Price
☐	📷	934	#6-'59 Impala	met. purple, gold-tint chrome Malaysia base, purple pearl, red, gold & black tampo on side & hood, "99 Treasure Hunt" in gold & black on door, gold HW logo on rear fender, white int., smoked window, asw-gbbs	$20
☐	📷	935	#7-Hot Wheels 500	black enamel, metal Malaysia base, large orange & white "1" w/"Treasure Hunt" logo & orange name on side, orange tampo on nose w/black & white "1," orange "Treasure Hunt ninety-nine" on front wing, red & white HW logo on rear wing, black plastic driver, orange letter "Treasure Hunt ninety-nine" with black 7sp wheels	$15
☐	📷	936	#8-Jaguar D-Type	met. black w/matching painted Malaysia base, red & gold stripe on side, gold, red & black over white "TH" on hood, gold plastic int. & side pipes, clear window, alw-5sp	$15
☐	📷	937	#9-'32 Ford Delivery	met. gold, purple plastic fenders, metal Malaysia base, clear window, black panels w/red pinstripe & yellow tampos on sides, white & red "T. HUNTER" on door, black panel on roof w/yellow pinstripe & red diamond pattern, black panels w/red pinstripe on hood & cowl, gold chrome headlights & grille, yellow HW logo on bottom right of door, g5sp	$15
☐	📷	938	#10-Hot Seat	clear plastic body, metal Malaysia base, black seat & plunger, black, white & red "TH" emblem below toilet paper roll on side, 5sp	$15
☐	📷	939	#11-Mustang Mach I	met. green, black plastic Malaysia base, black panel on side w/silver stripe outline, silver, black & gold "TH" tampo on rear fender behind wheel, silver "TH" and "Mustang" on black painted rocker panel, wide black stripe on roof & hood outlined w/thin & black stripe, silver painter hood stripes, black int., rear spoiler, hood scoop & rear window louvers, clear window, 5sp	$25
☐	📷	940	#12-Express Lane	purple plastic body, HW logo on side w/gold "Treasure Hunt," black plastic seat & butterfly steering wheel, metal Malaysia base, engine & pushbar, g5sp	$20

In 1999 there were several different paint variations. Not only different colors, but there were many light and dark variations of the same color. I have found that the first car releases are usually the light-colored ones. That's why it's important to try to get the cars when they first show up. You're bound to find something different after the car has been in production for awhile. For example, sometimes a car will change production countries. You might notice there is a slight color change along with the new country origin on the base. These are a few things that are good to look for when you buy a new car.

1999 First Editions, #2-'99 Mustang

1999 First Editions,
#6-Monte Carlo Concept Car

1999 First Editions, #2-'99 Mustang

1999 First Editions, #5-Olds Aurora GTS-1

1999 First Editions, #2-'99 Mustang

1999 First Editions, #5-Olds Aurora GTS-1

1999 First Editions

Photo	No.	Name	Description	Price
☐ 📷	649	#1-1936 Cord	a. met. dark red, chrome Malaysia base, casting still on top of window plastic inside, looks like a dome light, purple int., clear window, silver HW logo on bottom of front fender behind wheel, asw-bbs	$10
☐ 📷			b. same as (a), burgundy color, asw-bbs	$8
☐			c. same as (b), no casting peg on window, asw-bbs	$3
☐ 📷	909	#2-'99 Mustang	a. dark met. candy purple, black plastic Malaysia base, small Mustang logo on front fender by door, silver "MUSTANG" on rear bumper, silver HW logo on rear fender above tire, red int., clear window, asw-5sp	$31
☐			b. same as (a), lighter met. candy purple, red int., clear window, asw-5sp	$31
☐			c. same as (a), dark met. candy purple, tan int., asw-5sp	$10
☐			d. same as (c), lighter met. candy purple, tan int., asw-5sp	$10
☐ 📷			e. same as (c), asw-3sp	$4
☐			f. same as (d), asw-3sp	$4
☐ 📷			g. met. candy blue, black plastic Malaysia base, small Mustang logo on front fender by door, silver "MUSTANG" on rear bumper, silver HW logo on rear fender above tire, tan int., clear window, 5sp	$10
☐	656	#3-'38 Phantom Corsair	a. black enamel, metal Malaysia base, gray int., clear window, gray HW logo behind front wheel, asw-ww5sp	$15
☐			b. same as (a), silver HW logo behind front wheel, asw-ww5sp	$4
☐ 📷			c. same as (b), asw-5sp	$15

911 (c)

1999 First Editions, #5-Olds Aurora GTS-1

911 (d)

1999 First Editions, #5-Olds Aurora GTS-1

912 (c)

1999 First Editions, #10-Porsche 911 GT3 Cup

913 (a)

1999 First Editions, #13-Popcycle

913 (b)

1999 First Editions, #13-Popcycle

913 (d)

1999 First Editions, #13-Popcycle

914 (b)

1999 First Editions, #8-Semi-Fast

1999 First Editions, #8-Semi-Fast

1999 First Editions, #4-1970 Chevelle SS

1999 First Editions, #14-Phaeton

1999 First Editions, #12-Track T

1999 First Editions, #15-Screamin' Hauler

1999 First Editions, #15-Screamin' Hauler

	Photo	No.	Name	Description	Price
☐	📷	656	#3-'38 Phantom Corsair	d. met. blue, metal Malaysia base, black int., clear window, silver logo behind front wheel, asw-ww5sp	$8
☐				e. same as (d), dark met. blue, asw-ww5sp	$8
☐		915	#4-1970 Chevelle SS	a. met. blue, metal Malaysia base, wide white "SS" stripes on hood & trunk, white int., blue & white HW logo on trunk in stripe, blue-tint window, 5sp	$5
☐				b. dark met. blue, metal Malaysia base, wide white "SS" stripes on hood & trunk, white int., blue & white HW logo on trunk in stripe, blue-tint window, 5sp	$5
☐				c. dark met. blue, wide white "SS" stripes on hood & trunk, metal Malaysia base, pinstripe filled in on stripe on hood, white int., blue & white HW logo on trunk in stripe, blue-tint window, 5sp	$7
☐	📷			d. met. gold, metal Malaysia base, black "SS" stripes on hood & trunk, black int., gold HW logo on trunk in stripe, blue-tint window, 5sp	$10
☐	📷	911	#5-Olds Aurora GT3 (on card)	a. white enamel, black plastic Malaysia base, met. blue on trunk & side, red stripe below blue on rear fender & door, hood has dark blue "11," large HW logo outlined in pearl blue w/"Leading The Way" & Aurora logo, side has large HW logo coming off front wheel well, white "11" & misc. racing decals, black rear spoiler & int., clear window, asw-gbbs	$20
☐	📷		Olds Aurora GTS-1	b. same as (a), GTS-1 on card, asw-gbbs	$15
☐	📷		Olds Aurora GTS-1 (on card)	c. red enamel, black plastic Malaysia base, hood has red, white, black & pearl blue HW logo w/black & pearl blue "1," large black & pearl blue "1" on roof, side has large red, white, black & pearl blue HW logo, "Track System" logo on rear fender, black rear spoiler & int., clear window, asw-gbbs	$10

Photo	No.	Name	Description	Price
☐ 📷		Olds Aurora GT3 (on card)	d. mf. silver, black plastic Malaysia base, hood has red, white, black & pearl blue HW logo w/black & pearl blue "1," large black & pearl blue "1" on roof, side has large red, white, black & pearl blue HW logo, "Track System" logo on rear fender, black rear spoiler & int., Malaysia base, clear window, asw-gbbs	$8
☐		Olds Aurora GTS-1 (on card)	e. same as (d), GTS-1 on card, asw-gbbs	$3
☐	910	#6-Monte Carlo Concept Car	a. red enamel, silver met. painted Malaysia base, gray int., smoked window, black HW logo on rear fender, asw-5sp	$3
☐ 📷			b. met. red, silver met. painted Malaysia base, tan int., smoked window, black HW logo on rear fender, asw-5sp	$6
☐			c. same as (b), asw-3sp	$105
☐ 📷	675	#7-Pontiac Rageous	a. met. red, black plastic Malaysia base, gray int., smoked window with black painted roof, small silver "Rageous" on front door, silver HW logo on rear fender, alw-3sp	$3
☐			b. same as (a), nonpainted roof, alw-3sp	$5
☐	914	#8-Semi-Fast	a. red plastic, metal Malaysia base & lower grille, yellow & black stripes w/black circle & white "17" on cab & body, black vents on side w/black HW logo & "Jones" tampos behind front wheel, "Champion & Goodyear" tampos below stripe on cab, smoked window, gray engine & int., 5sp	$8
☐			b. same as (a), upper grille chromed	$4

1999 First Editions, #11-Fiat 500C

1999 First Editions, #16-Ford GT-40

1999 First Editions, #16-Ford GT-40

1999 First Editions, #17-Jeepster

1999 First Editions, #18-Turbolence

1999 First Editions, #18-Turbolence

1999 First Editions, #19-Pikes Peak Tacoma

1999 First Editions, #20-Shadow Mk IIa

1999 First Editions, #26-Mercedes CLK-LM

1999 First Editions, #22-'56 Ford Truck

1999 First Editions, #23-Chrysler Pronto

1999 Treasure Hunt Series, #1-Mercedes 540K

1999 Treasure Hunt Series, #2-T-Bird Stocker

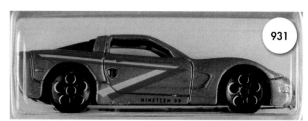

1999 Treasure Hunt Series, #3-'97 Corvette

1999 Treasure Hunt Series, #4-Rigor Motor

1999 Treasure Hunt Series, #5-Ferrari F512M

1999 Treasure Hunt Series, #6-'59 Impala

Photo	No.	Name	Description	Price
❑	914	#8-Semi-Fast	c. black plastic body, red plastic cab, metal Malaysia base & lower grille, chrome grille above metal one, yellow & black stripes w/black circle & white "17" on cab, light green & black stripes w/black circle & white "17" on body, tip of stripe missing on lower front fender, white HW logo & "Jones" tampos behind front wheel, "Champion & Goodyear" tampos below stripe on cab, smoked window, gray engine & int., 5sp	$6
❑			d. same as (c), yellow & black stripes w/black circle & white "17" on cab & body, 5sp	$3
❑ 📷	683	#9-Tee'd Off	a. white pearl, metal Malaysia base, white pearl plastic top w/magenta "Miller CC" and green pearl & white "Country Club" tampo, gold HW logo above "Miller" on top, gray int., chrome engine, 5sp	$15
❑ 📷			b. same as (a), maroon pearl int., 5sp	$6
❑ 📷			c. candy blue, metal Malaysia base, white pearl plastic top w/magenta "Miller CC" and green pearl & white "Country Club" tampo, gold HW logo above "Miller" on top, white pearl int., chrome engine, 5sp	$4
❑	912	#10-Porsche 911 GT3 Cup	a. candy gray pearl, black plastic Malaysia base, side has yellow & pearl green outlined in red and 6 misc. racing decals, red "8 Cup" in silver circle, white HW logo behind rear wheel, yellow plastic rear wing, orange int., blue-tint window & headlights, asw-bbs	$10
❑			b. same as (a), yellow plastic rear wing, red HW logo behind rear wheel	$7
❑ 📷			c. same as (a), black plastic rear wing, white HW logo behind rear wheel, asw-bbs	$45
❑			d. same as (b), black plastic rear wing, red HW logo behind rear wheel, asw-bbs	$5
❑			e. candy purple, black plastic Malaysia base, side has yellow & pearl green outlined in red and 6 misc. racing decals, red "8 Cup" in purple circle, red HW logo behind rear wheel, black plastic rear wing, orange int., blue-tint window & headlights, asw-bbs	$3
❑	919	#11-Fiat 500C	a. candy met. purple, metal Malaysia base, thin gold stripe on side, gray plastic roll cage & rear wing, chrome engine, exhaust & windshield, gold HW logo on side by engine, 5sp	$4

Photo	No.	Name	Description	Price
☐ 📷	919	#11-Fiat 500C	b. same as (a), dark purple (looks black), 5sp	$6
☐ 📷	917	#12-Track T	a. black enamel, metal Malaysia base, seat & engine, yellow & red flames outlined in green on hood, silver painted grille, tan plastic cover, dash & steering wheel, silver HW logo on trunk, 5sp	$4
☐			b. same as (a), without HW logo on trunk	$15
☐ 📷	913	#13-Popcycle	a. met. burgundy w/orange stripe & HW logo, metal Malaysia base, chrome engine, chrome "Stingray" bicycle under orange-tint canopy, 3sp	$15
☐ 📷			b. met. purple w/orange stripe & HW logo, metal Malaysia base, chrome engine, chrome "Stingray" bicycle under orange-tint canopy, 3sp	$3
☐			c. same as (b), undipped chrome engine, 3sp	$5
☐ 📷			d. dark met. purple w/brown stripe & HW logo, metal Malaysia base, chrome engine, chrome "Stingray" bicycle under orange-tint canopy, 3sp	$8
☐ 📷	916	#14-Phaeton	met. teal w/thin silver over gold stripes on side, metal Malaysia base, tan plastic top & int., tinted window, silver HW logo in front of rear wheel over exhust, 5sp	$3
☐ 📷	918	#15-Screamin' Hauler	a. met. purple, metal Malaysia base & int., chrome engines, blue-tint window, silver HW logo on rear, 5sp	$3
☐ 📷			b. same as (a), dark purple met., 5sp	$3
☐ 📷	921	#16-Ford GT-40	a. met. blue, gray plastic Malaysia base, white racing stripe on center of trunk, roof & hood, white circle & black "59" on hood & door, white racing stripe on lower side w/"FORD," white HW logo on rear fender, gray int., blue-tint window, thin rear 5sp	$5
☐ 📷			b. same as (a), wide rear 5sp	$3
☐			c. same as (a), asw-5sp	$15
☐ 📷	922	#17-Jeepster	red enamel, metal Malaysia base, black plastic fenders, bumpers, & int., black & silver "Jeepster" tampo behind front wheel, silver HW logo on door below handle, smoked window w/silver painted trim, alw-5sp	$3
☐ 📷	923	#18-Turbolence	a. black enamel, metal Malaysia base, gold "Dayla" tampo twice by gold chrome engine, gold "1" w/purple outline on nose, gold HW logo on rear, gold chrome int., alw-g5dot	$2
☐ 📷			b. same as (a), small rear chrome 5sp large/g5dot front	$25

There were a few Turbolence 923 (b) variations found and passed up as an error. Either way, they are worth mentioning!

Photo	No.	Name	Description	Price
☐ 📷	924	#19-Pikes Peak Tacoma	yellow enamel, black plastic Malaysia base, white roof, hood & grille, yellow painted side vent, black & red "TOYOTA Express Lube" and yellow, black & red "Pennzoil" logo on hood, red & black "1" & black HW logo on rear fender, "PENNZOIL" & misc. racing decals on side, int. & bed cover, clear window, asw-gbbs	$3
☐ 📷	925	#20-Shadow Mk IIa	a. black enamel, gray plastic Malaysia base & int., met. silver painted rear wing w/gray & black "Shadow" tampo, side has white "101" & misc. racing decals, white HW logo behind front wheel, 5sp	$3
☐			b. same as (a), white & black "Shadow" tampo on rear wing	$3
☐ 📷	1113	#21-360 Modena	a. red enamel, black plastic Malaysia base, small yellow Ferrari logo on hood, no HW logo on rear plate, black int., clear window, asw-5sp	$10

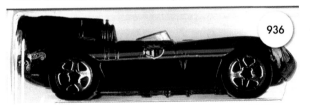

1999 Treasure Hunt Series, #7-Hot Wheels 500

1999 Treasure Hunt Series, #8-Jaguar D-Type

1999 Treasure Hunt Series, #9-'32 Ford Delivery

Photo	No.	Name	Description	Price
☐	1113	#21-360 Modena	b. same as (a), yellow HW logo on rear plate	$8
☐		Ferrari 360 Modena (on card)	c. red enamel, black plastic Malaysia base, small yellow Ferrari logo on hood, yellow HW logo on rear plate, black int., clear window, asw-5sp	$4
☐	927	#22-'56 Ford Truck	light pearl blue, gray plastic Malaysia base, blue flames w/magenta outline & "Genuine Ford Parts" tampo on side, chrome int. & engine, blue-tint window, 5sp	$5
☐	928	#23-Chrysler Pronto	yellow pearl, black plastic Malaysia base, black roof, dark smoked window, gray int., silver painted headlights & emblem on grille, black HW logo in front of rear wheel, 5sp	$2
☐	680	#24-Baby Boomer	candy blue w/orange, yellow & white flames on sides, chrome engine & fuel tanks, gray injection & belts, metal Malaysia base, white HW logo on side rear, 5sp	$2
☐	676	#25-Porsche 911 GT1-98	a. white enamel, black plastic Malaysia base, orange, purple & gray tampos w/misc. racing decals, black HW logo behind rear wheel, black rear wing & int., clear window, asw-bbs	$2
☐			b. same as (a), asw-bbs/2	$8
☐	926	#26-Mercedes CLK-LM	a. pearl gray, black plastic Malaysia base, silver HW logo on black rear wing, black int., clear window, asw-gbbs	$3
☐			b. same as (a), asw-bbs2	$5

938

1999 Treasure Hunt Series, #10-Hot Seat

1999 Treasure Hunt Series, #12-Express Lane

939

1999 First Editions, #11-Mustang Mach I

940

Buggin' Out Series

Photo	No.	Name	Description	Price
☐	941	Treadator	a. red enamel, yellow plastic side scoops & nose, black plastic Thailand base & treads, chrome fenders, drive wheels, engine, exhaust & canopy, yellow, silver & black ant tampo on side of rear wing, yellow, silver & black "anteater" tampo on top of rear wing, yellow HW logo on side between scoop & exhaust	$3
☐			b. same as (a), undipped chrome fenders, drive wheels, engine, exhaust & canopy	$5
☐			c. same as (a), black chrome fenders, drive wheels, engine, exhaust & canopy,	$25
☐	942	Shadow Jet II	gray plastic body, metal Malaysia base, green, yellow & black tampo on side & top, green & yellow "Stinger" below tampo, yellow HW logo behind rear wheel, yellow int., green-tint canopy, 5sp	$3
☐	943	Radar Ranger	met. purple, metal Malaysia base, yellow, black & white spider web & spider tampo on side & top of right side pod, black HW logo at center of web on side, black radar dish, blue plastic inserts & seat, blue-tint canopy, alw-ct/b	$3
☐	944	Baja Bug	a. light met. blue, metal Malaysia base, light yellow, orange & black tampos on front & side, light yellow HW logo in front of rear wheel, orange int., 5sp	$6
☐			b. met. blue, metal Malaysia base, yellow, orange & black tampos on front & side, light yellow HW logo in front of rear wheel, orange int., 5sp	$5

Buggin' Out Series, Treadator

Buggin' Out Series, Radar Ranger

Buggin' Out Series, Treadator

Buggin' Out Series, Baja Bug

Buggin' Out Series, Shadow Jet II

X-Ray Cruiser Series

	Photo	No.	Name	Description	Price
☐		945	Mercedes C-Class	a. met. black, black plastic Malaysia base, silver & very light purple tampos, silver & purple HW logo on rear fender, white int., yellow-tint window, asw-gbbs	$8
☐	📷			b. same as (a), much darker silver & purple tampos, gbbs	$5
The Mercedes C-Class for the X-Ray Cruiser Series was discontinued and was replaced by the '63 Corvette.					
☐	📷	946	Lamborghini Diablo	dark met. teal, teal plastic rear wing, black painted Malaysia base, silver & black tampos on side & front, gray int., smoked window, 5sp	$3
☐	📷	947	'67 Camaro	a. blue enamel, metal Malaysia base, yellow, red & white tampos on hood, roof & sides, red & yellow flames on side, white HW logo on rear roof pillar above wheel, white int., tinted window, 5sp	$7
☐				b. same as (a), 3sp	$4
☐	📷	948	Jaguar XJ220	yellow enamel, black plastic Malaysia base, black tampos on front & sides, blue int., clear window, black HW logo behind rear wheel, 3sp	$3
☐	📷	1114	'63 Corvette	black met., gold chrome Malaysia 2 rivet base, silver & gold tampos on hood & sides, silver HW logo on rear fender, tan int., clear window, g5sp	$6

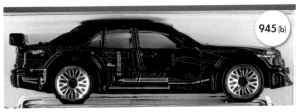

X-Ray Cruiser Series, Mercedes C-Class

X-Ray Cruiser Series, Lamborghini Diablo

X-Ray Cruiser Series, '67 Camaro

X-Ray Cruiser Series, '63 Corvette

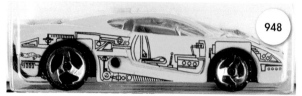

X-Ray Cruiser Series, Jaguar XJ220

Street Art Series

Photo	No.	Name	Description	Price
☐ 📷	949	Mini Truck	met. black, black plastic Malaysia base, orange, gold & white tampos on hood & side, white & black "Mini Truck" on hood & door, black & white HW logo on side behind door, chrome engine, exhaust, grille & speakers, black int., clear window, t/b	$3
☐ 📷	950	Propper Chopper	met. green, black plastic Malaysia base, rotors & tail, green, black & gold tampos, white & black HW logo above rear window, black int., yellow-tint window	$4
☐ 📷	951	Ambulance	a. met. purple, chrome Malaysia base, blue, white, green & black tampos on side, black & white "Speedy" & large white & green HW logo on side, purple int. & rear doors, orange-tint window & light bar on roof, asw-5sp	$4
☐			b. same as (a), asw-3sp	$5
☐ 📷	952	School Bus	a. yellow enamel, black plastic Malaysia base, no rear door, orange, black & gold tampo on side, orange HW logo behind rear wheel, yellow int., red-tint window, asw-5dot	$8
☐ 📷			b. met. silver, black plastic Malaysia base, no rear door, orange, black & gold tampo on side, orange HW logo behind rear wheel, yellow int., red-tint window, asw-5dot	$3
☐			c. same as (b), with rear door, asw-5dot	$6

Street Art Series, Mini Truck

Street Art Series, Ambulance

Street Art Series, Propper Chopper

Street Art Series, School Bus

Street Art Series, School Bus

Pinstripe Power Series

	Photo	No.	Name	Description	Price
❑	📷	953	3-Window '34	dark met. purple, metal Malaysia base, light purple plastic fenders, black plastic running boards & int., gold & silver pinstripe tampo on side, silver HW logo behind side window, chrome engine grille & headlights, blue-tint window, 5sp	$5
❑	📷	954	Tail Dragger	black enamel, metal Malaysia base, silver & gold pinstripe tampos on hood, fenders & trunk, gold HW logo on rear fender, tan int., clear window, bbs	$4
❑	📷	955	'65 Impala	met. light green, gold-tint chrome Malaysia base, silver & gold pinstripe tampos on hood & side, gold logo on rear fender, tan int., smoked window, asw-gbbs	$4
❑	📷	956	Auburn 852	black enamel & silver met., metal Malaysia base, white plastic fenders, gold & black pinstripe tampos on hood & trunk, black logo on trunk behind seat, chrome headlights, grille & steering wheel, white int., clear window, asw-bbs	$3

Pinstripe Power Series, 3-Window '34

Pinstripe Power Series, '65 Impala

Pinstripe Power Series, Auburn 852

Pinstripe Power Series, Tail Dragger

Game Over Series

	Photo	No.	Name	Description	Price
❑	📷	957	Lean Machine	black enamel & purple plastic, metal Malaysia base, yellow, green, black & silver side tampos, green HW logo on top behind black canopy, 5sp	$3
❑	📷	958	Shadow Jet	yellow enamel, metal Malaysia base, pearl blue, red, white & black tampos on side top rear, two black HW logos on rear wing, chrome engine & fuel tank, yellow int., smoked canopy, 5sp	$3
❑	📷	959	Speed Blaster	a. light green enamel, day-glo yellow plastic Malaysia base, green "Dino," yellow "HUNT" on side w/green, yellow, gold & black tampo, black HW logo behind front wheel, green, yellow, gold & black tampo on hood & roof, gold-tint chrome window & rear engine, gt/b	$2
❑				b. same as (a), g5sp	$40
❑	📷	960	Twin Mill II	pearl pink, black plastic Malaysia base, yellow & black tampo on side & top of front fenders, black & white "FINAL FIGHT IV FIGHT2DAFINISH" tampo on side w/black & white men w/blue boxing gloves, yellow & black "FF IV" on nose, roof has black & white over yellow man with blue boxing gloves and black HW logo, chrome engine, alw-bbs	$3

957

959 (a)

Game Over Series, Lean Machine

Game Over Series, Speed Blaster

958

960

Game Over Series, Shadow Jet

Game Over Series, Twin Mill II

Surf 'N Fun Series

	Photo	No.	Name	Description	Price
❑	📷	961	'40s Woodie	met. purple fenders & hood, metal Malaysia base, tan plastic body, black roof w/yellow, orange & white tampo, black over white tampo on top of front fenders, right front fender has yellow & orange flower tampo, chrome engine & grille, white HW logo on roof by windshield, black int., blue-tint window, 5sp	$4
❑	📷	962	VW Bug	light pearl blue, metal Malaysia base, white, light green & dark blue tampo on roof & side, "Olas del Sol" in white on roof & side in tampo, white HW logo on side between rear fender & door, white int., smoked window, 5sp	$5
❑	📷	963	'55 Chevy	met. red, chrome Malaysia base, white, light blue & dark blue wave tampo on side & hood, "Ride Yourself Wild" tampo on roof, "Ride Yourself Wild," "Macon" & "Spike Surfboards" tampos on side, light blue HW logo on front fender above wheel, black window, 3sp	$4
❑	📷	964	Chevy Nomad	a. white pearl, metal Malaysia base, long black & gold racing stripe in center of hood that goes over the hood almost to the grille, gold & black "West Side" with emblem on hood & rear fender, black & gold racing stripe down side w/"Spike Surfboards" over red & black flames, black HW logo on rear fender by rear pillar, white int., smoked window, g5sp	$8
❑				b. same as (a), short hood stripe. The stripe on the hood stops at the bend. Does not go down the front of the hood to the grille.	$4

961

Surf 'N Fun Series, '40s Woodie

963

Surf 'N Fun Series, '55 Chevy

962

Surf 'N Fun Series, VW Bug

964 (a)

Surf 'N Fun Series, Chevy Nomad

X-Treme Speed Series

	Photo	No.	Name	Description	Price
☐	📷	965	Dodge Sidewinder	white enamel, black plastic Malaysia base, purple, light greeen & dark blue tampos on hood & side, purple HW logo on driver's side rear fender, purple int. & bed cover, smoked window, 5sp	$3
☐		966	Callaway C7	a. light green enamel, black plastic Malaysia base, yellow, white & black side tampo, black tampo in center of hood, black int., rear wing, cowl & headlights, clear window, white HW logo on driver's side rear fender, t/b	$3
☐	📷			b. same as (a), 5sp	$8
☐	📷	967	Porsche Carrera	silver, metal Malaysia base, black, red & white tampos on hood & side, white HW logo on rear fender above rear tire, white int., tinted window, g5sp	$3
☐	📷	968	Mazda MX-5 Miata	blue enamel w/matching painted metal Malaysia base, black, yellow & pearl light green tampos on hood & side, pearl light green tampo on trunk, black HW logo on hood, day-glo green int., clear window, asw-bbs	$3

X-Treme Speed Series, Dodge Sidewinder

X-Treme Speed Series, Porsche Carrera

X-Treme Speed Series, Callaway C7

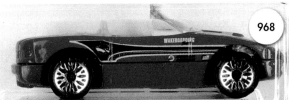

X-Treme Speed Series, Mazda MX-5 Miata

Sugar Rush Series II

	Photo	No.	Name	Description	Price
☐	📷	969	'70 Roadrunner	yellow enamel, chrome Malaysia base, brown stripe on side w/"Nestle" & "Oh Henry!," red "Oh" on side & trunk, brown HW logo on rear fender, black int., clear window, 5dot	$4
☐	📷	970	Jaguar XK8	red enamel, black plastic Malaysia base, white, brown & yellow "100 GRAND" tampo on side & hood, yellow "Nestle" on trunk by boot, yellow "Hot Wheels" tampo on rear fender, tan int., smoked window & headlights, gbbs	$3
☐	📷	971	Pikes Peak Celica	white enamel, black plastic Malaysia base & rear wing, magenta & light blue tampo on side, roof & hood, light green & magenta tampo over "Tarts" on hood & side, magenta HW logo above rear wheel, black int., clear window, asw-bbs	$3
☐	📷	972	Dodge Concept Car	a. white enamel, metal Malaysia base, two blue stripes on trunk, hood & side, red & blue "Nestle Baby Ruth" on hood & side, blue HW logo on rear fender, blue int., clear window, 5dot	$3
☐				b. same as (a), silver painted Malaysia base, 5dot	$8

Sugar Rush Series II, '70 Roadrunner

Sugar Rush Series II, Jaguar XK8

971

Sugar Rush Series II, Pikes Peak Celica

972 (a)

Sugar Rush Series II, Dodge Concept Car

Mega Graphics Series

	Photo	No.	Name	Description	Price
☐	📷	973	Funny Car	day-glo yellow, metal Malaysia base, black & gray tampo on side w/black & orange "3" and orange & gray "Team Bousquette" black over day-glo yellow on hood, orange HW logo on hood next to blower, yellow-tint window, 5sp	$5
☐		974	Mustang Cobra	a. white pearl, black plastic Malaysia base, black, silver & orange tampos on roof, hood & side, orange HW logo on right side of roof by windshield, black int., clear window, asw-t/b	$3
☐	📷			b. same as (a), asw-5sp	$6
☐	📷			c. same as (b), light brown in tampo replacing orange, asw-5sp	$8
☐	📷	975	Turbo Flame	black plastic body, red painted Malysia base, yellow, gold & red tampos on side & behind gold chrome engine, red HW logo above front wheel, black int., yellow-tint canopy & rear, g5sp	$3
☐	📷	976	Firebird Funny Car	dark purple met. (looks black), blue-tint metal Malaysia base, side has large white, pearl rose & orange HW logo over wide white stripes, large black, white & pearl rose "1" w/orange & black "F/C" and orange "Team Handy," two white panels on hood w/large black, white & pearl rose "1" and orange & black "F/C," orange "Team Handy" w/white "Racing" on nose, smoked window, b5sp	$5

973

Mega Graphics Series, Funny Car

975

Mega Graphics Series, Turbo Flame

974 (b)

Mega Graphics Series, Mustang Cobra

976

Mega Graphics Series, Firebird Funny Car

974 (c)

Mega Graphics Series, Mustang Cobra

Terrorific Series

	Photo	No.	Name	Description	Price
☐	📷	977	At-A-Tude	met. green, black plastic Malaysia base & rear wing, light green w/black outline "Freaks Of Horror" & Wolfman face w/white lightning bolts on hood & side, orange lettering & swirl on side, black HW logo below orange swirl on hood left of Wolfman face, chrome int. & engine, green-tint window, b5sp	$3

	Photo	No.	Name	Description	Price
❑	📷	978	Cat-A-Pult	orange enamel, metal Malaysia base, green & black "Hunchback of Los Angeles" tampo on hood & side, black HW logo in front of rear wheel, black int., smoked window, asw-5sp	$3
❑		979	Sweet 16 II	a. black enamel, metal Malaysia base, purple, red, white & black side tampo, purple, white & black tampo on hood, red HW logo above rear tire, gold-tint chrome engine & front drive, yellow-tint canopy, 5sp	$4
❑	📷			b. same as (a), dark gold chrome, 5sp	$3
❑				c. same as (b), silver painted Malaysia base, 5sp	$5
❑	📷	980	Splittin' Image II	met. gold, black plastic Malaysia base, red, green & black side tampos, small black HW logo in front of rear wheel, pink-tint chrome canopies, engine & exhaust, 3sp	$3

Terrorific Series, At-A-Tude

Terrorific Series, Sweet 16 II

Terrorific Series, Cat-A-Pult

Terrorific Series, Splittin' Image II

Classic Games Series

	Photo	No.	Name	Description	Price
❑	📷	981	Super Modified	pearl light blue, metal Malaysia base & engine, purple & white "Ker Plunk" on top panel & side, orange, purple & light green tampos on top panel, white HW logo on side behind rear tire, purple "Classic Games" on orange oval behind front wheel, black int., roll cage, rear push bar, rear & front wings, gbbs2	$3
❑	📷	982	Silhouette II	silver-blue pearl, black plastic Malaysia base, magenta & white "Toss Across" tampo on side, magenta & light blue stripes on hood, chrome engine, magenta HW logo behind front wheel, white int., blue-tint canopy, 5dot	$2
❑	📷	983	Sol-Aire CX4	white enamel, black plastic Malaysia base, blue & red "Skip-Bo" tampos on top of rear wing & side, Skip-Bo emblem on nose& in front of rear wheel, blue HW logo behind rear wheel, black int., blue-tint window, 3sp	$2
❑	📷	984	Escort Rally	red enamel, gray plastic Malaysia base, yellow, white & purple "UNO" on hood & door, yellow, red, black & white side tampos, yellow HW logo on rear fender behind rear wheel, black int., clear window & rear spoiler, asw-bbs	$8

Classic Games Series, Super Modified

Classic Games Series, Silhouette II

983

Classic Games Series, Sol-Aire CX4

984

Classic Games Series, Escort Rally

Car-Toon Friends Series

	Photo	No.	Name	Description	Price
☐	📷	985	Saltflat Racer	purple plastic body, silver painted Malaysia base, black & white "Natasha Fatale" tampos on top & side, red & white HW logo above red dynomite stick on side, chrome int., roll bar, engine & front drive, clear canopy, 5sp	$3
☐	📷	986	XT-3	orange enamel, black painted Malaysia base, white, black & gray "Rocky" tampos on top & side, blue-tint metal engine, black HW logo on left side top panel, black canopy & nose, g5sp	$3
☐		987	Double Vision	a. black enamel, black plastic Malaysia base, red, white & yellow tampos w/picture of Bullwinkle on side, yellow stripe around white & orange "Bullwinkle" behind engines, gray engines, chrome blowers white HW logo above front wheel, gray seat, clear canopy, gbbs	$3
☐	📷			b. same as (a), engines & blowers are backwards, gbbs	$8
☐	📷	988	Lakester	white & black enamel, black painted Malaysia base, black & white picture of Boris on top w/orange HW logo, white & orange "The Bomb" w/black bomb on side, chrome engine & int., red-tint canopy, alw-5sp	$2

985

Car-Toon Friends Series, Saltflat Racer

987 (b)

Car-Toon Friends Series, Double Vision

986

Car-Toon Friends Series, XT-3

988

Car-Toon Friends Series, Lakester

Non-Series Collector Number Packs

	Photo	No.	Name	Description	Price
☐	📷	991	Rodzilla	chrome plastic body, white teeth & eyes, metal China base, gold chrome engine, red HW logo on rear arm (fender brace), gbbs	$3
☐	📷	992	Ferrari F512M	red enamel, black painted metal Malaysia base, larger yellow & black Ferrari emblem on hood, black HW logo on rear plate, tan int., smoked window, 5sp	$3
☐	📷	993	Ferrari 348	yellow enamel, black plastic Malaysia base, larger yellow Ferrari emblem on hood, black & yellow int., smoked window, 5sp	$3
☐	📷	994	Way 2 Fast	met. black, met. gold painted metal Malaysia base, black, orange, white & gold tampos on roof & side, gold HW logo on roof in curve of tampo, chrome int. & engines, g5sp	$3
☐	📷	995	Porsche 911	yellow enamel, metal Malaysia base, black HW logo on door, black int., smoked window, 5sp	$3

Rodzilla

Ferrari F512M

Ferrari 348

Way 2 Fast

Porsche 911

'32 Ford Delivery

	Photo	No.	Name	Description	Price
❏	📷	996	'32 Ford Delivery	pearl light blue body, black plastic fenders, metal Malaysia base, chrome headlights & radiator, silver & dark blue tampo on side, black ""Hot Wheels Delivery" in silver rectangle in side panel, black "Hot Wheels Delivery" in silver tampo on rear, silver HW logo on door, blue-tint window, bbs	$3
❏	📷	997	Jaguar D-Type	a. red enamel w/matching painted metal Malaysia base, green-tinted tampo w/black stripes down the center from the nose to the tail, black ring & "27" in white circle outlined in green on hood, side has green-tint tampo w/black stripes &"JAGUAR D-TYPE" and black ring & "27" in white circle outlined in green, white HW logo below side stripe in front of rear wheel along with two other racing decals, black HW logo on rear also, gray int., smoked window, alw-bbs	$5
❏	📷			b. red enamel w/matching painted metal China base, yellow tampo w/black stripes down the center from the nose to the tail, black ring & "27" in white circle outlined in yellow on hood, side has green-tint tampo w/black stripes & "JAGUAR D-TYPE" and black ring & "27" in white circle outlined in yellow, white HW logo below side stripe in front of rear wheel along with two other racing decals, black HW logo on rear also, gray int., smoked window, alw-bbs	$3
❏	📷	998	Firebird Funny Car	met. red, metal Malaysia base, black & white side tampo w/silver "MARTIN Racing" & misc. racing decals, small black HW logo above tampo behind front wheel, black & white tampo on hood w/black "Martin" & white "Racing" & misc. racing decals, smoked window, g5sp	$5
❏		999	Hot Seat	a. chrome plastic body (bowl), metal Malaysia base, gold HW logo below white toilet paper roll on rear of side (pun intended), red plastic seat & plunger, 5sp	$5
❏	📷			b. same as (a), black HW logo, 5sp	$3
❏	📷	1000	'59 Impala	a. white pearl, gold-tint chrome Malaysia base, yellow & gold tampo on side w/dark red ribbon & "59 Impala," gold HW logo below "59 Impala" on rear fender, small yellow, gold& dark red pinstripe tampo on hood, black int., smoked window, asw-gbbs	$5
❏				b. same as (a), white enamel, asw-gbbs	$15

Jaguar D-Type

Jaguar D-Type

Firebird Funny Car

Hot Seat

'59 Impala

Slideout

997 (a)

997 (b)

998

999 (b)

1000 (a)

1001

Ferrari F40

Dairy Delivery

Mercedes-Benz Unimog

Dodge Viper RT/10

Tow Jam

Chaparral 2

1003

1004

1005

1006

1007

1008

Photo	No.	Name	Description	Price
❑ 📷	1001	Slideout	met. blue body, white plastic Malaysia base, yellow plastic rear push bar, engine, front wing & top wing, black & yellow "27" on rear, yellow stripe on rear side of roll cage, black triangle tampo w/two white racing decals & yellow HW logo on side, yellow & black splochy stripe on body above engine, dark blue & white "27" & splotchy stripe w/Rman Racing on side of top wing, 5sp	$3
	1002	unreleased		—
❑ 📷	1003	Ferrari F40	black enamel, metal Malaysia base, larger yellow & black Ferrari emblem on front, yellow HW on rear plate, red int, smoked window, 5sp	$4
❑ 📷	1004	Dairy Delivery	white enamel w/black cow spots & red "Got Milk?" on side, gold HW logo in black spot left of "Got Milk?," chrome Malaysia base, black int., clear window, 5sp	$4
❑ 📷	1005	Mercedes-Benz Unimog	red enamel cab & box, black plastic fenders, int. & rear box cover, white HW logo on center of hood, metal Malaysia base, clear windows, large ct/b	$3
❑ 📷	1006	Dodge Viper RT/10	met. blue, black plastic Malaysia base, small Dodge emblem between two wide white stripes on hood & trunk, white HW logo& "Viper R/T 10" on front fender behind front wheel, orange directional lights in front bumper, black int., smoked window, 5sp	$4
❑ 📷	1007	Tow Jam	met. green, chrome Malaysia base, black, yellow & green outlined flame tampo on hood & side, small green & black HW logo on rear of roof, metal boom w/black plastic sling, black window, 3sp	$3
❑ 📷	1008	Chaparral 2	red enamel, white painted metal Malaysia base, two wide white stripes from nose to tail, white HW logo on door, gray injection & exhaust, black int., clear window, bbs/2	$3
❑ 📷	1009	Peterbilt Dump Truck	dark blue enamel, white plastic dump box, metal Malaysia base, white HW logo on hood, blue-tint window & int., alw-5sp	$4
❑ 📷	1010	Ford Stake Bed Truck	teal enamel, gray stake bed, chrome Malaysia base, int., exhaust stacks & grille, silver HW logo on door, blue-tint window, asw-5dot	$4
❑ 📷	1011	Oshkosh Cement Truck	black plastic body, barrel & Malaysia base, met. burgundy painted fenders & seat, gold HW logo on front bumper, asw-t/b	$4
❑ 📷	1012	Flame Stopper	white enamel, black plastic Malaysia base, brown & yellow over black airplane tampo w/light green & black "Airport" & black "Fire & Rescue Team" on cab doors, small red HW logo, flame in circle & "Emergency" w/two thin stripes on cab behind window, black boom w/rivets & part number, black window, alw-ct/b	$3
❑ 📷	1013	Mercedes 500 SL	silver pearl, black plastic Malaysia base, red HW logo on rear plate, chrome grille & headlights, black int., smoked window, alw-bbs	$3
❑ 📷	1014	'67 Camaro	candy gray, metal Malaysia base, black, yellow, red & white tampos w/"Stunt 99" on hood & side, gray HW logo on hood, black int., blue-tint window, 5sp	$5

Peterbilt Dump Truck

Oshkosh Cement Truck

Ford Stake Bed Truck

Flame Stopper

Mercedes 500 SL — 1013

'32 Ford Coupe — 1018 (b)

'67 Camaro — 1014

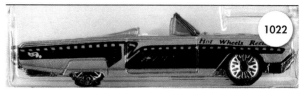

'63 T-Bird — 1022

Mercedes C-Class — 1015

Shelby Cobra 427 S/C — 1024

'32 Ford Coupe — 1018 (a)

Mercedes SLK — 1025 (a)

Photo	No.	Name	Description	Price
❑ 📷	1015	Mercedes C-Class	yellow enamel, black plastic Malaysia base, dark blue HW logo on rear fender, red int., clear window, asw-bbs	$2
❑ 📷	1018	'32 Ford Coupe	a. white pearl, black plastic China base, blue-tint, white, dark blue & magenta flames on roof & side, chrome engine & radiator, magenta HW logo above rear tire, black int., clear window, 5sp	$4
❑ 📷			b. same as (a), dark blue & dark purple flames on roof & side, dark purple HW logo above rear tire, black int., clear window, 5sp	$10
❑ 📷	1022	'63 T-Bird	met. gold, metal Thailand base, black side tampo, black & white tampo on hood, HW logo on rear fender near taillight, white int., tinted window, bbs	$3
❑ 📷	1024	Shelby Cobra 427 S/C	white enamel, metal Thailand base, black, rose & orange flames on tops of front fenders, trunk & side, black on nose, hood & cowl w/white scoop, black "47" in white circle & "Celebrity Tour De Milan" tampo on hood, black "Celebrity," white"Hollywood Tour" in orange rectangle and white "47" in black circle on rear fender, white & black HW logo on rear deck, black int., smoked window, alw-5sp	$4
❑ 📷	1025	Mercedes SLK	a. dark mf. blue, metal India base, white HW logo on rear fender by taillight, white int., tinted window, asw-t/b	$4
❑			b. same as (a), painted metal India base	$2
❑ 📷	1026	Dodge Caravan	orange pearl, black plastic Malaysia base, black & yellow "METRO HOTEL" w/pink "SHUTTLE" on side, black & silver tampo w/3 small airplanes from fender to fender, black white Handicapped decal & silver HW logo behind rear fender, black stripe on bottom, white int., dark smoked window, alw-5sp	$9

Photo	No.	Name	Description	Price
❏	1027	Customized C3500	pearl magenta, black plastic Thailand base, large yellow lightning tampo across hood & roof, large yellow lightning tampo across side w/black outlined "Jerry's Electric" & white "24 HR. Service since 1999," "i" in "Electric" is a white lightning bolt, white "How Am I Driving?" over rear wheel, yellow HW logo on box between cab & rear fender, black int., blue-tint window, 5sp	$7
❏ 📷	1028	'56 Flashsider	yellow enamel, chrome Thailand base, brown & black tampo on hood & side, white & black "Hot Rod" on door, black & orange "HANDYMAN" on front fender, two black & white decals & HW logo on rear fender behind rear wheel, black & yellow HW logo on rear of bed cover, black window, 3sp	$5
❏ 📷	1029	'40s Ford Truck	red enamel, chrome China base, black, yellow & white "Pizza on Wheels" tampo on door over seven thin white pinstripes, black & white check stripe from door to hood, black "Fast Delivery" on rear fender over tire, black HW logo on rear fender behind tire, white int., roll bar, tubs & rear wing, yellow-tint window, 5sp	$4
❏ 📷	1030	Porsche 959	gray pearl, metal China base, black & white "959" on door, red & black "Twin Turbo" on rocker panel, red & yellow Porsche emblem on hood w/red & black "Twin Turbo," red HW logo on rear fender by taillight, black int., blue-tint window, asw-5dot	$3
❏ 📷	1031	Aeroflash	green plastic body, black painted Malaysia base, black, brown & white tampos on tops of front fenders & top rear, black & brown "3" & white HW logo on rear, black int., clear window, 3sp	$4
❏ 📷	1032	Ford GT-90	yellow enamel, metal China base, side has black & white tampos on it w/yellow, black & red circle, black "15" above black stripe on side, black & white HW logo behind front wheel, yellow "COLLISION PATROL" in black stripe on rocker panel, black & yellow tampo w/black "15" on nose, black int., clear window, asw-3sp	$2

Dodge Caravan (1026)

'56 Flashsider (1028)

'40s Ford Truck (1029)

Porsche 959 (1030)

Aeroflash (1031)

Ford GT-90 (1032)

1970 Plymouth Barracuda (1035)

Roll Patrol Jeep (1037)

Dodge Viper RT/10

Panoz GTR-1

Super Comp Dragster

Twang Thang

Rail Rodder

Whatta Drag

Dodge Ram 1500

Photo	No.	Name	Description	Price
❑ 📷	1035	1970 Plymouth Barracuda	met. purple, chrome China base, black side w/silver dots & white outline Octopus on door, "PURPLE OCTOPUS beach rentals" tampo on rear fender above wheel, white & black HW logo on rear fender behind rear wheel, black int. & hood scoop, smoked window, asw-3sp	$3
❑ 📷	1037	Roll Patrol Jeep	yellow enamel, metal Thailand base, black, silver & pearl blue tampo on hood & side, gray "Mudcat" over rear wheel, gray "30" w/black outline on front fender high behind front wheel, "JT Motorsport" & two other decals on rocker panel, black HW logo behind rear wheel, tan int., tinted window, asw-ct/b	$25
❑ 📷	1038	Dodge Viper RT/10	mf. silver, black plastic China base, red, white & blue flag tampo w/black & white "Team Benjamin" on side & hood, red, white& black "27" on hood & rear fender, black "World of Racing Federation" on rear fender above "27" & below "27" on hood, black HW logo on rocker panel behind front wheel, black int., clear window, alw-3sp	$3
❑ 📷	1040	Panoz GTR-1	green pearl, black plastic China base, red, white & blue stripe tampos on side, hood & tops of front fenders, small blue & white "17" on hood & behind front wheel, misc. racing decals on tops of front fenders, white "WRF" & small "World of Racing Federation" on tops of rear fenders, white HW logo on rear fender low behind rear wheel, black int. & rear wing, clear window, 3sp	$3
❑ 📷	1041	Super Comp Dragster	candy gray w/black plastic Thailand fenders, chrome base & fuel tank, red & white tampo on side w/purple & white lettering, purple HW logo on side behind chrome headers, brown & white "WRF" & small "World of Racing Federation" on side in front of headers, red & purple Oriental writing on top of body next to driver & rear deck, purple "Power," red "Speed" & white "Attitude" on rear deck, black roll cage & wheelie bars, 5sp	$3
❑ 📷	1042	Twang Thang	met. green, black plastic China base, white & gold flames on hood & rear deck, gold HW logo in center of rear deck, gold chrome guitars on each side connected over the hood, chrome int., engine & headers, green-tint window, 5sp	$3
❑ 📷	1043	Rail Rodder	a. white plasic body, metal Malaysia base, blue-tint, white, dark blue & light blue "Ice Breaker" tampo on side, blue-tint, white, dark blue & light blue "Engine 32 below" on side of cab, light blue HW logo on side before "Ice Breaker" tampo, light blue chrome engines, stack & drive wheels, tiny dark blue chrome front wheels, b5sp	$4

Photo	No.	Name	Description	Price
☐	1043	Rail Rodder	b. same as (a), silver painted metal China base, b5sp	$3
☐ 📷	1044	Whatta Drag	black enamel, gray painted China base & headers, black "6" in white circle on right front & roof, misc. racing decals on left front, orange painted headlights, gold chrome engine, rear suspension & wing, gold plastic air scoop, large HW logo on top of wing, red-tint window, 5dot	$3
☐ 📷	1045	Dodge Ram 1500	black enamel, light gray China base, silver "Federal Drug Enforcement" on side of rear box w/silver HW logo and white "Drug Sniffing" & red "K9," silver & white "Federal Drug Enforcement" emblem on door w/"1037" large silver & white "Federal Drug Enforcement" emblem on hood, light gray int., box bed, bumpers & grille, clear window, alw-5sp	$5
☐ 📷	1046	Police Cruiser	white enamel, black plastic Thailand base & bumpers, flag tampo on side w/red HW logo on door, white "Hot Wheels Police Force" in blue stripe below large black "POLICE" on door, red "02" high on front fender behind wheel, black int., blue-tint window, headlights & light bar on roof, asw-3sp	$5
☐ 📷	1047	Olds Aurora	black enamel w/white doors, black plastic Thailand base, "Highway Patrol" & "To Protect & Serve" in gold on doors, black & gold police emblem on rear door, large white "39" & small gold HW logo on roof, gold "unit" & white"L91" on rear fender, small white "POLICE" half on door & half on front fender, tan int., clear window, asw-5dot	$5
☐ 📷	1048	Rescue Ranger	a. white enamel, chrome China base, black "BOMB SQUAD" w/red & black tampo on door, red "Caution" & black "Explosive Materials" on front fender above wheel, black w/red pinstripe tampo on side of box w/white "Squad 3649," large black"BOMB SQUAD" w/red "Emergency Detonation Team" on side, small HW logo on side behind door, small red & black"Caution" tampo below HW logo, black "Safety Kit" & tampo behind rear wheel, red insert, blue-tint window & int., alw-5sp	$4
☐			b. same as (a), w/o "Explosive Materials" on fender, alw-5sp	$15
☐			c. same as (a), alw-5dot	$3
☐ 📷	1049	Treadator	black enamel, purple plastic side scoops & nose, blue Thailand base & treads, white w/light blue, black & purple tampos on side of driver's compartment, chrome canopy, engine, headers, fenders & track drives	$3
☐ 📷	1051	'65 Mustang	black enamel, metal China base, yellow & orange flames outlined in red on front fender to door, rear fender and hood, white "Mustang" & horse on rocker panel in front of rear wheel, red& yellow HW logo on front of hood in flame, tan int., tinted window, asw-g5sp	$4

Police Cruiser

Olds Aurora

Rescue Ranger

Treadator

'65 Mustang

Rigor Motor

Hydroplane — 1053

Porsche 959 — 1054

School Bus — 1055

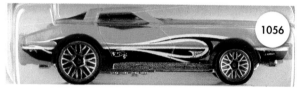

Corvette Stingray — 1056

Thunderstreak — 1057

'96 Mustang — 1058

Dodge Ram 1500 — 1059

Ramp Truck — 1060

Rescue Ranger — 1061

Photo	No.	Name	Description	Price
📷	1052	Rigor Motor	red enamel, metal China base, black & yellow "Thorny Graves" on top & side over white, red & black roses tampo, chrome engine, fuel tank & seat, black skull headlights & radiator, black HW logo below skulls, smoked canopy, 5sp	$3
📷	1053	Hydroplane	black enamel, black plastic China base, white & gold tampo w/two red pinstripes on top of pontoons, white "7" in black circle on front of left pontoon, red & yellow over white HW logo on top of rear wing, chrome int. & engine, yellow-tint canopy	$3
📷	1054	Porsche 959	black enamel, metal China base, gold HW logo on nose, white int., clear window, asw-bbs	$2
📷	1055	School Bus	black enamel, black plastic China base, silver, black & light purple tampo on roof w/white, yellow & black 5-spoke wheel & flame tampo, black, silver & light purple tampo on side w/large white HW logo behind rear wheel, white "Graphics" outlined in light green in front of rear wheel, black int., red-tint window, asw-5dot	$2
📷	1056	Corvette Stingray	tan plastic body, metal China base, orange, white & black tampo on hood & side, black "Stingray" on rear of hood by windshield, white HW logo on bottom of door in front of rear wheel, smoked window w/black lines, gbbs	$3
📷	1057	Thunderstreak	met. red, blue plastic side pods, metal China base, light green "Thunderstreak" over black on side pod & top of rear wing, misc. silver racing decals on side pod w/small silver HW logo, blue plastic driver, yellow lettering, b5sp	$3
📷	1058	'96 Mustang	met. dark red, metal China base, black & gold flames on hood& side, white horse in flame on door, small white "Mustang" & horse in flames on hood, white "Mustang" & gold "96" above black stripe on rocker panel in front of rear wheel, white HW logo high on rear fender, black int., smoked window, asw-gbbs	$3

Photo	No.	Name	Description	Price
☐ 📷	1059	Dodge Ram 1500	met. light green, gray plastic China base, pale green stripes on side with black & white check tampo from front fender well to top center of rear fender, chrome int., box bed, bumpers & spacer between body & base, light green HW logo on rear fender above bumper, tinted window, alw-5dot	$4
☐ 📷	1060	Ramp Truck	black enamel, metal China base, yellow plastic ramp w/yellow, red & blue "24 HR. Emergency Towing" tampo, large gold HW logo on roof, black window, asw-5dot	
☐ 📷	1061	Rescue Ranger	white enamel, red plastic China base, red & gold stripe on side w/gold & black "Fire Dept." on box and "51" on front fender, "City of Hot Wheels" logo on door w/gold "Emergency," gold"Oxygen Supply" & "First Aid" w/small black "+" on top doors on box, white HW logo in red stripe on side rear, red plastic insert, red-tint window & int., alw-5dot	$4
☐ 📷	1062	Rail Rodder	dark blue plastic body, metal Malaysia base, orange & white "Rail Rodder" w/light green & white "RXR" & stripes on side, small white HW logo & "Engine 5" on side of cab, gold chrome engines & wheel drivers, small gold 5sp front wheels & b5sp rear	$3
☐ 📷	1063	1970 Plymouth Barracuda	orange enamel, chrome China base, white stripe on side w/orange "426" on rear fender, white HW logo on front fender below stripe, behind front wheel, black int. & hood scoop, tinted window, asw-3sp	$4
☐ 📷	1064	Lakester	met. silver w/matching painted China base, blue, black & green tampo on side w/black "93005" & green & black "Alien X plorer," black HW logo above "X plorer", chrome engines & int., green-tint canopy, alw-5sp	$2
☐ 📷	1065	Firebird	white enamel, gray plastic China base, silver, blue & red tampo on side w/red & blue "1" & "Huffman Racing" along with misc. racing decals, blue & white tampo on hood w/red & blue"Huffman Racing," red HW logo on side behind rear wheel, black int., smoked window, alw-yellow letter black 5sp	$4
☐ 📷	1066	Mustang Cobra	met. gold, black plastic India base, black striped tampo on side w/gold "Mustang" in cove on door, black HW logo high on door above stripes, black int., clear window, asw-5sp	$3
☐ 📷	1067	Express Lane	orange plastic body, metal China base, engine & push handle, red & black "Floyd$ Market" tampo over yellow on side, red seat & butterfly steering wheel, black HW logo on rear, 5sp	$3

Rail Rodder

1970 Plymouth Barracuda

Lakester

Firebird

Mustang Cobra

Express Lane

Dodge Concept Car

Ford GT-90

'40 Ford

Blimp

'32 Ford

Scorchin' Scooter

Panoz GTR-1

'59 Cadillac

Photo		No.	Name	Description	Price
❑	📷	1068	Dodge Concept Car	met. silver, metal China base, black & gold stripes on side w/black & gold stripes on rocker panel, white "Dodge" in front of rear wheel on rocker panel, black panel w/gold stripes on hood & trunk, tampo on hood has white "Dodge" on each side, black HW logo on rear fender above rear wheel, black int, tinted window, g/bbs	$2
❑	📷	1069	'40 Ford	a. yellow enamel, black plastic China base, dark red & black over gold "Haulin' 40" tampo on roof, red, gold & black tampos on both fenders, red & black stripes on side of running board, black int, roll bar, tubs, rear wing, wheelie bars, scoop & grille, black HW logo on rear fender behind wheel, smoked window, 5dot	$10
❑				b. same as (a), maroon & black over gold "Haulin' 40" tampo on roof, 5 dot	$4
❑	📷	1070	'32 Ford	met. red, gray plastic China base, silver, white & black tampo on side w/gray & black "Frankie's Garage," chrome engine& grille, black HW logo on lower part of side by headers, black int., clear window, 5dot	$4
❑	📷	1071	Panoz GTR-1	black enamel, black plastic China base, red, white & silver tampo on door, white "Power" & "Atittude," red "Speed" on side of front fender, white "Samurai Racing" on top of left front fender, red & silver sword tampo on top of right front fender, silver, red & white Samurai warrior tampo on hood with two white swiggles, white HW logo on rear fender behind rear wheel below white "Honor," red int. & rear wing, clear window, 3sp	$2
❑		1072	Unreleased		—
❑	📷	1073	Ford GT-90	red enamel, metal China base, white, gold & black tampo on side, white painted headlights, gold stripe below rear window, silver"FORD GT-90" on rocker panel in front of rear wheel, black HW logo in center front by windshield, black int., smoked window, asw-t/b	$2
❑	📷	1074	Blimp	black plastic balloon, red plastic tail, red enamel metal Malaysia gondola, large red & yellow over white HW logo on side	$3

Photo	No.	Name	Description	Price
☐ 📷	1075	Scorchin' Scooter	red enamel, blue-tint metal Malaysia base, black tampos w/white "Duncans" & gold & black "Motorcycles" on tank & side of rear fender, black tampo w/gold & white "Tall Dude Shocks" on side of front fender, black, white & gold tampo on side of tank, white HW logo on rear fender below "Motorcycles" black plastic forks & handlebars, black painted seat, black spoked wheel w/chrome rim	$5
☐ 📷	1076	'59 Cadillac	a. met. blue w/white cove & silver pinstripe, chrome Malaysia base, black "Eldorado" on front fender behind front wheel, white pinstriping on hood & trunk, silver HW logo on rear fender behind rear wheel, white int, blue-tint window, bbs	$9
☐			b. same as (a), gray pinstripe around cove & gray HW logo on rear fender, bbs	$4
☐ 📷	1077	'57 Chevy	red enamel metal body, chrome Malaysia base, white & gold tampos on side w/white & gold flames on rear fender, thin white pinstripe on side with gold "Custom Rod," white & gold tampo on roof w/thin white pinstripes, white HW logo above rear wheel, blue-tint metal engine, black int, black window, g/bbs	$4
☐ 📷	1078	Camaro Z28	met. blue, metal Malaysia base, red & white flag tampo on side w/white & gold stars, red & white flag tampo on hood w/white & gold stars on both sides, large white "3" over gold "30" tampo on roof, small white "3" over gold "30" tampo on rear roof pillar, white HW logo on front fender above flag tampo, black window, 3sp	$3
☐ 📷	1079	'63 Corvette	candy gray, black plastic Malaysia base, black panels w/yellow pinstripes & light green & white tampos on hood, roof & side, yellow HW logo on rear fender behind rear wheel, black int, clear window, asw-5dot	$3
☐ 📷	1080	Humvee	a. green pearl plastic body, metal Malaysia base, black, silver & yellow tampo on side w/black "Hummer" above rear wheel, yellow circle w/black "B" & silver "Man" tampo on side of front fender and center of hood, silver "HUMVEE" on rear deck, no HW logo, gray window, asw-ct/b	$3
☐			b. same as (a), no "HUMVEE" on rear deck, asw-ct/b	$8
☐			c. green pearl plastic body, silver met. painted India base, yellow circle w/black "b" & silver "Man"tampo on side of front fender and center of hood, flat yellow, silver & flat black side tampo, green showing through black part of tampo, "Hummer" missing from side, silver "HUMVEE" at top of trunk, silver HW logo above notch on lower trunk, gray window, asw-ct/b	$10
☐ 📷	1081	Power Plower	met. green, metal Thailand base, white & orange "Oak Bros." light green pinstripes & tree w/white "Mulching" & "earth pros" on door, white "Landscaping" & "Tree Trimming" with light green& white leaf, & orange, white & brown acorn on side of box, white "Bio Recycling" & light green pinstripes on side of front fender, white HW logo high, behind rear wheel, light green int., roll bar & bed, yellow-tint window, asw-ct/b	$3

'57 Chevy

Camaro Z28

'63 Corvette

Humvee

Power Plower

Jaguar XJ220

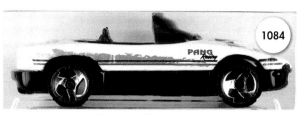

Mazda MX-5 Miata

Blown Camaro

Porsche 928

Blown Camaro

Toyota MR2

	Photo	No.	Name	Description	Price
☐	📷	1082	Jaguar XJ220	met. gold, black plastic Malaysia base, black & light blue tampos on side & hood, large black "Jaguar XJ220" above rear wheel, small white "Jaguar" & emblem behind front wheel, white circle emblem in center on front of hood, white HW logo behind rear wheel, gold int., smoked window, g3sp	$2
☐	📷	1083	Blown Camaro	a. met. teal, metal Malaysia base, thin silver stripes on left side hood w/silver & black "Blown," gold & black "Camaro" & black & silver "650" w/small gold & silver squares, side has thin silver pinstripes w/gold & silver squares, large black & silver "650," silver & black "Blown" w/gold & black "Camaro," black stripe on rocker panel & bottom of rear fender, thin black stripes going diagonal under silver stripes on door, small HW logo high behind rear wheel, black int., smoked window, bbs	$3
☐	📷			b. same as (a), stripes on hood are in the center, bbs	$10
☐	📷	1084	Mazda MX-5 Miata	white enamel, black painted Malaysia base, thick silver splotch on side w/thin purple & black pinstripes, purple "PANG" & black "Racing" on front fender above stripes, large purple over black "Racing" on front fender above stripes, large purple over black "Racing" on front fender above stripes, large purple over silver "OFFICIAL PACE CAR" on hood, thin purple & black stripes on hood & trunk over silver splotches, black "CAR 23" on trunk w/silver over purple HW logo, black int., smoked window, asw-3sp	$2
☐	📷	1085	Porsche 928	gold pearl, metal Malaysia base, black HW logo on nose, black window, 5dot	$2
☐	📷	1086	Toyota MR2	candy purple, black plastic Malaysia base, silver diagonal stripes on door & roof, white, black & orange "4" on roof & door, white, black & orange "MR2" & white & black "Racing" on rear fender, thin silver pinstripe through center of side, HW logo on front fender high behind wheel, gray int., clear window, asw-3sp	$2
☐	📷	1087	Rig Wrecker	yellow enamel, chrome Malaysia base, gray, white & black tampo on side, white & black "Finish Towing" on door w/small black "Radio Dispatched" & three blue & white stripes, "City of Hot Wheels," small gray www.hotwheels.com, black "24 Hour Service," and small blue HW logo high on side by black plastic exhaust stack, large white & blue "Finish Line" w/blue "Towing" & small white "Moving The Community Since 1999" above rear wheels, black outlined doors w/blue "TOOLS" & "CABLES" blue plastic boom & lights above roof, black int. & grille, clear window, asw-5dot	$5
☐	📷	1088	Speed Machine	black enamel, metal Malaysia base, red outlined eagle on small white & orange circle w/orange & yellow flames on front, orange & yellow flames on side w/white "SPEED SEEKER" & "Hot Wheels" logo, white int., yellow-tint canopy, g5dot	$3
☐	📷	1089	25th Anniversary Lamborghini Countach	candy gray, black plastic Malaysia base, white HW logo in lower-left side of windshield, black int., clear window, asw-5dot	$3

Photo	No.	Name	Description	Price
❑ 📷	1090	'97 Corvette	black enamel, black plastic Malaysia base, white & light red tampo on side w/misc. racing decals, silver "CORVETTE" above rear wheel, black "1" in white & silver "World Racers" tampo on door, red HW logo high on door, bronze stripe tampo on hood w/large white bow tie & small "CORVETTE," silver "USA 1" & black "1" in white & silver "World Racers" tampo, "Heraldawest" twice on front bumper in white, white int., blue-tint window, alw-3sp	$3
❑ 📷	1091	X-Ploder	a. black plastic body, metal Malaysia base, yellow & orange flames on side, orange HW logo in front of rear wheel, chrome engine & driver, red-tint canopy, t/b	$7
❑ 📷			b. same as (a), orange HW logo behind rear wheel	$3
❑ 📷	1092	'58 Corvette	a. black enamel, black plastic Malaysia base, aqua engine compartment (some of these were repaints of the aqua cars & you can still see the aqua paint under the hood), chrome int., exhaust, bumpers & grille, red HW logo in white box on trunk, smoked window, silver painted headlights, bbs	$15
❑			b. same as (a), silver met. painted engine compartment, bbs	$4
❑ 📷	1093	BMW 850i	met. gold, met. gold plastic Malaysia base, black HW logo on nose, black int. & taillights, smoked window, asw-bbs	$2
❑ 📷	1094	Ferrari F355 Berlinetta	red enamel, metal Malaysia base, larger yellow & black Ferrari horse logo on hood w/ green & white stripe above, small yellow& black Ferrari horse logo on door close to front fender, black HW logo high behind rear wheel, black int., clear window, asw-5sp	$4
❑ 📷	1095	Mercedes SLK	met. gray, black painted India base, red HW logo high behind rear wheel, black int., smoked window & headlights, asw-t/b	$2
❑ 📷	1096	Avus Quattro	chrome body, black plastic Malaysia base, smoked canopy w/black & met. silver tampos, black int., black HW logo top rear, alw-5sp	$2
❑ 📷	1097	'31 Doozie	met. red, metal Malaysia base, black plastic fenders, top & int., gray HW logo on side of fender-mounted spare tire, clear window, alw-bbs	$3

Rig Wrecker · 1087

X-Ploder · 1091 (a)

Speed Machine · 1088

X-Ploder · 1091 (b)

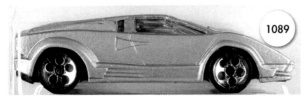

25th Anniversary Lamborghini Countach · 1089

'58 Corvette · 1092

'97 Corvette · 1090

BMW 850i · 1093

Ferrari F355 Berlinetta

'37 Bugatti

Mercedes SLK

Road Rocket

Avus Quattro

Power Pipes

'31 Doozie

Power Pipes

	Photo	No.	Name	Description	Price
❑	📷	1098	'37 Bugatti	black enamel w/yellow cove, metal Malaysia base, chrome int., grille & headlights, small HW logo above cove in front of rear wheel, clear window, alw-bbs	$3
❑	📷	1099	Road Rocket	red plastic body, black plastic top, metal Malaysia base, black tampo on side w/red & black HW logo behind front wheel, chrome engine & roll bar, red int., bbs	$2
❑	📷	1100	Power Pipes	a. white plastic body, red painted metal Malaysia base, red & yellow tampo on side w/red HW logo behind front wheel, gold chrome scoops & int., red-tint canopy, 5dot	$2
❑	📷			b. same as (a), asw-5dot	$15
❑	📷	1101	Radar Ranger	teal enamel, metal Malaysia base, large white & black "radar ranger" w/small "mission control" & "11" tampo on side, small white & black "radar ranger" w/small "mission control" & "11" tampo on top of right pod, black circle w/white "6" & "recon. vehicle" on side by canopy & front of right pod, black HW logo on front of right pod, white plastic radar dish & white insert, clear canopy, alw-ct/b	$3
❑	📷	1102	Mini Truck	black enamel, black plastic Malaysia base, gold chrome engine, shifter, front grille, exhaust & speakers in rear bed, gold HW logo on front of hood, red int., smoked window, gbbs	$2
❑	📷	1103	1980 Corvette	met. gold, metal Malaysia base, black roof, smoked window, black int., black HW logo on rear plate, asw-bbs	$4
❑	📷	1104	Twang Thang	orange pearl, purple plastic Malaysia base, purple plastic guitars on side, (no color on strings or hardware), gold chrome engine, exhaust & int., smoked window, black HW logo on nose, g5sp	$3
❑	📷	1105	Mustang Mach I	met. blue, black plastic Malaysia base, thin white, wide silver & thin orange stripes on hood & side, black rocker panel w/two thin white stripes & "MACH 1" behind front wheel, small white "Mustang" above "MACH 1" on lower front fender, black int, hood scoop, tach, grille, rear window louvers & spoiler, white HW logo high on rear fender behind wheel, clear window, bbs	$4

Photo	No.	Name	Description	Price
☐	1106	Go Kart	a. lt. orange enamel painted metal Malaysia body, metal chassis HW logo & "123 racing," orange "MJ engineering," 5dot	$8
☐			b. dark orange enamel painted metal Malaysia body, metal chassis & engine, black plastic seat, black panel w/white & black HW logo & "123 racing," orange "MJ engineering," 5dot	$5
☐	1107	Chrysler Thunderbolt (very hard to find)	dark met. blue, black plastic Malaysia base, silver flames outlined in white on side w/black & white "Lucero," silver "36" outlined in white on front fender above flame behind wheel, lower portion of side has wide black stripe w/one silver pinstripe on top, two silver pinstripes below black stripe on rocker panel w/silver"thunderstreak" in front of rear wheel, four triangles above Thunderstreak in black stripe, white int., smoked window, asw-3sp	$5
☐	1115	Ferrari F335 Challenge	a. silver pearl, metal Malaysia base, green pearl, white enamel & red enamel stripes on hood & roof, misc. racing decals on side, small rectangle yellow & black Ferrari horse logo on hood, no HW logo, black int., smoked rear spoiler & window, asw-5sp	$3
☐			b. same as (a), asw-5dot	$71

Some Ferrari cars now have a sticker on the back of the package that says, "Official Licensed Product," with a registration number. If you have a card that does have the "Official" sticker, add $1 to the value of the car.

Radar Ranger

Mini Truck

1980 Corvette

Twang Thang

Mustang Mach I

Go Kart

1999 First Editions, #21-360 Modena

Ferrari F355 Challenge

Photo	No.	Name	Description	Price
❏ 📷	1118	Ferrari 456M	red enamel, metal Malaysia base, small rectangle yellow & black Ferrari horse logo on hood w/green & white stripes above it, yellow HW logo on rear of trunk, tan int., clear window, asw-5sp	$3
❏ 📷	1119	Ferrari F355 Spider	red enamel, metal Malaysia base, green & white stripe over yellow & black Ferrari logo on hood & front fender behind front wheel, small black lettering in front of rear wheel, no HW logo, tan int., clear window, asw-5sp	$5
❏ 📷	1120	Ferrari F50	a. red enamel, black painted Malaysia base w/"Ferrari F50" green & white stripe over yellow & black rectangle Ferrari logo on hood, small triangle yellow & black rectangle Ferrari logo w/green & white stripe above it on front fender behind front wheel, small black lettering in front of rear wheel, no HW logo, black int. & rear grille, clear window, asw-5sp	$5
❏			b. same as (a), w/"F50 SPIDER" on base	$5
❏ 📷	1121	Chevy 1500	orange plastic body, met. silver painted India base, black, white & red bull's-eye tampo on side w/black & white "2" behind rear wheel, small white HW logo on rear fender by taillight, black int., roll bar & bed cover, tinted window, asw-5dot	$3

Ferrari 456M

Ferrari F50

Ferrari F355 Spider

Chevy 1500

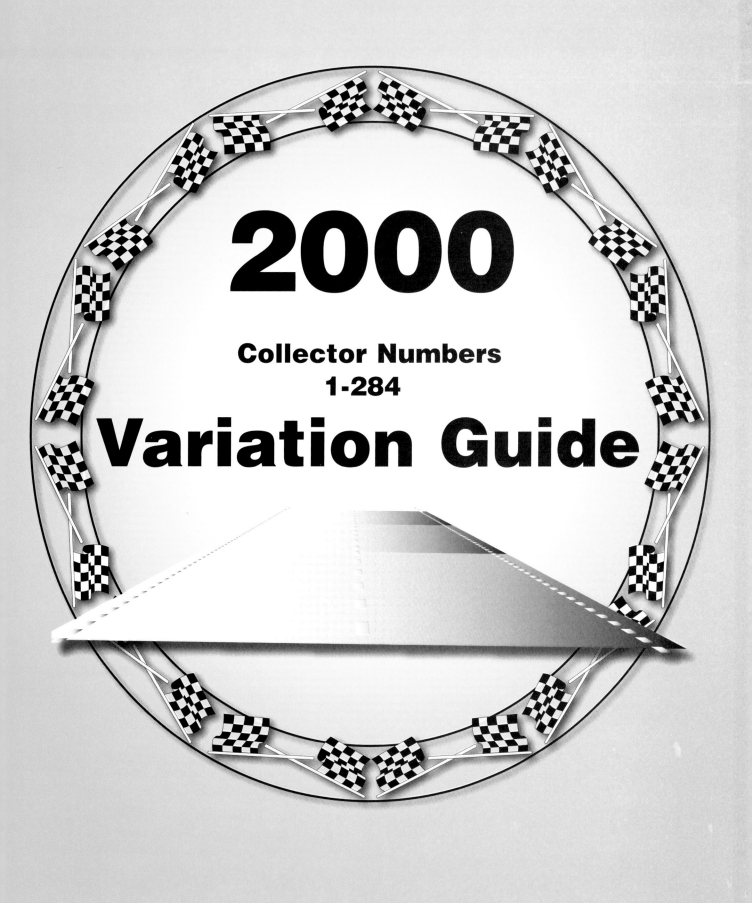

2000

Collector Numbers
1-284

Variation Guide

Future Fleet 2000 Series

Photo	No.	Name	Description	Price
❑	1	Ford GT-90	a. black enamel, metal Malaysia base, silver, brown & black side tampo, silver & green numbers on door & rocker panel, rear window has silver oval outlined w/two black pinstripes w/black HW flame design & two dots, & white over black "Speed Fleet 2000," brown HW logo below numbers on door, green-tint window, white int., asw-bbs	$3
❑ 📷			b. same as (a), metal China base, lighter brown in tampo, asw-bbs	$2
❑			c. same as (b), asw-3sp	$2
❑ 📷	2	Pontiac Rageous	a. black enamel, gray plastic Malaysia base, pearl blue & gold side tampos, front door has silver oval w/black HW flame design & two dots outlined w/black pinstripe, silver "Speed Fleet 2000" below oval, silver "Rageous" on back boor, brown HW logo high on rear fender behind wheel, red-tint canopy, red int., alw-3sp	$3
❑			b. same as (a), gray plastic China base, lighter gold color in side tampo, alw-3sp	$2
❑ 📷	3	Jeepster	a. black enamel, black plastic fenders, metal Malaysia base, brown, blue & silver striped side tampo, door has silver oval w/black HW flame design & two dots outlined w/black pinstripe, silver "Speed Fleet 2000" below oval, silver "Y2K" on lower front fender behind wheel, black int., blue-tint window, alw-5sp	$40
❑			b. same as (a), silver painted Malaysia base, alw-5sp	$3
❑ 📷	4	Chrysler Thunderbolt	black enamel, gray plastic Malaysia base, yellow stripes & purple design side tampo w/ silver oval w/black HW flame design & two dots outlined w/black pinstripe, silver "Speed Fleet 2000" below oval, purple HW logo behind yellow stripes high on rear fender, yellow int., yellow-tint window w/black plastic roof, asw-3sp	$2

Future Fleet 2000 Series, Ford GT-90

Future Fleet 2000 Series, Jeepster

Future Fleet 2000 Series, Pontiac Rageous

Future Fleet 2000 Series, Chrysler Thunderbolt

Hot Rod Magazine

Photo	No.	Name	Description	Price
❑ 📷	5	Phaeton	a. met. red, metal Malaysia base, flat black flame-type tampo w/gold outline on hood & side, gold HW logo in front of rear wheel above exhaust, tan plastic top, black int., smoked window, g/bbs	$3
❑			b. same as (a), metal Thailand base, g/bbs	$2
❑ 📷	6	Track T	a. yellow enamel, metal Malaysia base, green, yellow & black flames on side, "Wayne's Body Shop" in black over green tampo on rear deck w/black & yellow HW logo, white plastic cover & dash, metal seat, t/b	$3
❑			b. same as (a), metal Thailand base, t/b	$2
❑ 📷	7	Tail Dragger	a. white pearl met., metal Malaysia base, purple & orange flames on hood, roof & trunk, gold HW logo in tampo on trunk, purple int., orange-tint window, asw-gbbs	$45
❑			b. same as (a), silver painted metal Malaysia base, asw-gbbs	$3

Photo		No.	Name	Description	Price
☐	📷	8	'33 Ford Roadster	a. met. green, green plastic fenders, metal Malaysia base, black, orange & yellow side tampo, yellow & black HW logo in front of rear wheel, gold chrome dash, engine & grille, black int. & running boards, clear window, 5sp	$5
☐				b. same as (a), dull gold engine, 5sp	$7
☐				c. same as (a), t/b	$2

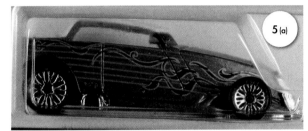

Hot Rod Magazine Series, Phaeton

Hot Rod Magazine Series, '33 Ford Roadster

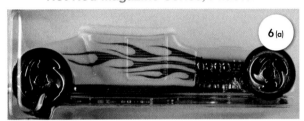

Hot Rod Magazine Series, Track T

Hot Rod Magazine Series, '33 Ford Roadster

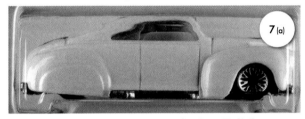

Hot Rod Magazine Series, Tail Dragger

Seein' 3-D Series

Photo		No.	Name	Description	Price
☐	📷	9	Propper Chopper	red enamel, black plastic Malaysia base, black, white, yellow & silver side tampo, white "UNIT" & large silver, white & yellow "3" outlined in black on side behind windows & small white numbers below, small white "Trackside Assistance" below window, small white HW logo back by tail, black tail, hook & wings, yellow rotor blades, black int., yellow-tint window	$2
☐	📷	10	1970 Dodge Charger Daytona	a. blue enamel, chrome Malaysia base, wide black stripe on hood w/thin orange & whites pinstripes on each side, orange, black & white side tampo w/large black, orange & white "22" on door, white HW logo on rear fender behind wheel, orange int., clear window, asw-5sp	$4
☐	📷			b. same as (a), asw-t/b	$2
☐	📷			c. same as (b), brown replaces orange in tampo, asw-t/b	$4
☐				d. same as (a), asw-bbs	$65
☐	📷	11	Lexus SC400	yellow enamel, black Malaysia plastic base, black & silver side tampo, orange stripe painted lower body line w/silver pinstripe, black HW logo behind rear wheel, white int., smoked window, asw-3sp	$2
☐	📷	12	Olds 442	a. met. green, chrome Malaysia base, lower half of body is black w/thin light green pinstripe at top, large blue, light green & yellow "OLDS" & yellow "442" on side, small yellow HW logo in front of rear wheel, white int., clear window, asw-3sp	$2
☐				b. same as (a), asw-5sp	$50

Seein' 3-D Series, Propper Chopper

Seein' 3-D Series,
1970 Dodge Charger Daytona

Seein' 3-D Series,
1970 Dodge Charger Daytona

Seein' 3-D Series, Lexus SC400

Seein' 3-D Series,
1970 Dodge Charger Daytona

Seein' 3-D Series, Olds 442

Snack Time Series

	Photo	No.	Name	Description	Price
❑	📷	13	Callaway C7	a. met. green, black plastic Malaysia base, yellow & orange lettering on hood w/yellow & black "MJ Foods," yellow & orange lettering on door, yellow & black pretzels on side, black & orange stripes on rocker panel, orange painted headlights, orange int. & rear wing, clear window, 5dot	$2
❑	📷			b. same as (a), 5sp	$4
❑	📷	14	Firebird	dark orange enamel, black plastic China base, large white & black "Yip's BBQ Cheesy Potato Chips" over yellow, red, black & white tampo on hood, yellow, red, black & white tampo on side w/large white & black "Yip's BBQ Cheesy Potato Chips" on door, black HW logo on roof pillar behind side window, white int., clear window, alw-5sp	$2
❑	📷	15	Monte Carlo Concept Car	met. blue, red enamel painted metal Malaysia base, brown & black cookie side tampo outlined in black & white, white panel on door w/black "Alan's Favorite" w/white & red "Deluxe Cookies," small white lettering above front wheel, dark red & white HW logo above rear wheel, small white, black & brown circle tampo on side roof pillar, light gray int., clear window, asw-bbs	$2
❑	📷	16	Dodge Sidewinder	a. butterscotch enamel, gray plastic Malaysia base, pink & dark red "Pop Corn" w/small white & black lettering top & bottom, dark red, black & white pop corn striping on side w/"Pop Corn" on door, red & white HW logo on rocker panel in front of rear wheel, red int., silver shifter, red-tint window, t/b	$3
❑	📷			b. same as (a), yellow enamel, "Pop Corn" on hood is much pinker, all reds in tampo are much brighter, t/b	$2

Snack Time Series, Callaway C7

Snack Time Series, Callaway C7

Snack Time Series, Firebird

Snack Time Series, Dodge Sidewinder

Snack Time Series, Monte Carlo Concept Car

Snack Time Series, Dodge Sidewinder

Mad Maniax Series

Photo	No.	Name	Description	Price
☐	17	Hot Wheels 500	blue enamel, metal Malaysia base, black plastic driver, yellow letter b7sp	$2
☐ 📷	18	Camaro Z28	a. met. silver, black painted metal Malaysia base, hood has yellow & black flames w/red & white face & red & white "Fire Eater" at front, side has yellow & black flames w/red & white face, red & white "Fire Eater" on rocker panel in front of rear wheel, red HW logo high on rear fender behind wheel, black window, bbs	$3
☐ 📷			b. same as (a), t/b	$65
☐	19	Slideout	black enamel, red plastic Malaysia base, white plastic top wing has brown & black character w/orange eyes breathing flames & light orange HW logo at left, yellow, gold & red flames on side w/white star accents, white pinstriped rollcage, white square w/black & red circle behind engine, white plastic front wing, gray plastic engine & rear pushbar, 5sp	$2
☐ 📷	20	Twin Mill II	orange enamel, gray plastic Malaysia base, pink & gold flame tampo on side w/brown, white black & gold head, brown & white pinstriping behind front wheel, chrome engines, black window, alw-g5dot	$2

Mad Maniax Series, Camaro Z28

Mad Maniax Series, Slideout

Mad Maniax Series, Camaro Z28

Mad Maniax Series, Twin Mill II

Attack Pack Series

Photo	No.	Name	Description	Price
☐ 📷	21	Nissan Truck	met. brown, black plastic Malaysia base, large dark orange, white & black tiger tampo on side w/smaller gold, white & black tiger head on door, dark orange & black-over-white HW logo on front fender, dark orange & black over white HW logo on hood w/large black, orange & white "Tiger," chrome rear engine, gray int. & rollbar, clear window, alw-ct/b	$2
☐ 📷	22	Power Plower	a. pearl purple, metal Malaysia base, white, red, orange & black "Piranha" tampo on hood, white, red, orange & black "Piranha" tampo on side, orange HW logo on hood above "Piranha" tampo day-glo orange int., roll bar & bed, clear window, asw-ct/b	$3
☐			b. same as (a), silver painted Malaysia base	$8
☐ 📷	23	'79 Ford F-150	black enamel, black plastic bed cap, chrome Malaysia base, light pearl green, silver & yellow Praying Mantis on side w/yellow & green "Mantis" on rear fender, silver painted rocker panel, black HW logo on rocker panel behind rear wheel, black int., clear window, alw-5sp	$4
☐ 📷	24	Dodge Ram 1500	dark met. red, black plastic lower half & China base, yellow, black & red Scorpion tampo over a black & purple tampo, black & yellow "Scorpion" w/black & orange "Sting" on door, black int., clear window, alw-5sp	$3

Attack Pack Series, Nissan Truck

Attack Pack Series, '79 Ford F-150

Attack Pack Series, Dodge Ram 1500

Attack Pack Series, Power Plower

Circus On Wheels Series

Photo	No.	Name	Description	Price
☐ 📷	25	'56 Flashsider	met. red, gold chrome Malaysia base, black panel on rear bed w/yellow lettering & yellow, orange & purple flames, orange & yellow "Circus" on hood outlined in silver & black w/small yellow "on wheels," black & yellow HW logo above the "C" in Circus, black window, g5dot	$3
☐	26	'32 Ford Delivery	a. black enamel, green plastic fenders, metal Malaysia base, yellow lightning tampo w/light green outline & white "Circus" on door, silver "on wheels" below Circus & small silver HW logo above, rear side panel has green over yellow "Alectra" tampo & small yellow writing below it w/silver pinstripe around it all, rear door has green lightning tampo w/yellow & green HW logo, chrome radiator & headlights, green int., clear window, bbs	$3
☐ 📷			b. same as (a), silver painted Malaysia base, bbs	$8
☐ 📷	27	Fat Fendered '40	a. blue enamel, metal Malaysia base, black over silver panel on side w/orange stripes, black "The Weise Brothers" in center orange stripe in tampo, small black "Worlds Greatest Gymnasts" in lower orange stripe, silver HW logo on rear fender behind wheel, tan int., clear window, asw-bbs	$4

Photo	No.	Name	Description	Price
☐	27	Fat Fendered '40	b. same as (a), gray replaces silver in side tampo & HW logo	$8
☐ 📷			c. same as (a), asw-t/b	$10
☐			d. same as (c), light brown replaces orange stripes in side tampo, asw-t/b	$4
☐			e. same as (a), asw-5sp	$40
☐	28	Dairy Delivery	a. met. purple, gray plastic China base, white & black "Worlds Smallest Clowns" on side in yellow & purple tampo, red & white "Circus on Wheels" in red & yellow tampo on door, red & white HW logo above the "C" in Circus, day-glo yellow int., yellow-tint window, g5sp	$5
☐ 📷			b. same as (a), light green replaces yellow in tampo, g5sp	$3

Circus On Wheels Series, '56 Flashsider

Circus On Wheels Series Fat Fendered '40

Circus On Wheels Series, '32 Ford Delivery

Circus On Wheels Series, Fat Fendered '40

Circus On Wheels Series, Dairy Delivery

Circus On Wheels Series, Dairy Delivery

Circus On Wheels Series, Fat Fendered '40

CD Customs Series

Photo	No.	Name	Description	Price
☐ 📷	29	Chrysler Pronto	met. green, black plastic Malaysia base, silver & black stripe tampo on hood w/black & white HW logo up by windshield, silver & black stripe tampo on side fenders & rocker panel, black panel around side window, large white HW logo on door up to roof pillar, small silver "Chrysler Pronto" on trunk, black int., clear window, 3sp	$2
☐ 📷	30	Pikes Peak Tacoma	a. black enamel, black painted metal vent, black plastic Malaysia base, large red, yellow & white "CRASH!" on side, black & red "2" on side of rear wing, white & red "CD ROM" on rocker panel below door, black & red "CD ROM" in yellow tampo & large black, red & white "2" on hood, red HW logo behind rear wheel, red plastic int. & bed cover, clear window, asw-gbbs	$2
☐			b. same as (a), unpainted metal vent in door, asw-gbbs	$7
☐ 📷			c. same as (a), metal insert in side vent missing, red plastic int. showing, asw-gbbs	$20
☐ 📷			d. same as (b), asw-g5dot	$10
☐ 📷	31	Shadow Mk IIa	a. white enamel, gray plastic Malaysia base, black fade to orange panel on side w/black, white & orange "Stunt Track," white & orange "Driver" & white "CD ROM," white & gray circle outlined in orange w/red "17" in center, black w/orange dots in scoop & red fade to orange tampo on top of front fenders, right fender w/white circle outlined in black w/red "17" at center, left fender w/black HW logo & white lettering below, red painted rear wing w/white HW logo, black & white "Stunt Track" & small white "Driver CD ROM," gray int., 5sp	$45
☐ 📷			b. same as (a), black plastic Malaysia base, 5sp	$3
☐ 📷	32	Pontiac Banshee	a. pearl orange met., metal Malaysia base, black & silver flames on front, black panels on rear w/white "Design" & eye tampo on driver side, silver circle outlined in orange w/"CCD," silver "Custom Car Designs" & small white "CD ROM" on passenger side, black int. & roof band, clear window, asw-5dot	$2

CD Customs Series, Chrysler Pronto

CD Customs Series, Shadow Mk IIa

CD Customs Series, Pikes Peak Tacoma

CD Customs Series, Shadow Mk IIa

CD Customs Series, Pikes Peak Tacoma

CD Customs Series, Pontiac Banshee

CD Customs Series, Pikes Peak Tacoma

Kung Fu Force Series

	Photo	No.	Name	Description	Price
❑	📷	33	Toyota MR2	black enamel, black plastic Malaysia base, brown, orange, gold & white tampos on hood & side, gold HW logo low behind rear wheel, red int., clear window, asw-3sp	$2
❑	📷	34	'99 Mustang	red enamel, black plastic Thailand base, black, yellow & orange side tampo, yellow, black, & orange fists tampo on hood, yellow HW logo low behind rear wheel, black int., clear window, asw-3sp	$2
❑	📷	35	Shadow Jet II	a. blue plastic body, metal Malaysia base, yellow, brown & black lightning bolt side tampo w/yellow lettering over rear wheel, yellow & blue HW logo at front, brown panel on top w/yellow & black lightning bolts, brown, orange & black figure, yellow, brown & black "Dragon Style Kung Fu" tampo chrome int., red-tint canopy, 3sp	$2
❑				b. same as (a), silver painted Malaysia base, 3sp	$4
❑	📷	36	Mini Truck	a. met. green, black Malaysia base, gold, brown, yellow & black side tampo, black HW logo on rear fender up by spoiler, black, & brown stripes on top of front fenders w/gold & brown Asian characters, brown, yellow & black tampo on nose, black rear bed insert w/chrome speakers, chrome shifter, engine & grille, black int., clear windshield, t/b	$2
❑	📷			b. same as (a), asw-t/b	$15

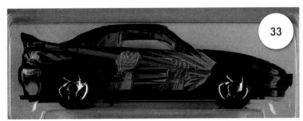

Kung Fu Force Series, Toyota MR2

Kung Fu Force Series, '99 Mustang

Kung Fu Force Series, Shadow Jet II

Kung Fu Force Series, Mini Truck

Kung Fu Force Series, Mini Truck

Speed Blaster Series

	Photo	No.	Name	Description	Price
❑	📷	37	Firebird Funny Car	pearl orange met., blue-tint metal Malaysia base, white, light blue, yellow & black side tampo, large black & white HW logo on side of rear wing above large black & white "Power," light blue, white & black tampos on each side of hood, blue-tint metal int., clear window, 5sp	$3
❑	📷	38	At-A-Tude	candy gray met., black plastic Malaysia base, black, yellow, orange & blue side tampo, large yellow & black "Performance" in cove, yellow & black HW logo on orange shirt behind cove, orange rear wing, chrome int. & exhaust, orange-tint window, 5sp	$2
❑	📷	39	Mustang Cobra	a. pearl blue, black plastic Malaysia base, yellow, black, orange & white side tampo, black HW logo in yellow part of tampo on door, gray int., clear window, asw-5sp	$3

	Photo	No.	Name	Description	Price
☐	📷	39	Mustang Cobra	b. same as (a), light blue pearl, asw-5sp	$2
☐				c. same as (b), black plastic India base, asw-5sp	$3
☐	📷	40	Shelby Cobra 427 S/C	white enamel, metal Thailand base, dark blue, light blue white & black side tampo, black & white HW logo behind rear wheel, blue int., blue-tint windshield, alw-5sp	$3

Speed Blaster Series, Firebird Funny Car

Speed Blaster Series, Mustang Cobra

Speed Blaster Series, At-A-Tude

Speed Blaster Series, Shelby Cobra 427 S/C

Speed Blaster Series, Mustang Cobra

Skate Series

	Photo	No.	Name	Description	Price
☐	📷	41	Rigor Motor	a. candy blue, metal Malaysia base, blue, black & white tampo on top, blue, black & white "Birdhouse" tampo on side, white HW logo behind rear wheel, blue-tint chrome engine & fuel tank, white plastic skulls & radiator, blue-tint canopy, 5sp	$8
☐	📷			b. same as (a), silver painted Malaysia base	$2
☐	📷	42	Sol-Aire CX4	a. white pearl, black plastic Malaysia base, black panel on side w/yellow, orange & silver designs, white "6" outlined in silver, orange HW logo in front of rear wheel on rocker panel, black panel on nose w/white "6" outlined in red, black painted headlights, black int., yellow-tint window, 3sp	$75

The Sol-Aire CX4 (a) variations were the baggie cars from the Criss Cross Crash sets, only a few have been found in the numbered packages so far.

	Photo	No.	Name	Description	Price
☐	📷			b. white enamel, black plastic Malaysia base, black side panel w/yellow & black cat face w/red eyes in front of rear wheel, red over white tampo w/black "birdhouse," black panel on roof & nose, red & black HW logo on roof facing front, black panel on nose has yellow cat face w/red eyes, black painted headlights black int., yellow-tint window, 3sp	$2

	Photo	No.	Name	Description	Price
❏	📷	42	Sol-Aire CX4	c. same as (b), maroon replaces red in side tampo & cats eyes, 3sp	$4
❏	📷	43	Speed Blaster	orange enamel, black plastic Malaysia base, black panel on side w/white tampo, black & white "Birdhouse" over white & burnt orange background on front w/white HW logo, black window & rear engine, 3sp	$2
❏	📷	44	Combat Medic	gray met., black plastic Thailand base, white, black & silver bird skeleton on side w/dark & light red designs, silver & red w/black outlined "Tony Hawk Birdhouse" & small black HW logo behind rear wheel, black "Birdhouse" over silver & white background w/red & silver flames on hood, black int., red-tint window, asw-5sp	$5

Skate Series, Rigor Motor

Skate Series, Sol-Aire CX4

Skate Series, Rigor Motor

Skate Series, Speed Blaster

Skate Series, Sol-Aire CX4

Skate Series, Combat Medic

Skate Series, Sol-Aire CX4

Secret Code Series

	Photo	No.	Name	Description	Price
❏	📷	45	Fiat 500C	red enamel, blue-tint metal Malaysia base, pink panel on door w/black & white letters, pink panel on rear roof pillar, gold HW logo in front of black painted side vent, chrome engine & rear chute, black wing, chrome windshield, metal seat, 5sp	$5
❏	📷	46	Baby Boomer	a. light blue pearl met., metal Malaysia base, white side panel outlined in silver w/orange & black letters, chrome engine, gray plastic shifter, bug catcher & blower, 5sp	$3
❏	📷			b. same as (a), darker blue pearl met. color, metal China base, 5sp	$2
❏	📷	47	Tee'd Off	a. black enamel, metal Malaysia base & exhaust, gold & white hands w/gold HW logo on black plastic roof, chrome engine, white int., 5sp	$3
❏				b. same as (a), metal China base, lighter gold color in tampo on roof, 5sp	$2
❏	📷	48	Screamin' Hauler	a. light yellow enamel, blue-tint metal Malaysia base & seat, black rear tampo w/dark gold numbers & white pinstripe, black triangle by cockpit w/white circle & light orange "3," chrome engines, smoked window, 5sp	$4
❏	📷			b. light yellow enamel, silver painted China base & seat, black rear tampo w/light gold numbers & white pinstripe, black triangle by cockpit w/larger white circle & dark orange "3," smoked window, 5sp	$2

Secret Code Series, Fiat 500C

Secret Code Series, Tee'd Off

Secret Code Series, Baby Boomer

Secret Code Series, Screamin' Hauler

Secret Code Series, Baby Boomer

Secret Code Series, Screamin' Hauler

2000 Treasure Hunt Series

Photo	No.	Name	Description	Price
❏	49	#1-Double Vision	a. candy purple met., chrome Malaysia base & engines, silver white & black star w/"TH 2000" emblem & silver tampos on side, silver HW logo at rear of side fender, gray seat, clear canopy, chrome wheel Real Riders	$14
❏ 📷			b. same as (a), blowers backwards	$20
❏ 📷	50	#2-Tow Jam	yellow enamel, chrome Malaysia base, black painted hood w/small silver HW logo at front, black panel on roof w/black & orange star & white & black "TH 2000" emblem, black painted boom, black plastic sling, black window, chrome wheel Real Riders	$15
❏ 📷	51	#3-1936 Cord	a. met. silver, chrome Malaysia base, white, orange & black flames on hood, orange & black star & white & black "TH 2000" emblem & small black HW logo on door, white int., orange-tint window, chrome wheel whitewall Real Riders	$25
❏			b. same as (a), gray front fenders, chrome wheel whitewall Real Riders	$50
❏ 📷			c. same as (a), chrome wheel blackwall Real Riders	$15
❏ 📷	52	#4-Sweet Sixteen II	red enamel, metal Malaysia base, white & orange tampo on hood, white & orange side tampo w/black & white "TH 2000" emblem & small black HW logo, chrome engine & front drive, white int., orange-tint window, chrome wheel Real Riders	$12
❏ 📷	53	#5-Lakester	met. green, black painted Malaysia base, white tampo on top w/orange & black star & white & black "TH 2000" emblem & small black HW logo, gold chrome engines & int., yellow-tint window, alw-g5sp	$8
❏	54	#6-Go Kart	white pearl, gold frame, gold chrome wheeled Real Riders	$25
❏ 📷	55	#7-Chaparral 2	dark candy met. blue, white enamel painted Malaysia base, orange, black & white "TH 2000" emblem on nose, silver HW logo in black panel between two silver painted vents, orange over white "C" w/black over white "HAPARRAL 2" on side & rear, gray int. & rear engine, blue-tint window, chrome wheel Real Riders	$15

Photo		No.	Name	Description	Price
☐	📷	56	#8-'57 T-Bird	pearl green met., chrome Malaysia base, black & silver tampo on hood w/white, black & silver "TH 2000" emblem, black panel on side w/white, black & silver "TH 2000" emblem on door, black & silver panel on rear fender w/silver HW logo by taillight, yellow-tint window & int., chrome wheel Real Riders	$14
☐	📷	57	#9-Pikes Peak Celica	a. met. blue, black plastic Malaysia base, hood has six black over white rectangles on left side, white "7" in black circle w/white outline over orange in center of hood, black over white stripe tampo on side w/white "7" in black circle w/white outline over orange in center of door, black, white & orange "TH" emblem on upper right side of door, five black rectangle tampo on rocker panel, black roof & rear wing, black int., clear window, asw-gold chrome Real Riders	$14
☐				b. same as (a), asw-chrome wheel Real Riders	$98
☐		58	#10-'67 Pontiac GTO	a. pearl white, gold-tint Thailand base, black & gold ribbon side tampo w/black, gold & orange "TH 2000" emblem on rear fender, white HW logo & "GTO" on top of windshield, black int., smoked window, gold chrome Real Riders	$15
☐	📷			b. same as (a), darker gold chrome Thailand base	$15
☐				c. same as (b), gold chrome Malaysia base, gold chrome Real Riders reported to only be found in JCPenney sets	$40
☐	📷	59	#11-Ford GT-40	gold flake, black plastic Thailand base, wide black enamel stripe on hood, roof & rear deck, orange, black & white star w/white & black "TH 2000" emblem on hood, small silver HW logo on nose, silver painted vents on rear deck, black rear & front grilles, black int., clear window, chrome wheel Real Riders	$12
☐	📷	60	#12-1970 Chevelle	black enamel, chrome China base, orange & red tampo on side & hood, white star on rear fender w/white "TH 2000" in red circle, red HW logo above star, white int., tinted window, chrome wheel Real Riders	$20

2000 Treasure Hunt Series, #1-Double Vision

2000 Treasure Hunt Series, #3-1936 Cord

2000 Treasure Hunt Series, #2-Tow Jam

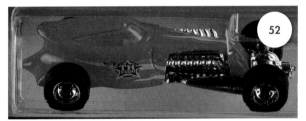

2000 Treasure Hunt Series, #4-Sweet 16 II

2000 Treasure Hunt Series, #3-1936 Cord

2000 Treasure Hunt Series, #5-Lakester

2000 Treasure Hunt Series,
#7-Chaparral 2

2000 Treasure Hunt Series,
#10-'67 Pontiac GTO

2000 Treasure Hunt Series,
#8-'57 T-Bird

2000 Treasure Hunt Series,
#11-Ford GT-40

2000 Treasure Hunt Series,
#9-Pikes Peak Celica

2000 Treasure Hunt Series,
#12-Chevelle SS

2000 First Editions

	Photo	No.	Name	Description	Price
❏	📷	61	#1-Ferrari 365 GTB/4	a. red enamel, metal Malaysia base, Ferrari emblem on hood, tan int., clear window, asw-5sp	$3
❏				b. same as (a), two stripes over Ferrari emblem on hood, asw-5sp	$2
❏	📷	62	#2-Ferrari 550 Maranello	a. red enamel, metal Malaysia base, yellow & black Ferrari emblem on hood, yellow HW logo on rear plate, tan int., clear window, asw-5sp	$3
❏				b. same as (a), green & white stripes over Ferrari emblem on hood, asw-5sp	$2
❏	📷	63	#3-1964 Lincoln Continental	white enamel, chrome Malaysia base, red int., clear window, red HW logo on rear plate, asw-bbs	$2
❏	📷	64	#4-Pro Stock Firebird	a. mustard yellow enamel, metal Malaysia base, white, purple & red tampo on nose, white, purple & red side tampo w/sponsor decals, pale orange hood scoop, gray int., smoked window, wide rear 5sp	$4
❏	📷			b. same as (a), bright orange hood scoop, wide rear 5sp	$4
❏	📷			c. black enamel, metal Malaysia base, white, purple & red tampos on hood & side, bright orange plastic hood scoop, gray int., smoked window, wide rear 5sp	$4
❏	📷			d. same as (c), Maroon replaces red in tampos, wide rear 5sp	$3
❏				e. same as (d), thin rear 5sp	$9
❏	📷	65	#5-Deora II	a. candy gray, black plastic Malaysia base, silver & black HW logo on side of rear spoiler, two blue surfboards over a black bed, chrome rear engine & int., smoked window, asw-5dot	$2
❏	📷			b. same as (a), no HW logo, asw-5dot	$4
❏	📷	66	#6-Deuce Roadster	blue-tint metal body & Malaysia base, chrome engine & grille, black int. & rear 'chute, clear window, 5sp	$2
❏	📷	67	#7-Chevy Pro Stock Truck	a. day-glo orange, chrome Thailand base, purple, light red & white tampos on hood & sides, white & light red HW logo on nose, light red & white HW logo above rear wheel, gray int., purple-tint window, 5sp	$15
❏				b. same as (a), chrome Malaysia base, 5sp	$3

Photo		No.	Name	Description	Price
❏	📷	68	#8-'68 El Camino	pearl white met., metal Malaysia base, chrome rear engine, large gray plastic rear wing, black painted rocker panel w/white HW logo behind the front wheel, gray int., blue-tint window, 5sp	$2
❏	📷	69	#9-Phantastique	candy blue met., chrome Malaysia base, silver stripe on side w/small silver HW logo in front of rear wheel, chrome windshield frame & grille, tan int., clear window, alw-gbbs	$2
❏	📷	70	#10-Thomassima III	a. met. red, chrome Malaysia base, small silver "Thomassima III" on rear w/silver HW logo on rear plate, black int., clear window, 5sp	$5
❏	📷			b. same as (a), bbs/2	$4
❏	📷			c. met. red, chrome Malaysia base, silver "Thomassima III" on door w/silver HW logo on front fender, black int., clear window, bbs/2	$3
❏	📷			d. same as (c), pr5	$2
❏	📷	71	#11-Ferrari 333SP	red enamel, black plastic Malaysia base, black int. & wing, bbs	$2
❏	📷	72	#12-Dodge Charger R/T	a. met. red, gray plastic Malaysia base, gray int., smoked window, 5sp	$2
❏	📷			b. same as (a), pr5	$20
❏		73	#13-Surf Crate	a. met. blue w/dark brown wood, no origin metal base, black int., red surfboard, 5sp	$15
❏	📷			b. met. purple w/orangish wood, no origin metal base, black int., red surfboard, 5sp	$3
❏	📷			c. met. purple w/light brown wood, no origin metal base, black int., red surfboard, 5sp	$3
❏	📷			d. met. purple w/dark brown wood, no origin metal base, black int., red surfboard, 5sp	$3
❏	📷	74	#14-'41 Willys	a. orange pearl met., gray plastic Malaysia base, orange, blue, yellow & black "Wild Willy" lettering on door, yellow, blue & purple tampos on side w/misc. racing sponsor decals, yellow & black HW logo on side or rear wing, chrome engine & int., smoked window, 5sp	$4
❏	📷			b. same as (a), purple replaces all orange in lettering & tampos, 5sp	$2
❏	📷	75	#15-Lotus Elise 340R	a. silver flake, matching silver flake painted metal Malaysia base, small green & yellow emblem on nose, black painted headlights, black HW logo on rear fender, black seats, clear window, 5sp	$30

2000 First Editions, #1-Ferrari 365 GTB/4

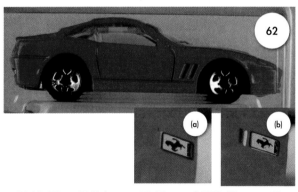

2000 First Editions, #2-Ferrari 550 Maranello

2000 First Editions,
#3-1964 Lincoln Continental

2000 First Editions, #4-Pro Stock Firebird

2000 First Editions, #4-Pro Stock Firebird

2000 First Editions, #4-Pro Stock Firebird

2000 First Editions, #4-Pro Stock Firebird

2000 First Editions, #5-Deora II

2000 First Editions, #5-Deora II

2000 First Editions, #6-Deuce Roadster

2000 First Editions, #7-Chevy Pro Stock Truck

2000 First Editions, #8-'68 El Camino

2000 First Editions, #9-Phantastique

2000 First Editions, #10-Thomassima III

2000 First Editions, #10-Thomassima III

Photo		No.	Name	Description	Price
❏	📷	75	#15-Lotus Elise 340R	b. same as (a), pr5	$10
❏	📷			c. same as (b), metal Malaysia base, pr5	$2
❏	📷	76	#16-1999 Isuzu VehiCROSS	met. silver, black plastic fenders, blue-tint metal Malaysia base, black hood w/silver HW logo, orange painted taillights, black int., smoked window, alw-pr5	$2
❏	📷	77	#17-Anglia Panel Truck	candy purple met., gray plastic Malaysia base, orange, white & black side tampo w/white & orange pinstripe, orange HW logo below pinstripe behind door, chrome int., orange-tint window, 5sp	$4
❏	📷	78	#18-So Fine	black enamel, chrome Malaysia base, silver painted side molding & three side vents, silver HW logo high on rear fender, red int., clear window, asw-bbs	$3
❏	📷	79	#19-'65 Vette	black met., gray plastic Malaysia base, silver HW logo on trunk below emblem, red int., clear window, 5sp	$3
❏	📷	80	#20-MX48 Turbo	a. met. purple, silver painted metal Malaysia base, day-glo green oval on nose w/black tampo & purple ring, day-glo green HW logo on rear plate, gray int., blue-tint window, 5sp	$40
❏	📷			b. dark blue met., silver painted Malaysia base, gray int., blue-tint window, 5sp	$5
❏	📷			c. dark blue met., silver painted Malaysia base, gray int., blue-tint window, pr5	$2
❏		81	#21-SS Commodore (VT)	a. candy gray met., black plastic Malaysia base, light orange & red side tampo w/misc. white & blue racing decals, white & blue square on door w/blue "12" & orange HW logo, transparent red rear spoiler, yellow int., smoked window, asw-5sp	$100
❏	📷			b. same as (a), red plastic rear spoiler, asw-5sp	$2

Photo	No.	Name	Description	Price
☐ 📷	82	#22-Cabbin' Fever	a. black enamel, gray plastic Malaysia base front grille & rear ramp, light orange & yellow flame tampo on side w/white teeth behind front wheel, small yellow HW logo above rear wheels, small white "Not For Hire" on door w/white & light orange "Motor 'Ep," orange & yellow stripe tampo by door vent w/white flames, chrome window & bed ramp, pr5	$8
☐ 📷			b. same as (a), larger white "Not For Hire" tampo on door, pr5	$4

2000 First Editions, #10-Thomassima III

2000 First Editions, #10-Thomassima III

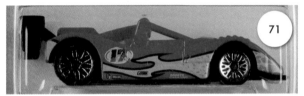

2000 First Editions, #11-Ferrari 333 SP

2000 First Editions, #12 Dodge Charger R/T

2000 First Editions, #12-Dodge Charger R/T

2000 First Editions, #13-Surf Crate

2000 First Editions, #13-Surf Crate

2000 First Editions, #13-Surf Crate

2000 First Editions, #13-Surf Crate

2000 First Editions, #14-'41 Willys

2000 First Editions, #14-'41 Willys

2000 First Editions, #15-Lotus Elise 340R

2000 First Editions, #15-Lotus Elise 340R

2000 First Editions, #15-Lotus Elise 340R

2000 First Editions, #16-1999 Isuzu Vehicross

2000 First Editions, #17-Anglia Panel Truck

2000 First Editions, #18-So Fine

2000 First Editions, #19-'65 Vette

2000 First Editions, #20-MX48 Turbo

Photo	No.	Name	Description	Price
☐ 📷	81	#22-Cabbin' Fever	c. same as (b), dark orange side tampo & "Motor 'Ep" on door, pr5	$7
☐ 📷	83	#23-Metrorail	a. aqua & white enamel, chrome Malaysia base, purple "Metrorail" over a green stripe in front fender, white HW logo on rear fender, chrome engine & int., smoked window, medium front 5sp	$10
☐ 📷			b. same as (a), small front 5sp	$3
☐ 📷	84	#24-Muscle Tone	a. light orange pearl met., gray plastic Malaysia base, thick blue stripe around nose, thin blue stripe on side above rocker panel, blue HW logo on front fender above bumper, black int., smoked window, 5sp	$10
☐			b. same as (a), blue int., 5sp	$4
☐ 📷			c. same as (b), darker orange, 5sp	$4
☐ 📷			d. same as (c), pr5	$2
☐ 📷	85	#25-Dodge Power Wagon	a. met. silver, gray plastic Malaysia base, small white "Power Wagon" on door, black bed cover w/HW logo embossed at rear, black int. & headlights, smoked window, asw-ct/b	$4
☐			b. same as (a), w/larger front & rear bumpers, three squares on front bumper are larger also, asw-ct/b	$2
☐ 📷	86	#26-Shoe Box	a. yellow enamel, black plastic Malaysia base, purple flames & HW logo, chrome int., purple-tint window, bbs/2	$10
☐ 📷			b. same as (a), red flames & HW logo, bbs/2	$4
☐ 📷			c. same as (b), pr5	$2
☐ 📷	87	#27-Sho-Stopper	a. pearl yellow, gray plastic Malaysia base, black painted side vent, red stripe on top of left front fender, black painted hood w/silver hatch marks, black front & rear grilles, silver HW logo in rear window, black window, alw-3sp	$4
☐ 📷			b. pearl mustard, gray Malaysia base, black window, alw-3sp	$3
☐ 📷			c. same as (b), alw-pr5	$2
☐ 📷	88	#28-'67 Dodge Charger	candy gray, chrome Malaysia base, orange "Dodge" & HW logo on rear fender behind wheel, orange painted taillights w/silver "Charger" red int., clear window, asw-pr5	$3

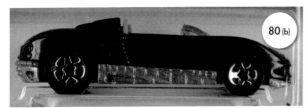

2000 First Editions, #20-MX48 Turbo

2000 First Editions, #20-MX48 Turbo

2000 First Editions, #21-SS Commodore (VT)

2000 First Editions, #22-Cabbin' Fever

2000 First Editions, #22-Cabbin' Fever

2000 First Editions, #22-Cabbin' Fever

2000 First Editions, #23-Metrorail

2000 First Editions, #23-Metrorail

2000 First Editions, #24-Muscle Tone

2000 First Editions, #24-Muscle Tone

2000 First Editions, #24-Muscle Tone

2000 First Editions, #25-Dodge Power Wagon

2000 First Editions, #26-Shoe Box

2000 First Editions, #26-Shoe Box

2000 First Editions, #26-Shoe Box

2000 First Editions, #27-Sho-Stopper

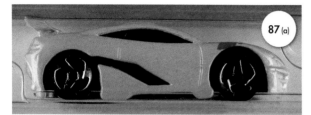

2000 First Editions, #27-Sho-Stopper

2000 First Editions, #28-'67 Dodge Charger

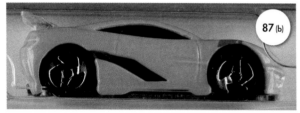

2000 First Editions, #27-Sho-Stopper

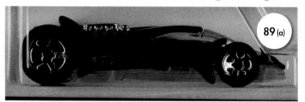

2000 First Editions, #29-Vulture

	Photo	No.	Name	Description	Price
❏	📷	89	#29-Vulture	a. black enamel, transparent plastic Malaysia base, orange "Vulture" at top of windshield, silver HW logo in front of rear wheel, chrome rear engine, chrome & orange int., clear window, 5sp	$3
❏	📷			b. same as (a), pr5	$2
❏	📷	90	#30-Mini Cooper	yellow enamel, blue-tint metal Malaysia base, white & black checked roof w/yellow & red HW logo at rear facing rear, gray front scoop w/blue insert, blue int., gray dash, blue-tint window, asw-bbs	$4
❏	📷	91	#31-Roll Cage	a. yellow enamel, blue-tint metal Malaysia base, red & yellow HW logo on nose, black seats, chrome engine, asw-ct/b	$3
❏				b. same as (a), silver painted metal Malaysia base	$20
❏	📷	92	#32-Austin Healey	a. black enamel, chrome & metal Malaysia base, gray enamel on lower side of body, chrome engine & grille, silver HW logo in black part of rear fender behind wheel, red int., smoked window, 5sp	$10
❏	📷			b. same as (a), silver replaces gray in cove, 5sp	$2
❏	📷	93	#33-Hammered Coupe	candy purple met., metal Malaysia base, chrome int., clear window, 5sp	$2
❏	📷	94	#34-Arachnorod	met. red, gray plastic Malaysia base, top has chrome spider trim & engines, black, lavender, light green & yellow tampo on top of rear fenders w/black, light green & yellow "4," black & yellow stripe on top of front fenders, yellow int., smoked canopy & rear turbines, pr5	$2
❏	📷	95	#35-Greased Lightnin'	a. candy gray met., metal Malaysia base, light blue, purple & black tampo on top of nose w/white & purple HW logo up by canopy, chrome rear engine & int., purple-tint canopy, 5sp	$7
❏	📷			b. same as (a), pr5	$2
❏	📷	96	#36-Blast Lane	a. pearl tangerine met., blue-tint metal Malaysia engine, red & white flames on tank & rear fender, gray plastic handlebars, chrome rim w/black spokes	$10
❏				b. same as (a), purple & white flames	$4

2000 First Editions, #29-Vulture

2000 First Editions, #33-Hammered Coupe

2000 First Editions, #30-Mini Cooper

2000 First Editions, #34-Arachnorod

2000 First Editions, #31-Roll Cage

2000 First Editions, #35-Greased Lightnin'

2000 First Editions, #32-Austin Healey

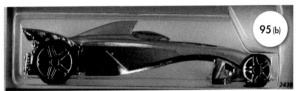

2000 First Editions, #35-Greased Lightnin'

2000 First Editions, #32-Austin Healey

2000 First Editions, #36-Blast Lane

Virtual Collection & Non-Series Collector Number Packs

	Photo	No.	Name	Description	Price
❏	📷	97/vc	1936 Cord	met. green, chrome China base, white HW logo behind front wheel, white int., clear window, asw-bw	$3
❏	📷	98	'99 Mustang	a. met. red, black plastic China base, black panel on door w/orange, yellow, black, & silver tampos, black painted rocker panel w/small silver names, black & orange "PSSC" on rear fender above wheel, black int., clear window, asw-3sp	$2
❏	📷			b. same as (a), asw-5sp	$4
❏	📷	99	Phantom Corsair	a. dark red met., metal China base, gold HW logo on rear plate, white int., clear window, asw-bbs	$2
❏				b. same as (a), metal Malaysia base, asw-bbs	$3
❏	📷	100	BMW M Roadster	a. red enamel, black painted metal Malaysia base, black HW logo in center of trunk, black painted headlights, black int., clear window, asw-5sp	$2
❏	📷			b. same as (a), asw-5dot	$30
❏	📷	101/vc	Hot Seat	blue plastic body, blue-tint metal Malaysia base & rear engine, white seat & plunger, white HW logo behind rear wheel, 5sp	$2

Virtual Collection Cars, 1936 Cord

'99 Mustang

'99 Mustang

Phantom Corsair

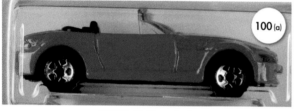

BMW M Roadster

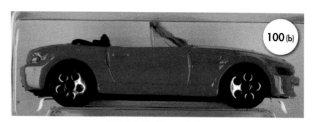

BMW M Roadster

Virtual Collection Cars, Hot Seat

'90 T-Bird

Virtual Collection Cars, Tractor

Photo		No.	Name	Description	Price
❑	📷	102	'90 T-Bird	chrome body, metal Malaysia base, orange, black, purple & white side tampos, black HW logo behind front wheel, black window, gbbs	$2
❑	📷	103/vc	Tractor	day-glo yellow enamel, black plastic Malaysia base, black plastic cab & hydraulics, black HW logo on nose, ctt rear-ct/b front	$3
❑		104/vc	Speed-A-Saurus	light green plastic body, mustard painted metal Malaysia base, gold chrome engine, g5sp	$2
❑	📷	105	'57 Chevy	a. aqua plastic body, metal Malaysia "1957 Chevy" base, chrome engine through hood, orange, black & white girl tampo on side, white dotted stripe down center of roof & trunk, white over black HW logo on rear fender behind wheel, black window, 5dot	$4
❑	📷			b. same as (a), aqua plastic body, metal Malaysia "1957 Chevy" base, chrome engine through hood, white & gold flame tampo behind rear wheel, white & gold stripe tampo behind front wheel, white pinstripe from front to rear w/"Custom Rod" below windshield post, white pinstripe on each side of roof w/white gold tampo in center, white HW logo above rear wheel, black window, 5dot	$4
❑				c. same as (b), "1957 Chevy" missing from base, 5dot	$5
❑				d. same as (b), silver painted metal Malaysia "1957 Chevy" base, 5dot	$15

Photo	No.	Name	Description	Price
☐	106	Ferrari 348	a. black enamel, black plastic Malaysia base, large yellow Ferrari shield on nose, tan & black int., smoked window, 3sp	$5
☐			b. same as (a), small rectangle Ferrari emblem on nose, 3sp	$2
☐ 📷	107	'70 Chevelle	a. met. gold, chrome China base, two wide black SS (Super Sport) stripes on hood & trunk, HW logo on trunk in stripe, black int., clear window, 5sp	$5
☐ 📷			b. same as (a), light lime-gold met. color, 5sp	$8
☐	108	Olds Aurora	light yellow enamel, yellow plastic China base, black rear wing, gray int., clear window, asw-t/b	$2
☐ 📷	109/vc	Monte Carlo Concept Car	a. pearl pink met., gray pearl painted metal China base, met. gold stripes w/black enamel splotches on side, met. gold HW logo on rear roof pillar, black int., clear window, asw-t/b	$2
☐			b. same as (a), darker pink color, butterscotch replaces gold in HW logo & stripe in side tampo, asw-t/b	$8
☐ 📷			c. same as (a), lime gold replaces gold in HW logo & stripe in side tampo, asw-t/b	$6
☐ 📷	110/vc	Forklift	orange enamel, metal China base, black & white "Marcus Construction" over a blue tampo, small white & black HW logo low in front of rear wheel, black cage, seat & lift, 5sp	$3
☐ 📷	111/vc	Wheel Loader	white enamel top half, red enamel lower half, metal China base, white plastic bucket, black plastic rear engine & seat, red HW logo on cab door, alw-ct/b	$3
☐ 📷	112/vc	Turbo Flame	transparent red plastic body, metal Malaysia base, yellow & orange flames over a lavender HW Logo on side, orange-tint canopy & rear tail, chrome engine, g5sp	$2
☐ 📷	113/vc	Flame Stopper	dark orange enamel, black plastic China base, gold & black "Air Port Fire & Rescue" w/maroon & black plane tampo on side, small maroon HW logo on side w/circle emblem & "Emergency," black window & winch, gray boom, alw-ct/b	$3

'57 Chevy

Virtual Collection Cars,
Monte Carlo Concept Car

'57 Chevy

Virtual Collection Cars,
Monte Carlo Concept Car

'70 Chevelle

'70 Chevelle

Virtual Collection Cars, Fork Lift

Virtual Collection Cars, Way 2 Fast

Virtual Collection Cars, Wheel Loader

'59 Chevy

Virtual Collection Cars, Turbo Flame

Virtual Collection Cars, Tee'd Off

Virtual Collection Cars, Flame Stopper

Virtual Collection Cars, Lamborghini Diablo

Virtual Collection Cars, Semi-Fast

Photo		No.	Name	Description	Price
❏	📷	114/vc	Lamborghini Diablo	met. blue, matching blue painted metal Malaysia base, black plastic rear wing w/white HW logo facing front, white int., clear window, 5dot	$2
❏	📷	115/vc	Way 2 Fast	dark red met., metal Malaysia base, orange, black, gold & white tampo on roof & side, small gold HW logo on roof at front right corner facing rear, two chrome engines & int., 5sp	$2
❏	📷	116	'59 Chevy Impala	silver flake, chrome Malaysia base, yellow, gold & maroon side tampo w/maroon "'59 Impala" & gold HW logo on rear fender behind wheel, small gold & maroon pinstripe tampo on front of hood, gray int., smoked window, asw-t/b	$2
❏	📷	117/vc	Tee'd Off	red enamel, metal China base, orange, gray & black flames on nose, orange, gray & black flame tampo on white plastic roof w/two golf clubs & a large white golf ball w/black HW logo, chrome rear engine, blue int. & rear bumper, 5sp	$2
❏	📷	118/vc	Semi-Fast	a. blue plastic body w/white plastic top, metal Malaysia base & grille, yellow & black stripes on side lower body w/black circle & white "17," black painted vent, white HW logo & Jones tampo behind front wheel, yellow & black stripe on cab w/black & yellow circle w/"17," small black & yellow tampo & blue "Good Year," gray int., clear window, 5sp	$4

Photo	No.	Name	Description	Price
☐	118/vc	Semi-Fast	b. same as (a), dark blue plastic body, silver painted Malaysia base & grille, 5sp	$2
☐ 📷	119	Pontiac Rageous	a. met. blue, black plastic Malaysia base, small silver "Rageous" above black paint on lower door, silver HW logo on rear fender high behind wheel, white int., light-tinted window, no black roof, alw-3sp	$2
☐ 📷			b. same as (a), tinted window w/black painted roof, alw-3sp	$3
☐			c. same as (b), black plastic China base, w/black painted roof, alw-3sp	$4
☐ 📷	120	Mercedes SLK	met. teal, black painted metal India base, silver painted side marker light & "Mercedes SLK" on front fender, black painted door handle, black HW logo high on rear fender by taillight, black int., clear window & headlights, asw-3sp	$2
☐ 📷	121	Mustang Cobra	a. met. red, met. red plastic India base, black multistripe tampo on side w/"Mustang" in cove, black HW logo next to door handle, white int., tinted window, asw-t/b	$2
☐			b. same as (a), clear window, asw-t/b	$4
☐ 📷	122	Ferrari F40	yellow enamel, metal Malaysia base, white & green stripe over yellow & black Ferrari emblem on nose, black int., clear window, 5sp	$2
☐	123/vc	Oshkosh Cement Truck	black plastic body, green enamel fenders, light green plastic barrel & Malaysia base, asw-5dot	$2
☐ 📷	124	Camaro Z28	black plastic body, black painted metal Malaysia base, red & white flag tampo w/large white stars outlined in gold on side, white HW logo above red & white stripes on front fender, small white & gold "30" on roof pillar behind door window, hood has red & white stripes w/white & gold stars, large white & gold "30" on roof, black window, gbbs	$2
☐ 📷	125	Porsche 930	white enamel, metal Malaysia base, black painted headlights & hood w/yellow, black & red Porsche emblem on nose, black painted louvers in rear wing, black HW logo on rear fender behind wheel, black int., smoked window, asw-3sp	$2
☐ 📷	126/vc	Rodzilla	a. light green plastic body, metal China base, gold-tint engine, g3sp	$2
☐ 📷			b. same as (a), dark gold chrome engine, g3sp	$2
☐ 📷	127/vc	Track T	white enamel, blue-tint metal Malaysia base, orange, black, yellow & silver side tampo w/black "07" & small black HW logo, black panel on hood w/silver check stripe, black panel on trunk w/silver checks, yellow, silver & orange stripe, black int. cover & dash, metal seat, t/b	$2

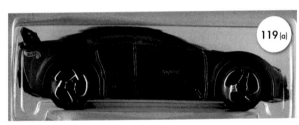

Pontiac Rageous

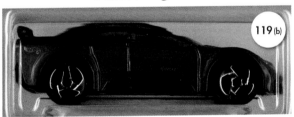

Pontiac Rageous

Mercedes SLK

Mustang Cobra

Ferrari F40

Camaro Z28

Porsche 930

Virtual Collection Cars, Track T

Rodzilla

Porsche 911 GT3 Cup

Virtual Collection Cars, Turbolence

'63 T-Bird

Rodzilla

Mercedes C-Class

	Photo	No.	Name	Description	Price
❑	📷	128	Porsche 911 GT3 Cup	white enamel, black plastic India base, side tampo is pearl green w/red pinstripe at front, yellow enamel at rear, white circle w/red "8 cup" & six misc. sponsor decals & red HW logo on rear fender behind wheel, red int. & rear wing, clear window & headlights, asw-3sp	$2
❑		129/vc	Turbolence	a. pearl gray, metal Malaysia base, five thin black wavy lines over thick orange, white & light pearl green stripes on side, black & white stripe tampo over light green pearl, white & orange thick stripes on hood, black oval w/white & black HW logo on nose, chrome engine & int., alw-5dot	$2
❑	📷			b. same as (a), gray engine & int., alw-5dot	$5
❑	📷	130	'63 T-Bird	met. charcoal, blue-tint metal Thailand base, white enamel cove w/gray outline, gray pinstripe on side w/gray HW logo at rear, white pinstripes on hood & on each ramp on the headrests on the rear deck, white int., clear window, asw-bbs	$2
❑	📷	131	Mercedes C-Class	red enamel, black plastic Malaysia base, black HW logo on rear fender behind wheel, black int., clear window, asw-5dot	$2
❑	📷	132	3-Window '34	met. green w/green plastic fenders & white plastic running boards, metal Malaysia base, gold, yellow & orange flame side tampo w/orange HW logo above, gold, yellow, orange & red flames on hood, chrome dash, engine & grille, white int., yellow-tint window, 3sp	$2
❑	📷	133/vc	Mercedes-Benz Unimog	dark red met., blue-tint metal Malaysia base, black plastic fenders, grille & int., tan rear bed canopy, white HW logo on hood, smoked window, alw-ct/b	$2

Photo	No.	Name	Description	Price
☐ 📷	134	Mercedes 500SL	a. dark candy blue met., light blue plastic Malaysia base, white HW logo on rear plate, chrome grille & headlights, black int., smoked window, alw-5dot	$10
☐ 📷			b. same as (a), met. blue, alw-5dot	$8
☐ 📷			c. same as (b), met. blue, gray plastic Malaysia base, alw-5dot	$3
☐ 📷	135/vc	Thunderstreak	purple met., metal China base, white panel on side w/blue & orange tampo, white over orange "6" on side of rear wing w/orange HW logo, chrome engine, metal vents, purple driver, bbs	$2
☐ 📷	136	Ferrari Testarossa	white enamel, black painted Malaysia base, yellow & black Ferrari emblem on nose w/one green stripe, black HW logo on rear plate, black plastic front & rear grilles, black int., clear window, 5sp	$2
☐ 📷	137/vc	Dogfighter	yellow enamel, black plastic China base, black & red flames on side, red HW logo on side of tail, gold chrome suspension & engine, red propeller, g5sp	$2
☐ 📷	138/vc	Skullrider	red plastic body, gray painted metal China base, black & white tampo on hood w/white circle & black "8," gold HW logo on nose, black & white tampo on roof side w/white circle & black "8," two chrome drivers, engine & side engine cover, 5sp	$2
☐ 📷	139	Ford GT-40	a. red enamel, black plastic China base, trunk, roof & hood have wide white center stripe w/light blue stripes on each side, white circle w/black "78" & black outline on hood & door, blue tampo w/white outline on tops of front fenders & on rear fenders, light blue, white & light blue stripes on lower sides, small white HW logo in front of rear wheel above stripes, black int., clear window, 5sp	$5
☐			b. same as (a), light blue in tampos, bbs/2	$2
☐ 📷			c. same as (b), dark blue in tampos, bbs/2	$4
☐			d. same as (b), bbs/2 rear-bbs front	$10

3-Window '34

Virtual Collection Cars,
Mercedes-Benz Unimog

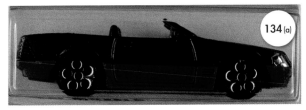

Mercedes 500SL

Mercedes 500SL

Mercedes 500SL

Virtual Collection Cars, Thunderstreak

Ferrari Testarossa

Virtual Collection Cars, Dogfighter

Virtual Collection Cars, Skullrider

Ford GT-40

Ford GT-40

Jeepster

'95 Camaro Convertible

Virtual Collection Cars, Blimp

Virtual Collection Cars, Recycling Truck

Virtual Collection Cars, Ice Cream Truck

	Photo	No.	Name	Description	Price
☐	📷	140	Jeepster	green enamel, black plastic fenders, silver met. painted China base, black & white dotted tampo on center of hood, white & blue enamel stripe on side w/white & black dotted tampo, blue "Jeepster" on door above white stripe, small white HW logo at rear of side fender, silver trimmed smoked window, black int., alw-5dot	$2
☐	📷	141	'95 Camaro Convertible	yellow enamel, black plastic Malaysia base, dark blue enamel stripes on hood, trunk & rear spoiler, blue to purple to light red flame tampo on side w/dark blue HW logo & black "Pace Car" on rocker panel, black int., clear window, alw-g3sp	$2
☐	📷	142/vc	Blimp	white plastic body, red plastic tail, yellow over red HW logo on side, red enamel gondola	$2
☐	📷	143/vc	Recycling Truck	very dark blue metal cab, dark blue plastic rear container, gray plastic Malaysia base, dark red, gray & black side tampo w/white & black HW logo, large white "Trasher" on roof of cab, black window, asw- t/b	$2
☐	📷	144/vc	Ice Cream Truck	a. butterscotch enamel, black plastic Malaysia base, red, black & blue clown & balloon tampo on right side of window, red, black & blue ice-cream & balloon tampo on left side of window, red & white w/black outline "I Scream" above rear wheel, rear has large red HW logo w/red & blue stars, red int., clear window, asw-5dot	$3

Photo	No.	Name	Description	Price
☐ 📷	144/vc	Ice Cream Truck	b. same as (a), asw-3sp	$2
☐ 📷			c. white pearl, black plastic Malaysia base, red, black & blue clown & balloon tampo on right side of window, red, black & blue ice-cream & balloon tampo on left side of window, red & white w/black outline "I Scream" above rear wheel, rear has large red HW logo w/red & blue stars, red int., clear window, asw-3sp	$4
☐ 📷	145/vc	Fire Eater	white enamel, chrome Malaysia base, orange, yellow & black side tampo, red insert, red-tint window & int., alw-3sp	$3
☐ 📷	146	Porsche Carrera	met. blue, metal Malaysia base, white HW logo in front of rear wheel, white int., clear window, 3sp	$2
☐	147	unreleased		—
☐ 📷	148	Pikes Peak Tacoma	a. red enamel, gray plastic Malaysia base, yellow, orange & white tampos on hood & sides red painted side vent, yellow HW logo behind rear wheel, yellow int. & bed cover, clear window, asw-3sp	$2
☐ 📷			b. same as (a), unpainted metal side vent, asw-3sp	$15

Virtual Collection Cars, Ice Cream Truck

Virtual Collection Cars, Ice Cream Truck

Virtual Collection Cars, Fire-Eater

Porsche Carrera

Pikes Peak Tacoma

Pikes Peak Tacoma

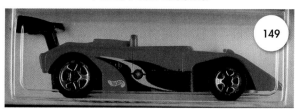

Shadow Mk IIa

Chrysler Pronto

Virtual Collection Cars, Go Kart

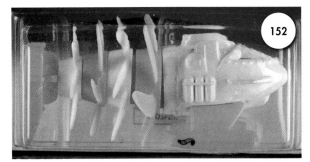

Virtual Collection Cars, Fathom This

Virtual Collection Cars, Shadow Jet II

Virtual Collection Cars, Shadow Jet II

Corvette Stingray

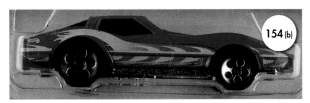

Corvette Stingray

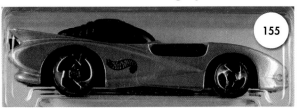

Virtual Collection Cars, Splittin' Image II

Virtual Collection Cars, Screamin' Hauler

Virtual Collection Cars, Popcycle

	Photo	No.	Name	Description	Price
❏	📷	149	Shadow Mk IIa	red enamel, gray plastic Malaysia base, dark blue pearl, black & yellow enamel side tampo w/white HW logo in front of rear wheel, teal pearl w/yellow & black enamel stripes on front half & teal pearl & white stripes on rear half, gray int. & rear engine, black enamel painted rear wing, g5sp	$2
❏	📷	150	Chrysler Pronto	candy purple met., black plastic China base, black roof, white HW logo on trunk, gray int., tinted window, 3sp	$2
❏	📷	151/vc	Go Kart	pearl purple body & Malaysia base silver & black dotted tampo w/black & silver HW logo on side pod, top of side pod has a silver stripe w/white dots, front faring is painted silver w/white dots, left side of faring has a black circle w/white "6" & white w/black outlined "kieran racing" at center, gray plastic seat, unpainted metal chassis, 5dot rear, mini 5sp front	$5
❏	📷	152/vc	Fathom This	white enamel, light orange plastic Malaysia pontoons, windows & rotors, black HW logo on left side of pontoon	$2
❏	📷	153/vc	Shadow Jet II	a. red plastic body, met. silver painted metal Malaysia base, purple to white fade tampo on upper side white over black "Techno" & five black squares, lower side tampo is gray w/white & black graphics, black HW logo behind rear wheel, chrome int., smoked canopy, b5dot	$5
❏				b. same as (a), unpainted Malaysia base, b5dot	$4
❏	📷			c. same as (a), silver met. replaces gray in lower side tampo, b5dot	$2
❏	📷	154	Corvette Stingray	a. blue plastic body, metal China base, white, orange & yellow side tampo, white HW logo behind rear wheel, black window, 3sp	$3
❏	📷			b. same as (a), 5dot	$4
❏	📷	155/vc	Splittin' Image II	candy gray, black plastic Malaysia base, black canopy's, headlights & engine black HW logo in front of rear wheel, g3sp	$2

Photo	No.	Name	Description	Price
☐ 📷	156/vc	Screamin' Hauler	candy red met., silver painted China base, chrome engines, gold HW logo on rear, silver painted int., smoked windshield, 5sp	$2
☐ 📷	157/vc	Popcycle	a. met. green, metal Malaysia base & seat, yellow stripe on top in front of engine w/yellow over white HW logo, gold-tint chrome engine, yellow-tint canopy, gold-tint chrome bicycle in side car, g3sp	$2
☐ 📷			b. met. green, metal China base & seat, yellow stripe on top in front of engine w/yellow HW logo, dark gold chrome engine, yellow-tint canopy, dark gold chrome bicycle in side car, g3sp	$4
☐ 📷	158/vc	Super Modified	red enamel, metal Malaysia base, white int. & wings, white HW logo above rear wheel, gbbs/2	$2
☐ 📷	159	BMW 850i	light blue pearl, dark blue plastic Malaysia base, black HW logo high behind rear wheel, black int. & taillights, clear window, asw-3sp	$2
☐ 📷	160	Jaguar XJ220	a. red enamel, black plastic Malaysia base, light purple stripes sides, dark purple stripe on hood, small black Jaguar emblem in stripe on nose, gray "XJ220" w/black & white outline on door, gray "Jaguar" tampo on lower door behind front wheel, light purple HW logo on front fender by wheel, black int., blue-tint window, gbbs	$4
☐ 📷			b. same as (a), dark purple stripes on side, light purple stripe on hood, gbbs	$2
☐ 📷	161	Ferrari F50	a. yellow enamel, black painted Malaysia base, white & green stripes over yellow & black Ferrari emblem on hood, green stripe above yellow & black Ferrari shield high behind front wheel, black int., rear engine & taillights, clear window & rear engine cover, asw-5sp	$4
☐			b. same as (a), red & green stripes over small Ferrari emblem on hood, asw-5sp	$2
☐ 📷	162	Ferrari 355 Challenge	yellow enamel, blue-tint metal Malaysia base, red & white enamel w/pearl green stripes on hood & roof, white & black tampo w/black "7" on center of hood, small yellow & black Ferrari emblem on nose, white & red tampo w/black "7" on door w/black & white misc. racing decals, small gold & red SHELL tampo in front of rear wheel, gray int., smoked window & rear wing, asw-5sp	$4

Virtual Collection Cars, Popcycle

Virtual Collection Cars, Super Modified

BMW 850i

Jaguar XJ220

Jaguar XJ220

Ferrari F50

Ferrari 355 Challenge

Mercedes CLK-LM

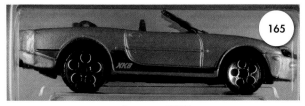

Jaguar XK8

Virtual Collection Cars, Phaeton

Pikes Peak Celica

Photo	No.	Name	Description	Price
☐ 📷	163	Mercedes CLK-LM	red enamel, black plastic China base, black plastic rear wing w/white HW logo, black int., clear window, asw-bbs	$2
☐ 📷	164/vc	Phaeton	black enamel, silver painted China base, purple checked tampo on hood w/silver outline, purple & silver side tampo, silver painted outline on exhaust, silver HW logo behind rear wheel, black plastic top, purple int., clear window, 5sp	$2
☐ 📷	165	Jaguar XK8	gray pearl, black plastic Malaysia base, blue & black stripe on left side of hood & trunk, white "XK8" in blue stripe on hood, blue & black stripe on lower rear fender onto rocker panel, white "XK8" in front of rear wheel, blue int., smoked windshield, 5dot	$2
☐ 📷	166	Pikes Peak Celica	white enamel, black plastic Malaysia base, light blue & light red side tampos, light blue HW logo behind rear wheel, light blue & light red tampos on hood w/black "TOYOTA" & emblem, roof has light red & light blue tampo, black "TOYOTA" on each side & black & red "8" at center, black int., black plastic rear wing, clear window, asw-3sp	$2
☐ 📷	167	Dodge Concept Car	a. white pearl, metal Malaysia base, dark gold & black tampo on side w/white "DODGE" on black painted rocker panel, black panel on hood & trunk w/thick gold outline, "DODGE" in white twice on hood, black HW logo high on rear fender behind wheel, gold int., clear window, g3sp	$4
☐ 📷			b. brighter white pearl paint, metal China base, gold stripes are much lighter, gold plastic int. is also lighter, clear window, g3sp	$2
☐ 📷	168/vc	Lakester	black enamel, black painted China base, white stripe on top w/black & gold "Skunk Racing" gold HW logo on side above right set of gold chrome exhaust, gold chrome int., yellow-tint canopy, alw-5sp	$2
☐ 📷	169	Panoz GTR-1	met. blue, black plastic China base, white lettering on top of left front fender, dark red & white sword w/Asian characters on right top front fender, dark blue, light blue & dark red Panoz logo at center of hood w/small dark red "SP" below it, dark red & silver on door, dark blue, light blue & dark red Panoz logo behind front wheel, dark red lettering & silver HW logo behind rear wheel, white plastic rear wing & int., clear window, 3sp	$2
☐ 📷	171	'56 Ford Truck	a. pearl white, gold plastic China base, gold panel tampo on side w/purple stripe, gold & purple tampo on rear fender, gold HW logo on rear fender behind wheel, gold chrome engine & int., yellow-tint window, g5sp	$2
☐			b. same as (a), maroon HW logo & stripes, g5sp	$5
☐ 📷	172	Porsche 911 GT1-98	a. candy purple met., black plastic Malaysia base & rear wing, pink tampos w/red outline on top, large black "27" on front & rear, misc. racing decals on tops of rear fenders, red "24" & black "HEURES DU MANS" on nose, black HW logo on rear next to "27," white int., smoked window, asw-bbs	$2
☐			b. same as (a), white tampos w/red outline on top, asw-bbs	$4
☐ 📷			c. same as (b), asw-t/b	$6
☐ 📷			d. same as (b), asw-pr5	$10
☐ 📷			e. same as (a), pink tampos w/red outline on top, asw-pr5	$8
☐ 📷	173/vc	Baby Boomer	a. red enamel, metal China base, pink circle w/red & black pacifier tampo on side w/white & black "Bad Bad Boy," gray plastic shifter, Bug Catcher Injectors & belt drives, gold-tint chrome engine, 5sp	$2

Photo	No.	Name	Description	Price
☐ 📷	173vc	Baby Boomer	b. same as (a), dark gold chrome engine, 5sp	$3
☐ 📷	174	'63 Vette	a. black flake, black 2-rivet plastic Malaysia base, yellow, light green & white tampos on side, hood & roof, yellow HW logo on high on rear fender, white int., clear window, asw-bbs	$3
☐ 📷			b. same as (a), asw-t/b	$8
☐ 📷	175	Olds Aurora	dark orange pearl met., black plastic China base, large blue & black "1" on roof, large blue & white HW logo outlined in black on hood w/blue & black "1," large blue & white HW logo on side w/blue & black flames, white & blue tampo behind rear wheel, black rear wing & int., blue-tint window, asw-bbs	$2

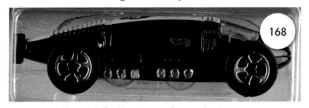
Dodge Concept Car

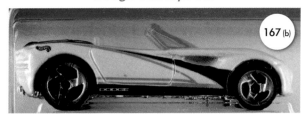
Dodge Concept Car

Virtual Collection Cars, Lakester

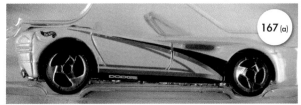
Panoz GTR-1

'56 Ford Truck

Porsche 911 GT1-98

Porsche 911 GT1-98

Porsche 911 GT1-98

Porsche 911 GT1-98

Virtual Collection Cars, Baby Boomer

Virtual Collection Cars, Baby Boomer

'63 Vette

T-Bird Stocker

'32 Ford Coupe

Chevy Nomad

'65 Impala

Ford Bronco

Roll Patrol

Purple Passion

Photo		No.	Name	Description	Price
❏	📷	193	'40s Woodie	candy bronze met. metal fenders & hood, tan plastic body, black fake rear spare tire, silver met. painted metal China base, white & black tampo on roof w/red & yellow "Linked" & four dots, black panels on top of both front fenders w/white designs, yellow, red & black HotWheels.com logo in rear side window, chrome supercharger popping through hood, black int., clear window, bbs	$2
❏	📷	194	T-Bird Stocker	met. blue, gray plastic China base, white stripes w/yellow, red & black HotWheels.com logo & yellow "connected" on side, red int., clear window, asw-3sp	$2
❏	📷	195	'32 Ford Coupe	candy purple met., chrome China base, red panel on side w/yellow, red & black HotWheels.com logo outlined in white, small yellow "Surf the net" over rear wheel, yellow dashed line along rocker panel, chrome engine & grille, black int., clear window, bbs	$2
❏	📷	196	Chevy Nomad	orange enamel, silver painted metal China base, white tampo on side w/large yellow & red HW logo, white stripes on hood w/red, yellow & black HotWheels.com logo outlined in white, black, yellow & white tampo in center of hood, white int., clear window, g3sp	$2
❏	📷	197	'65 Impala	met. green, gold chrome China base, white tampo on side w/yellow, red & black HotWheels.com logo outlined in white, yellow "web site" on front fender above wheel, two white designs on each side of hood w/three yellow & red ovals, yellow int., yellow-tint window, asw-3sp	$2
❏	📷	198	Ford Bronco	white pearl met., metal Thailand base, silver design side w/light purple, blue & gold Lizard tampo on door, dark purple & blue "SANTA FE" over rear wheel, gold HW logo high on rear fender at left, green plastic cap, purple int. & motor cycle on rear, clear window, asw-ct/b	$4
❏	📷	199	Roll Patrol	red enamel, metal Thailand base, white panel on side w/dark blue, orange & light green flowers, orange outlined "Hawaii" above rear wheel, orange outlined HW logo up by windshield, tan int. & spare tire, smoked windshield, asw-ct/b	$4

Photo	No.	Name	Description	Price
☐ 📷	200	Purple Passion	white pearl met., chrome Thailand base, black & white spade w/white & red "#13" over yellow & red flames w/black outline on roof, red & black dice over yellow, red & black flames on side, red HW logo high on rear fender behind wheel, red int., clear window, asw-gbbs	$4
☐ 📷	201	'65 Mustang	green enamel, metal Thailand base, yellow & black wings w/black, yellow & white guitar on side, purple notes, two yellow, black & white lava lamps on hood w/black, yellow, purple & white guitar, purple HW logo on trunk w/yellow & purple "Classic" & white & purple "Rock," yellow int., yellow-tint windshield, asw-t/b	$4
☐ 📷	202	Hydroplane	white enamel, light orange plastic China base, chrome int., orange-tint canopy	$2
☐ 📷	203	Surf Patrol	candy gray met., metal Thailand base, black, blue, purple & white side tampo w/black & white "Storm Chaser" & black HW logo on door, purple int. roll bar & bed floor, purple-tint window, asw-ct/b	$2
☐ 📷	204	Saltflat Racer	black plastic body, silver painted metal Thailand base, yellow & orange tampo on top w/yellow outlined "Max" at center, yellow HW logo next to driver, black, yellow & orange tampo behind front wheel, chrome int., engine & front drive, orange-tint windshield, g5sp	$2
☐ 📷	205	Pikes Peak Celica	white enamel, black plastic Thailand base, dark blue, gold & yellow side tampo w/yellow & black "Slingshot Racing," black dots behind rear wheel, black "JINN Shocks" in front of rear wheel, black HW logo left of gold dots on front fender, light blue plastic wing, front air-dam & int., clear window, asw-bbs	$2
☐ 📷	206	Rig Wrecker	black enamel, gold-tint chrome Thailand base, black & white side tampo outlined in gold, gold HW logo on door in white part of tampo, white plastic boom, gold-tint chrome int., clear window, asw-g3sp	$3

'65 Mustang

Pikes Peak Celica

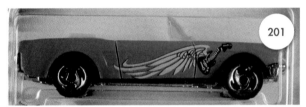

Hydroplane

Rig Wrecker

Surf Patrol

Police Car

Saltflat Racer

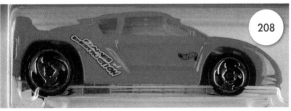

Zender Fact 4

Customized C3500

Tow Jam

Lexus SC400

Double Vision

Lexus SC400

Whatta Drag

Photo	No.	Name	Description	Price
❑ 📷	207	Police Car	light blue pearl met., black plastic Thailand base, silver & black side stripe, black "POLICE," silver "To Protect & Serve" & white & black shield on front door, black "K9 unit" & silver "011794" on rear door, black HW logo above stripe on rear fender, gray int., transparent red roof lights, smoked window, asw-t/b	$3
❑ 📷	208	Zender Fact 4	red enamel, gray plastic Thailand base, red & yellow flames w/silver outline over black splotches on hood & roof, yellow, red & black "Flames of Destruction" on rear fender, black HW logo on door behind front wheel, gray int., orange-tint window & headlights, t/b	$4
❑ 📷	209	Customized C3500	yellow enamel, black plastic China base, purple & orange tampos on hood & side, "THORN Bros. Industrial Maintenance" tampo on door & hood, black "Radio Dispatched 24 HRS" on bottom of door, orange HW logo on rocker panel behind front wheel, black int., clear window, t/b	$7
❑ 📷	210	Lexus SC400	a. met. blue, black plastic Malaysia base, white HW logo behind rear wheel, white int., smoked window, asw-bbs	$2
❑ 📷			b. same as (a), asw-t/b	$7
❑ 📷	211	Tow Jam	met. blue, chrome Malaysia base, black & yellow dotted flames outlined in light green on hood & side, small green & black HW logo on roof facing rear, metal boom, black plastic sling, black window, 5sp	$2
❑ 📷	212	Double Vision	light candy green met., gray plastic Malaysia base, misc. white, gold & black racing decals on side & top, large "20/20" on side & in front of engines, white HW logo above two decals on rear fender behind wheel, two gray engines w/chrome blowers & bug catchers, gray int., clear canopy, 3sp	$3
❑ 📷	213	Whatta Drag	orange enamel, metal Malaysia base, white circle w/orange "6" on roof & right side of front, five misc. white & black racing decals on left side of front, gray plastic two port fuel injection on chrome engine, large chrome rear wing w/large yellow & red over white HW logo facing front, smoked window, chrome int., small front 5sp, large black spoke w/chrome rim motorcycle wheel	$2
❑ 📷	214	Super Comp Dragster	yellow enamel, black plastic fenders (Thailand), chrome base, black flames w/red outline on side w/five red & black misc. racing decals, black & yellow checked tampo w/black & red "5," small silver & red decal & black "D1" facing rear on top next to rollcage, red HW logo third decal down on side, chrome headers, black rollcage & wheelie bars, 5sp	$2

Photo	No.	Name	Description	Price
☐ 📷	215	XT-3	red met., yellow enamel painted metal Malaysia base, yellow & black side tampo w/red pinstripe, small black lettering, red HW logo & black, red & white "XT3" at right, three small yellow triangles w/row of white & row of yellow numbers, blue-tint metal engine, black canopy & nose point, 5sp	$2
☐ 📷	216	School Bus	red enamel, black plastic Thailand base, dark blue, black & silver side tampo outlined in white, large white HW logo behind rear wheel, white "Graphics" outlined in black above black & red "TEAM," roof has silver & dark blue tampo outlined in white w/a pink, red & black flame wheel design, white & black "HOT WHEELS twice on tire of roof tampo, white int., blue-tint window, asw-5dot	$2
☐ 📷	217	'57 T-Bird	a. met. purple, chrome Malaysia base, white, yellow to black fade tampo outlined in orange on side, hood & hood scoop, orange HW logo on rear fender by taillight, blue-tint window & int., bbs	$2
☐			b. same as (a), w/porthole in top, bbs	$52

I have only seen a couple of these '57 T-Bird (b) variations, so keep your eyes open for them.

Photo	No.	Name	Description	Price
☐ 📷	218	Rescue Ranger	met. silver, chrome China base, black & red "Bomb Squad" side tampos, small black HW logo below red "TEAM" behind door, red plastic emergency lights & rear insert, smoked int. & window, alw-3sp	$3
☐ 📷	219	Side Kick	a. gold met., metal Malaysia base, black tampo on front w/red & white "Side Kick," red & white HW logo over a silver design, misc. placed small red & white squares & triangles on the top of the body, blue-tint metal engine, black plastic rear exhaust metal int., red-tint window, alw-5sp	$4
☐ 📷			b. same as (a), black plastic Malaysia base, alw-5sp	$2

Super Comp Dragster

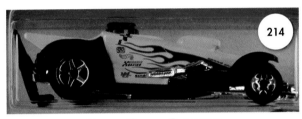

XT-3

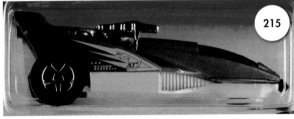

School Bus

'57 T-Bird

Rescue Ranger

Side Kick

Side Kick

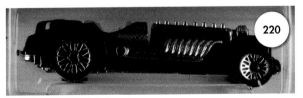

Sweet 16

Rail Rodder

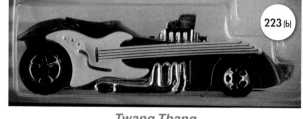

Twang Thang

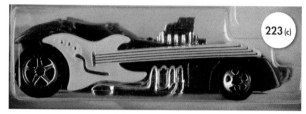

Twang Thang

Dogfighter

	Photo	No.	Name	Description	Price
❑	📷	220	Sweet 16	black enamel, blue-tint metal Malaysia base & engine, orange & silver flames on top of each fender, small orange HW logo above silver "Sweet 16" w/silver & orange flames on side, red int., bbs	$2
❑	📷	221	Rail Rodder	black plastic body, silver painted metal China base, red, yellow & black flames on side w/ large black outlined "ex" small black & yellow "12," large black & red over white HW logo & white & red "Rail Rodder" below side window, gold chrome engines & wheel drivers, b5sp rear/gold mini wheel front	$2
❑	📷	222	Dogfighter	met. silver, black plastic China base, black & orange flames on side, black HW logo on side of tail, chrome suspension & engine, light orange propeller, bbs	$2
❑		223	Twang Thang	a. met. blue, blue plastic China base, white guitar w/chrome trim, chrome int., engine & side pipes, white HW logo on nose, smoked window, 5sp	$3
❑	📷			b. same as (a), darker blue met., 5sp	$2
❑	📷			c. same as (b), gold trim replaces chrome trim on guitar, 5sp	$7
❑	📷	224	Ford GT-90	pearl green met., metal China base, black enamel front fenders w/gold pinstripe & white painted headlights, black painted body break & rocker panel w/silver "FORD GT-90" in front of rear wheel, black HW logo at center front by windshield, white upper w/silver lower tampo on door, white upper, silver lower tampo on rear fenders, gold below rear window, white int., clear window, asw-5dot	$2
❑	📷	225	Chrysler Thunderbolt	a. red enamel w/dark red plastic top, black plastic Malaysia base, silver flame tampo w/pink outline on side & top of rear fenders, silver "36" over white high on front fender behind wheel, black & pink "Lucero" over flame tampo on door, black stripe from body line down w/thin silver stripe at top & four silver outlined vents in front of rear wheel, two thin pink stripes on rocker panel w/silver "Thunderstreak" below vent outlines, HW logo embossed in rear clear window, black int., asw-5sp	$2
❑	📷			b. red enamel w/light red plastic top, black plastic Thailand base, silver flame tampo w/white outline on side & top of rear fenders, silver "36" over white high on front fender behind wheel, black & white "Lucero" over flame tampo on door, black stripe from body line down w/thin silver stripe at top & four silver outlined vents in front of rear wheel, two thin white stripes on rocker panel w/silver "Thunderstreak" below vent outlines, HW logo embossed in rear clear window, black int., asw-5sp	$3

There is going to be a change in the Hot Wheels flame logo from here on out. The older logo has the little ball that has "Mattel" in it. The new logo will not have it. This is sometimes called the "Meatball," as I was told by the designers. You are going to notice that there will be many cars that will be transition pieces with the logos. So, keep your eyes open, or in my case, get out your glasses.

Photo	No.	Name	Description	Price
☐ 📷	226	'67 Pontiac GTO	a. orange enamel, chrome Thailand base, white on side w/black tiger stripes on front fender, "TIGER Racing" in black & orange on door, black "Gabbi's" tampo in front of rear wheel, red & white HW logo above "Gabbi's," six misc. racing decals on rear fender behind wheel, black int., clear window, 5sp	$5
☐ 📷			b. same as (a), chrome Malaysia base, new HW logo missing Mattel, 5sp	$5
☐ 📷	227	Skullrider	black plastic body, metal China base, dark maroon & silver side tampo in cove behind front wheel, dark maroon & silver tampo on cab side by driver opening w/small dark maroon new HW logo, drivers & engine, 5sp	$2
☐ 📷	228	'57 Chevy	pearl orange met., chrome Malaysia base, metal engine through hood, black & white fading to magenta tampo on roof & side, red "Pro Speed" outlined in silver over front wheel, new black HW logo w/o Mattel behind front wheel, red "W" w/silver & black above red & silver "'57 Extreme" tampo on rear fender by taillight, black int., smoked window, 5sp	$2
☐ 📷	229	Blown Camaro	red enamel, metal Malaysia base, door has silver & gold checks, black & silver "650," silver & gold over black "Blown Camaro," all over a black design & thin silver striping, thin silver striping on rear fender w/small old black HW logo, hood has silver & black "Blown," gold & black "Camaro," black & silver "650" w/silver & gold checks over eight thin silver pinstripes on left side of hood, black int., smoked window, t/b	$2
☐ 📷	230	Ferrari F355 Spider	a. met. gray, metal Malaysia base, yellow & black Ferrari emblem on nose w/red & green stripes, yellow & black Ferrari shield w/green & red stripes on front fender behind high wheel, small black writing above rocker panel in front of rear wheel, old yellow HW logo on rear plate, black int., smoked window, asw-5sp	$4
			b. same as (a) new yellow HW logo on rear plate, asw-5sp	$2

Ford GT-90

'67 Pontiac GTO

Chrysler Thunderbolt

Skullrider

Chrysler Thunderbolt

'57 Chevy

'67 Pontiac GTO

Blown Camaro

Ferrari F355 Spider

Oshkosh Snowplow

Treadator

'33 Ford Roadster

Porsche 959

Ferrari 550 Maranello

Oshkosh Snowplow

Ferrari 365 GTB/4

	Photo	No.	Name	Description	Price
❏	📷	231	Treadator	met. gold, black plastic Thailand base, silver panel w/black outline on rear wing w/small red inner panels, in the red panels are new black HW logo, green & black "02" & green, silver & black design, black, silver, red & green tampo on top of rear wing, red plastic scoops & nose, chrome rear engine, fenders, tread drives & canopy	$2
❏	📷	232	Porsche 959	black enamel, metal China base, white over silver "959" on door, maroon over silver "Twin Turbo" on rocker panel, old maroon HW logo on rear fender behind wheel, red, yellow & black Porsche shield on nose w/maroon "Twin Turbo" black int., clear window, asw-5dot	$2
❏	📷	233	Oshkosh Snowplow	a. pearl mustard painted metal nose & fenders, metal Malaysia base, black plastic box & cab, red & white "Hanks Hauler" w/yellow & orange tampo on cab door, orange, yellow & black road tampo on hood w/white, yellow & orange flames, alw-ct/b	$5
❏	📷			b. same as (a), light pearl mustard, black plastic Malaysia base	$3
❏	📷	234	'33 Ford Roadster	black enamel, black plastic fenders, blue-tint metal Malaysia base, gold, yellow & orange side stripes, new gold HW logo on door above stripes, gold, yellow, orange & red flames on hood, chrome engine & grille, black int., chrome dash, tinted window, pr5	$2
❏	📷	235	Ferrari 550 Maranello	dark gray met., blue-tint metal Malaysia base, yellow & black Ferrari emblem on nose w/green & red stripes, old yellow HW logo on rear, red int., clear window, asw-5sp	$2
❏	📷	236	Ferrari 365 GTB/4	yellow enamel, metal Malaysia base, black int., clear window, 5sp	$2
❏	📷	237	'64 Lincoln Continental	a. black enamel, chrome Malaysia base, white HW logo on trunk, red HW logo on rear plate, red int., clear window, 5dot (this base was a leftover from the white car)	$35

Photo	No.	Name	Description	Price
❏	237	'64 Lincoln Continental	b. same as (a), white HW logo on trunk only, 5dot	$2
❏ 	238	Deuce Roadster	a. met. gold, metal Malaysia base, orange & black tampo on hood w/orange HW logo, brown, yellow & black Devil face on side w/yellow & red flames, chrome engine, scoop & grille, black int. & rear parachute, red-tint window, g5sp	$4
❏			b. same as (a), orange replaces brown in Devil face & light orange replaces red in flames on side, windshield is taller & lighter red-tint, g5sp	$2
❏	239	Tail Dragger	a. met. blue, metal Thailand base, silver & light blue stripe tampos on hood, side & on fender skirt, white & blue over silver new HW logo on rear fender above skirt, silver int., blue-tint window, 3sp	$2
❏			b. same as(a) blue-tint Malaysia base, larger white & blue new HW logo outlined in white over a silver background, 3sp	$3
❏	240	Scorchin' Scooter	dark orange pearl met., blue-tint metal Malaysia engine, black panel on side w/white "Dunkins," gold panel w/black "Motorcycles" & old white HW logo, black tampo on tank w/white "Dunkins," & gold panel w/black "Motorcycles" black tampo on side of front fender w/gold lettering & small white design, black handlebars & forks plastic, chrome rim w/three black spokes	$4
❏	241	Propper Chopper	black enamel, maroon pearl plastic Malaysia base, rear wing, tail, rotor blades, & int., orange & yellow "Sky Spy" w/white, black, orange & yellow eye tampo over a light blue design & four yellow dots on side, maroon dashed line w/maroon & white arrow head, new yellow HW logo above arrow head, blue-tint window	$2
❏	242	Olds 442	a. white enamel w/chrome Malaysia base, gold panels on hood scoops, gold over black "442" above black stripe on fender behind front wheel, gold & black stripe tampos on side from front to back, gold HW logo in front of rear wheel above black stripe, gold int./clear window, asw-pr5	$2

1964 Lincoln Continental

Tail Dragger

Deuce Roadster

Scorchin' Scooter

Deuce Roadster

Propper Chopper

Tail Dragger

Olds 442

Olds 442

Deora II

Chevy Pro Stock Truck

Photo	No.	Name	Description	Price
☐ 📷	242	Olds 442	b. same as (a), asw-5sp	$10
☐ 📷	243	Deora II	candy blue met., black plastic China base, black rear bed w/two orange plastic surfboards, one surfboard has a large yellow & red over white new HW logo, orange, red & white track design, & misc. red & white sponsor decals and the other surfboard has a smaller yellow & red over white new HW logo, orange, red & white track design, misc. red & white sponsor decals & a large white design w/orange markings, chrome engine & int., clear window, asw-pr5	$2
☐ 📷	244	Chevy Pro Stock Truck	candy purple met., chrome China base, purple & white, red & white & white & red over white old HW logo on hood, white & purple "PRO TRUCK" on door, three red & white stripes on side w/12 misc. racing decals, large white & red over white old HW logo above rear wheel, purple & white stripe on rear fender down along rocker panel, orange int., clear window, 5sp	$2
☐ 📷	245	Phantastique	met. red, chrome China base, silver tampo on side w/old silver HW logo where a door would be, cream int. w/a chrome shifter & center console, chrome grille, clear windshield w/chrome frame, alw-bbs	$2
☐ 📷	246	'68 El Camino	dark orange pearl met., metal China base, black painted rocker panel w/old white HW logo behind front wheel, chrome rear engine, large gray plastic rear wind & int., clear window, 5sp	$2
☐ 📷	247	Ford F-150	black enamel, black plastic Thailand base, hood, roof & tailgate have two wide white stripes w/thin pinstripe on each side new white & red over white HW logo on rear plate, orange & white painted taillights, chrome front bumper & grille, rear bumper, int. & rear bed floor, yellow-tint window, alw-3sp	$2
☐ 📷	248	Way 2 Fast	a. pearl gray met., black painted metal Malaysia base, blue, black & white stripe side tampo w/white "Heralda" in black oval, side tampo covers the whole side, small "Way 2 Fast ® Racing" in black at bottom of door, black panel on roof w/thick black, blue & white stripes outlined in thin silver pinstripes, silver "Heralda" in black oval, silver "Racing" & blue & white HW logo outlined in silver at rear of roof, chrome int., engines & grille, gray plastic radiator cover, 5sp	$4
☐ 📷			b. pearl gray met., black painted metal Thailand base, blue, black & white stripe side tampo w/white "Heralda" in black oval, side tampo goes as far as rear of window, small "Way 2 Fast Racing" in black at bottom of door, ® is missing, black panel on roof w/thick black, blue & white stripes outlined in thin silver pinstripes, white "Heralda" in black oval, white "Racing" & blue & white HW logo outlined in silver at rear of roof, chrome int., engines & grille, gray plastic radiator cover, 5sp	$2
☐ 📷	249	'59 Impala	black enamel, dark gold chrome Malaysia base, orange & gold side tampo w/orange & black new HW logo high on rear fender, orange & gold tampo on hood, red int., smoked window, asw-gbbs	$2

Photo		No.	Name	Description	Price
☐	📷	250	Porsche 911 GTI-98	a. white enamel, black plastic China base, aqua, dark red, mustard yellow & dark blue tampos, small dark blue lettering on roof, dark red "Porsche" on front above scoop, American flag below scoop on left, dark red "Champion" & small lettering on nose, dark blue "Champion," blue over yellow "Motorsport" & red "Parts" over yellow on rear white plastic wing, dark blue "Michelin" & Michelin Man tampo on side behind rear wheel, American flag & dark blue "38" over light yellow at center on side, dark red "Champion" & small lettering on rocker panel, gray int., clear window, red HW logo behind front wheel, asw-bbs	$3
☐	📷			b. white enamel, black plastic China base, olive, dark red, mustard yellow & dark blue tampos, small dark blue lettering on roof, dark red "Porsche" on front above scoop, American flag below scoop on left, dark red "Champion" & small lettering on nose, dark blue "Champion," blue over yellow "Motorsport" & red "Parts" over yellow on rear white plastic wing, dark blue "Michelin" & Michelin Man tampo on side behind rear wheel, American flag & dark blue "38" over light yellow at center on side, dark red "Champion" & small lettering on rocker panel, gray int., clear window, red HW logo behind front wheel, asw-bbs	$5
☐	📷			c. white enamel, black plastic Malaysia base, teal, light red, light yellow & dark blue tampos, small dark blue lettering on roof, red "Porsche" on front above scoop, American flag below scoop on left, red "Champion" & small lettering on nose, blue "Champion," blue over yellow "Motorsport" & red "Parts" over yellow on rear white plastic wing, dark blue "Michelin" & Michelin Man tampo on side behind rear wheel, American flag & dark blue "38" over light yellow at center on side, red "Champion" & small lettering on rocker panel, gray int., clear window, red HW logo behind front wheel, asw-bbs	$8

245

Phantastique

246

'68 El Camino

247

Ford F-150

248 (a)

Way 2 Fast

248 (b)

Way 2 Fast

249

'59 Impala

250 (a)

Porsche 911 GTI-98

250 (b)

Porsche 911 GTI-98

250 (c)

Porsche 911 GTI-98

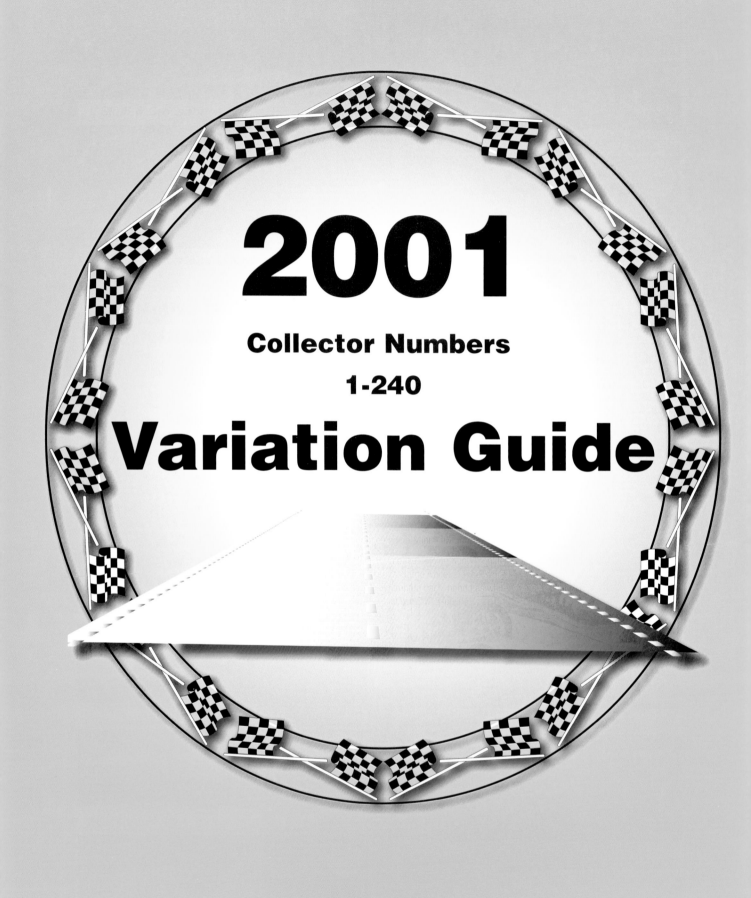

2001

Collector Numbers

1-240

Variation Guide

2001 Treasure Hunt Series

Photo	No.	Name	Description	Price
☐ 📷	1	#1-'65 Corvette	red enamel, gray plastic Malaysia base, gold & silver pin stripes on hood, trunk, & sides, gold & black-over-white TH emblem w/white & gold HW logo behind rear wheel, white int., clear window, chrome bumpers, chrome wheel "Real Rider" rubber tire	$15
☐ 📷	2	#2-Roll Cage	orange enamel, white enamel Malaysia base, black painted side panel w/orange, white & black "TH" emblem & red & white HW logo, black panel on nose w/red "HARE" & white oval w/red "R" & black "C," gold chrome rear engine, floor pan & hood scoop, black plastic int., small ct/b spare tire on rear, all small chrome wheeled knobby "Real Rider" tires w/white letters	$15
☐ 📷	3	#3-So Fine	met. green, chrome Malaysia base, silver painted side molding & three vents on side of front fender, gold pinstripe on side w/gold lettering on rear fender skirt, gold & silver pinstriping on hood, gold, silver & black "TH" emblem w/gold-over-white HW logo on trunk, dark smoked window, white int., chrome wheel, whitewall "Real Rider" tire	$15
☐ 📷	4	#4-Rodger Dodger	black enamel, chrome Malaysia base, orange & white flames, gold & black over white TH emblem w/white & red HW logo on rear fender behind wheel, red int., smoked window, chrome wheel whitewall "Real Rider" rubber tire	$15
☐ 📷	5	#5-Blast Lane	met. gold, blue-tint Malaysia base, black oval on gas tank w/gold pinstripe tampo & silver gas cap, black square on rear fender w/red, white & black "TH" emblem & white & red HW logo, black headlight cover w/two silver painted headlights, dark gold chrome handlebars, light gold chrome rims w/three black spokes	$20
☐ 📷	6	#6-Hammered Coupe	gray body, black rear fenders, roof, hood scoop & nose piece w/white panel pinstripes, blue-tint metal Malaysia base, silver & black "TH" emblem on rear w/orange-over-white new HW logo, orange-over-white rear painted taillights on rear fenders, two orange panels over black w/white pinstripes on hood, chrome engine & int., orange-tint window, pr5	$10
☐ 📷	7	#7-Vulture	white pearl, transparent orange plastic Malaysia base, black panel on side w/silver, red & white tampos, black panel on nose w/red & silver, red, white & black "TH" emblem w/red & white HW logo, black, red, & silver tampo on roof, black panels w/silver dots on top of rear fenders & headlights, chrome int. & rear engine, red-tint window, pr5	$10

2001 Treasure Hunt Series, #1-'65 Corvette

2001 Treasure Hunt Series, #4-Rodger Dodger

2001 Treasure Hunt Series, #2-Roll Cage

2001 Treasure Hunt Series, #5-Blast Lane

2001 Treasure Hunt Series, #3-So Fine

2001 Treasure Hunt Series, #7-Vulture

Photo	No.	Name	Description	Price
❑ 📷	8	#8-Dodge Charger	yellow enamel, chrome Malaysia base, black & orange stripe tampo on hood w/black "7" in white circle w/black outline in center, black & orange stripe tampo on side w/black "7" in white circle w/black outline in center of door, black "Roberts," red "Shocks" above rear quarter panel, red "Dodge" in black rectangle behind rear wheel, gray & black "TH" emblem w/white over red HW logo on door, "taumuvieri valves" below TH emblem, five misc. racing decals on front fender, black int., clear window, all small chrome wheel "Real Rider" rubber tire	$12
❑	9	#9-Olds 442	a. light blue flake, chrome Malaysia base, wide white stripes on each hood scoop w/"455" on each side, gray stripe from rear side window to headlights, silver painted door handle, orange-over-silver painted side marker lights, orange, silver & black "TH" logo on rear fender above marker light, gray stripe on lower rear fender, rocker panel & front fender, white int., clear window, all large chrome wheel "Real Rider" tires	$15
❑ 📷			b. same as (a), dark blue flake	$20
❑ 📷	10	#10-Pontiac Rageous	met. brown, gray plastic Malaysia base, black, gold, silver & orange tampo on side, black, orange & silver "TH" emblem on rear fender behind wheel, hood has black panel w/brown & gold pinstripe outlining silver fade w/orange tampo, gray int., black painted roof w/smoked window, all large chrome wheel Real Riders	$12
❑	11	#11-Deora	met. blue, metal Thailand base, black panels w/white outlines on roof, bed cover & sides, black stripe on side w/blue & white "deora 1" & TH logo, blue plastic surfboards & int., blue-tint window, redline bw	$10
❑ 📷	12	#12-Cabbin' Fever	white enamel, gold chrome Malaysia base, window, grille & ramps, black plastic rear ramp & roof cover w/gold over white "Cabbin Fever" over pearl green flame tampo, pearl green, white & black tampo on side from behind front wheel to rear, pearl green, black & gold "TH" emblem on door w/gold HW logo, large front & center pr5, xl/rear pr5	$15

2001 Treasure Hunt Series, #8-Dodge Charger

*2001 Treasure Hunt Series,
#10-Pontiac Rageous*

2001 Treasure Hunt Series, #9-Olds 442

2001 Treasure Hunt Series, #12-Cabbin' Fever

2001 First Editions

Photo	No.	Name	Description	Price
❑ 📷	13	#1-Cadillac LMP	a. candy gray, black plastic Malaysia base, black "Cadillac," "Toshiba Copiers + Fax" w/Cadillac emblem on nose, black HW logo, small "Toshiba," US flag, "AC Delco" & "1" on side in front of rear wheel, black "Perelli" & two small sponsor names behind front wheel, black int., bbs	$3
❑			b. same as (a), no side tampo, bbs	$26
❑			c. same as (a), no front tampo, bbs	$20
❑ 📷	14	#2-Surfin' School Bus	yellow enamel w/dark & light brown wood side, black plastic fenders, gray plastic Malaysia base, chrome rear engine, purple-tint window, 5sp	$2
❑	15	#3-La Troca	a. met. red, gold-tint chrome Malaysia base, gold painted visor w/white pinstripe, black window, gbbs	$3
❑ 📷			b. same as (a), gold chrome Malaysia base, gbbs	$3

Photo	No.	Name	Description	Price
❑ 📷	15	#3-La Troca	c. met. rose, gold chrome Malaysia base, gold painted visor w/white pinstripe, black window, gbbs	$5
❑ 📷	16	#4-Sooo Fast	white pearl met., red met. painted Malaysia base, blue tampo w/gold outline & white HW logo on hood, chrome int., engine, grille, front suspension & rear exhaust, clear window, 5sp	$3
❑ 📷	17	#5-Super Tuned	a. candy blue met., gray plastic Malaysia base, large white letters on side & hood outlined in dark red w/small dark red "Racing," eight misc. sponsor decals including dark red HW logo on right side of door, five misc. sponsor decals on front of hood w/white dots across nose, red int., bed cover & rear wing, smoked window, pr5	$2
❑ 📷			b. same as (a), very dark candy blue met., pr5	$3
❑			c. same as (a), open space between rear wing & bed cover (also known as open wing), pr5	$10
❑			d. same as (c), open rear wing, all thin asw-pr5	$15
❑ 📷			e. same as (b), very dark candy blue met., large white letters on side & hood outlined in bright red w/small bright red "Racing"	$10
❑ 📷	18	#6-Hooligan	a. flat black, metal Malaysia base, dark red flames on side w/white outline, red plastic int. & engine (no chrome on engine), 5sp	$15
❑			b. same as (a), chrome on engine, 5sp	$2
❑ 📷	19	#7-Krazy 8s	dark candy blue, blue-tint metal Malaysia base, smoked rear wing w/yellow, orange & purple "Krazy 8's" w/orange "Racing" over a silver design on top, silver HW logo on side of rear wing, smoked canopy w/silver tampo, chrome engine & int., alw-pr5	$2

2001 First Editions, #1-Cadillac LMP

2001 First Editions, #2-Surfin' School Bus

2001 First Editions, #3-La Troca

2001 First Editions, #3-La Troca

2001 First Editions, #4-Sooo Fast

2001 First Editions, #5-Super Tuned

2001 First Editions, #5-Super Tuned

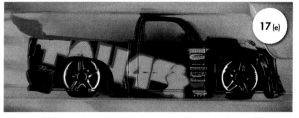

2001 First Editions, #5-Super Tuned

2001 First Editions, #6-Hooligan

2001 First Editions,
#9-Panoz LMP-1 Roadster S

2001 First Editions, #7-Krazy 8s

2001 First Editions, #10-Shredster

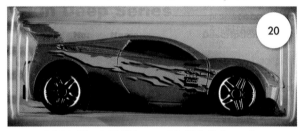

2001 First Editions, #8-MS-T Suzuka

2001 First Editions, #11-Dodge Viper GTS-R

2001 First Editions,
#9-Panoz LMP-1 Roadster S

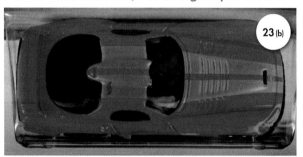

2001 First Editions, #11-Dodge Viper GTS-R

	Photo	No.	Name	Description	Price
☐	📷	20	#8-MS-T Suzuka	candy lime, black plastic Malaysia base, yellow & black side tampo w/six misc. racing decals including small black HW logo behind front wheel, large yellow & black "2" w/black & silver sponsor decals & lettering, black int., tinted window, alw-pr5	$2
☐	📷	21	#9-Panoz LMP-1 Roadster S	a. red enamel, black plastic Malaysia base, white "Panoz Racing School" outlined in black on side behind front wheel, white HW logo left of Panoz on front fender, white box w/black "11" on black plastic side, flag tampo on left, & "11" in white box on right side of hood, "Hella" in white above each headlight, blue & red Panoz emblem on nose, black rear wing & int., bbs	$2
☐	📷			b. same as (a), asw-bbs	$15
☐		22	#10-Shredster	a. pearl tangerine metal top, pearl mustard metal Malaysia fenders, black plastic body, hood scoop & int., silver "Shredster" & HW logo on black body side behind front fender, gray plastic base, smoked window, wide rear pr5	$2
☐				b. same as (a), thin rear pr5	$15
☐				c. same as (a), wide rear 5sp	$10
☐	📷			d. same as (a), thin rear 5sp	$5
☐	📷	23	#11-Dodge Viper GTS-R	a. red enamel, black plastic Malaysia base, two wide silver stripes on roof & hood, red HW logo on left rear of roof, black int., clear window, 5sp	$5
☐	📷			b. same as (a), gray stripes on roof & hood, 5sp	$3
☐	📷	24	#12-Maelstrom	a. dark candy blue met., chrome Malaysia base, silver & orange flames on top of each front fender, thin orange stripe on side onto front fender, silver HW logo above stripe chrome engines & exhaust, black int., smoked window, 3sp	$2

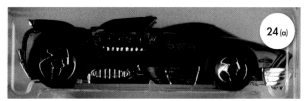

2001 First Editions, #12-Maelstrom

2001 First Editions, #14-1971 Plymouth GTX

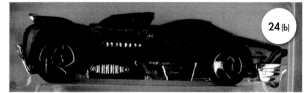

2001 First Editions, #12-Maelstrom

2001 First Editions, #14-1971 Plymouth GTX

2001 First Editions, #13-Lotus M250

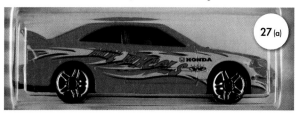

2001 First Editions, #15-Honda Civic

	Photo	No.	Name	Description	Price
❑	📷	24	#12-Maelstrom	b. same as (a), much darker candy blue met., 3sp	$3
❑		25	#13-Lotus M250	a. candy gray, black plastic "LOTUS M250" Malaysia base, silver painted "Lotus" on rear w/silver HW logo, small green circle tampo on nose, black side vent, headlights & grille, red int., smoked window, 5sp	$75
❑	📷			b. same as (a), unpainted "Lotus" on rear w/silver HW logo, 5sp	$4
❑				c. same as (b), black plastic "LOTUS PROJECT M250" Malaysia base, 5sp	$4
❑				d. same as (c), name change "LOTUS PROJECT M250" on card	$4
❑	📷	26	#14-1971 Plymouth GTX	Sub-Lime enamel, chrome Malaysia base, black panel & small black emblem on front of hood, black int., blue-tint window w/HW logo stamped in rear, 5sp	$2
❑	📷			b. same as (a), no door lock below handle on side, 5sp	$4
❑	📷	27	#15-Honda Civic	a. red enamel, black plastic Malaysia base, white over black tampo on side w/red "Hot Wheels," black "HONDA" & emblem & "W" in an oval behind front wheel, hood has white & red "Hot Wheels" over black & white panel tampo, white int., smoked window, asw-pr5	$3
❑	📷			b. same as (a), asw-bbs	$7
❑	📷	28	#16-Evil Twin	a. dark met. purple, black plastic Malaysia base, silver painted molding on rear fender skirt, two chrome engines, front bumper & side pipes, silver painted headlights, red painted taillights, purple HW logo on white rear plate, tan int., clear window, bbs	$15
❑				b. same as (a), red HW logo on rear plate, bbs	$4
❑	📷			c. same as (b), much lighter met. purple, bbs	$2
❑	📷	29	#17-Hyper Mite	a. pearl light green, black plastic Malaysia base, pearl lavender checked tampo on side below canopy, large white "2" outlined in red on side, dark red HW logo on rocker panel, chrome engine, int., grille & headlights, two blue-tint metal header pipes, purple-tint canopy, large 5sp rear & mini front	$10
❑	📷			b. same as (a), dark blue checked tampo below canopy, large 5sp rear & mini front	$8
❑	📷			c. same as (a), purple checked tampo below canopy, large 5sp rear & mini front	$4
❑	📷	30	#18-Outsider	a. pearl orange, blue-tint metal Malaysia base, black panel w/green, white, black & dark orange striped tampo on top, white circle w/black "1" & thin black outline on nose, white & orange "VJ" on front by gray plastic driver, white "Roberts," "Jones," "Saffer" & "Heralda" tampos behind driver, black, green, white & light orange stripe tampo on sidecar by gray plastic passenger, white outlined HW logo over orange on rear fender	$8
❑				b. same as (a), light orange replaces dark orange in stripe, "VJ" missing in tampo, "Roberts," "Jones," "Saffer" & "Heralda" tampos are smaller & clearer, HW logo on rear is smaller & outlined in black	$3

	Photo	No.	Name	Description	Price
☐	📷	31	#19-Monoposto	a. pearl orange met., black plastic Malaysia base, black, green & white HW tampo on top, silver painted headlights, chrome driver & int., green-tint canopy, pr5	$2
☐	📷			b. same as (a), dark orange pearl met., pr5	$4
☐	📷			c. same as (a), bbs	$10
☐	📷			d. same as (c), dark pearl orange met., bbs	$15
☐	📷	32	#20-Vulture Roadster	candy purple met., orange-tint plastic Malaysia base & windshield, silver checkered tampo on top left side w/orange HW logo by left front wheel, white "Roadster" w/white & black over orange "VR1" on side, chrome engine & int., metal header on roof, 5sp	$2
☐	📷	33	#21-Fright Bike	a. purple-tint plastic body, black plastic front fairing, blue-tint metal Malaysia frame, forks & engine, old HW logo stamped on back of rear fender, gray plastic wheelie bars w/old HW logo stamped on side, chrome rims w/black spokes	$5
☐	📷			b. darker purple-tint plastic body, old HW logo stamped on back of rear fender, gray plastic wheelie bars w/new HW logo stamped on side	$4

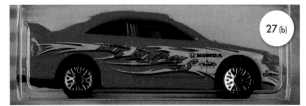

2001 First Editions, #15-Honda Civic

2001 First Editions, #16-Evil Twin

2001 First Editions, #16-Evil Twin

2001 First Editions, #17-Hyper Mite

2001 First Editions, #17-Hyper Mite

2001 First Editions, #17-Hyper Mite

2001 First Editions, #18-Outsider

2001 First Editions, #19-Monoposto

2001 First Editions, #19-Monoposto

2001 First Editions, #19-Monoposto

2001 First Editions, #20-Vulture Roadster

2001 First Editions, #19-Monoposto

2001 First Editions, #19-Monoposto

2001 First Editions, #21-Fright Bike

	Photo	No.	Name	Description	Price
☐	📷	34	#22-Jet Threat 3.0	a. pearl silver w/matching painted metal Malaysia base, black "DC-121" w/red & yellow tampos on top of both center wings, "Step Back" in black w/red & white tampo by exhaust at end of center wing, yellow HW logo on left wing behind front wheel, chrome engines, int. & backing plates, smoked canopy, 5dot	$4
☐	📷			b. same as (a), metal Malaysia base, 5dot	$2
☐				c. same as (b), blue-tint metal Malaysia base, 5dot	$2
☐	📷	35	#23-Montezooma	a. orangish yellow pearl met., chrome Malaysia base, light orange panels on hood w/gold outline, light orange & gold stripe tampo on side, gold & light orange HW logo on rear fender behind wheel, gold int., smoked window, asw-bbs	$2
☐	📷			b. same as (a), yellow pearl met., asw-bbs (Race & Win Card)	$10
☐	📷			c. same as (a), short smoked windshield	$4
☐	📷	36	#24-Toyota Celica	a. yellow enamel, black plastic Malaysia base, black & silver "RHLman TURBO" on side w/six misc. black racing sponsors on right side of door, black HW logo above rear wheel, yellow-tinted headlights, yellow plastic rear spoiler, white int., yellow-tint window, asw-pr5	$2
☐	📷			b. same as (a), lighter yellow color, black plastic front grille & vents, asw-pr5	$80

The Toyota Celica #24 (b) variation with the black front grille is very rare in the US package. They were an International carded release. These can be equated to the gold 7sp cars that were found in 1995.

| ☐ | 📷 | 37 | #25-Ford Focus | black enamel, black plastic Malaysia base, yellow tampo w/red outline on side & top of front fenders, gray painted headlights, roof has large yellow "Meguiar's" & thick brown stripe, hood has large yellow "Meguiar's" & "NuForms," side has eight misc. decals w/smaller yellow "Meguiar's" & blue oval Ford above rear wheel, red HW logo on rear fender behind wheel, large black plastic rear wing & int., clear window, asw-5dot | $2 |

	Photo	No.	Name	Description	Price
❑	📷	38	#26-Mega-Duty	gray pearl, metal Malaysia base, black plastic fender flares, bumpers, int. & bed, red-tint windows & headlights, black tampo on hood outlined in orange, orange over black HW logo at front of hood, alw-pr5	$2
❑	📷	39	#27-Riley & Scott Mk III	a. dark candy blue met., black plastic Malaysia base, dark orange & black tampo w/silver squares on top of each side, left side of top has four red, white & black sponsor decals, three on right, large white & black "1" w/orange & black over silver HW logo at center of front, large orange & black HW logo w/white & silver on white plastic rear wing, white int., bbs	$4
❑	📷			b. same as (a), asw-bbs	$7
❑	📷	40	#28-XS-IVE	red plastic body, blue-tint metal Malaysia base, chrome rear engine, black window, front bumper & headlight support, large green circle outlined in white & black w/yellow & black HW emblem & black "Hot Wheels Rescue" on cab door, rear body has yellow, white & red HW logo outlined in black, small "U5" & larger white & yellow "RESCUE" over black tampo, yellow "FIELD & FOREST" outlined in black & black "28767," large ct/b on front & rear, small ct/b center wheel	$3

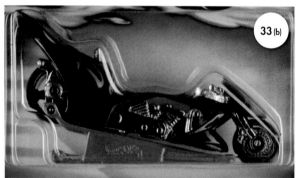

2001 First Editions, #21-Fright Bike

2001 First Editions, #22-Jet Threat 3.0

2001 First Editions, #22-Jet Threat 3.0

2001 First Editions, #23-Montezooma

2001 First Editions, #23-Montezooma

2001 First Editions, #23-Montezooma

2001 First Editions, #24-Toyota Celica

2001 First Editions, #24-Toyota Celica

2001 First Editions, #25-Ford Focus

2001 First Editions, #26-Mega Duty

2001 First Editions, #27-Riley & Scott Mk III

2001 First Editions, #27-Riley & Scott Mk III

2001 First Editions, #28-XS-IVE

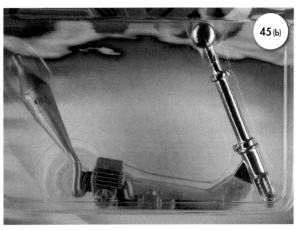

2001 First Editions, #33- Mo' Scoot

2001 First Editions, #34-Ford Thunderbolt

2001 First Editions, #35-Morris Wagon

Photo	No.	Name	Description	Price
❏	45	#33-Mo' Scoot	a. day-glo orange transparent body, blue-tint metal Malaysia base & front end, gray plastic engine & tunie exhaust pipe, day-glo green transparent wheels, large rear, small front, raised silver HW logo on top of body	$35
❏ 📷			b. same as (a), flat silver HW logo on top of body	$3
❏ 📷	46	#34-Ford Thunderbolt	black enamel, chrome Malaysia base, silver & red "Thunderbolt" on rear quarter, silver early Ford emblem on rear roof post, silver "Hugh Riehlman" on top of door, silver & red "Robert Ford" & silver "Homer" on lower door, red "Crew" w/silver "Judy-Pat-Ruth" in front of rear wheel, red & silver HW logo behind rear wheel, silver "Engine By" w/red "Kermit" on front fender above wheel, Ford 427 emblem on lower fender behind wheel, silver painted molding on side from taillights to headlights, red int., smoked window, 5sp	$3
❏ 📷	47	#35-Morris Wagon	a. black enamel metal body, tan plastic back half w/black painted roof, blue-tint metal Malaysia base, chrome engine & int., yellow-tint window, HW logo molded on rear left door, extra large rear 5sp, small front 5sp	$2
❏ 📷			b. same as (a), large rear 5sp, small front 5sp	$25
❏ 📷	48	#36-Fandango	a. pearl orange met., gray plastic Malaysia base, large green, white & black "Fandango" tampo on side, black outlined side exhaust vent in front of rear wheel, black & white HW logo on door, black int., orange-tint window, pr5	$2
❏ 📷			b. same as (a), very light pearl orange met., more silver than orange, pr5	$5
❏ 📷			c. same as (a), asw-pr5	$15
❏ 📷	49	#29-Old # 3	red enamel, black painted metal Malaysia base, white "3" on side of cowl, black "3" on front of gray radiator, gray steering wheel, black painted seat, metal header on left side, chrome wheel w/black spare tire on rear, no HW logo, alw-5sp	$2

	Photo	No.	Name	Description	Price
❏	📷	50	#30-Ferrari 156	red enamel, metal Malaysia base, white "2" on side & nose, yellow & black rectangle Ferrari logo on nose, yellow & black triangle Ferrari logo on each side behind small scoop, silver HW logo behind rear wheel, metal int., gray plastic engine & roll bar, clear window & injection covers, bbs	$2
❏	📷	51	#31-Cunningham C4R	a. white enamel, charcoal met. plastic Malaysia base, two thick pearl blue stripes down center from nose to tail, pearl blue HW logo in stripes on tail, blue int., clear window, alw-5sp	$2
❏				b. same as (a), stripes on hood are pearl blue, stripes & HW logo on rear are blue enamel	$4
❏				c. same as (a), stripes on hood & trunk are blue enamel, blue enamel HW logo in stripes on tail	$4
❏				d. same as (a), stripes on hood are blue enamel, stripes & HW logo on rear are blue pearl	$4
❏	📷	52	#32-'57 Roadster	a. bright red enamel, blue-tint metal Malaysia base, silver painted side trim, chrome engine, white over orange HW logo behind rear wheel, pink int., smoked window, 5sp rear, old style mini wheel front	$4
❏	📷			b. same as (a), 5sp rear, new mini 5sp front wheel	$2

2001 First Editions, #35-Morris Wagon

2001 First Editions, #35-Fandango

2001 First Editions, #35-Fandango

2001 First Editions, #35-Fandango

2001 First Editions, #29-Old #3

2001 First Editions, #30-Ferrari 156

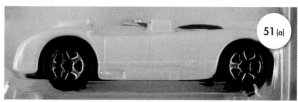

2001 First Editions, #31-Cunningham C4R

2001 First Editions, #32-'57 Roadster

2001 First Editions, #32-'57 Roadster

Fossil Fuel Series

	Photo	No.	Name	Description	Price
❑	📷	41	School Bus	green enamel, black plastic Malaysia base, gray & white dinosaur skeleton w/black outline on roof w/white & black "Triceratops" five times, gray, white, gold & black dinosaur skeleton on side w/white & black "Triceratops," white HW logo on rear fender above bumper, white int., yellow-tint window, asw-5dot	$2
❑	📷	42	Ambulance	dark candy purple met., gray plastic Malaysia base, candy blue, silver, white enamel & black side tampo w/large "SaberTooth," white, silver & black tampo on hood w/candy blue HW logo, white int. & rear doors, blue-tint window, asw-t/b	$2
❑	📷	43	Firebird Funny Car	silver flake, metal Malaysia base, white w/orange & red dinosaur skeleton on side w/white over black "T-Rex" over rear wheel, black panel on hood w/white, orange & red dinosaur skeleton on right side, black, orange & white "T Rex" on left side of hood, white HW logo above the "T" on the hood, metal int., orange window, 5sp	$4
❑	📷	44	Camaro Z-28	red enamel, black painted metal Malaysia base, two black panels on hood w/silver & gold designs, silver & black lettering above rear wheel, black, gold, silver & pink side tampo, silver HW logo on roof pillar, black window, 3sp	$2

Fossil Fuel Series, School Bus

Fossil Fuel Series, Funny Car

Fossil Fuel Series, Ambulance

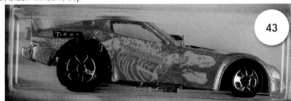

Fossil Fuel Series, Camaro Z-28

Turbo Taxi Series

	Photo	No.	Name	Description	Price
❑	📷	53	'57 Chevy	a. black enamel w/chrome Malaysia base, metal engine through hood, side has black & white check tampo from front to back, white "Kostya's Fleet & Taxi Service" in light brown ring w/gold outline & black center on door & roof over gold, black & pearl white tampo, black "No. 3" behind front wheel, gold HW logo on rear fender above bumper, black int., smoked window, 3sp	$3
❑				b. same as (a), dark brown ring on door & roof, 3sp	$7
❑	📷	54	Limozeen	a. green met., gold chrome Thailand base, white checked tampo on side & left half of hood, small white & gold lettering above large white & black "TAXI" over gold on side & hood, gold HW logo on front fender above bumper, white int., smoked window, asw-g5sp	$8
❑	📷			b. same as (a), asw-gt/b	$5
❑				c. same as (b), gold chrome Malaysia base, asw-g5sp	$3
❑	📷	55	'57 T-Bird, w/port hole	a. yellow enamel, chrome Malaysia base, side has white & black "Tad's" w/silver & black "taxi" over orange checked tampo w/white fade, white & black "Tad's taxi" w/black, silver & white circle tampo over an orange & black tampo on hood, small black "Radio Dispatched No. 9" on front fender, orange & black tampo over porthole on side of top, small black HW logo behind rear wheel, orange-tint window & int., 3sp	$3

| ❑ | 📷 | 55 | '57 T-Bird, w/port hole | b. same as (a), light brown replaces orange in tampos, 3sp | $5 |
| ❑ | 📷 | | | c. same as (a), no port hole in top, 3sp | $87 |

The '57 T-Bird (c) variation car with no porthole cars were also found in international packages.

| ❑ | 📷 | 56 | '70 Chevelle | met. blue, chrome China base, small white "China Town Blue" & gold HW logo in black panel on center of hood, black & white checkered tampo on rest of hood w/white & gold "TAXI" on nose, black & white checkered dragon tampo outlined in gold on side, small white & black "China Town Blue" w/white & gold "TAXI" over rear wheel, white int., blue-tint window, 5sp | $3 |

Turbo Taxi Series, '57 Chevy

Turbo Taxi Series, '57 T-Bird

Turbo Taxi Series, Limozeen

Turbo Taxi Series, '57 T-Bird

Turbo Taxi Series, Limozeen

Turbo Taxi Series, '57 T-Bird

Rat Rods Series

	Photo	No.	Name	Description	Price
❑	📷	57	Track T	a. flat black primer, metal Malaysia base, brown primer flames w/white outline, black int. cover, metal seat, brown primer HW logo on nose, wwbw	$5
❑	📷			b. flat black primer, metal Malaysia base, orange flames w/white outline, black int. cover , metal seat, orange HW logo on nose, wwbw	$2
❑	📷	58	'33 Roadster	flat black, red oxide (brown) primer painted metal Malaysia base, red HW logo & white over red "Lil Black & Red" over rear fender, chrome engine, dash, grille & headlights, red int. & running boards, clear window, wwbw	$3
❑	📷	59	Phaeton	red oxide (brown) primer, black painted metal China base, red flames w/black outline on side, white HW logo on side above rear wheel, black int. & top, clear window, wwbw	$3
❑	📷	60	Shoe Box	a. flat lavender primer, chrome Malaysia base, black "Lucky Nines" w/red & white dice w/black outline behind front wheel, black pinstripe on upper & lower body lines, new white HW logo in side rear window, chrome int. & engine, blue-tint window, wwbw	$3
❑	📷			b. same as (a), darker flat lavender, wwbw	$5
❑	📷			c. same as (a), no HW logo, wwbw	$10

Turbo Taxi Series, '70 Chevelle SS

Rat Rods Series, Phaeton

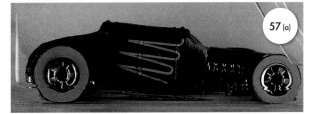

Rat Rods Series, Track T

Rat Rods Series, Shoe Box

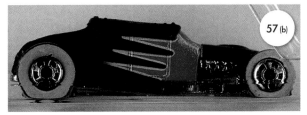

Rat Rods Series, Track T

Rat Rods Series, Shoe Box

Rat Rods Series, '33 Roadster

Rat Rods Series, Shoe Box

Anime Series

	Photo	No.	Name	Description	Price
☐	📷	61	Muscle Tone	a. met. green, black plastic Malaysia base, black panel w/silver dots on side, light green "e" w/gold outline in black circle w/silver "unit four" & silver outline, light green, silver & gold tampo on lower door, gold wolf man figure w/light green face, silver hair & silver & green body parts on hood, light green "e" w/gold outline in black circle w/silver "unit four" & silver outline on upper right hand side of hood, silver HW logo high on rear fender behind wheel, white int., yellow-tint window, t/b	$2
☐	📷			b. same as (a), tampo colors are much darker, gray replaces silver on hood, t/b	$2
☐	📷	62	Ford GT-90	a. white enamel, metal China base, blue, silver, gold & black side tampos, silver, blue & black Anime logo in front of rear wheel, silver & black tampos on front w/silver, blue & black Anime logo on nose, black & white HW logo behind front fender, gray int., blue-tint canopy, asw-pr5	$2
☐				b. same as (a), light blue replaces blue in all tampos, asw-pr5	$4
☐	📷	63	Dodge Charger R/T	a. pearl mustard, black plastic Malaysia base, side tampo is a pink-faced boy w/pearl green & dark red clothes holding a pink sword w/black outline over a black panel, white "Unit Two" & pearl green HW logo on rear fender behind wheel, pearl green & white Anime logo w/black "R/T" behind front wheel, hood tampo is same as side w/pink faced boy & larger pearl green & white Anime logo, black painted headlight covers, small black "R/T" on right of rear bumper, black int., HW logo stamped in rear green-tint window, 3sp	$2
☐				b. same as (a), white replaces pink in boys face & sword on hood, 3sp	$5
☐	📷	64	Olds Aurora GTS-1	light blue pearl, black plastic China base, black, red & gray tampos on side & hood, black HW logo on rear fender behind wheel, black rear wing & int., clear window, asw-pr5	$2

Anime Series, Muscle Tone

Anime Series, Dodge Charger R/T

Anime Series, Muscle Tone

Anime Series, Olds Aurora GTS-1

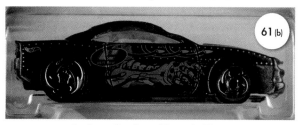

Anime Series, Ford GT-90

Rod Squadron Series

The Rod Squadron series cards may be found with a misspelling of "Squardron." These error cards are quite common, so the fact that they exist does not warrant any price difference. The only exception needs to be made for the #66, which had a short press run with the error.

Photo	No.	Name	Description	Price
❑ 📷	65	Dodge Daytona Charger	a. silver flake, black plastic Malaysia base, black & bright yellow side tampos, yellow & black squares on top of rear wing & front fenders, "Mildred" in red on front fender above wheel, black hood & nose, black int., clear window, black HW logo in front of rear wheel, asw-bbs	$2
❑ 📷			b. same as (a), pale yellow in tampos, asw-bbs	$4
❑ 📷	66	Lakester	a. olive w/brown camouflage, silver pearl painted Malaysia base, white & gray circle w/black eagle & HW logo on side, black & white misc. tampos on sides, white star in gray & black circle on top, clear canopy, chrome int., alw-5sp	$2
❑ 📷			b. same as (a), silver pearl painted China base, alw-5sp	$2
❑ 📷	67	Greased Lightnin'	a. Rod Squadron misspelled on card, spelled as "Squardron," black enamel, yellow enamel painted metal Malaysia base, "BUZZBOMB" in yellow w/three red & yellow bombs on nose, ten white skulls w/red bombs on side of nose, yellow side wing has red triangle outlined in black w/a yellow, white & black Bee & three small black bombs, black HW logo on right side yellow side wing, black plastic engine & int., yellow-tint canopy, 5sp	$15
❑ 📷			b. same as (a), card still misspelled as "Rod Squardron," pr5	$10
❑			c. same as (b), "Rod Squadron" spelled right on card, pr5	$2
❑ 📷	68	Propper Chopper	blue enamel, black plastic Malaysia base rear wing & hook, yellow plastic tail & rotors, rear section of body has a yellow line & "222" w/yellow HW logo & yellow, black, gray & red tampo design, yellow ">" above rear door, "The Sky Is Falling" in yellow below doors, yellow "222" & "7-SK-DGS BRAVO" on side of nose, black int., clear window	$3

Rod Squadron Series, Dodge Daytona Charger

Rod Squadron Series, Lakester

Rod Squadron Series, Dodge Daytona Charger

Rod Squadron Series, Greased Lightnin'

Rod Squadron Series, Lakester

Rod Squadron Series, Greased Lightnin'

Skull & Crossbones Series

	Photo	No.	Name	Description	Price
☐	📷	69	Rigor Motor	a. orange enamel, black painted metal Malaysia base, black panel on top has white, silver & gold bones w/black HW logo in orange circle facing rear, white, silver & gold bones along top side, black panel on side has silver skulls w/white eyes & gold accents, gold chrome engine, int., & fuel tank, black plastic skull headlights & radiator, red-tint canopy, g5sp	$2
☐	📷			b. same as (a), gold-tint chrome, more white in tampos, g5sp	$3
☐	📷	70	Blast Lane	black enamel, blue-tint metal Malaysia engine, black plastic forks, two white & silver bones in the shape of an X on rear fender, white & silver skull w/purple & silver flames on top of tank, silver HW logo on side of tank, chrome magenta rims w/black spokes	$5
☐	📷	71	Deuce Roadster	dark purple pearl, blue-tint metal Thailand base, white & silver skull tampo w/red pinstriped panels on side, red & silver panel pinstripes on hood, silver HW logo on cowl, chrome engine, scoop & grille, red int. & parachute pack, clear window, 5sp	$2
☐	📷	72	Screamin' Hauler	pearl gray, silver met. painted China base, large black striped tampo on side w/light green outline, white & black skulls on top of front fenders w/black & light green flames, chrome engines on each side, black HW logo above left of rear wheel, silver met. int., green-tint window, 5sp	$2

Rod Squadron Series, Propper Chopper

Skull & Crossbones Series, Rigor Motor

Skull & Crossbones Series, Rigor Motor

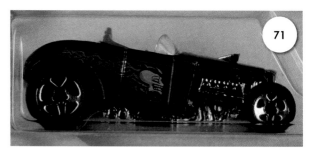

Skull & Crossbones Series, Deuce Roadster

Skull & Crossbones Series, Blast Lane

Skull & Crossbones Series, Screamin' Hauler

Logo-Motive Series

Photo	No.	Name	Description	Price
❑ 📷	73	Phantastique	red enamel, chrome China base, large white & orange HW logo on hood over black, orange & white tampo, large white, orange & black HW tampo on front fender, chrome windshield frame, shifter, rear deck piece & front grille, black int., smoked window, alw-bbs	$2
❑ 📷	74	Pontiac Banshee	candy blue, metal Malaysia base, gray plastic roof bar & hood, large silver & black HW logo on side, black w/white outline flame tampo over light pearl blue on top of each front fender, black w/white outline flame tampo over silver panel outlined in light pearl blue on top of rear fenders, gray int., blue-tint canopy, asw-5sp	$2
❑ 📷	75	Turbolence	a. black enamel, black enamel painted Malaysia base, white & gold pinstripe flames on hood w/large white & gold HW logo, white & gold pinstripe on side w/flame tampo on rear fender, white w/gold "Hot Wheels" on side below stripe, chrome engine & int., alw-5dot	$2
❑ 📷			b. same as (a), gold chrome engine & int., alw-5dot	$7
❑ 📷	76	Metrorail	white enamel, chrome Malaysia base, engine & int., front fender has black flames w/ orange outline, rear fender has large white, orange & black "HW's" logo over orange panel w/black pinstripe from front to back, hood has white, orange & black "HW's" logo twice over orange, orange-tint window, 5sp	$2

Logo-Motive Series, Phantastique

Logo-Motive Series, Turbolence

Logo-Motive Series, Pontiac Banshee

Logo-Motive Series, Metrorail Nash Metropolitan

Logo-Motive Series, Turbolence

Monsters Series

	Photo	No.	Name	Description	Price
❑	📷	77	'59 Impala	black enamel, gray plastic Malaysia base, red & orange flame tampo on roof, yellow, gray, white & red Mummy on hood holding orange & yellow flames & a red & black HW logo in its mouth, yellow, white & red Mummy arm wrapped in gray & white on side, white int., green-tint window, bbs	$2
❑	📷	78	Tail Dragger	pearl blue met., metal Malaysia base, roof tampo has gray & black Zombie w/yellow eyes & teeth & red over black "Zombie Attack!" twice, three red handprints & HW logo on rear fender, door has gray & black Zombie w/yellow & red eye & teeth, yellow stitches & hair & six red skulls, white int., red-tint window, asw-bbs	$2
❑	📷	79	'59 Cadillac	a. met. green, chrome Thailand base, green, yellow, white & black Frankenstein head on hood w/yellow & black lightning bolt on each side, yellow & black circles w/white, yellow & black bones & white, green & black eyeball on trunk, yellow scar w/black stitches on side w/yellow & black "Creature Screacher" above rocker panel, yellow HW logo on rear fender behind wheel, gray int., yellow-tint window, asw-g5sp	$6
❑				b. same as (a), chrome Malaysia base, asw-g5sp	$3
❑	📷	80	Purple Passion	bright red enamel, chrome Malaysia base, three white, green & black bloodshot eyeballs w/green & white flames on side, roof tampo is three-eyed purple monster w/two mouths, green lips & green & white flames w/black outline, green HW logo on rear skirt over wheel, white int., clear window, asw-g5sp	$10

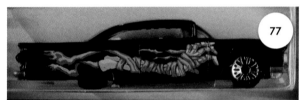

Monsters Series, '59 Impala

Monsters Series, '59 Cadillac

Monsters Series, Tail Dragger

Monsters Series, Purple Passion

Extreme Sports Series

	Photo	No.	Name	Description	Price
❑	📷	81	MX-48 Turbo	silver met., black enamel painted China base, red, black & orange tampo w/orange, white & black eye on side, red, & black tampo on hood w/orange, white & black eye & black & orange "Hipno" & white & orange "Ride," black HW logo above "Hipno" on hood, black int., orange-tint window, 3sp	$2
❑	📷	82	Double Vision	a. green met., black plastic Malaysia base, two gray engines w/chrome blowers, black, light green & white flames outlined in gold on side w/light green & white shamrocks outlined in black, Leprechaun w/white face, gold beard, hair & hat, outlined in black, black, light green & white flames outlined in gold on top by engines, "Lucky Leprechaun" in green over black, outlined in gold & white "Racing" in front of yellow-tint canopy, white & gold flame behind canopy, gold HW logo on top front driver side, gbbs	$2
❑	📷			b. same as (a), backwards blowers, gbbs	$5
❑				c. same as (a), engines & blowers backwards, gbbs	$4
❑				d. same as (a), g5dot	$4

Photo	No.	Name	Description	Price
❏ 📷	83	Twin Mill II	a. red w/silver & gold flake, black plastic Malaysia base, gold checked tampo on side, white & orange w/black outlined flames on rocker panel, orange & black dragon w/white eyes breathing white over black flames in front of rear wheel, hood has gold check tampo changing to black w/orange over black "Drag'n" & two orange & black dragons w/white eyes breathing white & black flames, white & orange w/black outlined flames on top of front fenders, gold HW logo above rear wheel, two gold chrome engines, black canopy, alw-bbs	$3
❏ 📷			b. same as (a), two gold-tint chrome engines, alw-bbs	$2
❏ 📷	84	Funny Car	yellow enamel, blue-tint metal Malaysia base, dark red, black, gray & white tampo on side, white & red over black "Chuy" w/red & white "Drag Team" over rear wheel, black HW logo behind rear wheel, white & red over black "Chuy" w/red & white "Drag Team" on hood w/dark red, black, & white tampo, clear window, 5sp	$3

Extreme Sports Series, MX48 Turbo

Extreme Sports Series, Twin Mill II

Extreme Sports Series, Double Vision

Extreme Sports Series, Twin Mill II

Extreme Sports Series, Double Vision

Extreme Sports Series, Funny Car

Company Cars Series

Photo	No.	Name	Description	Price
❏ 📷	85	Jaguar XJ 220	a. black enamel, black plastic Malaysia base, large gold Jaguar (animal) outline on side, gold "Jaguar" w/silver Jaguar (animal) outline on nose, gold HW logo high on rear fender behind wheel, tan int., yellow-tint window, g3sp	$2
❏ 📷			b. same as (a), no side tampo or logo, g3sp	$10
❏ 📷	86	'99 Mustang	white enamel, black plastic China base, thick red & thick blue stripe w/black outline on left side of hood, blue, red & black Mustang emblem on door, large black "Mustang" w/red outline & red wedge w/white "GT" on side, red HW logo behind rear wheel, white int., tinted window, asw-3sp	$3
❏ 📷	87	Monte Carlo Concept Car	a. mustard yellow enamel, black painted metal China base, side has thick black stripe on top body line from front to rear, large red Chevy bow tie w/black outline & small black "Monte Carlo" on door, half of hood has a black panel w/small red Bow Tie & gold "Monte," other half of hood has small black "Carlo," gold HW logo high on rear fender in black stripe, black int., clear window, asw-5sp	$3
❏ 📷			b. same as (a), light yellow, orange replaces red in bow tie on side & hood, black painted metal Malaysia base, asw-5sp	$4
❏ 📷	88	Dodge Sidewinder	a. met. maroon, black plastic Malaysia base, orange "Dodge" w/red outline & silver Ram emblem on door, hood has black panel tampo w/orange "Dodge" w/red outline & silver "Sidewinder" w/red outline, silver HW logo on upper-left side of hood by smoked windshield, black int. & bed cover, pr5	$4

Photo	No.	Name	Description		Price
❑		88	Dodge Sidewinder	b. same as (a), wide rear pr5	$20
❑	📷			c. same as (a), 3sp	$2

Company Cars Series, Jaguar XJ 220

Company Cars Series, Jaguar XJ 220

Company Cars Series, '99 Mustang

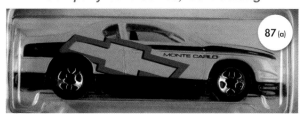

Company Cars Series,
Monte Carlo Concept Car

Company Cars Series,
Monte Carlo Concept Car

Company Cars Series, Dodge Sidewinder

Company Cars Series, Dodge Sidewinder

Hippie Mobiles Series

Photo	No.	Name	Description		Price
❑		89	'68 Mustang	a. candy gray, blue-tint metal Malaysia base, blue enamel hood w/large red & white peace sign, three small gray peace signs, white "United Groove" & HW logo, side has red over white "United Groove" on door, flag tampo, orange stripes w/red outline & white & red peace sign in blue enamel square, small red, white & blue peace signs on front & rear fenders, one large blue peace sign on rear fender behind wheel, black int., blue-tint window, asw-5sp	$10
❑	📷			b. same as (a), white replaces the silver in the three small peace signs on the hood, asw-5sp	$3
❑	📷	90	'63 Corvette	met. green, chrome Malaysia base, yellow & green striped tampo on hood & sides, yellow & black smiley face w/ "Funky Speed" on center of door & hood, gold HW logo front of hood, white int., yellow-tint window, asw-5sp	$3
❑	📷	91	'64 Lincoln Continental	light met., blue, chrome China base, black panels w/silver trim on front & rear fenders, dark & light blue diamond tampo on side, hood & trunk w/silver pinstriping, silver w/black outline "Right On" on trunk, dark blue met. & black HW logo behind rear wheel in black panel, white int., blue-tint window, asw-bbs	$2
❑	📷	92	'67 Pontiac GTO	yellow enamel, chrome Malaysia base, black hood, yellow scoop, white "Flower Power" on each side, orange & white pinstripe flames w/white & orange flowers, side has white & orange skull, orange flames w/black outline & orange & white flowers, black "GTO" on front fender behind wheel, black HW logo on rear fender low behind wheel, black int., smoked window, 5sp	$3

Hippie Mobiles Series, '68 Mustang

Hippie Mobiles Series, '64 Lincoln Continental

Hippie Mobiles Series, '63 Corvette

Hippie Mobiles Series, '67 Pontiac GTO

Skin Deep Series

	Photo	No.	Name	Description	Price
☐	📷	93	Super Comp Dragster	met., gold w/black plastic Malaysia fenders, chrome base, red, gray & black flames on side, silver & black ribbon w/Hot Wheels over a red heart w/silver dagger on nose, silver ribbon wrapping around red & black flames goes over top of hood, two white, silver & black skulls over red, white & black flames on rear deck, red HW logo on top next to cage, black plastic wheelie bars, int. & roll cage, 5sp	$2
☐		94	Willys Coupe	silver flake, chrome (DCC) Malaysia base, dark red panel on side w/black & gray tampo, dark red panel on roof w/black tampo & gray HW logo facing rear, black plastic wheelie bars, chrome int. & engine, red-tint window, 5sp	$3
☐		95	Chevy Pro Stock Truck	day-glo yellow, black plastic China base, silver panel on side w/black swirl tampo, black & white tiger w/yellow eyes over silver panels w/white pinstripes on rear bed, black int. & roll bar, clear window, pr5	$3
☐		96	Pro Stock Firebird	black enamel, silver met. painted metal China base, pearl purple, silver & black skull tampo on side, pearl purple, silver & black tampo on hood, gray plastic hood scoop, silver HW logo on front fender in front of wheel, white int., smoked window, pr5	$2

Skin Deep Series, Super Comp Dragster

Non-Series Collector Number Packs

	Photo	No.	Name	Description	Price
☐		97	Anglia Panel	yellow enamel, gray plastic China base, blue & black tampo on side panel w/black, blue & white pinstripe outline, white, black & blue pinstripe at mid body line, blue HW logo below pinstripe behind door on side, chrome int., blue-tint window, 5sp	$4
☐	📷	98	Thomasimma III	(name spelled wrong on card) candy blue met., chrome China base, white "Thomassima III" on door, white HW logo high behind louvers on front fender, black int., clear window, pr5	$2
☐	📷	99	Pro Stock Firebird	white enamel, silver painted metal China base, red & black tampos on hood & side, black "PROCH racing" outlined in red on side, two racing decals on front fender behind wheel, three decals on rocker panel, two decals low on rear fender behind wheel, red HW logo high on rear fender behind rear wheel, red plastic hood scoop, black int., clear window, pr5	$2
☐	📷	100	'70 Road Runner	a. red enamel, chrome Malaysia base, thick black stripe on side w/"440" & black HW logo on rear fender, small black "Road Runner" in front of side scoop, black painted hood w/white "Plymouth 440" & two thin pinstripes twice, black int., clear window, 5sp	$4

Photo	No.	Name	Description	Price
☐ 📷	100	'70 Road Runner	b. same as (a), larger front wheelwell opening & more pronounced windshield wipers, 5sp	$8
☐ 📷	101	Chevy Pick-Up	a. yellow plastic body, metal Malaysia base, black & silver "Barb'd & Wired" tampo on side, black panel w/silver & black barbed wire tampo on hood w/silver & black HW logo on nose, black int., grille & bed cover, clear window, asw-3sp	$3
☐ 📷			b. same as (a), asw-pr5	$5
☐ 📷	102	Road Rocket	a. light gold chrome body, metal Malaysia base, clear top w/orange, gold & black flames over black panels on rear fenders, gold & silver pinstripes over black panel on rear spoiler, orange pinstripe around panels, black & orange HW logo on rear spoiler, gold chrome int., pr5	$3
☐ 📷			b. same as (a), dark gold chrome body, 5dot	$27
☐ 📷	103	Porsche 928	a. green met., silver painted metal China base & headlights, red, yellow & dark purple tampo on side, red, yellow & black Porsche emblem on nose, yellow & black HW logo on bottom of door in front of rear wheel, black window, 5dot	$4
☐ 📷			b. same as (a), brown replaces red in tampo, 5dot	$2
☐ 📷	104	Audi Avus	candy purple met., black plastic Malaysia base, dark orange, black & gray side tampo, dark orange HW logo in black part of tampo behind front wheel, black & light purple tampo on smoked canopy, white int., alw-pr5	$2
☐ 📷	105	Demon	a. met. black, metal Thailand base, roof has dark red panel w/black & orange flames outlined in silver, black, dark red & gold long narrow flames outlined in silver on side, silver HW logo on rear of roof, chrome engine, red int., clear window, 3sp	$6
☐			b. met. black, metal Malaysia base, roof has dark red panel w/black & orange flames outlined in silver, black, dark red & gold thicker flames outlined in silver on side, larger silver HW logo on rear of roof, chrome engine, red int., clear window, 3sp	$4
☐ 📷	106	Power Pipes	chrome, black painted Malaysia base, blue & black side tampos, dark blue-tint canopy, 3sp	$2

98

Thomasimma III

99

Pro Stock Firebird

100 (a)

'70 Road Runner

100 (b)

1970 Plymouth Road Runner

101 (a)

Chevy Pick-Up

101 (b)

Chevy Pick-Up

102 (a)

Road Rocket

102 (b)

Road Rocket

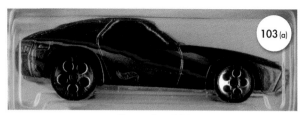

Porsche 928

Power Pipes

Porsche 928

Surf Crate

Audi Avus

Dodge Charger R/T

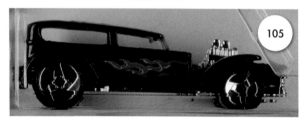

Demon

Dodge Charger R/T

	Photo	No.	Name	Description	Price
❏	📷	107	Surf Crate	gold flake, metal "no origin" base, tan & brown wood simulated sides, black int., no window, 5sp	$2
❏	📷	108	Dodge Charger R/T	a. met., purple, black plastic Malaysia base, small silver "R/T" on front fender behind wheel, silver "Charger" on rear bumper, black int., clear window w/HW logo stamped in rear, pr5	$40
❏	📷			b. same as (a), white int., pr5	$3
❏	📷			c. same as (b), light purple met., pr5	$5
❏				d. same as (b), 5sp	$10
❏	📷	109	'65 Corvette	white enamel, black plastic Malaysia base, black int., clear window, 5sp	$3
❏	📷	110	'41 Willys	a. black enamel, gray plastic Malaysia base, dark yellow, orange & brown side tampo, black & orange "Wild Willy" outlined in yellow over white on door w/six misc. black, yellow & white racing decals, three decals on front fender behind wheel, orange & white tampo behind rear wheel in yellow part of stripe, orange to brown triangle over yellow w/yellow & white HW logo on side of rear wing, chrome supercharger , int. & rear wing support, red-tint window, 5sp	$3
❏	📷			b. same as (a), light yellow replaces dark yellow & brown replaces orange in all tampos, 5sp	$8
❏	📷	111	Express Lane	orange plastic body w/"Gator Bait Market" tampo, metal China base, engine & push bar, tan seat & butterfly steering wheel, white HW logo on rear, 5sp	$2
❏	📷	112	Mustang Mach I	a. met. silver, black plastic Malaysia base, thin orange, wide black & thin white stripe tampo on hood & side, white "Mustang" above orange stripe on front fender behind wheel, black rocker panel w/thin white stripes & white "MACH 1" behind front wheel, old white HW logo high on rear fender behind wheel, black int., rear window louvers, spoiler, tachomitor & hood scoop, clear window, pr5	$3

	Photo	No.	Name	Description	Price
❏	📷	112	Mustang Mach I	b. same as (a), wider orange stripe in side tampo, pr5	$5
❏	📷			c. same as (a), 5sp	$15
❏	📷	113	BMW Z3 Roadster	a. teal enamel, black painted metal Malaysia base, black HW logo on trunk, black int., smoked window, asw-pr5	$3
❏	📷			b. same as (a), asw-3sp	$3
❏	📷	114	'96 Mustang	a. white pearl, metal Malaysia base, black & gold flames on hood & side, white horse in flame on door, small white "Mustang" & horse in flames on hood, black "Mustang" & gold "96" above black stripe on rocker panel in front of rear wheel, black HW logo high on rear fender, black int., smoked window, asw-pr5	$5
❏	📷			b. same as (a), asw-3sp	$2
❏				c. same as (b), blue-tint Malaysia base, asw-3sp	$2
❏	📷	115	1935 Cadillac	gold flake, black plastic fenders, metal Malaysia base, chrome headlights & grille, white panels on side w/red pinstripe outline, white panel on roof side w/red tampo & pinstripe outline, white panel on top of roof w/red tampo & red HW logo facing rear, white int., clear window, asw-bbs	$3
❏	📷	116	Auburn 852	a. white enamel, black plastic fenders, blue-tint metal Malaysia base, dark red panels on hood w/black & silver pinstripes, wide dark red stripe along side, silver HW logo facing rear on black boot behind seat, chrome dash, headlights & grille, black int., clear window, asw-bbs	$3
❏	📷			b. same as (a), light red panels & stripe, asw-bbs	$2
❏	📷	117	Shoe Box	a. white pearl, black plastic Malaysia base, light & dark red flames outlined in purple on side, purple HW logo behind rear wheel, chrome engine, int., front grille & bumper, smoked window, pr5	$2

108 (d)

Dodge Charger R/T

109

'65 Corvette

110 (a)

'41 Willys

110 (b)

'41 Willys

111

Express Lane

112 (a)

Mustang Mach I

112 (b)

Mustang Mach I

Mustang Mach I

BMW Z3 Roadster

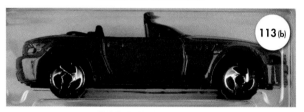

BMW Z3 Roadster

'96 Mustang

'96 Mustang

1935 Cadillac

Auburn 852

Auburn 852

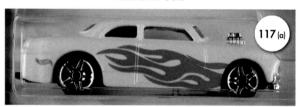

Shoe Box

Shoe Box

Photo	No.	Name	Description	Price
☐ 📷	117	Shoe Box	b. same as (a), 5sp	$20
☐ 📷	118	Muscle Tone	a. black enamel, gray plastic Malaysia base thick orange stripe across nose, thin orange stripe on side above rocker panel, orange HW logo (old) on front fender above bumper, red int., clear window, 5sp	$25
☐ 📷			b. same as (a), new HW logo, 5sp	$15
☐ 📷			c. same as (a), old HW logo, pr5	$5
☐ 📷			d. same as (a), (new) HW logo, pr5	$2
☐ 📷	119	Sho-Stopper	a. red enamel, gray plastic China base, black side vent, black & white tampoed hood w/red scoop, yellow enamel stripe on top of left front fender, old-style yellow HW logo w/ball in center of rear window, black int., clear window, alw-pr5	$5
☐			b. same as (a), new yellow HW logo in rear window, alw-pr5	$3
☐			c. same as (b), "Seared Tuner" on gray plastic China base, alw-pr5	$3
☐ 📷	120	Hammered Coupe	a. dark pearl blue, metal Malaysia base, chrome engine, int. scoop & grille, white HW logo on rear fender behind wheel, smoked window, pr5	$2
☐ 📷			b. same as (a), 5sp	$15

Muscle Tone

Muscle Tone

Muscle Tone

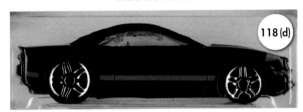

Muscle Tone

Sho-Stopper

Hammered Coupe

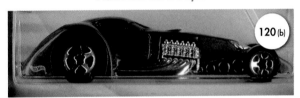

Hammered Coupe

Firebird

	Photo	No.	Name	Description	Price
☐	📷	121	Firebird	silver flake, black plastic China base, red & black "Handy Racing" on hood & door, black panel on white hood w/black & white checks, white "1" & red & black over white HW logo, black & white stripe tampo on side w/black & white checks, six misc. racing decals w/red & black over pink HW logo above rear wheel, black int., tinted window, alw-white letter b5sp	$2
☐	📷	122	Fork Lift	red enamel, metal China base, black plastic roll cage, seat & forks, yellow, white & red flames outlined in blue on side w/white "TAK construction," black flame tampo w/yellow "caution" on rear, yellow & blue HW logo on side by rear wheel, 5sp	$3
☐	📷	123	Wheel Loader	candy gray body, dark candy blue cab & engine cover, metal China base, black plastic bucket & hydraulics, dark red, orange, & yellow flames on cab side & side of engine cover, dark red & black over white HW logo on side of cab w/red "527 construction," white & black "Hot Wheels" over orange & yellow flames on roof, alw-ct/b	$3
☐	📷	124	Lamborghini Diablo	a. dark purple met., blue-tint metal Malaysia base, white, gold & black tampo stripe on side w/ "Lamborghini" in silver on top of door, "Diablo" in gold at bottom of door, gold & black HW logo in white stripe at left of door, black & gold Lamborghini emblem on nose, black plastic rear spoiler, taillights & int., smoked window, 3sp	$3
☐	📷			b. same as (a), silver met. painted Malaysia base, 3sp	$7
☐	📷			c. same as (a), light purple met., metal Malaysia base, pr5	$15
☐	📷	125	'32 Ford Vicky	a. black primer, metal Malaysia base & engine, gold fade to yellow flame w/red outline on side, orange fade to yellow flames w/red outline on roof, red & white HW logo on rear of roof, orange int., tinted window, pr5	$2
☐	📷			b. same as (a), 5sp	$15
☐	📷	126	'68 Mustang	candy red, blue-tint metal Thailand base, gray & black stripe tampo on side, silver painted door handle, white HW logo on rear fender w/"68" where the Mattel meatball used to be, black int., clear window, asw-5sp	$10

	Photo	No.	Name	Description	Price
❑	📷	127	Roll Cage	red enamel, blue-tint metal Malaysia base, blue & yellow HW logo over white on nose, small ct/b spare tire on rear, chrome rear engine & front air scoop, black int., asw-ct/b	$3
❑	📷	128	Lotus Elise 340R	a. dark pearl red, silver met., painted metal China base, small yellow circle w/black emblem on nose, black headlights, black plastic side, rear spoiler & front spoiler, yellow HW logo behind fuel cap on top rear fender, gray int. w/black seats, tinted window, pr5	$3
❑	📷			b. same as (a), brighter red pearl, pr5	$2
❑	📷	129	Slide Out	a. day-glo yellow body, blue plastic Malaysia base, black plastic engine, front wing, top wing & rear push bar, top of wing has large white "Hot Wheels" & large white "6" outlined in blue w/two wide green stripes, white stars w/light yellow "Austin Curtis" & white "Racing," side of wing has three light green over blue stripes, light yellow "6" & "Austin Curtis," white "Racing" & stars w/white & blue HW logo, 3sp	$2

Fork Lift

Wheel Loader

Lamborghini Diablo

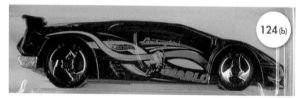

Lamborghini Diablo

Lamborghini Diablo

'32 Ford Vicky

'32 Ford Vicky

'68 Mustang

Roll Cage

Lotus Elise 340R

Lotus Elise 340R

Slideout

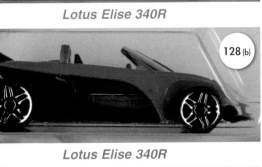

Slideout

Slideout

	Photo	No.	Name	Description	Price
☐	📷	129	Slideout	b. same as (a), pr5	$50
☐	📷			c. same as (b), bright yellow in tampos, bright green in side stripes, pr5	$75
☐	📷	130	25th Anniversary Lamborghini Countach	a. dark pearl blue, black plastic Malaysia base, silver "Lamborghini" on door & across nose, black "1" in white box outlined in silver on side & upper left front fender, silver & white HW logo behind air scoop in front of rear wheel, white int., clear window, asw-5dot	$15
☐	📷			b. same as (a), asw-pr5	$5
☐	📷			c. same as (b), silver HW logo, no white background asw-pr5	$2
☐	📷	131	Greased Lightnin'	a. pearl orange met., black painted metal Malaysia base, blue & black lettering over white stripes on nose, small red & white HW logo above "C" in "Casey" at end of stripes on right, red oval w/black outline & white lettering below the "C" in "Casey" at end of stripes on left, black rectangle w/white lettering above "Casey" on nose, chrome engine & int., smoked canopy, 5sp	$10
☐	📷			b. same as (a), pr5	$2
☐	📷	132	MX48 Turbo	silver flake, black painted metal Malaysia base, green & black oval tampo on hood, green HW logo on rear plate, black int., smoked window, 3sp	$2
☐	📷	133	'97 Corvette	a. silver met., black plastic Malaysia base, red, white & blue ribbon & stars tampo on side, blue ribbon is pearl, red & white ribbons are enamel, white box outlined in black w/black "97" & small red lettering on door, white "Corvette" on top of windshield, white int., smoked window, HW logo stamped into rear window, black HW logo low behind rear wheel, alw-bbs	$4
☐	📷			b. same as (a), blue enamel replaces candy blue in ribbon on side, alw-bbs	$2
☐	📷	134	Oshkosh Cement Truck	yellow plastic body, silver met. painted metal fenders, black plastic Malaysia base, black plastic barrel w/yellow, black & white construction tampo, "14," & yellow & black HW logo, asw-3sp	$2

	Photo	No.	Name	Description	Price
❏	📷	135	Corvette Stingray	black enamel, metal Malaysia base, orange, white & yellow flames outlined in gray on hood & side, gray HW logo behind rear wheel, black int., smoked window, 5sp	$3
❏	📷	136	Ice Cream Truck	white pearl, black plastic Malaysia base, red, black & blue clown & balloon tampo on right side of window, red, black & blue ice-cream & balloon tampo on left side of window, red & white w/black outline "I Scream" above rear wheel, rear has red & blue stars w/large red HW logo w/out meatball, blue int., clear window, asw-3sp	$2
❏	📷	137	Arachnorod	black enamel, chrome China base, purple pearl w/silver web tampo on top of rear fenders w/green & red pinstripe, purple, green & red tampo on each side of hood, top has chrome spider trim & engines, no HW logo, gray int., orange-tint canopy & rear turbines, 5sp	$2

25th Anniversary Lamborghini Countach

25th Anniversary Lamborghini Countach

25th Anniversary Lamborghini Countach

Greased Lightnin'

Greased Lightnin'

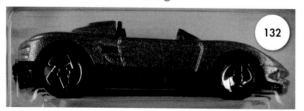

MX48 Turbo

'97 Corvette

'97 Corvette

Oshkosh Cement Truck

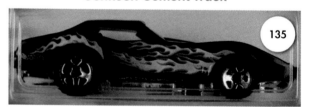

Corvette Stingray

Ice Cream Truck

Arachnorod — 137

Vulture — 138

Ford GT-40 — 139

Hot Seat — 140

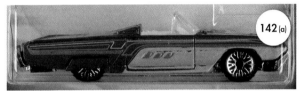

Go Kart — 141 (a)

'63 T-Bird — 142 (a)

'63 T-Bird — 142 (b)

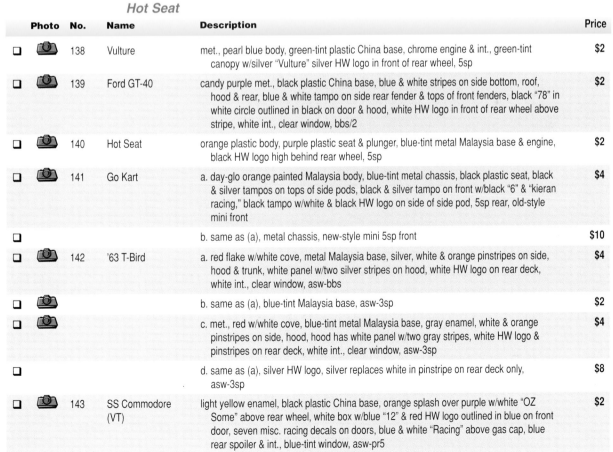

'63 T-Bird — 142 (c)

	Photo	No.	Name	Description	Price
☐	📷	138	Vulture	met., pearl blue body, green-tint plastic China base, chrome engine & int., green-tint canopy w/silver "Vulture" silver HW logo in front of rear wheel, 5sp	$2
☐	📷	139	Ford GT-40	candy purple met., black plastic China base, blue & white stripes on side bottom, roof, hood & rear, blue & white tampo on side rear fender & tops of front fenders, black "78" in white circle outlined in black on door & hood, white HW logo in front of rear wheel above stripe, white int., clear window, bbs/2	$2
☐	📷	140	Hot Seat	orange plastic body, purple plastic seat & plunger, blue-tint metal Malaysia base & engine, black HW logo high behind rear wheel, 5sp	$2
☐	📷	141	Go Kart	a. day-glo orange painted Malaysia body, blue-tint metal chassis, black plastic seat, black & silver tampos on tops of side pods, black & silver tampo on front w/black "6" & "kieran racing," black tampo w/white & black HW logo on side of side pod, 5sp rear, old-style mini front	$4
☐				b. same as (a), metal chassis, new-style mini 5sp front	$10
☐	📷	142	'63 T-Bird	a. red flake w/white cove, metal Malaysia base, silver, white & orange pinstripes on side, hood & trunk, white panel w/two silver stripes on hood, white HW logo on rear deck, white int., clear window, asw-bbs	$4
☐	📷			b. same as (a), blue-tint Malaysia base, asw-3sp	$2
☐	📷			c. met., red w/white cove, blue-tint metal Malaysia base, gray enamel, white & orange pinstripes on side, hood, hood has white panel w/two gray stripes, white HW logo & pinstripes on rear deck, white int., clear window, asw-3sp	$4
☐				d. same as (a), silver HW logo, silver replaces white in pinstripe on rear deck only, asw-3sp	$8
☐	📷	143	SS Commodore (VT)	light yellow enamel, black plastic China base, orange splash over purple w/white "OZ Some" above rear wheel, white box w/blue "12" & red HW logo outlined in blue on front door, seven misc. racing decals on doors, blue & white "Racing" above gas cap, blue rear spoiler & int., blue-tint window, asw-pr5	$2

	Photo	No.	Name	Description	Price
❏	📷	144	Isuzu VehiCROSS	yellow enamel, metal China base, black plastic bumpers, fender flares & rocker panels, red painted taillights, black panel on hood w/silver HW logo, black int., smoked window & headlights, alw-pr5	$2
❏	📷	145	Toyota MR-2	red enamel, black plastic Malaysia base, yellow lightning bolt outlined in black in side, large yellow & black HW logo over rear wheel, yellow "TOYOTA" on door, five yellow racing decals on rocker panel, white tampo behind rear wheel, hood has two yellow lightning bolts outlined in black w/yellow "TOYOTA" & emblem, small yellow-over-black HW logo on nose, white int., smoked window, asw-3sp	$2
❏	📷	146	Camaro Z28	a. met. purple plastic body, silver met. painted Malaysia base, white, silver & black stripe tampo on side & hood, black & white over silver HW logo behind rear wheel, black window, 5sp	$7
❏	📷			b. same as (a), darker purple met. plastic body, gray replaces silver in tampo & logo, 5sp	$5
❏				c. same as (b), unpainted metal Malaysia base, 5sp	$3
❏	📷	147	Sharkruiser	orange enamel w/matching painted metal Thailand base, black-over-white tiger stripe tampo on head, black tiger stripe only on rest of body, black HW logo on dorsal fin, chrome engine, teeth & seat, gt/b	$3
❏	📷	148	Speed Shark	red enamel, chrome Thailand base, flat black & gray side tampo, flat black stripe w/white teeth on top of each front fender, gray plastic side insert & int., chrome rear engine & window, red HW logo in gray part of side tampo in front of rear wheel, 3sp	$2
❏	📷	149	Police Car	white enamel, black plastic Thailand base, black painted roof w/red lights, small white "Hot Wheels County," gold "Sheriff" w/white underline, white "240" w/gold outline, side has gold & black stripe tampo w/small black "Hot Wheels County" & gold "Sheriff" w/black outline, white over gold HW logo w/black outline on rear fender behind wheel, black int., clear window & headlights, asw-5sp	$4

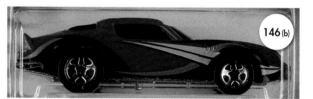

SS Commodore (VT)

Camaro Z28

Isuzu VehiCROSS

Sharkruiser

Toyota MR2

Speed Shark

Camaro Z28

Police Car

Enforcer

Power Pistons

Surf Crate

'56 Ford

Deora II

'40 Ford Truck

Chevy Stocker

Ferrari 333 SP

	Photo	No.	Name	Description	Price
❏	📷	150	Enforcer	met. green, black painted metal Thailand base, black "POLICE" on side behind front wheel, white & gold "Enforcer" on side above rear wheel, silver "Riot Control" below Enforcer, gold panel w/silver & black badge on side rear screen, gold "E" in white background w/black outline, & small black "RC" in gold painted side window, white-over-gold HW logo w/black outline on front, black plastic front & rear window & side mounted machine guns, alw-5sp	$3
❏	📷	151	Surf Crate	silver met., metal no origin base, roof has two wide white stripes over brown w/black & orange Dragon, black circle w/brown "HW" twice & orange outline, brown "HW" over orange w/black outline w/black Dragon on side, white & black over orange HW logo above rear wheel, black int., orange surfboard, chrome engine, 5sp	$3
❏	📷	152	Deora II	met., red, black plastic China base, side has black barbed wire tampo on top body line, larger black barbed wire tampo on rocker panel & large silver & black HW logo over black & silver diamond between them both, roof has silver barbed wire ring w/silver & black design & black & gold "HW/33" over it all, two white surfboards on rear, chrome int. & rear engine, clear window, asw-5sp	$3
❏	📷	153	Chevy Stocker	white plastic body, metal Thailand base, yellow, black & gold "Yellow Jacket" over black & gold tampo on hood, large yellow jacket insect w/small "Yellow Jacket" over black & gold tampo on side, gold HW logo on rear fender behind wheel, black window, gt/b	$4
❏	📷	154	Power Pistons	transparent orange plastic body, metal Thailand base, white & black wing tampo on side w/small white over black "ROCKET" & large black, gold & white "FLYZ," black HW logo behind rear wheel, gray int., insert & exhaust, clear canopy, 3sp	$2
❏	📷	155	'56 Ford	candy gray, black plastic China base, orange & silver tampo over black panel on side behind door window, orange, white & black "Harley Davidson Motor Cycles" logo on door, thick tapering black stripe w/orange & silver pinstripe on side from lower right of door to rear of body, black "Genuine Product" over rear wheel, white, black & orange HW logo high on rear fender behind wheel, chrome engine & int., clear window, 5sp	$2

Photo	No.	Name	Description	Price
☐ 📷	156	'40 Ford Truck	white enamel sides, black enamel top, black plastic China base & grille, black panels outlined in orange on side w/"Harley-Davidson" Tampo on door, silver & black over orange HW logo on rear fender, orange int., roll bar, tubs & rear wing, clear window, 5sp	$4
☐ 📷	157	Ferrari 333SP	black enamel, black plastic China base, yellow plastic rear wing & int., orange to yellow flames outlined in blue from headlight covers down side to rear, white oval w/blue & black "17" in front of rear wheel, four misc. racing decals on side, front panel has white oval w/blue & black "17," orange & yellow flame, white "Sports Carazing" & white HW logo, pr5	$2
☐ 📷	158	Mini Cooper	a. pearl dark blue, blue-tint metal Malaysia base, black & white checked tampo on roof w/red & yellow HW logo at rear, gray steering wheel & hood scoop, orange int., orange-tint window, asw-bbs	$3
☐ 📷			b. same as (a), asw-5dot	$9
☐ 📷	159	Cabbin' Fever	a. green met., gray plastic Malaysia base, black plastic rear ramp & roof cover, chrome ramp deck & window, red & yellow flame tampo on side w/two sets white, one set yellow teeth behind front wheel, small white "Not For Hire" by door handle, orange & yellow tampo above vent, red & white tampo behind vent, white & orange "MoToR' EP" & white outline "Transport" on lower door, small yellow HW logo centered above rear wheels, large front & center pr5, xl/rear pr5	$4
☐			b. same as (a), red "Hot Wheels" & white "Transport" on side of black plastic rear ramp	$87
☐ 📷	160	Metrorail	red enamel top half, white enamel lower half, chrome China base, white part of front fender has purple "Metrorail" above two red pinstripes, small white HW logo on red part of rear fender behind wheel, chrome engine & int., purple-tint window, 5sp	$3
☐ 📷	161	Jaguar XK8	dark red met., black plastic China base, dark blue & black stripe tampo on side w/small white "XK8" on rocker panel, dark blue & black stripe tampo on right side of hood & trunk w/small white "XK8" by clear windshield & headlights, tan int., no HW logo, pr5	$2
☐ 📷	162	Hummer	yellow plastic body, black painted metal Malaysia base, thin black stripes w/red & black "Rescue" over rear wheel, black "Camron" & red "TR" on door, red & black "TR" tampo, black "Camron" & six black stripes twice on roof, large black "021" facing rear on roof, black HW logo on rocker panel below front door, gray plastic window, asw-ct/b	$2
☐ 📷	163	'37 Bugatti	white pearl, black plastic fenders & trunk, metal Malaysia base, black stripe tampo on side w/black "Classic" & HW logo on door, "Classic 1937" & HW logo in black on center of hood w/black pinstriping, two black plastic spare tires on trunk w/metal wheel, gold chrome int., radiator & headlights, clear window, alw-5dot	$2

Mini Cooper

Mini Cooper

Cabbin' Fever

Metrorail

Jaguar XK8

Hummer 162

'37 Bugatti 163

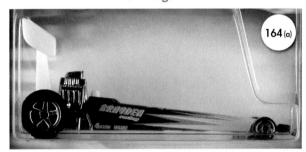

Dragster 164 (a)

Dragster 164 (b)

Flashfire 165 (a)

Flashfire 165 (b)

Ferrari 456M 166 (a)

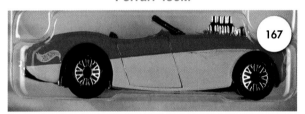

Austin Healey 167

So Fine 168 (a)

Photo	No.	Name	Description	Price
☐ 📷	164	Dragster	a. candy purple met., white tampo w/orange outline on front, blue-tint metal Malaysia base & engine, large orange over white "Brayden Racing" on side w/two orange & white racing decals below, white w/orange outline "1" & HW logo on top by white plastic driver w/orange & white "Roberts" & "TR," white plastic rear wing, 5sp rear, old-style mini front	$4
☐ 📷			b. same as (a), white plastic driver w/dark burnt orange & white "Roberts," bright orange "TR," new-style mini 5sp front wheel	$3
☐ 📷	165	Flashfire	a. pearl gray, black plastic Malaysia base, day-glo orange plastic side insert, rear wing, int. & rear exhaust, black & orange stripe tampo on side w/black dots from rear of front wheel into door, black dots over rear wheel well, top is painted black w/one thin orange stripe on each side from nose to tail, silver dots on inside of orange stripe on top of front fenders, silver dots on each side of indent on rear behind wing, orange-over-white "Sanders" on nose w/large white & orange "S" emblem, orange, black & white HW logo in black stripe on front fender behind wheel, chrome engine, tinted canopy, bbs	$3
☐ 📷			b. same as (a), 5dot	$2
☐ 📷	166	Ferrari 456M	a. blue met., silver painted metal China base, yellow & black rectangle Ferrari logo on hood w/white stripe above, yellow HW logo on rear, tan int., clear window, asw-pr5	$2
☐			b. same as (a), no stripe above Ferrari logo on hood, asw-pr5	$3

	Photo	No.	Name	Description	Price
☐	📷	167	Austin Healey	red enamel w/white lower half, chrome China base & engine, white HW logo on rear fender behind wheel, black int., tinted window, bbs2	$2
☐	📷	168	So Fine	a. met. green, chrome Malaysia base, silver painted molding & louvers on side, silver HW logo high on rear fender by taillight, white int., clear window, bbs	$2
☐	📷			b. same as (a), 5sp	$3
☐	📷	169	Blast Lane	dark candy blue met., blue-tint metal Malaysia base, red, orange & white flame tampo on tank & rear fender, large red & white HW logo w/black outline on tank, gray plastic handlebars & headlights, chrome rim w/three black spokes	$4
☐	📷	170	Solar Eagle III	orange plastic body, black painted metal Malaysia base, silver solar cells on top, black & silver tampo on nose w/silver "Solar Eagle," side has black, silver & white tampo w/black & silver "Cal State L.A." & white "Solar Eagle," small black HW logo on side behind tampo, black canopy w/thin orange stripe, small black wheels	$3
☐	📷	171	Mercedes C-Class	a. light blue pearl, black plastic Malaysia base, white fading to silver dots covering hood w/ gold, white & red stripe tampo on each side & large gold, white & red HW logo outlined in silver in the center, white fading to silver dots on rear fender, gold, white & red tampo on side w/large gold, white, & red HW logo outlined in silver on doors, four misc. red & white racing decals on rocker panel, black int., smoked window, asw-bbs	$2
☐	📷			b. same as (a), asw-5sp	$2
☐	📷	172	Radio Flyer Wagon	candy purple met., blue-tint metal Malaysia base, white "Radio Flyer" on side, chrome engine & rear wing, black seat & handle, white HW logo on rear, 5sp	$2
☐	📷	173	Talbot Lago	red enamel, metal Malaysia base, silver striped tampo on front & rear fenders, silver & red HW logo in center of rear fender skirt, chrome int., grille & headlights, clear window, bbs	$3
☐	📷	174	Baja Bug	a. silver flake, blue-tint metal Malaysia base, yellow, black & orange tampo on side w/two racing decals & yellow & orange over black HW logo on lower door, hood has yellow, black & orange tampo w/one racing decal & yellow, black & orange HW logo on the center, black int., asw-ct/b	$3

So Fine

Mercedes C-Class

Blast Lane

Solar Eagle III

Radio Flyer Wagon

Mercedes C-Class

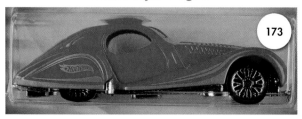

Talbot Lago

Baja Bug

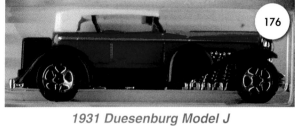

1931 Duesenburg Model J

Baja Bug

Dodge Viper RT/10

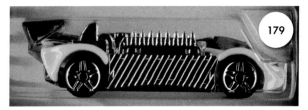

Chaparral 2

VW Bug

Krazy 8s

	Photo	No.	Name	Description	Price
❏	📷	174	Baja Bug	b. same as (a), matching silver painted metal Malaysia base, asw-ct/b	$4
❏	📷	175	VW Bug	red oxide primer (flat brown), silver met., painted China metal base, side has orange-to-yellow flames outlined in black, roof has two orange-to-yellow flames outlined in black w/orange & black HW logo at rear, red int., tinted window, 5dot	$3
❏	📷	176	1931 Duesenberg Model J	met. red w/silver flakes (fine mf.), metal Malaysia base, black plastic fenders & int., white plastic top, smoked window, silver painted molding on side, white & red HW logo on rear, alw-5sp	$3
❏	📷	177	Dodge Viper RT/10	day-glo yellow, black plastic China base, black graphics w/red pinstripes on side & hood, red circle w/white "DE" & black "anti CONSTRUCT" on hood & door, red ram emblem on nose, small black "Viper R/T 10" behind front wheel, black headlights & checks on rocker panel, black HW logo behind rear wheel, black int., smoked window, alw-pr5	$2
❏	📷	178	Chaparral 2	green met., black painted China base, nose & side have white cross outlined in gold w/black circle & white "C" in the center w/white "Team," gold "Corrosive" over silver & black tampo, gold HW logo on rear deck by spoiler, gray plastic engine, black int., clear window, pr5	$2
❏	📷	179	Krazy 8s	day-glo yellow, blue-tint metal Malaysia base, black & orange flames over front fenders, red & blue flames over rear fenders, red & black HW logo facing rear on green-tint rear wing, green-tint canopy, chrome engines & int., alw-pr5	$3
❏	📷	180	Corvette Stingray	silver flake, black plastic "Corvette Stingray III" Malaysia base, green & yellow flames outlined in blue over black tampo on side & hood, yellow over black HW logo outlined in blue longways in center of hood, milky white (looks like glow in the dark) int., smoked window, bbs	$3

Photo	No.	Name	Description	Price
❑ 📷	181	Surfin' School Bus	dark pearl blue, gray plastic Malaysia base & fenders, tan wood molding on side w/brown & tan graining, silver HW logo behind front fender about half way up, orange-tint window, chrome rear engine, pr5	$2
❑ 📷	182	Sooo Fast	black primer, metal Malaysia base, red & silver tampo on hood w/silver HW logo, chrome int., grille & rear engine, smoked window, 5sp	$2
❑ 📷	183	Super Modified	orange enamel, metal Malaysia base & engine, black plastic rear wing, int., rear pushbar & front wing, white HW logo on side of driver cockpit, bbs/2	$2
❑ 📷	184	Jaguar D-Type	met. silver w/matching painted metal China base, wide dark red stripe w/thin black & thick white stripe on each side from nose to rear, large white circle w/large black "6" on nose, white over black HW logo in stripe on rear, small red circle w/black outline & small white "6" in center on tail, gray int., clear window, alw-5sp	$2
❑ 📷	185	Armored Car	a. black plastic body, blue-tint metal Malaysia base, side has gold pinstripe panels, left panel has gold "Armored" & silver stripe below, center panel has white & gold "Always Safe," white HW logo outlined in gold, "Transport" in gold, silver stripe below & gold flame tampo, right panel has "Driver Carries Only Hot Wheels" in white w/silver door handle, rocker panel has silver "8 5 18 1 12 4 1," hood has gold flames in gold pinstripe panels on both sides, center panel on hood has silver "14 15 1 8" by windshield w/white & gold "Always Safe" & white HW logo outlined in gold, gray int., orange-tint window, 5sp	$15
❑ 📷			b. same as (a), gold in tampos is lighter, alw-5sp	$4

Corvette Stingray

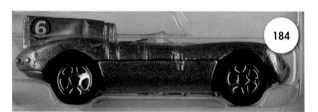

Jaguar D-Type

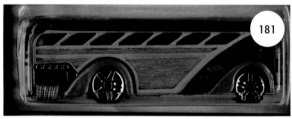

Surfin' School Bus

Armored Car

Sooo Fast

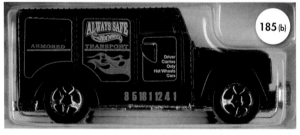

Armored Car

Super Modified

Rodger Dodger

Photo		No.	Name	Description	Price
❏	📷	186	Rodger Dodger	mustard yellow enamel, chrome Malaysia base, black & orange flames on side, black panel on roof, blue-tint metal engine sticking out of hood, orange & white over black HW logo at end of trunk, black int., smoked window, 5sp	$3
❏	📷	187	Bywayman	met., charcoal, met., silver painted metal Malaysia base, thin orange stripe from front to back on body line, gray "We Knock it Down & Rebuild it" above stripe on side of box, orange & white over gray HW logo below stripe on box in front of rear wheel, white & orange "Tony & Noah Construction Contractors" w/white house & black roof in orange circle on door, white & orange "Tony & Noah Construction Contractors" on tailgate w/ three orange circles w/white saw, plug & hammer, gray int., bed floor & roll bar, smoked window, asw-ct/b	$2
❏	📷	188	Flame Stopper	a. red oxide primer (brown), black plastic China base, white plastic boom, white, yellow-to-orange flames over black on side from front to back, white w/black outline "Corrosive Crew" on doors, yellow "unit 31" & white "n*er" in black panel on cab side behind rear window, black "Stand Clear" in yellow panel over side windows, white w/black outline "Toxic" over flames between wheels, white over black HW logo behind rear wheel, black plastic window, alw-yct/b	$7
❏	📷			b. same as (a), alw-ct/b	$2
❏	📷	189	Dodge Power Wagon	met. black, gray plastic Malaysia base (DCC), three large squares on front bumper, small red & white "POWER WAGON" on door, small white "DODGE" on left side of tailgate, gray plastic bed cover w/old HW logo stamped at rear, gray int., tinted window, asw-ct/b	$3
❏	📷	190	Ferrari 308	gray pearl, black painted metal Malaysia base, yellow & black rectangle Ferrari emblem on nose w/red & green stripe above, yellow HW logo on rear plate, black int., smoked window, 5sp	$2

Bywayman

Dodge Power Wagon

Flame Stopper

Ferrari 308

Ferrari F355

Ferrari F355

Flame Stopper

Ford Escort Rally

Roll Patrol

Rescue Ranger

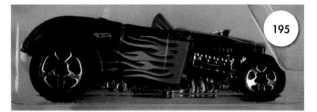

Deuce Roadster

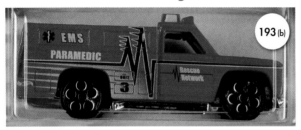

Rescue Ranger

3-Window '34

Photo	No.	Name	Description	Price
☐ 📷	191	Ferrari F355	a. yellow enamel, metal Malaysia base, white roof w/two green stripes & black "Good-Year," green, white & red stripe tampo on hood w/red outlined "1" in black & white checked rectangle w/smaller red rectangle w/white "Racing," yellow & black rectangle Ferrari logo on nose w/red & green stripe above it, red HW logo on rear plate, white int., smoked window & rear spoiler, asw-pr5	$2
☐ 📷			b. same as (a), asw-5sp	$8
☐ 📷	192	Ford Escort Rally	candy gray, black plastic Malaysia "Escort Rally" base, burnt orange, white, black & orange tampo on roof & side, white rectangle topped w/black on roof & side w/large black & red "1" & small black "Champion" w/two checkered flags, black above has white & red check mark & "Rally," large "Hot Wheels" in front of rear wheel above rocker panel, red, white & black tampo above rear wheel, three misc. orange, black & white racing decals behind rear wheel, large white & red HW logo on rear of roof by wing, black int., smoked rear wing & window, asw-5dot	$3
☐ 📷	193	Rescue Ranger	a. red enamel, chrome China base, yellow plastic insert, yellow "Rescue Network" on door w/black design, blue & white medical logo & yellow & black "EMS" on left upper access door on side, white "PARAMEDIC" above rear wheel, black "Unit 3" in front of rear wheel, yellow fading stripe tampo on side of box, blue & white stripe tampo on side from nose to tail, white HW logo on lower left of box behind rear wheel, black int., smoked window, alw-5dot	$3
☐ 📷			b. same as (a), chrome Thailand base, alw-5dot	$5
☐ 📷	194	Roll Patrol	blue enamel, metal Thailand base, orange to yellow stripe tampo on side w/blue "Unit 5" & small yellow "Rescue Network" behind front wheel, large yellow "Coast Rescue" above rear tire & stripes, red HW logo low behind rear wheel, red plastic int. & spare tire, blue-tint windshield, asw-ct/b	$4
☐ 📷	195	Deuce Roadster	candy purple, blue-tint metal Thailand base, red to white flames w/red outline on hood & side, white HW logo high in front of rear wheel, white int. & 'chute, chrome engine & scoop, smoked windshield, 5sp	$2
☐ 📷	196	3-Window '34	green enamel, black plastic fenders, black painted Thailand metal base, black, purple to orange tampo on side w/black & gold squares, purple HW logo in front of rear wheel, chrome int., grille & engine, clear window, 5sp	$3

Austin Healey

Austin Healey

Side Kick

Dairy Delivery

Dairy Delivery

Photo	No.	Name	Description	Price
☐ 📷	197	Austin Healey	a. light candy blue, chrome China base, metal chassis, dark red to light green flames w/dark red outline on front fender from wheel well, light green "Office Of The Mayor" around black & white globe w/yellow & red "Planet" & white-over-red "Hot Wheels" on door, four light green dots on each side of door tampo, chrome engine, grille & floorpan, red int., clear windshield, 5sp	$2
☐ 📷			b. dark candy blue, chrome Thailand base, blue-tint metal chassis, light red-to-yellow flames w/dark red outline on front fender from wheel well, larger yellow "Office Of The Mayor" around black & white globe w/yellow & red "Planet" & white-over-red "Hot Wheels" on door, four yellow dots on each side of door tampo, chrome engine, grille & floorpan, dark red plastic int., clear windshield, 5sp	$14
☐ 📷	198	Side Kick	silver blue met., black plastic Thailand base, metal door & seat w/red oval w/white outline & white "Postal Express" w/black outline, white & black globe w/white over red HW logo & yellow to red "Planet" outlined in black on roof, black Eagle wing on right side & above red -tint windshield w/white "23,"large red & brown ring on hood w/white & black "Hot Wheels Postal Express," black, white & yellow American Bald Eagle coming through center on the ring, blue-tint metal engines, alw-5dot	$2
☐ 📷	199	Dairy Delivery	a. yellow enamel, black plastic China base, nub in lower part of front grille, large tampo w/long black spears ending w/short dark red spears on roof, upper side has "Big Lou's" in white & gray w/black outline, man's head & dark red flames, black panel w/white "Speedy Delivery" & "When ya absolutely, positively gotta have it yesterday!!!" in small black letters, "Mr. Big" in dark red below side window, lower side has large tampo w/long black spears ending w/short dark red spears, black & red lettering by gas cap, white-over-dark red HW logo behind rear wheel, red int., tinted window, pr5	$3
☐ 📷			b. yellow enamel, black plastic Thailand base, small indented hole in lower front grille, large tampo w/short black spears ending w/long bright red spears on roof, upper side has "Big Lou's" in pink & gray w/black outline, mans head & bright red flames, black panel w/pink "Speedy Delivery" & "When ya absolutely, positively gotta have it yesterday!!!" in small black letters, "Mr. Big" in bright red below side window, lower side has large tampo w/short black spears ending w/long bright red spears, black & red lettering by gas cap, larger white over bright red HW logo behind rear wheel, dark red int., smoked window, pr5	$5
☐ 📷	200	'68 El Camino	a. light orange enamel, metal China base, light purple plastic front bumper & rocker panel, purple to black flames w/light green outline on side, purple to black flames w/green & yellow outline on hood, Xs in Xtreeme Xpress are purple outlined in green, other lettering is orange outlined in black over rear wheel, mustard yellow HW logo on rear fender by taillight, mustard yellow plastic rear wing & int., light purple plastic bed insert w/chrome engine, tinted window, pr5	$7

Photo	No.	Name	Description	Price
❑ 📷	200	'68 El Camino	b. orange enamel, blue-tint metal Thailand base, dark purple plastic front bumper & rocker panel, black flames w/light green & yellow outline on side & hood, Xs in Xtreeme Xpress are red outlined in green, other lettering is yellow outlined in black over rear wheel, yellow HW logo on rear fender by taillight, yellow plastic rear wing & int., dark purple plastic bed insert w/chrome engine, tinted window, pr5	$3
❑ 📷	201	Super Tuned	a. yellow enamel, gray plastic Malaysia base, red plastic bed cover, rear wing, large white letters w/black rectangle & light gray & red outline on side, large light gray letters w/black rectangle & red outline on hood, six misc. racing decals on door w/red & white HW logo last, four misc. racing decals at front of hood, red int., smoked window, pr5	$2
❑			b. same as (a), asw-thin pr5	$15
❑ 📷			c. same as (a), letters on hood are now white w/red outline, top decal on door has thick red line above lettering, pr5	$5
❑ 📷	202	La Troca	flat lavender primer, chrome China base, HW logo stamped on tailgate, black window, bbs	$2
❑ 📷	203	Hooligan	a. dark maroon met., silver met. painted metal China base, gas tank in bed & fuel injection, red flames w/silver outline on side, red plastic int., grille & engine w/chrome trim on heads, 5sp	$2
❑ 📷			b. same as (a), no chrome on cylinder head, 5sp	$15
❑ 📷	204	Ferrari 360 Modena	a. black met. w/matching black met. painted metal Malaysia base, yellow & black rectangle Ferrari logo on hood w/red & green stripes above, yellow HW logo on rear plate, pink int., clear window, asw-pr5	$4
❑ 📷			b. same as (a), asw-5sp	$2
❑ 📷			c. same as (a), asw-5dot	$30

'68 El Camino — 200 (a)

La Troca — 202

'68 El Camino — 200 (b)

Hooligan — 203 (a)

Super Tuned — 201 (a)

Hooligan — 203 (b)

Super Tuned — 201 (c)

Ferrari 360 Modena — 204 (a)

Ferrari 360 Modena

Power Rocket

Ferrari 360 Modena

Cadillac LMP

'38 Phantom Corsair

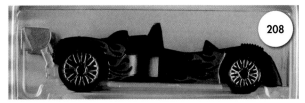

Ferrari F40

Panoz GTR-1

Blimp

Photo	No.	Name	Description	Price
❑ 📷	205	'38 Phantom Corsair	root beer met., metal China base, silver & black panels w/gold pinstripes on side & hood, silver & black HW logo outlined in gold on rear skirt, gray int., clear window, ww/5sp	$2
❑ 📷	206	Panoz GTR-1	a. dark candy red, black plastic China base, blue enamel & silver tampos on tops of front fenders & on side from front to rear, large silver & blue enamel HW logo on door, silver w/blue enamel outline "1" above stripe on rear fender behind wheel, blue & red w/green clover & silver outline Panoz emblem over white circle in center of hood, silver w/blue enamel outline "1" below Panoz emblem on hood, three blue misc. racing decals on rocker panel, light blue plastic rear wind & int., clear window, pr5	$3
❑			b. same as (a), red enamel, pr5	$2
❑ 📷	207	Power Rocket	red plastic transparent body, metal Thailand base, white fading to gray side tampo outlined in black, red & black "Hot Wheels" over rear wheel, white "3" w/black outline behind front wheel, chrome engine & int., smoked canopy, 5dot	$2
❑ 📷	208	Cadillac LMP	flat black, gold plastic Malaysia base, gold flames behind front wheel, gold flames in front of rear wheel, met. gold painted metal rear wing, no HW logo, gold int., g/bbs	$2
❑ 📷	209	Ferrari F40	pearl blue, blue -tint metal Malaysia base, yellow & black rectangle Ferrari emblem on nose w/red stripe above, white HW logo on rear plate, black int., clear window, pr5	$2
❑ 📷	210	Blimp	a. gold plastic blimp w/orange plastic tail fins, orange enamel painted metal Malaysia gondola, black insert w/large light gray & gold "Power Blimp" & small burnt orange & white squares, large white & black "Hot Wheels" w/bright orange & white outline & small squares on other side 10	$10
❑ 📷			b. same as (a), black insert w/large white & gold "Power Blimp" & small bright orange & white squares	$4

	Photo	No.	Name	Description	Price
☐	📷	210	Blimp	c. same as (a), black insert w/large white Hot Wheels logo w/orange & white outline & small burnt orange & white squares	$4
☐	📷	211	Krazy 8s	flat black, gloss black enamel painted metal China base, multi-colored tampos on top of each fender, gold chrome engines & int., yellow-tint canopy & rear wing w/black & gold "Krazy" & 8 Ball, gold HW logo above "Krazy" on rear wing, alw-gpr5	$2
☐	📷	212	Shredster	day-glo lime top, black plastic side w/silver "Shreadster" & HW logo, candy purple metal China fenders, chrome base, black int. & hood scoop, smoked window, pr5	$2
☐	📷	213	MS-T Susuka	red enamel, black plastic China base, mustard yellow & black tampo on side, six misc. silver & black racing decals including a HW logo on right side of door, small mustard, silver & black tampo above rear wheel, hood has large black lettering w/silver outline & mustard "2" along w/four misc. silver racing decals including a HW logo, black int., clear window, alw-pr5	$2
☐	📷	214	Porsche 911 GT3 Cup	a. pearl Tangerine, black plastic Malaysia base, dark blue, white & orange side tampo w/white "Hot Wheels" & large "1" on door, black plastic rear wing, dark blue int., smoked window, asw-pr5	$4
☐	📷			b. same as (a), asw-3p	$2
☐	📷	215	Popcycle	purple, metal China base, white fade to silver dot tampo on top from rear to front, silver HW logo on top by exhaust, chrome engine & bicycle, purple-tint canopy, 5dot	$2
☐	📷	216	'32 Ford	flat black, black plastic China base, door has white panel w/silver outline & black "State Trooper Talluville CA.," silver tire w/orange wings & white over black HW logo, flat black panel w/silver outline on quarter panel w/white "# 51," flat black panel w/silver outline in front of door, chrome engine & grille, orange int., clear window, 5sp	$3

210 (b)

Blimp

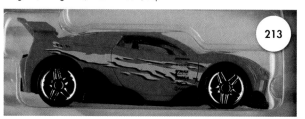

213

MS-T Suzuka

210 (c)

Blimp

214 (a)

Porsche 911 GT3 Cup

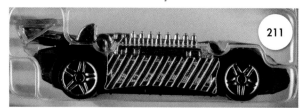

211

Krazy 8s

214 (b)

Porsche 911 GT3 Cup

212

Shredster

215

Popcycle

'32 Ford

Corvette

Shadow Jet

GT Racer

Ferrari 250

Riley & Scott Mk III

Corvette

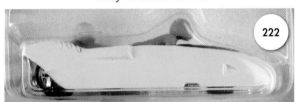

Outsider

Photo	No.	Name	Description	Price
📷	217	Shadow Jet	met. silver, metal Malaysia base, rear wing has black stripe w/red & white checks, black triangle between rear wing has red & white HW logo & white & red star, side pod has red & white checks, white & red star, black stripe w/white "85720" & white & red HW logo, top of each pod has small black "Caution" & three small triangles, black nose, chrome engine & fuel tanks, smoked canopy, silver int., 5sp	$2
📷	218	Ferrari 250	candy gray met., black plastic China base, yellow & black rectangle Ferrari emblem on nose w/red stripe at top, yellow HW logo on rear plate, black int., clear window & headlights, bbs	$2
📷	219	Corvette	a. pearl tangerine met., metal Malaysia base, dark red flames w/silver outlines coming off each wheel opening, black & silver HW logo high on rear fender behind wheel, smoked window w/no color roof, gray int., asw-pr5	$4
📷			b. same as (a), asw-3sp	$2
📷	220	GT Racer	dark blue enamel, blue-tint metal Malaysia base, brown, orange & yellow flames on roof & side, small yellow HW logo above flames behind front wheel, black plastic rear wing & engine, metal int., yellow-tint window, 5dot	$2
📷	221	Riley & Scott Mk III	red enamel, black plastic Malaysia base, transparent dark blue rear wing, black-over-white headlights w/blue stripe below, small black "Good Year & Hella" above, blue panel between headlights w/silver "74 Ranch Resort," white "Good Year" over front wheel, dark blue tampo on side outlined in light gray w/six misc. racing decals & thin black & white slashes, light gray "74" outlined in dark blue over dark blue ring w/three light gray stars on left, dark blue stripe over light gray w/silver "74 ranch Resort" on each side of cockpit w/small blue-over-white "B. Robinson & J. Baldwin," thin black & white slashes over front fenders along side stopping at rear fender, white HW logo, blue-over-white "Z4" & "GAR" at front of cockpit, blue int., bbs	$2

Photo	No.	Name	Description	Price
❑	236	Submarine	b. same as (a), gray plastic (Fathom This) under left & Malaysia under right pontoon	$2
❑ 📷	237	Fire Eater	a. day-glo lime, red plastic insert, chrome Malaysia base, side has red stripe w/black tampos, two black & red hoses, black "122" in red stripe at front, black int., smoked window, alw-5dot	$3
❑ 📷			b. same as (a), chrome Thailand base, alw-5sp	$5
❑ 📷	238	Ferrari F50	met. purple, metal Malaysia base, yellow & black rectangle Ferrari logo on nose w/red & green stripe above, no HW logo, black int., clear window, asw-5dot	$2
❑ 📷	239	T-Bird Stocker	red plastic body, blue-tint metal Malaysia base, black & white camera tampo on side, small black "On" w/large white "3," black & white "Photography" & white "Artle Scott," black & white "Smile!" high behind rear wheel, no HW logo, chrome window, 5dot	$2
❑ 📷	240	Shelby Cobra 427 S/C	red w/gold & silver flakes, blue-tint metal Malaysia base, yellow & orange flames outlined in black on side from front & rear wheel wells, no HW logo, tan int., clear window, alw-bbs	$2

1936 Cord

Semi-Fast

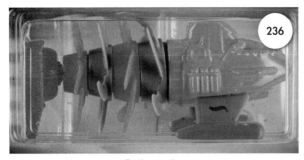

Submarine

Fire-Eater

Fire-Eater

Ferrari F50

T-Bird Stocker

Shelby Cobra 427 S/C

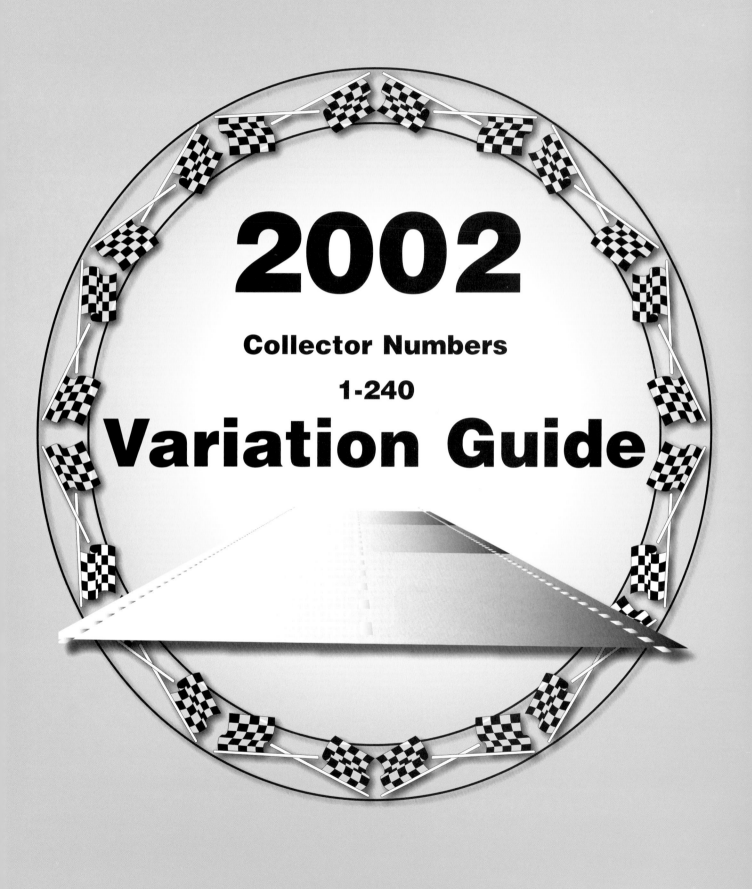

2002

Collector Numbers

1-240

Variation Guide

2002 Treasure Hunt Series

Photo	No.	Name	Description	Price
☐ 📷	1	La Troca	yellow enamel, gold chrome Malaysia base, white panels w/gold & black outline on fenders, doors, & hood, roof has white w/gold & black outline "La Troca" over white panel w/ gray, gold & black pinstripes, roof has met. olive painted visor over windshield, panel on door has gold & black "TH" tampo w/white & gold over black HW logo, gold painted door handle & gas cap, thick gold stripe on lower part of both fenders, black window, all small chrome-wheeled Real Riders	$11
☐ 📷	2	'71 Plymouth GTX	a. dark blue met. gloss black roof, chrome Malaysia base, gloss black panel w/"440" twice on hood w/silver outline, silver pinstripe on side, "440" above orange marker light on front fender, silver painted door handle & lock, silver "GTX" in front of rear wheel, three section red-over-silver rear side marker light behind rear wheel, white, black & light blue "TH" emblem on trunk, black int., clear window, chrome rim Real Riders	$13
☐ 📷			b. same as (a), light blue met. chrome Malaysia base, chrome rim Real Riders	$15
☐ 📷	3	'57 Roadster	a. candy lime met. blue-tint metal Malaysia base, white lower half of side w/black flames w/orange outline, silver painted trunk, hood & side moldings, red painted taillights, white rear plate w/light orange "Hot Wheels," light orange, white & black HW logo & TH logo on trunk, chrome engine & fronted, black int., smoked windshield, chrome wheeled white wall rear tire, new mini 5sp front	$12
☐			b. same as (a), 5sp rear wheels	$45
☐ 📷	4	Lotus Project M250	burgundy w/silver & gold flake, black plastic Malaysia base, black, gold & white Treasure Hunt logo on roof w/white & gold over black HW logo, black painted headlights, small black & white emblem on nose, smoked window, black side vent & int., redline Real Rider tires on chrome rims	$10
☐ 📷	5	Ford Thunderbolt	silver met. chrome Malaysia base, gloss black hood w/silver rear vents in scoop, silver painted hood locks, white stripe on side body line w/black outline, two inside headlights painted black, red painted taillights two black painted vents behind door, black oval w/"Heralda Racing" behind rear wheel, black, white & light blue "TH" emblem on trunk, white "Thunderbolt" across top of windshield, white int., blue-tint window, chrome rim Real Riders	$10

2002 Treasure Hunt Series, #1-La Troca

2002 Treasure Hunt Series, #3-'57 Roadster

2002 Treasure Hunt Series, #2-'71 Plymouth GTX

2002 Treasure Hunt Series, #4-Lotus Project M250

2002 Treasure Hunt Series, #2-'71 Plymouth GTX

2002 Treasure Hunt Series, #5-Ford Thunderbolt

*2002 Treasure Hunt Series,
#6-Panoz LMP-1 Roadster S*

*2002 Treasure Hunt Series,
#6- Panoz LMP-1 Roadster S*

2002 Treasure Hunt Series, #7-Phaeton

2002 Treasure Hunt Series, #8-Fat Fendered '40

2002 Treasure Hunt Series, #9-'40 Ford

2002 Treasure Hunt Series, #10-Tail Dragger

Photo	No.	Name	Description	Price
❏ 📷	6	Panoz LMP-1 Roadster S	a. white enamel w/candy blue sides & front ducts, black plastic Malaysia base, light red & silver stripes on tops of front fenders, light red panel on center of hood w/white, dark blue & silver "12" & six white & silver stars, white & blue HW logo w/black outline & gray, blue & black TH logo on left side of cowl, nine silver outline stars on rear deck, silver & white stripes on top of candy blue tops of rear fenders, white & blue HW logo outlined in black on side behind front wheel, light blue "12" outlined in white at center of black side panel, black int., chrome rim Real Rider tires w/white letter "Treasure Hunt 2002"	$20
❏ 📷			b. same as (b), dark candy blue met. Paint	$15
❏			c. same as (b), missing "12" on side	$25
❏ 📷	7	Phaeton	pearl white, blue-tint metal Malaysia base, yellow & green fade flames w/black outline over silver ghost flame, black panel on each side of hood w/white pinstripe, black panel on cowl, green, black & white "TH" emblem on rear w/white over green HW logo w/black outline, black plastic roof & int., clear windshield, chrome-wheeled whitewall "Real Rider" tires	$10
❏ 📷	8	Fat Fendered '40	"Fendered" spelled wrong. Spelled as "Fendeered" on card, flat black, metal Thailand base, orange & red over white flames on roof, behind front fender & behind side rear window, white "Millers Cams & Fuel Control" on side w/large white "2" outlined in red & small "A," white, orange & black "TH" logo over silver w/red & white over silver HW logo on trunk, white int., yellow-tint window, all small chrome-wheeled Real Riders	$11
❏ 📷	9	'40 Ford	a. aqua enamel w/white pearl above bodyline & on top of rear box, black plastic Thailand base & grille, black w/silver outline flames on each fender, blue & black TH emblem on roof w/white & blue HW logo outlined in black, gray rear wing, wheel tubs, roll cage & int., clear window, chrome wheeled "Real Rider" tires	$13
❏			b. same as (a), white enamel upper cab	$25
		The '40 Ford (b) variation with the white enamel upper half cars were only found from a mail-away promotion.		
❏ 📷	10	Tail Dragger	purple met. blue-tint metal Malaysia base, black panels w/white outline on side, fenders, roof & trunk, blue & white HW logo on side above white, blue & black TH emblem, white int., blue-tint window, all small chrome wheeled Real Riders	$13

	Photo	No.	Name	Description	Price
☐	📷	11	Mini Cooper	a. black enamel, blue-tint metal Malaysia base, orange, purple, red & silver flames on roof w/large "02" in orange outlined in white, red & silver HW logo on door w/white, orange silver & red TH emblem, purple & silver flames outlined in orange coming from TH emblem, silver painted headlights, orange seat & cage, chrome dash, clear window, all small chrome-wheeled Real Riders	$12
☐				b. same as (a), unpainted headlights	$20
☐	📷	12	Anglia Panel	candy red met. light gray plastic Thailand base, side has red to gold fade w/white outline tampo over black on lower half, white & red to gold fade HW logo over black & red, white, gold & black TH emblem on upper half, chrome int., clear window, chrome hub white lettered Real Riders	$15

2002 Treasure Hunt Series, #11-Mini Cooper   *2002 Treasure Hunt Series, #12-Anglia Panel*

2002 First Editions

	Photo	No.	Name	Description	Price
☐	📷	13	#1-Midnight Otto	a. pearl white, blue-tint metal Malaysia base, orange fade to white tampo over black panel on roof & side, black roof panel has thin gold pinstripe outline, white over gold HW logo outlined in black on front of roof facing rear, black window, pr5	$2
☐	📷			b. same as (a), metal Malaysia base, 5sp	$3
☐	📷	14	#2-Hyperliner	yellow enamel, black plastic Malaysia base, black tampo fades to yellow dots on roof w/red "hyperliner" by windshield, six misc. decals on left side of red plastic scoop, large yellow "1" w/black & red outline & large red w/black outline "Hot Wheels" at rear, red int., gray rear side vents, smoked window, yellow letter b5sp	$2
☐	📷	15	#3-Tantrum	a. day-glo lime, black plastic Malaysia base, large silver HW logo on side w/five misc. racing decals on front fender behind wheel, black & chrome int. & grille, black hood vents, chrome rear exhaust tips, blue-tint windshield, asw-pr5	$2
☐				b. same as (a), gray enamel HW logo on side, pr5	$26
☐	📷			c. same as (a), asw-3sp	$3
☐	📷			d. same as (a), asw-5sp	$10
☐	📷	16	#4-Overbored 454	a. dark blue pearl met. black plastic Malaysia base, white SS Stripes on roof & trunk, chrome int. & engine, blue-tint window, large white & gray HW logo on trunk, silver painted headlights, pr5	$2
☐				b. same as (a), gray painted headlights	$3
☐	📷	17	#5-Jester	purple transparent plastic body, blue-tint metal center spacer, black plastic Malaysia base, silver painted roof, white & green stripe tampo behind front wheel & upper rear fender, metal bed insert w/R/C car & tools, metal int., green-tint window, pr5	$2
☐	📷	18	#6-Altered State	a. candy purple, blue-tint metal Malaysia base & engine, black cove w/red outline & gold "Altered State" outlined in red, white & gold HW logo high in front of rear wheel, "AA/FA" in white below HW logo, black plastic roll cage & int., 5sp	$3
☐	📷			b. same as (a), large 5sp rear, small pr5 front (found at KB Toys)	$25
☐	📷	19	#7-Nissan Skyline	a. dark met. blue, black plastic Malaysia base, red stripe w/silver outline coming off both wheel wells, large white "APT" w/silver outline on side, 4 misc. racing decals on rocker panel including a HW logo in front of rear wheel, white w/silver outline "Tuned" on rocker panel behind front wheel, small red, silver & black tampo low in front of front wheel, flat black hood w/five misc. racing decals including a red & white HW logo, large silver "AP" & silver outline "T," red outline "2" & red & silver "Motorsports," black int. & rear wind, clear window, asw-pr5	$20

2002 First Editions, #1-Midnight Otto

2002 First Editions, #1-Midnight Otto

2002 First Editions, #2-Hyperliner

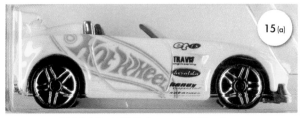

2002 First Editions, #3-Tantrum

2002 First Editions, #3-Tantrum

2002 First Editions, #3-Tantrum

2002 First Editions, #4-Overbored 454

2002 First Editions, #5-Jester

2002 First Editions, #6-Altered State

2002 First Editions, #6-Altered State

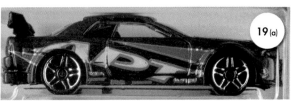

2002 First Editions, #7-Nissan Skyline

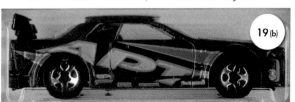

2002 First Editions, #7-Nissan Skyline

2002 First Editions, #8-Honda Spocket

2002 First Editions, #9-Corvette SR-2

2002 First Editions, #9-Corvette SR-2

2002 First Editions, #10-Nomadder What

2002 First Editions, #10-Nomadder What

2002 First Editions, #10-Nomadder What

2002 First Editions, #11-Super Smooth

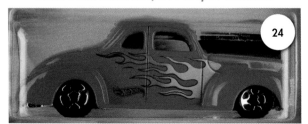

2002 First Editions, #11-Super Smooth

2002 First Editions, #12-'40 Ford Coupe

Photo		No.	Name	Description	Price
❑	📷	19	#7-Nissan Skyline	b. same as (a), asw-5sp	$2
❑	📷	20	#8-Honda Spocket	red plastic body, silver met. fenders, black plastic Malaysia base, tailgate has silver w/black outline taillights, silver & black HW logo on left side, black Honda emblem in center, yellow "Spocket" on right, dark smoked window, white int., alw-pr5	$2
❑	📷	21	#9-Corvette SR-2	a. red enamel w/silver cove, chrome Malaysia base & grille, thick pink stripe down center of hood w/gray, red, white & black Corvette emblem, pink circle w/black "2" on right side of stripe on nose, short white tampo on each hood bump, no HW logo, gray int., clear window, 5sp	$3
❑	📷			b. same as (a), asw-5sp	$15
❑				c. same as (a), white stripe & circle on hood, 5sp	$2
❑	📷	22	#10-Nomadder What	a. light pearl tangerine met. (more silver than orange in color), black w/silver side tampo, transparent orange plastic Malaysia base w/chrome transmission & drive shaft, gray HW logo on rocker panel in front of rear wheel, chrome int., headlights & taillights, smoked window, pr5	$4
❑	📷			b. same as (a), dark pearl tangerine met. (more orange than silver in color), pr5	$3
❑	📷			c. same as (b), 5sp	$2
❑	📷	23	#11-Super Smooth	a. dark candy blue, black plastic Malaysia base, silver, black & blue tampo on bed cover w/silver HW logo, black int., clear window, pr5	$2
❑	📷			b. same as (a), asw-pr5	$15
❑	📷	24	#12-'40 Ford Coupe	red enamel, chrome Malaysia base, white, yellow to orange flames on side, larger black HW logo in front of rear fender, gray int., smoked window, 5sp	$2

Photo	No.	Name	Description	Price
❏ 📷	25	#13-Ferrari P4	red enamel, black plastic Malaysia base w/chrome oil pan, white circle on side w/black-over-red "24," black, red & white "Champion" decal in front of rear wheel, white "FRAM" above yellow & black Ferrari emblem behind front wheel, white circle w/black-over-red "24" on top of left rear fender behind wheel, white circle w/black-over-red "24" on nose w/yellow & black rectangle Ferrari emblem black seats & rear spare tire, chrome dash & rear engine, clear window, g5sp	$2
❏ 📷	26	#14-Saleen S7	a. gray met. black plastic Malaysia base, black painted headlights w/two small white ovals, thin curved white pinstripe & small red oval in upper corner, small red & black square on nose, black & silver over white HW logo at top of rear window, black int., smoked window, pr5	$4
❏			b. same as (a), gloss black stripe above side window, pr5	$2
❏ 📷			c. same as (b), 5sp	$3
❏ 📷	27	#15-Backdraft	a. silver blue pearl plastic body, blue-tint metal Malaysia base, two wide white stripes on top of left front fender, dark blue plastic surfboard in center of rear chrome int., HW logo embossed in center of front bumper, smoked canopy, pr5	$3
❏ 📷			b. same as (a), metal Malaysia base, 3sp	$2
❏ 📷	28	#16-Custom Cougar	a. black enamel, black plastic Malaysia base, Race & Win card, purple pearl plastic rear wing & int., chrome dash, roll cage & engine, light greenish yellow Dragon head fading to light orange flame w/silver outlines on side, no HW logo, orange-tint window & hood, purple chrome pr5	$4
❏ 📷			b. same as (a), plain card, no "Race & Win," dragon head on side is all yellow	$3
❏ 📷	29	#17-'68 Cougar	a. light pearl green, chrome Malaysia base, gloss black painted roof, black HW logo high on rear fender behind wheel, smoked window, black int., asw-5sp	$2
❏ 📷			b. same as (a), flat black roof, asw-5sp	$4

2002 First Editions, #13-Ferrari P4

2002 First Editions, #14-Saleen S7

2002 First Editions, #14-Saleen S7

2002 First Editions, #15-Backdraft

2002 First Editions, #15-Backdraft

2002 First Editions, #16-Custom Cougar

2002 First Editions, #16-Custom Cougar

2002 First Editions, #17-'68 Cougar

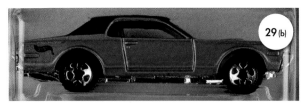

2002 First Editions, #17-'68 Cougar

2002 First Editions, #17-'68 Cougar

2002 First Editions, #18-Torpedo Jones

2002 First Editions, #19-Custom '69 Chevy

2002 First Editions, #20-Custom '59 Cadillac

2002 First Editions, #21-Open Road-ster

2002 First Editions, #21-Open Road-ster

2002 First Editions, #22-Jaded

Photo	No.	Name	Description	Price
❑	29	#17-'68 Cougar	c. same as (b), flat black painted hood scoop & silver painted hood pins, asw-5sp (These were leftover bodies from the HW.com promo. Most of these were found in the Booklet 3 packs.)	$75
❑ 📷			d. same as (b), bright candy Antifreeze green, asw-5sp	$5
❑ 📷	30	#18-Torpedo Jones	red enamel, matching painted metal Malaysia base, black & gold pinstripe on hood & cowl, two tan painted straps w/gold buckles on hood, chrome engine, exhaust, int., radiator & side wheel drives, white & gold over black HW logo behind tan plastic driver, alw-bbs	$2
❑ 📷	31	#19-Custom '69 Chevy	red enamel, black plastic Malaysia base & grille, gray int., smoked window, no HW logo, alw-pr5	$2
❑ 📷	32	#20-Custom '59 Cadillac	light purple pearl, chrome Malaysia base, orange panels on roof, hood & tops of front fenders w/yellow scallops, each panel starts w/white design w/light green outline, no HW logo, white int., clear window, asw-gbbs	$2
❑ 📷	33	#21-Open Road-ster	a. pearl mustard met. blue-tint metal Malaysia base, black, silver & green stripe tampo on nose, gray & black-over-green HW logo on rear spoiler facing rear, chrome engine & int., green-tint canopy, pr5	$2
❑ 📷			b. same as (a), metal Malaysia base, 5sp	$4
❑ 📷	34	#22-Jaded	purple met., gray plastic Malaysia base, dark red w/black outline tampo on side w/black "Jaded" on door to front fender, black-over-red HW logo on rear fender by taillight, chrome rear wing, int. & under hood scoop, purple-tint window, 5sp	$2
❑ 📷	35	#23-'57 Cadillac Eldorado Brougham	a. black enamel, chrome Malaysia base, silver met. painted roof, two silver painted moldings on top of each front fender, large silver HW logo on trunk facing rear, light gray int., clear window, asw-bbs	$3
❑			b. same as (a), large gray enamel HW logo on trunk facing rear, asw-bbs	$2
❑			c. same as (a), no HW logo on trunk, asw-bbs (I found this car at Target.)	$15

2002 First Editions, #23-'57 Cadillac Eldorado Brougham

2002 First Editions, #25-Lancia Stratos

2002 First Editions, #24-HW Prototype 12

2002 First Editions, #25-Lancia Stratos

2002 First Editions, #24-HW Prototype 12

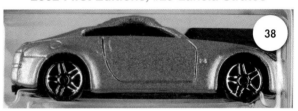

2002 First Editions, #25-Lancia Stratos

2002 First Editions, #24-HW Prototype 12

2002 First Editions, #26-Nissan Z

Photo	No.	Name	Description	Price
☐ 📷	36	#24-HW Prototype 12	a. candy bronze met., metal Malaysia base, frosted purple plastic center insert, silver painted headlights, no HW logo, gray plastic rear wing & int., very dark purple-tint window, pr5	$4
☐ 📷			b. same as (a), center insert is very dark purple, looks black, two brackets now added to top of gray plastic rear wing, pr5	$3
☐ 📷			c. same as (a), frosted purple plastic center insert, two brackets added to top of gray plastic rear wing, 5sp	$3
☐ 📷	37	#25-Lancia Stratos	a. red enamel, black plastic Malaysia base, silver HW logo on trunk facing rear, silver dot on nose, black int., black plastic rear window louvers, clear window, asw-5sp	$15
☐ 📷			b. same as (a), asw-pr5	$10
☐ 📷			c. same as (a), asw-g/pr5	$4
☐			d. red enamel, black plastic Malaysia base, silver HW logo on trunk facing rear, silver dot on nose, large white panel on top of each front fender w/thin green & gray stripe on the inside, white rectangle on top of each side of trunk, small green & white tampo above rear wheel by roof post, black int., black plastic rear window louvers, clear window, asw-gpr5	$2
☐ 📷	38	#26-Nissan Z	silver met. black plastic Malaysia base, black, white & orange tampoed headlights, white HW logo in rear smoked window, black int. & grille, asw-pr5	$2
☐ 📷	39	#27-Toyota RSC	candy gray met. black plastic Malaysia base, tan, white & black painted lights on top of all four fenders, black & white painted marker lights above rear lights, small round black emblem on nose, black int. & front lights, smoked window, alw-or5	$2
☐ 📷	40	#28-2001 Mini Cooper	a. pearl mustard met., metal Malaysia base, gloss bright white roof w/flat black painted pillars & cowl vents, black plastic fenders & rocker panels, silver painted headlights, grille, bumperettes & directional lights, no HW logo, black int., clear window, asw-pr5	$15

Photo	No.	Name	Description	Price
❑ 📷	40	#28-2001 Mini Cooper	b. same as (a), bright white gloss roof, asw-5sp	$8
❑			c. same as (b), grayish white satin roof, asw-5sp	$3
❑ 📷			d. same as (c), dark pearl mustard paint, grayish white satin roof, asw-5sp	$3
❑ 📷	41	#29-Super Tsunami	a. light candy gold met. black plastic Malaysia base, three bare metal grilles on hood, gray plastic rear window & int., large black & silver outlined "HW" w/smaller "PR" & silver & black "Tsunami" on side, one black & silver & two black small sponsor decals behind front wheel, black "Jones Race Products" in silver & black rectangle behind rear wheel, white & silver "Hot Wheels.com" on rear window, silver outline "Super Tsunami" at top of windshield, silver "www.hotwheels.com" at bottom of windshield, 2 blue-tint window, pr5	$2
❑ 📷			b. same as (a), dark candy gold met., pr5	$3
❑ 📷	42	#30-'64 Riviera	a. candy bronze met. chrome Malaysia base, light green & pink pinstripe flames in two panels on hood, roof & trunk, center of trunk has purple & light green HW logo above small light green & purple pinstripe flames, white int., purple-tint window, asw-pr5	$5
❑			b. purple replaces pink in pinstriping, pr5	$2
❑ 📷			c. same as (b), asw-5sp	$4
❑ 📷	43	#31-Moto-Crossed	a. red enamel, blue-tint metal Malaysia base, two wide black & yellow flame stripes on hood w/wide silver stripe on the outside & a thin silver strip on the inside of each strip. Large white & red HW logo outlined in black across hood, white "MX" outlined in yellow & black on right side of hood below the HW logo, black-over-silver emblem on nose w/ white "1" in center, small black over silver panel on side of hood w/yellow "Motocrossed," black-over-silver tampo on side w/small white lettering & emblem at bottom, black over silver panel over rear wheel w/yellow & black flame & white-over-red "1," gray plastic rollcage, rear engine cover & exhaust, black int., smoked windshield, alw-5sp	$3
❑ 📷			b. dark mustard yellow replaces all yellows in tampos	$5

2002 First Editions, #27-Toyota RSC

2002 First Editions, #28-2001 Mini Cooper

2002 First Editions, #28-2001 Mini Cooper

2002 First Editions, #29-Super Tsunami

2002 First Editions, #28-2001 Mini Cooper

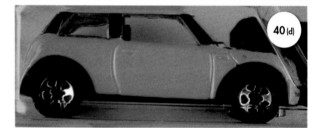

2002 First Editions, #29-Super Tsunami

2002 First Editions, #30-'64 Riviera

2002 First Editions, #30-'64 Riviera

2002 First Editions, #31-Moto-Crossed

2002 First Editions, #31-Moto-Crossed

2002 First Editions, #32-Lotus Esprit

2002 First Editions, #33-Volkswagen New Beetle Cup

2002 First Editions, #33-Volkswagen New Beetle Cup

2002 First Editions, #34-Pony-Up

2002 First Editions, #35-I Candy

2002 First Editions, #35-I Candy

Photo		No.	Name	Description	Price
☐	📷	44	#32-Lotus Esprit	black enamel, black plastic Malaysia base & rear spoiler, green & silver Lotus emblem on nose, white HW logo low on side in front of rear wheel, tan int., clear window, 5sp	$2
☐	📷	45	#33-Volkswagen New Beetle Cup	a. yellow enamel, gray plastic Malaysia base, white, red & black stripes up side up to roof line, small black painted vent window at front of door, large black circle outlined in silver w/gray "1" & dots on door, five white sponsor decals in the stripes, one red decal on rocker panel "PROCH," hood has large black circle outlined in silver w/tan "1" & dots w/white & red HW logo outlined in black, silver, black & tan painted headlights, gray int., yellow roll cage & blue-tint window, alw-pr5	$8
☐	📷			b. same as (a), side stripe stops at bottom of side window, does not go to roof, alw-pr5	$3
☐	📷	46	#34-Pony-Up	a. candy bronze, metal Malaysia base, black stripe w/pearl blue met. flames on hood, rear window & trunk, silver & black HW logo over black on rear window, silver painted headlights, black int., smoked window, pr5	$3
☐				b. same as (a), light blue enamel replaces pearl blue met. in flames on hood, rear window & trunk, pr5	$8

Photo	No.	Name	Description	Price
☐ 📷	47	#35-I Candy	a. satin lime met. transparent purple fenders & int., unpainted metal Malaysia base, black, orange & red flames on nose w/red, white & black HW logo, blue-tint metal engine, orange window, 5sp	$10
☐ 📷			b. same as (a), clear window, 5sp rear, skinny 5dot front	$4
☐ 📷	48	#36-Rocket Oil Special	a. purple pearl met., metal Malaysia base, (Race & Win card) white w/red outline "Rocket Oil" on each side of hood over red & white pinstriping, white & red HW logo w/black outline on side of rear, chrome int. & engine, smoked windshield, 5sp	$4
☐ 📷			b. same as (a), darker candy purple met. paint, blue-tint metal Malaysia base, 35th Anniversary Card, darker red in HW logo	$2
☐ 📷	49	#37-Hyundai Spyder Concept	a. candy gold met. black plastic Malaysia base, orange & silver painted taillights, silver painted running lights on top of front fenders, four silver painted scoops on hood, silver painted gas cap behind driver seat, white, black & orange HW logo on rear above Hyundai emblem, black int., smoked windshield, pr5	$2
☐ 📷			b. same as (a), darker candy gold met.	$3
☐ 📷	50	#38-Sling Shot	dark blue met. unpainted blue-tint metal Malaysia base, top side has black panel & flame tampo w/silver "Slingshot" & black, silver & light blue HW logo, tampo is outlined at front in light blue & fades to silver at the rear where the flames are, black & white oval tampo on nose, chrome int. & rear engine, smoked window, pr5	$3
☐ 📷	51	#39-40 Somethin'	a. yellow enamel, black plastic Malaysia base, wide black racing stripe w/thin outer pinstripe on top from nose to tail, black "40" in large white circle w/black outline on hood, black "40" in white circle w/black outline on left side (passenger side) of stripe on rear deck, black heart tampo w/"Heart Racing" outlined in white above rear wheel, black "40" in large white circle w/black outline on door, black painted side vent, "Maddy" in black where door handle would be, four black & white sponsor decals on rocker panel, black & white heart tampo behind front wheel, small black & white sponsor decal & black HW logo in front of front wheel, gray int. & rear pipes, dark smoked window, pr5	$4

2002 First Editions, #36-Rocket Oil Special

2002 First Editions, #38-Sling Shot

2002 First Editions, #36-Rocket Oil Special

2002 First Editions, #39-40 Somethin'

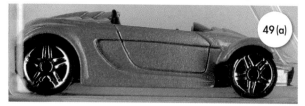

2002 First Editions, #37-Hyundai Spyder Concept

2002 First Editions, #39-40 Somethin'

2002 First Editions, #37-Hyundai Spyder Concept

2002 First Editions, #39-40 Somethin'

Photo	No.	Name	Description	Price
☐	51	#39-40 Somethin'	b. same as (a), black paint missing from side vent, pr5	$2
☐			c. same as (b), pale yellow, pr5	$5
☐			d. yellow enamel, black plastic Malaysia base, wide black racing stripe w/thin outer pinstripe on top from nose to tail, large white circle w/black outline on hood w/black "40," large black & white "X" on rear deck w/black "Velocity" in white panel outlined in black, black rectangle w/white "THQ" high on rear fender, "Pitschke" in black where door handle should be, black "40" in large white circle w/black outline on door, four black & white sponsor decals on rocker panel, small black HW logo in front of front wheel, red painted taillights, gray int. & rear pipes, dark smoked window, redline 5sp	$25

It's not too often a car is released as a promotion that has a collector number on it, but this 40 Somethin' 51 (d) variation was. It was released with a video game. Some people said they asked the manager if they could buy the car without the game and were able to; others said they found them on the pegs at Toys R Us. I got mine from HWC Amy when I sent her some Hot Wheels Comics for the Petersen Museum.

Photo	No.	Name	Description	Price
☐	52	#40-Side Draft	a. candy bronze met. black plastic Malaysia base, chrome rear section & oil pan, large silver & black over white "7" on door w/five misc. racing sponsors, white-over-silver HW logo outlined in black above decals behind front wheel, small black sponsor decal left of headlight, black, silver & white stripe along rear fender body line, black int. & louvers behind smoked canopy, pr5	$2
☐			b. same as (a), gray enamel "7" on side, pr5	$4
☐	53	#41-Ballistik	a. dark green met. black plastic Malaysia base, chrome engine w/closed scoop, chrome int., front grille & rear pipes, blue-tint canopy w/white-over-green HW logo w/light green & black outline facing rear, alw-Y5	$5
☐			b. same as (a), front of scoop is open & clean	$2
☐	54	#42-Syd Mead's Sentinel 400 Limo	dark aqua met. flat black rear half of roof & trunk, chrome Malaysia base, gray int. & circle through hood, smoked window, orange painted taillights, no HW logo, b5sp/rear, small chrome 5sp front	$4

2002 First Editions, #39-40 Somethin'

2002 First Editions, #41-Ballistik

2002 First Editions, #40-Side Draft

2002 First Editions, #42-Syd Mead's Sentinel 400 Limo

2002 First Editions, #40-Side Draft

Wild Frontier Series

Photo	No.	Name	Description	Price
☐ 📷	55	'59 Chevy Impala	bronze met. gold chrome Malaysia base, gold & white Sheriff badge outlined in black on roof w/white over black HW logo, side has white, red & gold horse w/black outline, gold & white Sheriff badge w/black "Posse" rear fender above wheel, white int., smoked window, g5sp	$2
☐ 📷	56	'32 Ford Delivery	a. black enamel w/tan plastic fenders, metal Thailand base, tan, white, red & black Man tampo on roof w/Ace of Spades w/red HW logo, two white & gold bullet holes & red outline, side panel has white over red HW logo, lower side has red "the Good, the Bad & the Speedy" w/red & tan pinstripe design below lettering & three white & gold bullet holes, chrome grille, tan int., tinted window, 3sp	$4
☐			b. same as (a), name change to '32 Ford Sedan Delivery	$2
☐			c. same as (b), date on blue-tint metal Thailand base is "198"	$4
☐	57	Ice Cream Truck	a. orange enamel, black plastic Malaysia base, side has yellow panel at top w/black outline & black letters "Come 'n Git It!" black "Saucy Sanders" over yellow state of Texas on left side of window, black "Rollin' Round-up Rodeo Grille" over yellow star on right side of window, white, yellow & orange pig w/black outline & orange & yellow flames below window, black "Chef Dave "Saucy" Saunders on Board" in center of door, white-over-yellow star above front wheel, rear has white-over-blue "Yall Come Back!!!" over window, orange-over-yellow HW logo over two crossed black forks below window, yellow "Home Of The Flamin' Sow" between taillights, white int., smoked window, asw-g5sp	$4

By the way, the "Saucy Sanders" on the #57 Ice Cream Truck is none other than HWC Dave Sanders.

Photo	No.	Name	Description	Price
☐ 📷			b. same as (a), burnt orange enamel color, asw-g5sp	$3
☐ 📷			c. same as (a), name change on card "Grillionaire"	$2
☐ 📷	58	Power Plower	a. met. dark red, blue-tint metal Malaysia base, hood has gold & white bull skull w/black outline, orange flames w/black outline on each side of skull over black & gold diamond snake skin tampo, orange over white HW logo above skull by windshield, side has two large white diamond shapes w/a smaller gold diamond shape in each one over black & gold diamond snake skin tampo, small white lines in each side of roof, gray bed, roll bar & int., yellow-tint window, asw-gct/b	$4
☐ 📷			b. same as (a), no white on roof asw-ct/b	$4
☐ 📷			c. same as (b), asw-g/or5	$2

Wild Frontier Series, '59 Chevy Impala

Wild Frontier Series, '32 Ford Sedan Delivery

Wild Frontier Series, Ice Cream Truck

57 (c)

Wild Frontier Series, Grillionaire

58 (b)

Wild Frontier Series, Power Plower

58 (a)

Wild Frontier Series, Power Plower

58 (c)

Wild Frontier Series, Power Plower

Spares & Strikes Series

Photo	No.	Name	Description	Price
☐ 📷	59	Surfin' School Bus	met. silver, black plastic fenders, gold chrome Malaysia base, roof has "Nathan's Smokin' Bowl-a-Rama" in white, orange & black, orange guy w/black hair & white shirt outlined in black, yellow-to-orange flames outlined in black, orange w/black outline "Burnin' Up The Lanes of The World," "Nathan's Cru," "Willmott, Heralda, Carris, McLone, Thienprasiddhi, Sanders," side has yellow & orange flames w/black outline from front wheel well along w/small white & black "Nathan's Smokin' Bowl-a-Rama," orange & yellow panel w/black & white bowling ball w/white pinstripes coming off ball to the left & black & white HW logo, orange & yellow triangle outlined in black in orange & yellow stripe behind rear fender, orange, yellow & black stripe below side windows, dark yellow-tint windows, g5sp	$2
☐ 📷	60	So Fine	aqua enamel, chrome China base, white cove, three black diamonds w/silver outline behind front wheel, silver & black "Three Lane King" on lower part of door, black stripe w/white outline from front to rear covering rear fender, silver pinstripe flames on rear fender, hood has black panel w/white outline, three white diamonds w/silver outline in the center of silver pinstripe triangle, silver pinstripe flames on each side, silver HW logo in center rear by windshield, white int., clear window, 5sp	$2
☐ 📷	61	Rodger Dodger	green met. chrome Malaysia base, blue-tint metal engine through hood, gold HW logo, white "Lila's" outlined in gold, white "Bowl-A-Rama" & white bowling pin outlined in gold & red in black panel w/white outline on roof, hood is black w/thin gold stripes & four white diamonds, white "Lila's Bowl-A-Rama" outlined in gold, four white bowling pins outlined in gold & red in black panel w/white outline on side, red & white heart w/gold flames behind rear wheel, gold int., clear window, 5sp	$2
☐ 📷	62	Sooo Fast	red enamel, metal China base, black & yellow stripe tampo on side w/black & white bowling ball & three white & red bowling pins, small white "Street Strike" outlined in black on lower door, black & white bowling ball w/white & red HW logo & three white & red bowling pins over yellow tampo on hood, clear window, chrome int., grille & rear engine, 5sp	$3

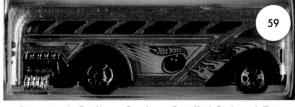

59

Spares & Strikes Series, Surfin' School Bus

60

Spares & Strikes Series, So Fine

Spares & Strikes Series, Rodger Dodger

Spares & Strikes Series, Sooo Fast

Tuners Series

Photo	No.	Name	Description	Price
☐ 📷	63	Ford Focus	white enamel, black plastic Malaysia base, black down center of hood w/bright red on each side, bright red "Hot Wheels Tuning," "Yokohama," "Eibach Springs," "Modern" & "Katzkin" w/blue & white Ford oval & white "racing" on hood, red & blue stripe tampo on rear fender w/blue & white Ford oval & white Racing, very dark red large "Y," "Yokohama," "Eibach Springs," "Modern" & "Katzkin" on side w/five more dark red & black racing decals at front of door, red plastic rear wing & int., clear window, asw-bbs	$2
☐ 📷	64	Honda Civic	met. dark blue, black plastic Malaysia base, black panel on hood w/four pale yellow sponsors & Hot Wheels, large pale yellow & black "W" tampo on side inside a circle, pale yellow stripe coming off front wheel well stopping at center of door, pale yellow & black Honda emblem on rear fender behind wheel, small yellow tampo on rear bumper behind wheel, six silver & pale yellow sponsor tampos on right side of door, pale yellow "Modern" on rocker panel in front of rear wheel, pale yellow "Y" & "Yokohama" above front wheel, pale yellow HW logo at bottom of front fender in front of wheel, black int., clear window, asw-3sp	$2
☐ 📷	65	MS-T Suzuka	a. yellow enamel, black plastic Malaysia base, black painted hood w/four bright orange sponsors & Hot Wheels, black panel painted on rear fender & half the door w/yellow "Hot Wheels," black "Eibach" & yellow "Springs" on left side of door at an angle, six silver, black & white sponsors decals on right side of door, black int., smoked window, alw-3sp	$2
☐			b. same as (a), light brown replaces yellow in hood tampo, alw-3sp	$5
☐ 📷	66	Toyota Celica	bright red enamel, black plastic Malaysia base, white & black stripe tampo on hood & side w/blue "Modern Image," black panel down center of hood w/blue Toyota emblem, "TOYOTA" & HW logo, "RHL" is blue-over-silver, white over blue HW high behind rear wheel above blue stripe on rear fender, six misc. blue over silver racing decals on right side of door, white plastic rear wing, black int. & headlights, smoked window, asw-bbs	$2

Tuners Series, Ford Focus

Tuners Series, MS-T Suzuka

Tuners Series, Honda Civic

Tuners Series, Toyota Celica

Corvette Series

	Photo	No.	Name	Description	Price
❑	📷	67	'65 Corvette	a. dark candy blue met., gray plastic Malaysia base, silver met. panel on hood w/gold, silver & black flames, silver flames w/gold outline on side, silver met. painted rear deck lid, silver HW logo on lower pass side of trunk, black int., clear windshield, 5sp	$3
❑				b. same as (a), gray met. painted hood w/gold & black flames, gray met. painted rear deck lid, gray met. HW logo on lower pass side of trunk, 5sp	$7
❑				c. same as (a), gray enamel painted hood w/gold & black flames, gray enamel painted rear deck lid, gray enamel HW logo on lower pass side of trunk, 5sp	$20
❑	📷	68	'97 Corvette	a. candy purple met. black plastic Malaysia base, roof & side have silver & black panel tampo w/black, gold & silver pinstriping, silver "CORVETTE" on rear deck facing rear, gray int., clear window w/old HW logo embossed in rear window, alw-3sp	$7
❑	📷			b. same as (a), gray replaces silver in roof & side tampos, alw-3sp	$3
❑	📷			c. same as (a), dark candy purple met., alw-3sp	$3
❑	📷			d. same as (a), alw-5sp	$3
❑	📷			e. same as (d), dark candy purple met., alw-5sp	$3
❑				f. same as (a), alw-bbs	$58
❑	📷	69	'58 Corvette	light yellow enamel w/white cover, black plastic China base, gloss black racing stripe from front to rear, wide center, thin on each side, black HW logo on rear quarter behind wheel, chrome int., front & rear bumpers & side exhaust, clear windshield, 3sp	$2
❑	📷	70	'63 Corvette	a. red enamel, chrome Malaysia base, white & silver flames on side, silver painted door handle, black painted rocker panel w/white "CORVETTE," silver HW logo behind rear wheel on quarter panel, hood has black painted raised center w/silver "SIXTY-THREE" on each side along w/white & silver flames, white int., tinted window, asw-3sp	$2
❑				b. same as (a), headlight doors missing, asw-3sp	$10

Corvette Series, '65 Corvette

Corvette Series, '97 Corvette

Corvette Series, '97 Corvette

Corvette Series, '97 Corvette

Corvette Series, '97 Corvette

Corvette Series, '58 Corvette

Corvette Series, '97 Corvette

Corvette Series, '63 Corvette

Trump Cars Series

Photo	No.	Name	Description	Price
☐ 📷	71	Dodge Charger R/T	a. black enamel, gray plastic China Base, side has white & silver panel w/red outline & red stripe w/silver outline, two black outlined Kings w/red crown, upright King has silver hair, upside down King has white hair, black clover w/red outline in silver part of side panel tampo on door, red over white "R/T" high on front fender behind wheel, hood has white & silver panel & red stripe w/silver outline, black outlined King w/red crown & silver hair in white part of panel, silver & red sword outlined in black, black "K" & black clover outlined in red in upper right of hood, gray int., red-tint window w/HW logo embossed in rear, 5dot	$7
☐			b. same as (a), upside down King on side has silver hair, not white	$5
☐ 📷			c. same as (b), side panel is all white enamel instead of silver & white	$2
☐ 📷	72	Hammered Coupe	dark red w/gold & silver flakes, black enamel painted metal Malaysia base, flat black roof & trunk w/yellow & white "Joker" outlined in red down trunk, flat black & red over yellow HW logo at bottom of trunk below "Joker," white panel outlined w/black & orange on hood & roof w/yellow & orange jokers w/white faces, flat black between tampo on hood & gold chrome grille, gold chrome engines, int., grille & front struts, clear window, g5sp	$2
☐ 📷	73	Montezooma	a. met. gold, black plastic Malaysia base, two white faces w/yellow hair w/red lines holding a yellow sword outlined in black on hood, white triangle panel outlined in black on top of front fenders w/black & red "J" above yellow & red harts outlined in black, white face outlined in black w/yellow hair w/black & red lines on door, side roof pillar & side of front & rear fenders have white panel w/black outline, in each panel are red & black "J" w/red & yellow hearts outlined in black, black int. & grille, red-tint window, asw-5dot	$2
☐ 📷			b. same as (a), darker met. gold, asw-5dot	$2
☐ 📷	74	'33 Ford	white met. pearl, maroon pearl plastic fenders, metal Malaysia base, queen tampo outlined in black, red & gold on door, one up, one down, three black spades w/black & red stripe on side w/black & red "Q" above rear fender, queen tampo on hood outlined in black, gold & red w/two red & black "Qs" & two black spades w/red & black stripes, black int. & running boards, clear windshield, chrome engine, dash & radiator shell, black painted grille, yellow painted headlights, 5sp	$2

Trump Cars, Dodge Charger R/T

Trump Cars, Dodge Charger R/T

Trump Cars, Dodge Charger R/T

Trump Cars, Hammered Coupe

Trump Cars, Montezooma

Trump Cars, Montezooma

Trump Cars, '33 Ford

Cold Blooded Series

Photo	No.	Name	Description	Price
☐ 📷	75	Firebird Funny Car	black enamel, metal Malaysia base, orange & white tampos on hood w/orange & white HW logo up by windshield, white, gold & black snake skin tampo outlined in orange on rear fender, orange & white tampo from front wheel well, large orange over black "Hot Wheels" logo w/white outline, black & white "Racing" in orange panel on side below HW logo, red-tint window, red 5sp	$3
☐ 📷	76	Speed Shark	candy bronze met. chrome Malaysia base, black tampo outlined in white w/small green & yellow stars on each side of cockpit, two small black tampos behind cockpit, large black HW logo on top of each rear fender, black angle tampo outlined in white on side w/green & yellow stars, yellow to green "Venomstripe" below side angle tampo, light gray int., side gills & rear insert, chrome canopy & rear engine, 5sp	$2
☐ 📷	77	Vulture	yellow enamel, smoked transparent Chine base, black side tampo w/green, white, black & brown snake, snake has brown eye, scales & tongue, light green over white HW logo on side in center, chrome engine & int., smoked canopy, 5sp	$2
☐	78	Phaeton	a. met. teal, silver met. painted metal China base & grille, large yellow, red & black snake on side w/white fangs over black & red stripe tampo, white & red HW logo w/black outline over snake on door, black tampo w/red stripes in hood, black plastic top & int., red-tint window, gt/b	$2
☐ 📷			b. same as (a), unpainted metal China base	$3

Cold Blooded Series, Firebird Funny Car

Cold Blooded Series, Vulture

Cold Blooded Series, Speed Shark

Cold Blooded Series, Phaeton

Star Spangled Series

Photo	No.	Name	Description	Price
☐ 📷	79	Chrysler Pronto	red met. black plastic China base, American flag tampo on hood & side outlined in silver, silver outlined star on top of each front fender, large silver outlined HW logo on rocker panel, silver outlined star behind each wheel on fenders, "Chrysler Pronto" in silver on lower part of trunk, gray int., clear window, bbs	$2
☐ 📷	80	3-Window '34	candy blue w/blue plastic fenders & white plastic running boards, metal Thailand base, hood has red & white stripes w/gold outline & six white & gold stars on each side, side has 12 white & gold stars w/red & white stripes w/gold outline, silver HW logo on roof post behind side window, white int., chrome dash, engine & grille, blue-tint window, t/b	$3
☐ 📷	81	Deora II	candy silver, chrome China base, silver stars over blue on roof, red & white stripes outlined in silver on side w/silver stars over blue on cab, white & red over blue HW logo in cove on side, red plastic surfboard on right rear, blue plastic surfboard on rear left, chrome int. & rear engine, clear window, asw-5dot	$2
☐ 📷	82	'68 El Camino	pearl white, metal China base, dark blue & bright red flames outlined in dark blue w/silver stars on hood & sides, bright red HW logo behind rear wheel, red plastic rear wing & int., chrome rear engine, clear window, 5sp	$2

Star Spangled Series, Chrysler Pronto

Star Spangled Series, Deora II

Star Spangled Series, 3-Window '34

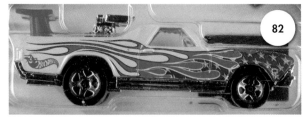

Star Spangled Series, '68 El Camino

Yu-Gi-Oh! Series

Photo	No.	Name	Description	Price
📷	83	Power Pistons	a. black plastic body, metal Thailand base & headlights, red & white "Maxmillion Pegasus" & larger light brown over white "Yu-Gi-Oh!" on side w/gray, white & red tampo, black, red & white HW logo high on rear fender behind wheel, white plastic vents, rear exhaust & int., red-tint canopies, red enamel 5sp	$4
📷			b. same as (a), no white background the red "Maxmillion Pegasus" & red & black HW logo	$2
📷	84	Seared Tuner	red enamel, black plastic Malaysia base, yellow w/black outlined "Time Wizard" above rear wheel, blue, yellow, white & black Wizard tampo behind front wheel, blue front & rear grilles, yellow HW logo facing front on rear spoiler, black int. & side vent, yellow-tint window, alw-g5dot	$2
📷	85	Fandango	a. light candy blue, gray plastic Malaysia base, orange & candy blue HW logo on hood by windshield, large light brown over white "Yu-Gi-Oh!" on side w/white, light brown, black & orange character & orange "YUGI" w/black outline, brown, white & black tampo on door, black int., green-tint window, magenta chrome 5sp	$4
📷			b. same as (a), very dark candy blue	$5
📷	86	Super Tuned	candy lime green met. gray plastic China base & lower front grille, blue, black & white flying Dragon on side w/gold & white "Yu-Gi-Oh!," white & lime HW logo facing front on hood up by windshield, black int., rear wing & bed cover, yellow-tint window, blue chrome 5sp	$2

Yu-Gi-Oh! Series, Power Pistons

Yu-Gi-Oh! Series, Seared Tuner

Yu-Gi-Oh! Series, Power Pistons

Yu-Gi-Oh! Series, Fandango

85 (b)

86

Yu-Gi-Oh! Series, Fandango

Yu-Gi-Oh! Series, Super Tuned

Spectraflame II Series

	Photo	No.	Name	Description	Price
☐	📷	87	Monoposto	a. candy lime green met., black plastic Malaysia base, top of car next to driver has lavender, silver & white tampo on black panel w/white outline, side has silver "Spectra" w/black outline, black "Flame II" w/white outline over a black oval w/gold outline & white tampo, white & lavender HW logo w/black outline above Spectra on side, purple-tint canopy, chrome driver, pr5	$2
☐	📷			b. same as (a), gray in "Spectra" instead of silver in side tampo	$4
☐	📷	88	Muscle Tone	a. candy gold met., black plastic Malaysia base, white over black "Muscletone" on windshield, trunk has gray over black "Spectra" & black w/gray outline "Flame II" over a black oval w/white tampo, white & green HW logo outlined in black above Spectra Flame II logo, white int., smoked window, gpr5	$2
☐	📷			b. same as (a), light candy lime met. gpr5	$8
☐	📷	89	Jet Threat 3.0	a. Misspelled on card as "JET THRREAT 3.0," light candy blue met., blue-tint metal Malaysia base w/"Jet Threat 3.0" in center, 2000 Mattel Inc. on lower wing, black panels on center & front wings, left wing has silver "Spectra" & black w/white outline "Flame II" over yellow background w/black over yellow HW logo, chrome int., wingtips, flaps, rear engine turbines & backing plates, yellow-tint canopy, bbs	$5
☐			Jet Threat 3.0	b. card spelled correctly, metal Malaysia base w/"Jet Threat 3.0" on upper wing, "2000 Mattel Inc." in center	$2
☐	📷	90	Screamin' Hauler	a. light candy purple, metal Malaysia base, silver panel outlined in black on nose w/black tampo, silver & black "Spectra Flame II" over magenta & white tampo on rear w/white & red HW logo outlined in black, orange & white painted taillights outlined in black w/silver between the orange & white, two silver painted triangles between the taillights, chrome engine on each side, metal int., smoked windshield, 5sp	$2
☐	📷			b. same as (a), black painted metal Malaysia base & int., 5sp	$5

The black painted base Screamin' Hauler cars were only found at Kmart stores. My guess here is that the bases for these cars were leftovers from the Halloween two-pack cars.

87 (a)

Spectraflame II Series, Monoposto

88 (a)

Spectraflame II Series, Muscle Tone

87 (b)

Spectraflame II Series, Monoposto

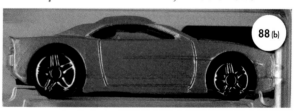

88 (b)

Spectraflame II Series, Muscle Tone

89

Spectraflame II Series, Jet Threat 3.0

90 (b)

Spectraflame II Series, Screamin' Hauler

90 (a)

Spectraflame II Series, Screamin' Hauler

Masters of The Universe Series

	Photo	No.	Name	Description	Price
☐	📷	91	'41 Willys Coupe	a. gloss black enamel, dark gray plastic China base, silver, red & light tan person w/silver dots outlining door & rear fender, white w/red outline "Ramman" high on door, silver HW logo on rear fender behind wheel, white over red "Masters of The Universe" facing rear on roof, chrome engine, int. & rear body panel, red-tint window, 5sp	$3
☐	📷			b. same as (a), dark gray plastic Malaysia base, no black detail in silver side tampo, 5sp	$2
☐	📷	92	Twin Mill	a. white pearl met. pearl gold met. plastic Malaysia base, side has a black outlined man w/yellow hair & light tan skin wearing brown armor, black over yellow "HE-MAN" on right of man, white & black HW logo on left of man, yellow over black "Masters of The Universe" on hood w/dark gray swards on top of fenders, gold chrome engines, pearl gold met. int., yellow-tint window, alw-g5sp	$2
☐				b. same as (a), dark gold chrome engines, alw-g5sp	$4
☐	📷			c. same as (a), gold chrome Malaysia base, alw-g5sp	$75

I can't tell you where the #92 Twin Mill (c) variation base came from. There were very few of these cars found with this gold chrome base.

	Photo	No.	Name	Description	Price
☐	📷	93	Double Vision	a. candy green met. gray plastic China base, two gray plastic engines w/chrome superchargers, dark gold & silver armored man on side w/silver & black "Man-At-Arms," silver dots outlining the whole side of the car, silver HW logo behind rear wheel, gray int., clear canopy, bbs	$2
☐	📷			b. same as (a), 5sp	$3
☐	📷	94	Phantastique	a. dark blue met. black plastic China base & front grille, black & silver skull tampo w/red eyes over white background on hood, white & silver bones on top of front fenders, white HW logo above white w/red outline "Skeletor" & "Masters of the Universe" on trunk, black int., red-tint windshield, alw-t/b	$2
☐				b. same as (a), black plastic Malaysia base, alw-t/b	$2
☐				c. same as (b), orange eyes, alw-t/b	$3

91 (a)

Masters Of The Universe Series,
'41 Willys Coupe

91 (b)

Masters Of The Universe Series,
'41 Willys Coupe

Masters Of The Universe Series, Twin Mill II

Masters Of The Universe Series, Twin Mill II

Masters Of The Universe Series, Double Vision

Masters Of The Universe Series, Phantastique

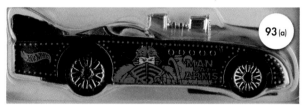

Masters Of The Universe Series, Double Vision

Sweet Rides Series

	Photo	No.	Name	Description	Price
☐	📷	95	Chevy Pro Stock Truck	a. white enamel, black plastic Malaysia base, dark blue stripe & light red wedge tampo on side w/"Baby Ruth," white "5" outlined in blue above a white & blue "Edelbrock" decal behind rear wheel, blue & white HW logo, red, white & black "Champion" & "Bell" decals on rocker panel, blue "Nestle," red "Carris" & red, black & white Hurst decal above Baby Ruth on side, light red "Good Year" above front wheelwell, black painted panel on rear bed cover w/large white over red "5" & "Champion," "Simpson," "Holley," "Hurst," "Hot Wheels," "Carris" & "Good Year" decals. rear spoiler has a blue stripe & "Nestle" w/light red "Baby Ruth" facing rear, red int., smoked window, red-chromed 5sp	$4
☐	📷			b. same as (a), Black plastic China base, lighter blue stripe on side, darker reds in all tampos, front bumper sticks out farther, tinted window, red chromed 5sp	$3
☐	📷	96	Pro Stock Firebird	a. silver/blue met. metal Malaysia base, dark blue & yellow tampo on hood w/yellow-over-black "Spree" over light candy blue met. tampo, small black lettering below "Spree." Large plastic yellow hood scoop. Yellow "1" outlined in light & dark blue & yellow "Good Year" twice on roof, white, light blue & dark blue HW logo & yellow & blue "Carris" decal facing rear behind the "1." Dark blue enamel on front fender onto door, light yellow-over-dark-blue "Spree" w/small black "Candy" below last "e" on side over a light candy blue tampo, small yellow lettering below "Spree" tampo, yellow "Good Year" at lower-left corner of door, three yellow & black sponsor decals on rocker panel, light yellow w/black outline "Hot Wheels" above rear wheel w/dark blue stripe above & below, light yellow "1" outlined in light & dark blue behind rear wheel, black int., blue-tint window, 5sp	$4
☐	📷			b. lighter silver/blue met. metal China base, all yellows in all tampos are much darker, light blue enamel replaces the candy blue met. under the Spree tampos on hood & side, Spree tampo & HW logo on side are now smaller	$3
☐	📷	97	Mustang Cobra	a. candy gray met., black plastic China base, dark flat blue enamel panel on hood w/white "Nestle," white & red "Crunch," red over white "12," red over white "Hot Wheels," dark red & white HW logo & dark red & white "Carris," dark flat blue, white, black & red enamel tampo on roof, 5 sponsor decals at center of tampo, dark flat blue, flat red, gloss black & white side tampo w/white white "Nestle," white & red "Crunch," black-over-white "12," behind front wheel, "Simpson," "Holley" & "Toms" decals on rocker panel, silver painted door handle, red & white HW logo, white "Good Year" & red & white "Millers Muffler" behind rear wheel, black int., blue-tint window, asw-bbs	$2

	Photo	No.	Name	Description	Price
☐	📷	97	Mustang Cobra	b. same as (a), black plastic Malaysia base, orange replaces red in all tampos, asw-bbs	$4
☐	📷	98	'70 Chevelle	yellow pearl met. chrome China base, yellow enamel painted hood & side w/sliced out stripes, hood has blue over white "Nestle," "Butterfinger," & "2," right side of hood has a blue & white sponsor decal w/ three black ones. Side has blue over white "Nestle," "Butterfinger," & white over blue "World Tour," blue & white w/black outline HW logo on rear fender above rear wheel, blue over white "2" & small black sponsor decal on front fender behind wheel, dark blue stripe on lower rear fender & along rocker panel w/four yellow & one white sponsor decals, white int., blue-tint window, g5sp	$2

Sweet Rides Series, Chevy Pro Stock Truck

Sweet Rides Series, Mustang Cobra

Sweet Rides Series, Chevy Pro Stock Truck

Sweet Rides Series, Mustang Cobra

Sweet Rides Series, Pro Stock Firebird

Sweet Rides Series, '70 Chevelle SS

Sweet Rides Series, Pro Stock Firebird

Grave Rave Series

	Photo	No.	Name	Description	Price
☐	📷	99	Evil Twin	a. white pearl met. black plastic China base, silver & black drops in red panels outlined in black on roof w/white, silver & black "Grave Rave," white, red & silver HW logo, & two white & black skulls, silver & black drops in a red panel outlined in black on side w/white & black skulls, chrome engines, exhaust, & bumper, red int., red-tint window, asw-bbs	$2
☐	📷			b. same as (a), asw-5sp	$4
The #99 Evil Twin (b) variation 5sp cars were found at K-B Toy Stores.					
☐	📷	100	Krazy 8s	candy red met. metal China base, one white & black skull over yellow & black tampo on top of each fender, lightly tinted rear wing w/white & black HW logo outlined in green, white & black "Grave Rave" below HW logo w/white & black skull on each side, chrome engine & int., lightly tinted canopy, alw-pr5	$2
☐	📷	101	Rigor Motor	a. silver met. flat black painted metal Malaysia base, black panel on top w/white, black & orange "Grave Rave" & HW logo, white & black skull tampos along side top, black & orange swirls on lower sides, chrome int., engine & front fuel tank, black plastic headlights, orange-tint canopy, 5sp	$3
☐				b. same as (a), semi-gloss painted Malaysia base, 5sp	$2
☐	📷			c. same as (a), gloss black painted Malaysia base, 5sp	$15

	Photo	No.	Name	Description	Price
❑	📷	102	Grave Rave Wagon	a. flat black, chrome Thailand base, four white & black oval skulls w/blue outline on hood, side has pale green, orange & blue tampo w/blue, white & black Reaper, white "Grave Rave" outlined in orange, pale green & black HW logo outlined in white & blue above Grave Rave, one white & black skull oval on far left, one white & black oval skull on far right, gray int. & rear doors, orange-tinted window, asw-5sp	$5
❑	📷			b. same as (a), chrome Malaysia base, more yellow & blue in side tampo, 5sp	$2

Grave Rave Series, Evil Twin

Grave Rave Series, Rigor Motor

Grave Rave Series, Evil Twin

Grave Rave Series, Grave Rave Wagon

Grave Rave Series, Krazy 8s

Grave Rave Series, Rigor Motor

Grave Rave Series, Grave Rave Wagon

Red Lines Series

	Photo	No.	Name	Description	Price
❑	📷	103	The Demon	silver met. blue-tint metal "Vintage" Malaysia base, black panel on roof & nose w/orange pinstriping, white & orange HW logo & "Redlines" on roof, chrome engine, white int., tinted windshield, redline 5sp	$2
❑	📷	104	'32 Ford Vicky	purple met. metal Malaysia base, light purple pearl tampo on side w/black & silver pinstriping, roof has white & pearl purple HW logo over black w/silver outline, silver & black "Redlines" outlined in pearl purple all over a black panel outlined in pearl purple, blue-tint metal engine, white int., clear window, redline 5sp	$3
❑	📷	105	Side Kick	light candy blue met. chrome Malaysia base, black panel outlined in white on roof & left side of hood, white & red over silver HW logo & "Redline" across front, blue-tint engines & seat, black plastic rear exhaust, blue-tint window, alw-redline 5sp	$2
❑	📷	106	Chevy Nomad	a. orange enamel, metal Malaysia base, hood has two wide white stripes w/ a thin white stripe on each outer side, thick & thin white stripe on upper body line from light to light, white, orange & black HW logo & "Redlines" on door, white "Heralda Engineering" on rear side window, black int., smoked window, redline 5sp	$2
❑				b. same as (a), no origin base	$7
❑				c. same as (a), no tampo in side window. These were said to be found in the 3-packs at K-B Toys	$10

Non-Series Collector Number Packs

Photo	No.	Name	Description	Price
☐ 📷	115	Honda Civic	black enamel, black plastic Malaysia base, white, green & yellow tampo on hood w/yellow & green "Hot Wheels," green & yellow tampo on side w/yellow & green "Hot Wheels" over rear fender, white "Honda" & "W" tampo high on front fender behind wheel, white int., green-tint window, asw-5dot	$2
☐ 📷	116	'71 Plymouth GTX	yellow enamel, chrome China base black panel on hood, black & white Plymouth emblem on nose, black int., smoked window, 5sp	$2
☐ 📷	117	'67 Dodge Charger	a. light mustard pearl met. chrome Malaysia base, black over dark red tampo outlined in black on hood, dark red tampo w/black outline on front fender & door, black-over-orange tampo outlined in black on rear quarter panel, white & black-over-red HW logo on front of hood by grille, small black "J P McClone" on top of rear fender below side rear window, black int., smoked window, asw-3sp	$8
☐ 📷			b. dark mustard pearl met. chrome Malaysia base, very dark red & black side & hood tampos, black over darker red tampo outlined in black on hood, darker red tampo w/black outline on front fender & door, black-over-orange tampo outlined in black on rear quarter panel, white & black over red HW logo on front of hood by grille, small black "J P McClone" on top of rear fender below side rear window, black int., smoked window, asw-3sp	$7
☐ 📷			c. same as (a), light mustard pearl met., chrome Malaysia base, silver over black "Charger" emblem on rear pillar above rear wheel, asw-3sp	$5
☐ 📷			d. same as (b), dark mustard pearl met. very dark red side & hood tampos, silver-over-black "Charger" emblem on rear pillar above rear wheel, asw-3sp	$4
☐ 📷			e. mustard pearl met., chrome Thailand base, brown w/black outline tampo on hood & side, white & black over red HW logo on nose, small black "J P McClone" on top of rear fender below side rear window, silver "Charger" emblem (no black background) on rear roof pillar, black int., smoked window, asw-3sp	$3
☐ 📷	118	Mercedes CLK-LM	met. burgundy, black plastic China base, black HW logo on nose, black plastic rear window & int., smoked window, asw-bbs	$2

Honda Civic

'67 Dodge Charger

'71 Plymouth GTX

'67 Dodge Charger

'67 Dodge Charger

'67 Dodge Charger

'67 Dodge Charger

Mercedes CLK-LM

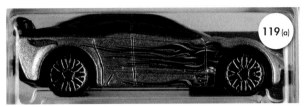

Pontiac Rageous

Shock Factor

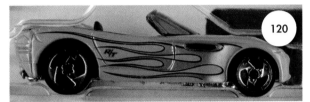

Dodge Concept Car

Deora

Shock Factor

Evil Twin

	Photo	No.	Name	Description	Price
☐	📷	119	Pontiac Rageous	a. "PONTIAC" misspelled on card, spelled as "PAONTIAC" on Race & Win Card, silver met., black plastic Malaysia base, long black flame tampo w/white highlights & orange outline on side, orange & black HW logo high on rear fender behind wheel, gray int., smoked canopy w/unpainted roof, alw-bbs	$5
☐				b. same as (a), "Pontiac" spelled correctly on Race & Win Card	$2
☐	📷	120	Dodge Concept Car	candy lime pearl, metal China base, silver flames outlined in black on side w/small black over silver "R/T" in front of rear wheel, silver negative flame tampo outlined in black of rear deck, no HW logo, black int., slightly-tinted window, 3sp	$2
☐	📷	121	Shock Factor	a. day-glo yellow metal top, black plastic side fuel tanks, scoop, engine cover & int., blue-tint metal Malaysia base, black-over-silver stripe on rear spoiler w/black, silver & gold flames, small black & gold tampo in front of scoop over driver, side pod has black "2" w/silver & gold outline & flames w/gold over black & silver HW logo, ct/b	$4
☐	📷			b. same as (a), or5	$2
☐		122	Deora	dark met. red, blue-tint metal Malaysia base, white, yellow & orange stripes on side w/black tampos, black lettering in front of front wheel above a black HW logo, black "Cawabunga" over rear wheel, little guy falling off surfboard in black behind rear tire, white plastic surfboards & int., clear window, asw-t/b	$2
☐	📷	123	Evil Twin	a. light yellow pearl, black plastic Malaysia base, chrome super chargers, exhaust, grille & front bumper, silver painted headlights & trim on rear fender skirt, orange painted taillights, light red HW logo on white rear plate, white int., smoked window, asw-gbbs	$20
☐	📷			b. same as (a), pearl mustard asw-gbbs	$15
☐	📷			c. same as (a), light gold met., asw-gbbs	$3
☐				d. same as (c), no painted taillights, no white box or HW logo, asw-gbbs	$15
☐	📷			e. same as (a), dark gold met., asw-gbbs	$5
☐	📷			f. dark caramel gold met., black plastic China base, red painted taillights, dark red HW logo in white on white rear plate, asw-gbbs	$5
☐	📷	124	Monoposto	a. red enamel, black plastic Malaysia base, gold, white, orange & dark blue tampo on top w/large dark blue to orange "Hot Wheels," silver painted headlights, white plastic int. & driver, blue-tint canopy, 3sp	$3

Photo	No.	Name	Description	Price
❑ 📷	124	Monoposto	b. red enamel, black plastic Thailand base, gold, orange, white & dark blue tampo on top, dark blue stripe on left by "H," smaller dark blue to orange "Hot Wheels" outlined in white, larger silver painted headlights, white plastic int., & driver, blue-tint canopy, pr5	$3
❑ 📷	125	Hyper Mite	a. dark candy purple met., black plastic Malaysia base, burnt orange enamel checked tampo w/ purple "2" w/white outline on side, white HW logo on rocker panel, gold-tint chrome engine, int., grille & headlights, blue tine metal exhaust, red-tint canopy, g5sp rear, old gold mini front	$20
❑ 📷			b. same as (a), new mini g5sp front wheel	$2
❑ 📷			c. same as (b), lighter candy purple met., lighter orange enamel checked tampo on side, g5sp rear, mini g5sp front	$3
❑ 📷			d. same as (a), black plastic Thailand base, orange enamel checked tampo & orange HW logo on rocker panel, g5sp rear, mini g5sp front	$5

Evil Twin

Evil Twin

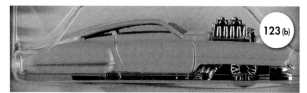

Evil Twin

Evil Twin

Monoposto

Monoposto

Hyper Mite

Hyper Mite

125 (c)

Hyper Mite

125 (e)

Hyper Mite

125 (d)

Hyper Mite

126 (a)

Surf Crate

126 (b)

Surf Crate

	Photo	No.	Name	Description	Price
☐	📷	125	Hyper Mite	e. same as (d), black plastic Thailand base, darker gold chrome, white HW logo on rocker panel, g5sp rear, mini g5sp front	$4
☐	📷	126	Surf Crate	a. red enamel, dark gold met. painted metal no origin base, gold chrome engine, white plastic surfboard in rear window, yellow, red, orange & white Sun tampo on roof w/orange & yellow over black HW logo, white, yellow & red flames outlined in orange on side, yellow "Curly" below side window, black int., g5sp	$2
☐	📷			b. same as (a), dark gold chrome engine	$3
☐	📷	127	Fore Wheeler	candy gold met. metal China base, white int., green plastic top w/gold & white flames & white w/gold outline "Caliente," white & orange HW logo on front w/white "La Paz" outlined in orange & white "Resort," chrome rear engine, g5sp	$2
☐	📷	128	Tow Jam	flat black, chrome Malaysia base, white "speed," orange "tow" & large orange, white & black "H&Y" on hood, white "speed," orange "tow," gray "service" & large orange, white & black "H" on door, roof has large white & orange over black HW logo on silver panel, metal boom w/gray plastic tow sling, silver painted windows, 3sp	$3

Photo	No.	Name	Description	Price
☐ 📷	129	Sweet 16	pearl white, blue-tint metal Malaysia base & engine, black tampo w/gold outline on top of each fender, black painted spare tire cover outlined in gold w/gold center, gold "Sweet Sixteen" on side, gold int., bbs	$2
☐ 📷	130	Porsche 911 Carrera	a. dark blue met. silver met. painted metal China base, red flames on side w/silver outline, red HW logo on rear fender behind wheel, black, yellow & red over silver Porsche emblem on nose, white int., tinted window, 3sp	$2
☐			b. same as (a), unpainted metal China base, 3sp	$4
☐ 📷	131	Thunderstreak	a. dark blue met. almost black, metal China base, large white & red HW logo on black plastic side pod, small red & white stripe above HW logo, one black stripe below, small silver & red stripe w/red "3" & "Racing" below HW logo, rear spoiler has thin white stripe, thin red stripe w/red-over-white "3" above a large red & white HW logo, silver, white & red stripe w/red "Racing" below HW logo, black plastic int. w/driver, bbs	$3
☐ 📷			b. lighter blue met., bbs	$3
☐ 📷			c. same as (b), two black pinstripes behind red "Racing" on side pod	$5
☐ 📷	132	Vulture Roadster	dark candy blue, transparent red plastic Thailand base & windshield, blue-tint metal exhaust over the roof, white w/red outline "VULTURE" on side above chrome injection, red, white & blue Vulture (bird) on side w/red & white flames, chrome seats w/transparent red inserts, 5sp	$2

Fore Wheeler

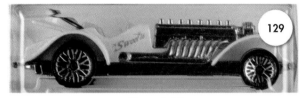

Tow Jam

Sweet 16

Porsche 911 Carrera

Thunderstreak

Thunderstreak

Thunderstreak

Vulture Roadster

Fright Bike

Old #3

Ferrari 348

Old #3

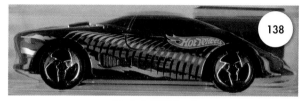

Buick Wildcat

Porsche 911 GT1-98

'67 Camaro

Chrysler Thunderbolt

'67 Camaro

	Photo	No.	Name	Description	Price
☐	📷	133	Fright Bike	red transparent plastic body w/old HW logo in rear fender, blue-tint metal Malaysia base & front forks, gray plastic wheelie bars w/new HW logo on side, black plastic front fairing, black spoke front & rear wheel w/chrome rim	$4
☐	📷	134	Old #3	a. light orange enamel, met. silver painted metal China base & seat, large black "3" on side in front of cockpit, black exhaust header & steering wheel, black radiator w/large white "3" on front, no HW logo, chrome spare wheel w/black tire on rear, alw-5sp	$2
☐	📷			b. same as (a), unpainted China base, alw-5sp	$4
☐	📷	135	Porsche 911 GT1-98	candy bronze met. black plastic Malaysia base, white, yellow, orange & black side tampo w/large "5" behind front wheel, yellow & orange-over-black HW logo in center of side, gray plastic rear wing & int., clear canopy & headlights, asw-bbs	$2
☐	📷	136	Chrysler Thunderbolt	dark red w/gold & silver flakes, black plastic Malaysia base, yellow to orange side tampo outlined in black w/large yellow "18" outlined in red in center of door, yellow "HOT WHEELS" outlined in black above rear wheel, small black tampo w/yellow letters above front wheel, sixteen misc. sponsor decals behind front wheel, small black tampo w/yellow lettering & four misc. sponsor decals in front of rear wheel, hood has yellow "Hot Wheels" outlined in red & black above a small black tampo w/yellow letters, red "18" outlined in yellow over a yellow to orange tampo, old HW logo embossed in rear window, black int., yellow-tint window w/transparent dark red top, asw-g5dot	$2
☐	📷	137	Ferrari 348	yellow enamel, black plastic Thailand base, yellow & black rectangle Ferrari emblem on nose w/red & green strip above, smoked window, black int., 3sp	$2
☐	📷	138	Buick Wildcat	candy purple met. black plastic China base, side has silver, black, white & light purple tampo w/white & light purple HW logo high behind front wheel, chrome rear engine, black canopy, alw-3sp	$2
☐	📷	139	'67 Camaro	a. dull met. blue, black painted metal China base, black hood w/large white & red HW logo w/red-over-silver "Racing" red w/silver outline "1" & white & silver fade to red striping, side has large white & red HW logo w/white, silver & red-over-black, red "Racing" w/silver outline above exhaust, red "1" w/silver outline behind rear tire, gray int., clear window, 3sp	$4

	Photo	No.	Name	Description	Price
☐	📷	139	'67 Camaro	b. same as (a), bright blue met. 3sp	$3
☐	📷	140	XS-IVE	a. glow in the dark looking white plastic body, blue-tint metal Malaysia base, black panel on side of door w/gold door handle & white & black over dark red HW logo, two black panels on hood w/thin black line between & a small red dot at the nose, right panel has red over white flame, left panel has gold star, white "WSMR" & gold "C33," rear half has white panel on side at top w/black "WSMR," red dot & black star, long white stripe on body line w/small black "MISSILE RANGE" & larger "ATEC," black panel on lower half w/gold "LC33," gold chrome rear engine, black plastic grille guard & bars going to headlights on cab roof, black int., yellow-tint window, large front & rear gct/b, small middle gct/b	$4
☐	📷			b. same as (a), chrome replaces gold chrome in wheels, large front & rear ct/b, small middle ct/b	$3
☐	📷			c. same as (a), large front & rear g/or5, small middle g/or5	$2
☐	📷	141	Ferrari 156	red enamel, metal Malaysia base, large white "36" on side & nose, three silver dots around yellow & black rectangle Ferrari emblem on nose, yellow & black triangle Ferrari emblem on top behind each front wheel, five silver dots half way around gas cap on nose, silver HW logo on side behind rear wheel, two clear small scoops & two clear bubbles over rear gray plastic engine, metal int., gray plastic roll bar, clear windshield, bbs	$2

XS-IVE

XS-IVE

XS-IVE

Ferrari 156

Ford Thunderbolt

Ford Thunderbolt

Ford Thunderbolt

Anglia Panel

143 (b)

Anglia Panel

145 (a)

Whatta Drag

143 (c)

Anglia Panel

145 (b)

Whatta Drag

144

Jeepster

146

Dogfighter

	Photo	No.	Name	Description	Price
❏	📷	142	Ford Thunderbolt	a. dark red w/gold & silver flakes, chrome Malaysia base, silver "Hugh Riehlman" on upper door, silver & gold "Robert FORD" on lower door w/silver "Homer" below, silver "Engine by" & gold "Kermit" on upper front fender, silver 427 Ford Emblem on lower fender behind wheel, small gold "crew" & silver "Judy-Pat-Ruth" in front of rear wheel, silver early FORD emblem on rear post above rear wheel, silver & gold "Thunderbolt" above rear wheel high on fender, gold & white HW logo on lower fender behind rear wheel, silver painted center body molding on side from front to rear w/silver painted molding behind door, white int., smoked window, 5sp	$2
❏	📷			b. same as (a), alw-5sp	$15
❏	📷			c. same as (a), 3sp	$5
❏	📷	143	Anglia Panel	a. silver/blue met. black plastic China base, flat black panel on roof w/large red "2" over silver & silver "Hot Wheels Racing," side has large white & red HW logo over white & silver, over black w/red outline & silver "Racing," red "2" w/silver outline & black stripes w/red outline behind side window, three sponsor decals behind rear wheel, black, silver & red stripe below "Racing," white & red "Carrie" on door below window, gray int., clear window, 5sp	$4
❏	📷			b. same as (a), light candy blue met. black plastic China base, 5sp	$3
❏	📷			c. same as (a), dark candy blue met. black plastic Thailand base, smaller "2" on side & all red colors are lighter, 5sp	$2
❏	📷	144	Jeepster	yellow enamel, gray plastic fenders & bumpers, metal Malaysia base, side has black panel w/red pinstripe at top w/large white & black HW logo over red w/gray outline, small black panel on top of rear quarter w/small white "Jeepster" & white "02" w/red outline, black panel on hood w/a thick gray stripe on each side w/red outlines, small white "TEAM," white "Hot Wheels" w/red outline in a black oval w/red & white outline & white "02" w/red outline, black panel behind rear seat w/white "02" & red outline & small white "TEAM" facing rear, black oval on trunk w/white "Hot Wheels" & red outline, gray int., smoked window, alw-5sp	$2

	Photo	No.	Name	Description	Price
☐	📷	145	Whatta Drag	a. pearl mustard, metal Malaysia base, silver over black tampo on nose w/black & silver "12" on right, black HW logo & white "Riehlman Headers" in red & black tampo on left, roof has a black panel w/orange stripe & yellow fade on right, large black & silver HW logo w/red outline on left, chrome int., rear engine, swingarm & wing, gray plastic scoops on top of engine, clear window, one large rear slick w/chrome ring, small front 5sp	$2
☐	📷			b. same as (a), 3sp	$4
☐	📷	146	Dogfighter	flat black, black plastic China base, red, yellow & white tampo w/red & yellow flame tampo on side of fuselage, yellow & red HW logo w/yellow & red pinstripes on tail, yellow & red pinstripe design on top of engine shroud, chrome engine, int. & suspension, red plastic prop, g3sp	$2
☐	📷	147	'65 Mustang	met. silver, metal Thailand base, black w/dark blue tampo on side w/white & black HW logo outlined in red behind rear wheel, white circle on door w/black "4," white int., tinted windshield, asw-5sp	$2
☐	📷	148	Porsche 959	red enamel, metal Thailand base, yellow & orange fade tampo outlined in black on hood & roof, yellow, red & black Porsche emblem on nose, large yellow & black over orange HW logo on door, yellow fade to orange "Twinn Turbo" outlined in black facing rear on rear spoiler, white int., smoked window, asw-5sp	$2
☐	📷	149	Jet Threat 3.0	a. silver blue pearl w/matching metal Thailand base, "Jet Threat 3.0" below "Thailand" on lower wing, silver "DC-121" w/small orange & black tampo on each side of upper center wing, small silver & black square tampo w/orange "Step Back" on lower part of center wing, chrome int., wing tips, flaps, rear exhaust & front backing plates, smoked canopy, small black-over-silver HW logo on wing behind front left wheel, 5dot	$3
☐				b. same as (a), slightly darker painted metal Thailand base w/"© 2000 Mattel Inc." above Thailand & "Jet Threat 3.0" on upper wing, 5dot	$2
☐	📷	150	Mega-Duty	a. orange enamel, black plastic fenders & bumpers, blue-tint metal Malaysia base, black tampo w/white outline on hood w/black dots & white over black HW logo on nose, black window & rear bed floor, alw-pr5	$4
☐	📷			b. same as (a), alw-3sp	$2

'65 Mustang

Porsche 959

Jet Threat 3.0

Mega-Duty

Mega-Duty

Toyota Celica

152

Silhouette II

153 (a)

Sol-Aire CX4

153 (b)

Sol-Aire CX4

154

Olds 442

155

T-Bird Stocker

156 (a)

Cunningham C4R

156 (b)

Cunningham C4R

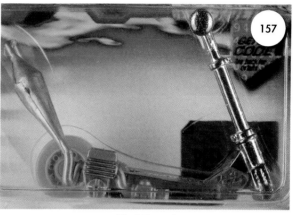

157

Mo' Scoot

158

Fandango

159

Thomassima III

160 (a)

Pikes Peak Celica

160 (b)

Pikes Peak Celica

161

M Roadster

	Photo	No.	Name	Description	Price
☐	📷	151	Toyota Celica	purple met. purple plastic rear wing, gray plastic Malaysia base, yellow w/black outline "RHLman," black w/yellow outline "TURBO" on side w/six misc. yellow & black racing sponsors on right side of door, yellow HW logo above rear wheel, white int., yellow-tint window & headlights, asw-bbs	$2
☐	📷	152	Silhouette II	candy lime, chrome Thailand base, white, black & orange tampo on side, white HW logo high behind rear wheel, chrome engine, white int., smoked canopy, 3sp	$2
☐	📷	153	Sol-Aire CX4	a. dark met. blue, gray plastic Malaysia base, white, black & orange tampo over black panel on side, blue met. panel on side w/dark blue rectangles, orange & black over white HW logo behind rear wheel, gray int., clear canopy, 3sp	$4
☐	📷			b. same as (a), light blue enamel panel on side w/dark blue rectangles, 3sp	$2
☐	📷	154	Olds 442	dark red w/silver & gold flakes, chrome Malaysia base, gray & black stripe tampo on side from front to rear w/white dots from rear to front fender behind wheel, silver painted door handle & large black "442" w/white outline on door, black & white HW logo high on front fender behind wheel, black "DJ" w/white outline, white pinstripe between black "Custom" & "Color" below window, smoked window, black int., asw-3sp	$2
☐	📷	155	T-Bird Stocker	met. blue, black plastic China base, side has large white & red HW logo over white & silver, over black w/red outline & silver "Racing," red "4" w/silver outline behind rear wheels, red & silver pinstripes behind side window, white "Weise" & "Heralda" oval tampos w/red & white "Racing" on rocker panel, white & black "Handy" tampo high behind front wheel, white "Miller Gauges" & "Proch" on front bumper in front of wheel, hood has black panel w/large red "4" over silver & silver "Hot Wheels" & small red "Racing," white & black "Handy" on nose, & white "Heralda" oval, "Proch," "Miller Gauges" & "Weise" on left side, gray int., clear window, asw-5sp	$2
☐	📷	156	Cunningham C4R	a. dark blue met., black plastic Malaysia base, two thick white enamel stripes down the center from nose to tail, white-over-blue HW logo in stripe on rear, black int., clear windshield, alw-5sp	$2
☐	📷			b. same as (a), lighter blue met., black plastic China base, alw-5sp	$2
☐	📷	157	Mo' Scoot	transparent light blue plastic body, metal Malaysia base & handlebars, orange transparent wheels, gray plastic engine, silver painted foot board w/large white & black HW logo	$2
☐	📷	158	Fandango	yellow enamel, black plastic Malaysia base, black, red & orange tampo on side w/silver pinstripes, large silver & black over orange HW logo above rear wheel, black int., front, side & rear grille inserts, smoked window, gpr5	$2
☐	📷	159	Thomassima III	teal met. chrome China base, small silver "Thomassima III" on lower door, silver HW logo in front of rear wheel, black int., clear window, pr5	$2
☐	📷	160	Pikes Peak Celica	a. very dark blue met. black plastic Thailand base, gray plastic front air dam, rear wing & int., black panel on roof w/red & silver "5," silver "Hot Wheels Racing," & three white sponsor decals, large dark red & white HW logo over black w/brown outline on side, brown & silver "5" on rear fender behind rear wheel, three white sponsor decals & silver "Racing" above HW logo on door, dark smoked window, asw-bbs	$2
☐	📷			b. same as (a), blue met. asw-bbs	$3
☐	📷	161	M Roadster	Champagne met. black painted metal Malaysia base & headlights, black HW logo on trunk by knob, black int., smoked window, asw-5dot	$2

Ferrari F512M

Ferrari F355 Spider

Lexus SC400

'57 T-Bird

Ferrari 308

Speed Blaster

Speed Blaster

Rodzilla

Enforcer

	Photo	No.	Name	Description	Price
❑	📷	162	Ferrari F512M	dark gray met. black painted metal Malaysia base, rectangle yellow & black Ferrari emblem on nose w/red & green strip above, black HW logo on rear plate, black int., clear window, 5sp	$2
❑	📷	163	Lexus SC400	met. gold, black plastic Malaysia base, side has maroon & black tampo in black panel w/silver outline, thin black stripe w/silver outline right above rocker panel, trunk has red tampos in two black panels w/silver outline, silver & red "Wicked & Low" across lower part of panels, silver & black HW logo on upper part of panels, white int., smoked window, asw-gbbs	$2
❑	📷	164	Ferrari F355 Spider	dull met. blue, black painted metal China base, yellow & black Ferrari rectangle on nose, white & red HW logo on rear deck behind seat, black int., smoked windshield, asw-5sp	$2
❑	📷	165	'57 T-Bird	dark blue met. chrome Malaysia base, black panel on roof w/four white sponsor decals, large silver "Hot Wheels," small red & white "Racing" & red & silver "7," red & silver "7" on side roof pillar (no porthole), four white sponsor decals behind rear wheel, large red & white HW logo on side over black w/red outline flames, silver "Racing" high on front fender behind wheel, blue-tint window & int., 5sp	$2
❑	📷	166	Ferrari 308	black enamel, black painted metal Malaysia base, yellow outlined "308" & red "turbo" on door, yellow & black rectangle Ferrari emblem w/red & white stripe on nose, white & black HW logo on rear fender behind wheel, black int., smoked window, bbs	$2
❑	📷	167	Rodzilla	plastic teal body & head, matching teal painted metal China base, white teeth & eyes, chrome engine, black HW logo on right rear arm, t/b	$2
❑	📷	168	Speed Blaster	a. candy blue met. chrome Malaysia base, window & rear engine, black hood w/silver "Hot Wheels," white & red "Racing," large dark red "6" w/silver outline on right, white "Heralda" oval, "Sheddon," "Miklo," & "Proch" on left side, silver painted headlights, side has large white & red HW logo w/black outline over red & black tampo, silver & black "Racing" high behind front wheel, dark red "6" w/silver & black outline on pillar behind side window, white "Heralda" oval, "Sheddon," "Proch" & "Miklo" above rocker panel, chrome window & rear engine, 3sp	$8
❑	📷			b. same as (a), brown replaces red in all tampos, 3sp	$3
❑	📷	169	Enforcer	a. met. gold, unpainted China base, black plastic guns on each side, black front & rear windows, white, black & red flames on the side, black panel w/red "e" at rear & white, black & red HW logo over rear wheel, black painted side window w/red, silver & white tampo, black-over-white "Enforcer" twice on front w/black, red & white tampo down the center, extra large rear 5sp, large 5sp front	$2
❑	📷			b. same as (a), silver met. painted China base	$4

	Photo	No.	Name	Description	Price
❏	📷	170	Splittin' Image	candy lime/gold met. metal "Vintage" Malaysia base, chrome engine, white int., blue-tint canopies, black HW logo in left front above headlight door, 5sp	$2
❏	📷	171	Oshkosh Snowplow	a. pearl light yellow met. painted metal hood, int. & fenders, gray plastic Thailand base, gray plastic cab & box, black panel at top of box side w/white "Hannah Plow & Scrape" orange, white & black tampo on door w/white "H" in black circle, black tampo on hood w/white outline & orange & black HW logo facing front, alw-ct/b	$5
❏	📷			b. same as (a), alw-or5	$3
❏	📷			c. same as (a), mustard yellow pearl met., gray plastic Malaysia base, lighter orange in door tampo, alw-or5	$3
❏	📷	172	Ferrari F355	silver met., metal Malaysia base, yellow & black rectangle Ferrari emblem on nose w/red & green stripe above, black HW logo on rear plate, black int., clear window, asw-5sp	$2
❏	📷	173	'70 Plymouth Barracuda	a. red enamel, chrome Malaysia base, black "Hemi" Hockey Stick side stripping, silver painted door handle & wheel well opening moldings, silver "hemi 'cuda" on front fender, light red plastic int. & "Shaker" hood scoop, tinted window, asw-5sp	$5
❏	📷			b. same as (a), gray replaces silver paint, gray painted door handle, wheelwell opening moldings, & "hemi 'cuda" on front fender, light red plastic int., asw-5sp	$5
❏				c. same as (a), dark red plastic int. asw-5sp	$5

Enforcer

Splittin' Image

Oshkosh Snowplow

Oshkosh Snowplow

Oshkosh Snowplow

Ferrari F355

'70 Plymouth Barracuda

'70 Plymouth Barracuda

Dodge Viper GTS-R

Dodge Viper GTS-R

1996 Chevy 1500

Auburn 852

Mustang Mach I

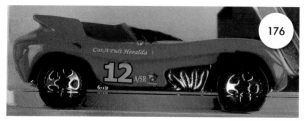

Cat-A-Pult

Mustang Mach I

'95 Camaro

Shoe Box

Photo	No.	Name	Description	Price
❑ 📷	174	Dodge Viper GTS-R	a. silver-tint champagne met. black plastic China base, two black stripes on hood & roof, small champagne & black HW logo on pass side of roof facing rear, black int., clear window, 5sp	$2
❑ 📷			b. same as (a), gold-tint champagne met. paint	$2
❑ 📷	175	Auburn 852	met. silver w/maroon plastic fenders, metal Malaysia base, maroon panels on hood & trunk w/silver & black pinstripes, black panel behind seat w/silver HW logo facing rear, chrome headlights, grille & steering wheel, maroon int., clear windshield, asw-bbs	$2
❑ 📷	176	Cat-A-Pult	red enamel, metal Malaysia base, wide white enamel stripe on hood, white w/black outline "12," white, gold & black tampo w/white "Vintage" & white A/SR at right of stripe, silver painted headlights & mirror, white "Cat-A-Pult Heralda" on side by cockpit, white w/black outline "12," white, gold & black tampo w/white "Vintage" & white A/SR on side, no HW logo, black int., smoked windshield, asw-5sp	$2
❑ 📷	177	'95 Camaro	white pearl met. black plastic Malaysia base, three red stripes & blue stars on hood, two red stripes & silver stars on side, white & red HW logo outlined in blue facing rear on rear spoiler, black int., smoked windshield, alw-5sp	$2
❑ 📷	178	1996 Chevy 1500	orange plastic body, metal Malaysia base, gray & black barbed wire tampo on side w/the lower half painted black w/gray outlined "BARB'd & WIRED," black painted panel on hood w/gray & black barbed wire on both sides, gray & black HW logo on nose, black plastic grille, int. & rear bed cover, clear window, asw-pr5	$2
❑ 📷	179	Mustang Mach I	a. black enamel, black plastic Malaysia base, white panel on roof w/small black "Bermudez County" w/gold star on each side, large "Police" w/gold outline, red, white & black HW logo & black "3280," door has white panel w/small black "Bermudez County" w/gold star on each side & large "Police" w/gold outline, gold-over-white "3280" on front fender, white-over-dark-red "LOOKN4SPDRS" on rear fender above rear wheel, gray rear louvers, spoiler, int., grille, hood scoop & tach, tinted window, 5sp	$3
❑			b. same as (a), dark red replaces red in HW logo on roof	$5

	Photo	No.	Name	Description	Price
❑	📷	179	Mustang Mach I	c. same as (a), "Burmudez" replaces "Bermudez" on roof & side tampo	$7
❑				d. same as (a), "Burmudez" on door "Bermudez" on roof	$51
❑	📷	180	Shoe Box	flat black, black plastic Malaysia base, narrow yellow, green & black flames on side from front to rear ending w/yellow, black & green HW logo, gray spider webs coming from front & rear fenderwells, gray spider web on hood w/yellow & green "Ghost Rider" at nose, chrome int., engine, grille & bumper, clear window, 5sp	$2
❑	📷	181	'79 Ford	white enamel, chrome Malaysia base & grille, gray plastic bed cap & tailgate, purple, silver & black side tampo, w/black Hawk head, "02" outlined in black w/purple through the center behind rear wheel, black outlined "Black Hawk Messengers" on door, black "wannaB racecardrivers" above front wheel on hood side, silver & black HW logo on hood w/black outlined "Black Hawk Messengers," black Hawk head, black "wannaB racecardrivers" & black outlined "02" w/purple through the center, dark purple-tinted window, alw-5sp	$3
❑	📷	182	Morris Wagon	met. green, metal China base, tan wood panel rear w/gloss black top, no HW logo, chrome engine & int., clear window, 5sp	$2
❑	📷	183	Montezooma	candy purple met., gold-tint chrome China base & grille, orange & gold panel tampo on hood, orange & gold stripe tampo on sides, black, orange & gold HW logo behind rear wheel, gold int., tinted window, asw-gbbs	$2
❑	📷	184	Ford Focus	a. white enamel, black plastic Malaysia base & rear wing, yellow, orange & black tampo on hood w/white, black, orange & yellow HW logo up by windshield, black painted headlights, black, dark orange & yellow tampo on side w/white "H&Y," dark orange "HW" & white "Motorsports," "J. Handy" in script at top of door, light & dark orange w/yellow tampo on roof w/black "H&Y," black triangle w/dark orange "HW" & "J. Handy" in script, & white "Motorsports," yellow-tint window, gray int., asw-5dot	$3
❑	📷			b. same as (a), clear window, asw-5dot	$20
❑	📷			c. same as (a), red replaces dark orange in side tampos	$5

'79 Ford

Ford Focus

Morris Wagon

Ford Focus

Montezooma

Ford Focus

'40s Woodie

Wheel Loader

Wheel Loader

Corvette Stingray III

Slideout

Express Lane

Pontiac Firebird

Photo	No.	Name	Description	Price
▢ 📷	185	'40s Woodie	black enamel metal fenders & hood, tan plastic wood grain body, metal Malaysia base, black painted roof w/"BEKAH CUSTOM" & brown, tan, black & white tampo, white "California Classics Established 1975" on side of hood, chrome engine & grille, black int. & rear tire cover, clear window, bbs	$3
▢ 📷	186	Wheel Loader	a. dark candy red met. black plastic China base, engine cover, cab & shovel, red, orange & yellow fade flames on cab to engine cover, red & black over white HW logo on cab side, red "527 Construction" at right of HW logo, red, orange & yellow fade flames on cab roof w/white & black "Hot Wheels" across at an angle, gray plastic seat, engine & rear radiator, alw-or5	$3
▢ 📷			b. same as (a), shovel bucket is on backwards. The teeth are up & the fence is down.	$7
▢ 📷	187	Corvette Stingray III	white enamel, black plastic Malaysia base, dark blue field w/white stars, red & black stripes on hood, white & red HW logo across hood, blue field w/white stars & red stripes w/black outline on side, gray & blue HW logo w/red outline across top stripe on side by windshield, black int., blue-tint windshield, 3sp	$2
▢ 📷	188	Slideout	green enamel, black plastic Malaysia base, rear pushbar, front & top wing, white to green fade flames on side of top wing w/white & green fade "77" w/black outline, green to white fade flames on top of top wing w/white & green HW logo facing rear, white & green fade "77" on front wing w/black outline, 5sp	$2

Photo		No.	Name	Description	Price
❑	📷	189	Express Lane	bright green plastic body, metal China base, engine & handle, green & black "Gator bait Market" over white panel w/gold & black outline on side, black plastic seat & steering wheel, white HW logo at rear, 5sp	$2
❑	📷	190	Pontiac Firebird	silver blue met. black plastic "1997 M.I." base, hood has black panel w/white stripe on each side, silver & black checks & red & black curls, red & black "handy racing," white "1" red, black & white HW logo, side has red & black "handy racing" w/silver & black checks on door going up to the front fender, black & white stripe down the side, red & black HW logo, "Prooch" & "Carris" decals on rear fender, white "Good Year & "Weise" on rocker panel, Champion decal above white stripe on front fender, red & black curl tampo above Champion, small white decal on front spoiler in front of wheel, white, red & black curl at front of tampo on front fender, black int., clear window, alw-5sp	$2
❑	📷	191	'56 Ford	flat black, red plastic China base, red & silver pinstriping on roof & hood, no HW logo, chrome engine & int., clear window, 5sp	$3
❑	📷	192	Nomadder What	candy lime met. black plastic Malaysia base, black w/silver tampo on side, silver HW logo on rocker panel in front of rear wheel, chrome int., front bumper & headlights, rear lights & drive line, smoked window, pr5	$2

'56 Ford

Nomadder What

Cabbin' Fever

Altered State

Altered State

Flashfire

Lamborghini Diablo

Scorchin' Scooter

Go Kart

Mini Cooper

Turbolence

Mini Cooper

Mini Cooper

Mini Cooper

	Photo	No.	Name	Description	Price
☐	📷	193	Cabbin' Fever	dark blue met. black plastic China base grille & ramp, old HW logo embossed at rear between taillights, red & white over silver HW logo w/silver over black "Racing" on cab side, red "8" outlined in silver over black & three white sponsor names below HW logo, all over a black flame tampo w/red outline, two silver sponsor names, large red & white HW logo outlined in silver w/white over red "Racing," red "8" outlined in silver & silver "Jinnco" on top of ramp over cab, black int., blue-tint window & rear bed, extra large rear pr5, large middle & front pr5	$3
☐	📷	194	Altered State	a. pearl yellow met. metal Malaysia base, blue enamel strip tampo on cowl down around cove over rear wheel, gold, white & black "Rat Trap" in cove w/two black & white rats, small gold lettering above Rat Trap, blue, gold & white HW logo facing driver between opening & blue stripe, black rollcage & seat, blue-tint metal engine, 5sp	$4
☐	📷			b. same as (a), pearl mustard met. 5sp	$2
☐	📷	195	Flashfire	white enamel, matching white plastic Malaysia base, black plastic rear wing, side insert, rear exhaust & int., gloss black panel on top of body w/orange pinstripe from front to rear, silver dots on hood & rear deck, orange over white "Sanders" & white over orange "S" on nose, orange pinstripe on front fender body line, orange pinstripe & black semi-gloss stripe tampo on side from front to rear, black dots behind front wheel & over rear wheel, black semi-gloss tampo w/orange stripe below black dots behind rear wheel, orange & black HW logo outlined in white in black stripe on front fender high behind wheel, smoked canopy, chrome engine, Y5	$2
☐	📷	196	Lamborghini Countach	candy tangerine met. black plastic Malaysia base, gray "Lamborghini" across hood, small black & gold emblem on nose, gold over silver rectangle w/black over silver "1" above the "L" in Lamborghini, "Lamborghini" on side w/silver & gold HW logo at left, gold-over-silver rectangle w/black over silver "1" low behind front wheel, black int., clear window, asw-5sp	$2

Photo	No.	Name	Description	Price
☐ 📷	197	Scorchin' Scooter	met. gold, blue-tint engine, black plastic forks, black flames on gas tank down to top & sides or rear fender, black painted seat, black circle on rear fender w/white skull & white "Hot Wheels," "MC" & "El Segundo, CA," black three spoke wheel w/chrome rim	$4
☐ 📷	198	Go Kart	yellow enamel Malaysia body, metal engine & chassis, white & blue HW logo outlined in silver & white outline "1" on side pod over a black & white tampo, black, white & silver tampo on nose w/white & gold "Brandon Racing," blue plastic seat, 5sp rear–mini 5sp front	$4
☐ 📷	199	Turbolence	a. light candy blue, blue-tint metal Malaysia base, white tampo w/black outline on top front half, black "68" w/silver shadowing on front, seven small silver circles outlined in black on nose & three on each side behind the fender humps, large white over black "68" behind rear wheel, white "XXO/F9," silver & black HW logo, white & black "WAYNCO, black & silver Carris," silver & black "JINNCO" & white & black "McCLONE" on side, chrome engine, int., gas filler & scoops, alw-3sp	$2
☐			b. same as (a), "68" on front is silver shadowed w/black outline, "68" on rear fender is white w/silver outline over black	$15
☐ 📷	200	Mini Cooper	a. dark green enamel, metal Malaysia base, white painted roof w/black fade checks, red & yellow HW logo at rear of roof facing rear, bright yellow int., black plastic hood vent & dash, clear window, asw-bbs	$7
☐ 📷			b. same as (a), dull yellow roll cage, asw-bbs	$10
☐ 📷			c. dark green enamel, metal China base, red & yellow HW logo at rear of roof facing rear, dull yellow cage, black plastic hood vent & dash, clear window, asw-5sp	$5
☐ 📷			d. dark green enamel, metal Malaysia base, white painted roof w/black & white checks down the center w/two thick orange stripes on each side, same tampo on hood beginning at bottom of black hood vent, orange & yellow flames on side w/white & red HW logo, black & white "COLLECTORS," black & white dot & red & black "com," blue-tint window, green int., black dash, asw-5sp	$8
☐			e. same as (d), HWC logo, asw-bbs	$81
☐ 📷	201	Lotus Elise 340R	satin candy blue met. metal China base, black plastic side panels, front & rear spoiler & seats, silver painted headlights, small yellow & green emblem on nose, silver HW logo behind gas filler, gray int., clear window, Y5	$3

Lotus Elise 340R (201)

'40 Ford Coupe (204)

Midnight Otto (202)

1932 Bugatti Type 50 (205)

Honda Spocket (203)

Metrorail Nash Metropolitan (206)

Baja Bug

'59 Cadillac

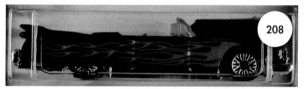

Jaguar D-Type

Dodge Sidewinder

Super Modified

Super Modified

Photo		No.	Name	Description	Price
❑	📷	202	Midnight Otto	purple met., metal China base, black panel outlined in gold on roof w/white fade to gray tampo, white, gold & black HW tampo facing rear at front of roof, black panel on side w/white fade to gray tampo, black window, pr5	$2
❑	📷	203	Honda Spocket	candy bronze met. fenders, rocker panels & bumpers, black plastic hood, cab & tailgate, black plastic Malaysia base, orange & silver painted taillights, silver & black HW on left top of tailgate, yellow "Spocket" on right top of tailgate, white int., smoked window, alw-pr5	$2
❑	📷	204	'40 Ford Coupe	flat black, chrome Malaysia base & grille, light yellow & purple fade flames w/white & purple outline on side, purple HW logo in front of rear wheel, pink int., yellow-tint window, 5sp	$4
❑	📷	205	1932 Bugatti Type 50	dark candy blue, black plastic fenders, trunk & two rear spare tires, metal Malaysia base, silver HW logo below rear side window w/light blue pinstriping in lower corner of body, chrome int., headlights & grille, clear window, alw-g5dot	$2
❑	📷	206	Metrorail Nash Metropolitan	met. silver, chrome China base, black, blue & white tampo on hood w/white Asian letters & "7175," black panel in center of hood w/white & black HW logo in center of white, blue & black over silver shield, blue panel on side of front fender w/ white "PURSUIT," dark blue w/black outline "7175" & black "Nash Metropolitan" on rear fender, four thick black angled stripes on door, black painted molding from front to rear, black painted rocker panel w/white Asian letters behind front wheel, chrome int. & engine, blue-tint window, 5sp	$3
❑	📷	207	Baja Bug	flat black, blue-tint metal Malaysia base, yellow to orange fade flames outlined in red on side, white square outlined in orange w/black & orange outlined "22" & white "E" tampo on side between rear fender & door, red int., red enamel 5sp	$2
❑	📷	208	'59 Cadillac	flat black, chrome Malaysia base, silver flames w/blue outline on side & hood, silver, black & blue HW logo on hood facing front, gray int., blue-tint windshield, asw-bbs	$2

Photo	No.	Name	Description	Price
☐ 📷	209	Jaguar D-Type	candy purple w/matching painted metal China base, wide black stripe on right side w/thin orange stripe on each side of it, moon fazes from full to eclipsed from one end of the stripe to the other. Rear fin has orange triangle w/white circle & black outline w/black "2" in the center, left side of hood has white & red over black HW logo, black & white over red "ECLIPSE," white "Racing" & a white circle outlined in orange w/a black "2" in the center, gray int. & exhaust, orange-tint windshield & headlights, alw-5dot	$2
☐ 📷	210	Dodge Sidewinder	met. blue, black plastic Malaysia base, large red & white HW logo on gray plastic bed cover, black panels w/white "Heralda," " Salas," "Thompson" & "Cano" on left, red & silver "9" on right, large red & white HW logo on side w/black flames outlined in red, smaller silver & black "Racing," "Heralda" emblem at top of door, white "Dodge" above front wheel, white "Salas," "Cano," & "Thompson" on rocker panel, red & silver "9" on rear fender behind wheel, gray int., clear window, pr5	$2
☐ 📷	211	Super Modified	a. dark blue met., blue-tint metal Malaysia base, large dark red, white, silver & black HW logo on nose, orange & silver "10" behind headers on side, white "Heralda" oval & "Racing" on side by cockpit, white "noah," "Weise" & "Handy" behind front wheel, gray plastic front & rear wings, rear push bar, seat & cage, bbs/2	$4
☐ 📷			b. same as (a), dark blue met., brown & silver "10" on side, bbs/2	$2
☐ 📷			c. same as (a), light blue met., bbs/2	$3
☐ 📷	212	Sweet 16 II	candy red, metal Malaysia base, black, yellow to orange fade flames on side w/black & yellow HW logo, orange-tint window, chrome engine & front drive, 5sp	$2
☐ 📷	213	Ferrari 456M	dark met. blue, black painted metal China base, yellow HW logo on rear of trunk, yellow & black rectangle Ferrari emblem w/red stripe at top on nose, light gray int., tinted window, asw-5sp	$2
☐ 📷	214	Overbored 454	a. candy tangerine met., black flake plastic Malaysia base, silver painted headlights, black S/S (Super Sport) stripes on roof & trunk, large black & gray HW logo on trunk facing rear, chrome engine & int., smoked window, pr5	$3

Super Modified

Sweet 16 II

Ferrari 456M

Overbored 454

Overbored 454

'68 Cougar

'68 Cougar

Corvette SR-2

Mustang Cobra

Mustang Cobra

Baby Boomer

Baby Boomer

Dodge Ram 1500

Ford F-150

Maelstrom

Dodge Caravan

	Photo	No.	Name	Description	Price
❏	📷	214	Overbored 454	b. rust met., black plastic China base, silver painted headlights, black S/S (Super Sport) stripes on roof & trunk, large black & silver HW logo on trunk facing rear, chrome engine & int., tinted window, pr5	$4
❏	📷	215	'68 Cougar	a. silver/blue met. chrome Malaysia base, flat black roof, black HW logo behind rear wheel, black int., clear window, thick asw-5sp	$3
❏	📷			b. same as (a), lighter color, more silver in the paint, chrome China base, thick asw-5sp	$2
❏				c. same as (b), China base, thin asw-5sp	$4
❏	📷	216	Corvette SR-2	silver/blue met., chrome Malaysia base & grille, silver cove, thick white stripe on hood onto cowl, silver & black Corvette emblem in stripe on nose, white circle w/black "2" on right of stripe half on nose, half on hood, black int., clear windshield, 5sp	$2
❏	📷	217	Mustang Cobra	a. candy purple met. black plastic China base, red, white & black tampo on side w/silver "Happy Birthday" outlined in red, small silver & red confetti tampos in the black part in side tampo, white "1 2 3" on lower rear bumper behind wheel, small red "4 5 6" high on rear fender behind wheel, red "7 8 9" on rocker panel, red "10" behind front wheel, white "11" on front fender above white "12" on front spoiler, gray int., red-tint window, asw-bbs	$4
❏	📷			b. candy purple met. black plastic China base, silver, black & red side tampo, silver & black HW logo high on rear fender behind wheel, gray int., red-tint window, asw-bbs	$2
❏	📷	218	Baby Boomer	a. baby blue enamel, silver met. painted China base, red & silver tampos on side w/silver "To" & red "Happy Birthday" outlined in silver over rear wheel, red & silver HW logo high in front of rear wheel, dark blue star below logo, white star above "Happy," some white & dark blue dots mixed in, gray plastic shifter, engine & front fuel tanks, 5sp	$4
❏	📷			b. dark candy blue met. silver met. painted metal China base, white & black zigzag tampo behind rear wheel, white & black "The Stork Express" in front of rear wheel, gray plastic scoop injectors, blower belts & shifter, chrome engine, fuel tanks & rear end, 5sp	$2

Photo	No.	Name	Description	Price
☐ 📷	219	Dodge Ram 1500	yellow enamel, black plastic China base, black, gold & red side tampo, door has black & red panel w/white "Maintenance Service" w/red & black shield w/white "HW Trans" & man w/hard hat, small white "Ram 1500" above Maintenance Service, box has small white "Radio Dispatched 24 Hrs. above rear wheel, black rectangle panel w/red dotted arrow, red "7" w/white outline, red & yellow HW logo high on rear of box, chrome bed liner, int., center line spacer & front & rear bumpers, blue-tint window, alw-3sp	$3
☐ 📷	220	Ford F-150	light purple enamel, black plastic Thailand base, chrome front & rear bumpers, int. & bed floor, emblem on hood has orange w/black outline, black panel & white "HW Trans" & white w/black outline guy wearing hardhat, same emblem on door, orange, black & silver tampo on side w/red "Radio Dispatched 24 Hrs." above rear wheel, orange w/white outline "1" in front of rear wheel, black panel w/silver "Maintenance Service" on rocker panel, orange-tint window, alw-3sp	$3

As of the summer of 2003, the following cars for the 2002 Main Line are hard to find in the collector number package. All of them were readily available in 5 packs, but for some reason, the "collector numbers " packaged cars (221-240) were pretty much only released in the "Factory Sealed Master Set." These cars were seldom found in stores. For this reason, their prices are higher than normal. Some people did break up their "Master Set" and either traded or auctioned them off. If you were able to find any of them in stores, consider yourself very lucky! You will notice that some of the cars that were released through stores have different bases than those released in the "Master Sets" including the #222 Ford GT-40. This car was found as 222 with a Thailand base and only in the "Master Set." It was not found in stores with that number or that base until late in the summer of 2003.

The "Ford GT-40" car was released in two different packages. Actually, it's the same package, with the number was changed with the addition of a sticker. The "Master Set" car is a Thailand base car and has a sticker over the printed collector number that has the number 222 on it. Then in the summer of 2003, the same car was being found with 222 printed on the package and with the Thailand base. The cars that were released as number 238 are the ones we all found in the stores with a China base. The Master Set also had the same Saltflat Racer as we found in stores as 238. That's why we have two cards with the number 238.

☐ 📷	221	Maelstrom	candy gray met., pink chrome Thailand base, black, blue, red & white octopus tampos on front & side, black & white HW logo on front, red-tint window, chrome int., pr5	$11
☐	222	Ford GT-40	silver-blue met. black plastic Thailand base, silver, blue, white & black octopus tentacle tampo on side, blue & black HW logo over white on rocker panel in front of rear wheel, gray int., blue-tint window, 5sp	$15
☐	223	SS Commodore (VT)	bright green enamel, black plastic Thailand base, white, green & black Hockey mask w/flames on hood, side has white & green flames & white "Hockey" over black panel w/black hockey puck w/green HW logo behind front fender, white & green "HWSL" logo on rear fender, black int., clear window, asw-bbs	$16
☐ 📷	224	Dodge Caravan	orange pearl met., gray Thailand plastic base, black, green & white Soccer ball side tampo w/white "Dodge," black HW logo above front wheel, tan int., clear window, alw-5sp	$10
☐ 📷	225	'57 Chevy	red enamel, met. gold metal engine coming through hood, gold chrome Thailand base, side has yellow stripes, black, gold, white & gray monster & woman w/black & gold HW logo on rear fender, roof has yellow & black "I Was a Teenage Freak from Outerspace!" w/a white rectangle w/"Rated HW" & a white & black HW logo, black int., smoked window, red 5sp	$35

'57 Chevy

Fiat 550C

227

Police Cruiser

228

Oldsmobile Aurora

229

Roll Patrol

230

Surf Patrol

231

Chevy Stocker

232

Jeep Jeepster

233

Hyper Mite

Photo	No.	Name	Description	Price
❏ 📷	226	Fiat 500C	candy lime green, blue-tint metal Thailand base, gold, black & white side tampo, white & black HW logo on lower door right above header collector, white, gold, green & black lettering on top of rear black plastic wing, gold chrome engine, front suspension, window & dash, metal seat, g5sp	$20
❏ 📷	227	Police Cruiser	dark blue met., gray plastic Malaysia base, side has white, red & gold tampo w/large white & red HW logo outlined in gold, white "Fire Chief" outlined in gold on door, white "No. 6" on rear fender above bumper, gray int., clear window, orange bar light on roof, orange headlights, asw-3sp	$3
❏ 📷	228	Oldsmobile Aurora	dark red met. white plastic Thailand base, white panel on roof w/orange, black & white flames, long black panel w/white outline at upper body line, "Unit 12" in white at rear, white & orange "Arson Investigator" on rear door, large white over orange & dark red HW logo outlined in white on front door, dark red flame cutout on front fender above wheel, long black panel outlined in white across bottom body line, white int., orange-tint window, asw-5dot	$3
❏ 📷	229	Roll Patrol	flat black, metal Thailand base, hood has red & orange flame tampo w/white & black HW logo, large white "5" outlined in bright orange, white oval w/red "Team" & bright orange "noah," "urban offroad" at left, side has white teeth w/red & brown mouth turning into brown flames, light brown "urban," white-over-red "Rat Race" & light brown "offroad" above rear wheel, tan int., orange-tint window, asw-or5	$16

Photo	No.	Name	Description	Price
📷	230	Surf Patrol	gold met., blue-tint metal Thailand base, hood has large white oval outlined in orange & blue w/black "Team Offroad" & orange "noah," white "2" outlined in blue & orange, white "surf 2 surf" outlined in blue & blue & white HW logo outlined in black & orange, side has large white oval outlined in orange & blue w/black "Team Offroad" & orange "noah," black "Handy Suspension" above front wheel, large blue & white HW logo outlined in black & orange above rear wheel, blue bed floor, rollbar & int., clear window, asw-or5	$5
📷	231	Chevy Stocker	yellow plastic body, metal China base, white, orange, black & gray tampo on roof w/white & black HW logo outlined in orange, large black "5" outlined in white & orange & white & orange "Flame Stocker," side has black, white, orange & gray flames, black & white "turbo," white & orange "jc5" over rear wheel, black window, 3sp	$19
📷	232	Jeepster	candy purple body, white plastic fenders & bumpers, metal China base, pearl-white-to-green fade tampo w/ black square & white "9" on hood & sides, white & black "Turbo JC9" on rear above wheel, green & black HW logo on rear deck w/white & black "Jeepster," white int., green-tint window, alw-5sp	$5
📷	233	Hyper Mite	pearl white met. black plastic Malaysia base, black panel outlined in gold on front w/pearl white met. "POLICE," black panel outlined in gold w/orange circle outlined in gold under each headlight, black panel outlined in gold on side w/white & black over gold HW logo, black "EXC" over gold in a white circle w/an orange ring around it, & white & black "Extreem City," black over gold "3" at the bottom, blue-tint metal exhaust, chrome int., rear engine, headlights & grille, orange-tint canopy, pr5 rear, mini 5sp front	$8
📷	234	Shredster	yellow pearl, flat black painted metal Malaysia fenders, gray plastic base, black "4" outlined in gold over white on nose, black tampo in front of windshield w/gold, black & white "EXC," white & black over gold HW logo, gold & black-over-white "EXC" in a gold & black ring & white over gold "Extreem City" on gray plastic side panel, gray int. & hood scoop, smoked windshield, pr5	$2
	235	Phantom Corsair	a. met. green, blue-tint metal Malaysia base (Master Set only), hood has yellow & orange flames, orange fade to yellow "Flame Breathin' Betty" over black, yellow circle w/red & black "Alive," side has red, light gray, yellow, & orange tampo over a black panel, woman's face on side is yellow, yellow & black HW logo outlined in red over rear wheel, smoked window, yellow int., asw-g5dot	$16
📷			b. same as (a), metal Malaysia base	$5
			c. same as (a), woman's face on side is white	$5
📷	236	Hiway Hauler	black met., black plastic Thailand base (Master Set only), black plastic rear box w/orange, yellow, black, gray & white tampo, large yellow & orange HW logo on side w/white & black "Side Show," red-tint window, alw-g5sp	$31
			b. same as (a), black metallic, black plastic Malaysia base, alw-g3sp	$10
📷	237	At-A-Tude	aqua enamel, black plastic Thailand base, large black "MOSQUITO" slanted on side over a white panel, large black mosquito w/white & blue HW logo as its wings on door, "Heralda" & "Sanders" tampo on rear quarter behind wheel, white "Handy," "Wielt" & "Soto Tires" on front fender behind wheel, aqua plastic rear wing, chrome int., smoked window, 5sp	$3
📷	238	Saltflat Racer	burgundy pearl plastic body, black painted metal Thailand base, chrome engine, int. & front end, top of body over engine has orange & white over black HW logo & orange & white ant (insect) over white & orange flames, black panel on top left of cockpit w/white "Fire Ants," white & orange flames left side of "Fire Ants" tampo, orange outlined flames on right above "Fire Ants" tampo, orange-tint canopy 5sp	$5
	238	Ford GT-40	silver-blue met. black plastic China base, silver, blue, white & black octopus tentacle tampo on side, blue & black HW logo over white on rocker panel in front of rear wheel, gray int., blue-tint window, 5sp	$3

Yes, this #238 Ford GT-40 is the same car as 222, but a different base. This car was number 222 in the Master Set and the Saltflat Racer was the 238 car for that set.

Photo	No.	Name	Description	Price
	239	Greased Lightnin'	a. met. silver upper half, blue lower half, metal Malaysia base, black panel on nose w/white & orange "808," Hot Wheels Air Show & white "R. Littleton" on black panel on side, chrome int., blue-tint canopy, pr5	$18
			b. same as (a), metal Thailand base	$10
📷	240	Ford GT-90	silver-green met. metal Malaysia base, black, silver, white & gold stripes on side w/black, white & gold star on lower door, black, white & gold "89" above stripes in front of rear wheel, rear window has a flat black airplane tampo over a gold tampo w/white & black HW logo & silver & black "Air Circus," black int., clear canopy, asw-3sp	$2

Shredster

At-A-Tude

Phantom Corsair

Saltflat Racer

Hiway Hauler

Ford GT-90

Wheel Abbreviations

asw	all small wheel
alw	all large wheel
bw	basic wheel or blackwall
bbw	black basic wheel
wbw	white basic wheel
ww	whitewall tire with basic wheel
uh	ultra hot wheel
guh	gold ultra hot
sho	silver hot ones
gho	gold hot ones
rr	chrome wheel Real Riders (synthetic rubber tires)
yrr	yellow wheel Real Riders
crr	chrome wheel Real Riders
grr	gold wheel Real Rider
hh	hot hub wheel from the Hot Hub Series
t/b	tri-blade or buzz saw or razor wheel
ot/b	orange tri-blade wheel
yt/b	yellow tri-blade wheel
ct/b	tri-blade wheel with construction tire
oct/b	orange tri-blade wheel with construction tire
wct/b	white tri-blade wheel with construction tire
yct/b	yellow tri-blade wheel with construction tire
3sp	3-spoke wheel
5sp	5-spoke wheel
b5sp	black 5-spoke wheel
w5sp	white 5-spoke wheel

pr5	new (2000) 5-spoke wheel (IROC) (Matchbox type)
mini 5sp front wheel	these are found on the front of cars like the Dragster and Railrodder
6sp	6-spoke pro circuit wheel
7sp	7-spoke wheel
b7sp	black 7-spoke wheel (no chrome)
g7sp	gold 7-spoke wheel
ww7sp	whitewall tire with 7-spoke wheel
bbs	chrome wire wheel with thin or narrow profile tire
gbbs	gold wire wheel
wbbs	white wire wheel
wwbbs	whitewall tire with wire wheel
bbs/2	new wire wheel with thicker or fatter profile tire (found on #669 #28-Chaparral 2)
5dot	chrome 5-dot or Lamborghini wheel
w5dot	white 5-dot wheel
ct	construction tire with chrome (8 dots) wheel
bct	construction tire with black (8 dots) wheel (no chrome)
oct	construction tire with orange (8 dots) wheel
yct	construction tire with yellow (8 dots) wheel
cts	construction tire with chrome spoke wheel (looks like old Matchbox construction wheel)
ctt	chrome wheel with tractor tire
ytt	yellow wheel with tractor tire

3sp

5sp

b5sp

7sp

yellow letter b7sp

bbs/2

gbbs

5dot

green star abbr.

bw

pr5

gho

rr

t/b

uh

ww

ct

ctt

cts

ct/b

Glossary

Backing Plate: The backing plate is the round metal plate behind a wheel where brake shoes were mounted.

Blister: Blister is the clear plastic cover over the car holding it to the card.

Blower: The Blower or Supercharger is the big aluminum thing that is between the air scoop (Bug Catcher) and the engine block. It is driven by the wide belt (Blower Belt) attached to the crankshaft at the bottom of the engine. The blower forces the air and gas mixture into the engine. You see them mostly on Funny Cars and Rails (Dragsters).

Boot: The boot is the cover that goes over the convertible top when it is down.

Bug Catcher: The Bug Catcher, as it's called, is the air scoop with fuel injection built together.

Candy Paint: Candy Paint looks like the color on a candy apple. It is translucent and usually has a very deep appearance.

Canopy: A canopy is a window that covers over the driver.

Cove: The cove is part of the body on the side of a car that is indented and is usually accented with different color paint.

Cowl: The cowl is the part of the body between the hood and the windshield.

Deck or rear deck: The rear deck is the part of the body that comes between the back window and the trunk lid.

Enamel: Plain color paint with no sparkles or flakes.

HW: Hot Wheels

Gold Chrome: The gold chrome is just that, chrome that has a gold color to it.

Gold-tint Chrome: The difference between gold-tint chrome and gold chrome is that the gold tint is just a little bit of tint in the chrome. You really have to pay attention to notice it. There were many cars that came out starting in 1997 with gold-tinted parts. After a while some of these parts became very dark gold chrome.

Headers: Headers are exhaust pipes that are used on race engines. Each exhaust port or outlet has one tube. Each tube is the same length, so they each so they each have the same amount of backpressure. That's why some headers look really bent up.

Insert: Insert as it's used in this case, is the plastic piece that is inserted into trucks like the Rescue Ranger or Fire Eater that would show up as a few different things: Hose reel, light bar on roof, and the air tanks on rear.

Logo: Small Hot Wheels flame design that is placed somewhere on the car.

MF: Metal flake paint, this has big flakes like the #163 Talbot Lago.

Met.: Metallic paint, this is paint that has small shinny flakes in it.

Pearl Paint: Pearl paint changes color slightly when you move it in the light. See the Pearl Driver Series cars.

Pillar or Roof Pillar: The pillar is the metal part that connects the roof to the body.

Push Bar: The push bar is a small bumper usually on the rear of a racecar, so it can be pushed to start it or push it back to the pits after it has stalled out.

Rocker Panel: The Rocker Panel is the part of the body that is below the door. The part you stepped on as a little kid to get into the car.

Roll Bar: The roll bar is one metal tube bent around the driver's seat to protect them if the car ever rolls over.

Roll Cage: The roll cage is made of many metal tubes that are constructed all around the driver's compartment to protect them from just about any type of accident or impact.

Smoked Window: Smoked windows are tinted very dark and are sometimes hard to see through, especially with a black interior.

Tach: The Tach or Tachometer is the gauge that shows the RPMs (Revolutions Per Minute) of the engine.

Tampo: Tampo is the design or stripes placed on the cars over the paint.

Tinted Window: Tinted windows have a light tint to them and are easy to see through.

Tubs: Tubs or wheel well tubs are the large metal or aluminum inner fenders that are built into racecars when they narrow the frame. This is done to be able to fit much larger tires under the body, so the body will be level and low to the ground.

Undipped Chrome: The chrome is not cured to its final step and looks dull.

Wheelie Bars: Wheelie Bars are the long rods with small wheels at the end that are usually bolted to the rear end housing of a drag car or bike to keep it from standing on its bumper and prevent it from flipping over when coming off the start line.

Names To Know

The following group of individuals help keep the Hot Wheels cars rolling down the track. Their creativity and inspiration take the hobby to new levels, and we would be doing our readers a disservice by not including a peek into the minds behind the magic.

Amy Boylan *Senior Vice President—Boy's Entertainment, New Media Division, Mattel, Inc.*

Q: How did you become involved with Mattel in your current position?

A: I started working for Mattel as their senior vice president of Mattel Media Group. It included all of the video and PC games. That in turn became cell phones, all technology, and the Web. The Web was how I started the new Hot Wheels collector sites. My new position still includes all of the above, plus Barbie collectors online and blue sky, such as the new exhibit at the Petersen Museum in LA.

Q: Are you a collector of Hot Wheels cars? If so, what brought you into the hobby?

A: I am. I also have a love of real cars, I own several. I first played with Hot Wheels cars when a neighbor got a Hot Wheels track set. He asked me to help set it up, I did, and we raced all day. At the end of the day, he gave me my favorite car, a 1968 purple Silhouette. I still have that car. Hot Wheels embodied everything I loved about cars growing up. Cool sleek, California custom.

Q: What are your top five favorite car series?

A: I don't have series favorites per say, more I am a castings, designer, and customs collector.

Q: What do you enjoy most about Hot Wheels cars?

A: They are the best die-cast cars made; they are the coolest cars that are always on trend, or setting trends. They are as new and fresh as they were 35 years ago. I am always excited when the new ones come out.

Michael Heralda *Hot Wheels Design*

Q: How did you become a designer at Mattel?

A: Mostly by luck! I was designing product graphics, catalogs, magazine ads, & packaging for Wham-O (the toy company). Mattel had an interest in a number of Wham-O's products and purchased the company. A window of opportunity opened up in Hot Wheels for a person with my experience (computer graphics), and I jumped at the chance to become part of the Hot Wheels Team.

Q: What influences have inspired your designs?

A: When asked what influences have inspired my designs, all I can say is everything influences me! I like observing things, people, art, trends, and pretty much anything that displays a sense of beauty, originality, creativity, humor, and wit. Of course there are certain topics and styles of art that I gravitate towards, such as ancient indigenous art and sculpture. Sometimes these images appear on certain vehicles. Sometimes the influence comes from the vehicle itself in its form and shape. I try to imagine what graphic treatment would enhance its overall appearance.

Q: What are your favorite top ten cars that you have designed?

A: Toy Fair cars are at the top of my list, mostly because there are no boundaries or limits to what I could do (with regards to cost and production treatments). I am given free reign on those vehicles.

S. Heralda photo

Q: What do you enjoy the most about Hot Wheels cars?

A: What I enjoy most about a Hot Wheels car is its simple beauty, functionality, and the enjoyment that kids of all ages have with them. I also enjoy knowing that I had a hand in bringing about such enthusiastic responses. People smile when they see a Hot Wheels car. There are a lot of "good" attachments and associations connected to them on an emotional level. I also like the way collectors are connected to the cars. I enjoy the fact that for them it has become a family event. I see parents, moms and dads, sharing time with their kids. It's all good!

Mark Jones *Hot Wheels Design*

Q: How did you become a designer at Mattel?

A: I was fortunate enough to be directed to Art Center, accepted there, and by my parents' sacrifice, attend and graduate in 1979. My first job out of school was at Ford Motor Company. After being laid off from Ford, I worked briefly at Honda Research of America and Chrysler Pacifica, before coming to Mattel in 1984. My first Hot Wheels design, the "Pipe Jammer" was released in 1993.

Q: What influences have inspired your designs?

A: Probably everything I've ever seen has shaped and affected my designs. I find inspiration in race cars (old and new), motorcycles, helicopters, and the landscape of the southwestern United States. I like the sculptural aspect of design.

Q: What are your favorite top ten cars that you have designed?

A: I Candy, Sweet 16 II, Hyper Mite, Vulture, Phantastique, Open Road-ster, Golden Arrow, Swoopy Do, Cabbin' Fever, and Popcycle.

Q: What do you enjoy most about Hot Wheels cars?

A: The freedom of design they allow me. The relatively short time from designing them to seeing them on the shelves. The way the sun hits them and they shine. Finally, the fact that other people seem to enjoy them also.

Carson Lev *Hot Wheels Design*

Q. How did you become a designer at Mattel?

A. I was actually first hired as director of engineering and product development for the Disney Entertainment Group at Mattel. We did all the toys, action figures games etc., for all the big Disney films. Being a die-hard car guy I was thrilled when the director of design position opened for Hot Wheels, and Larry Wood went to the big boss and said, "Carson is the only guy to hire!"

Q. What influences have inspired your designs?

A. Having grown up Southern California I was immersed in car culture from day one. It seemed that all my friends were the children of racers, car customizers or drivers! I spent most of my free time hanging out at **speed shops, garages and race tracks.** Most of my early influence came from drag racing, although anything with an engine that goes fast has to be cool! **As a teenager,** I learned pinstriping, lettering, design and graphics **from Ed "Big Daddy" Roth and Kenny Youngblood.**

Q. What are your favorite top ten cars that you have designed?

A. As the director of design, I was responsible for the management of the design staff, however, I managed to influence and direct staff to projects that were based on my passion. I have also included projects other than Hot Wheels diecast:

The Real Full Size Twin Mill
The Real Full Size Deora II
The Hot Wheels Gallery and Hot Wheels Hall of Fame at the Petersen Automotive Museum
1:64 Collector Single Hot Wheels Funny Car
1:64 Ed "Big Daddy" Roth 4 Car Collector Set
1:64 Bruce Meyer Gallery 4 Car Collector Set
1:64 Basic Car 1959 Chevrolet Bel Air "Redphin"
1:64 Collector Single 1969 Pro Stock Camaro
Chip Foose two car 100% Hot Wheels Set
1:18 Flaming Ferrari

Marco Patino photo

Q. What do you enjoy the most about Hot Wheels cars?

A. The best thing about Hot Wheels is the reaction people have to the great little cars. Simply put, after 35 years, these little cars continue to stir the passion that people have for cool cars. I could give 500 people each a dollar bill and it would not come close to the reaction if I gave them each a dollar Hot Wheels car!!! Hot Wheels is The World's Coolest Car Company! Clearly they embody SPEED, POWER, PERFORMANCE, and ATTITUDE! **It's all about the cars!!**

Wayne Scott *Hot Wheels Design*

Q: How did you become a designer at Mattel?

A: I was working for Revell at the time, and decided I wanted to try something new. I interviewed for a position with Mattel and the next thing you know...I'm working on Hot Wheels cars.

Q: What influences have inspired your designs?

A: Too many to list really! Music for one really makes me tick! Album cover art influenced me quite a bit growing up, and to this day it's one of my favorite references. I'm a car guy...so, car culture is obviously a major influence! Movies! TV! Comics! Other artists! Probably the most influential were my art teachers as a kid. I can't leave that out! Geeeez...What doesn't influence me is probably a better question. I think I could list almost everything!?!? Did I say art, music, and cars?

Q: What are your favorite top ten cars (FOR THE DAY) that you have designed?

A: Dairy Delivery (Colldotcom—Heavy Metal), '56 Ford Panel (Black W/ Red & Silver Pinstripin'), '49 Merc Set (2003 Irvine Convention), '59 Caddy (Pride Rides '03—Met. Orange), Rodger Dodger (Cinci

Convention '03), School Bus (Halloween Highway '03), Phantom Corsair (Blvd. Buccaneers '03), '70 Roadrunner (Scorchers '03), Big Mutha (Black w/Red Scallops/Blue Pinstripin'), '64 Riviera (Matte Black w/ Blue Flames—Hall Of Fame).

Q: What do you enjoy the most about Hot Wheels cars?

A: They allow me to be even more of a kid! How they relate to so many others! The opportunities that these little cars create! So many different canvases!

Dave Weise *Hot Wheels Design*

Q: How did you become a designer at Mattel?

A: I became a designer at Mattel after doing brief free-lance work as a vendor first. This led to a position as a temp designer before joining the team full time.

Q: What influences have inspired your designs?

A: I have been greatly influenced by what other Hot Wheels designers have done in the past as well as what I have seen at car shows and cool stuff running on the street.

Q: What are your favorite top ten cars that you have designed?

A: Radio Flyer Wagon, '67 Dodge Charger, Baby Boomer, '70 Cuda Convertible, '64 Impala, BMW M3, Montezooma, '41 Ford Pickup, Ford (Cartooned) F150 Pickup, 24/Seven

Q: What do you enjoy most about Hot Wheels cars?

A: I enjoy the flair and imagination that goes into them. There is always a little extra pizzazz.

Alphabetical Index

A

B

C

G

H

I

J

K

L

M

N

O

P

Hot Wheels Variations

R

S

T

V

W

X

Z

Catch Your Breath Productions

Michael "Mick" Zarnock has been collecting Hot Wheels cars since the late 1960s. He enjoys collecting the different card varieties, as well as buying and selling car variations. In addition to this second edition, he is also the author of *Warman's® Hot Wheels Field Guide*.